The Eclipse of the American Century

The Eclipse of the American Century

An Agenda for Renewal

Gene W. Heck

ROWMAN & LITTLEFIELD PUBLISHERS, INC.
Lanham • Boulder • New York • Toronto • Plymouth, UK

ROWMAN & LITTLEFIELD PUBLISHERS, INC.

Published in the United States of America
by Rowman & Littlefield Publishers, Inc.
A wholly owned subsidary of The Rowman & Littlefield Publishing Group, Inc.
4501 Forbes Boulevard, Suite 200, Lanham, Maryland 20706
www.rowmanlittlefield.com

Estover Road
Plymouth PL6 7PY
United Kingdom

British Library Cataloguing in Publication Information Available

Library of Congress Cataloging-in-Publication Data:

Heck, Gene W.
  The eclipse of the American century : an agenda for renewal / Gene W. Heck.
    p. cm.
  Includes bibliographical references and index.
  ISBN-13: 978-0-7425-6310-0 (cloth : alk. paper)
  ISBN-10: 0-7425-6310-3 (cloth : alk. paper)
  eISBN-13: 978-0-7425-6562-3
  eISBN-10: 0-7425-6562-9
  1. United States—Politics and government. 2. World politics. I. Title.
JK31.H38 2008
973.93—dc22   2008014893

Printed in the United States of America

♾™ The paper used in this publication meets the minimum requirements of
American National Standard for Information Sciences—Permanence of Paper
for Printed Library Materials, ANSI/NISO Z39.48-1992.

To the Founding Fathers' Remarkable Vision

Contents

Acknowledgments

The author acknowledges his debt and gratitude to many for making publication of this book possible. Foremost among them are the publisher, Rowman & Littlefield, and its superb editors Chris Anzalone, Karen Ackermann, and Jeremy Rehwaldt-Alexander for making its publication not only possible but enjoyable; to Tiffani Migliore, as always, for her wit and wisdom; and finally, but certainly not least, to my wife Adrienne whose counsel and support have been a source of strength for many years. Thank you all.

Introduction

Can the Twenty-First Century
Again Be the *American Century*?

> In the end, more than they wanted freedom, they wanted security. But when the Athenians finally wanted not to give to society but for society to give to them—when the freedom that they wanted most was freedom from responsibility—then Athens ceased to be free.
>
> —Historian E. A. Gibbon in epitaph to the ancient city state of Athens

"Change" is a codeword for altering the existing order. In an era wherein political candidates are incessantly calling for ethereal structural change, however ill-defined, it is illuminating to consider the types of change that advocates of analogous persuasions already have produced. As within the past half century, liberal proponents of countercultural revolution against America's civic institutions in the name of "political correctness" have transformed her social fabric in ways that now threaten her demise—leading many analysts and citizens to query: Can anyone survey the extent of the ongoing cultural assault and conclude: "Well done! We need more of this"? A return to the nation's historic values is invoked.

For civilizations die when the socioeconomic infrastructures—the values systems, civic allegiances, and financial frameworks that support them—are, over time, destroyed. Civilizational death is an incremental process. It may not happen in a day, but over time, it happens—and it is happening in America today—as her core culture, and the intrinsic values that underpin it, are systematically deconstructed by those who would politically bring her down. Here, there are no easy answers. Quick fixes are no cure. Holistic remedy is imperative.

From her inception, confident aspiration has been the theme of America's sense of calling—a conviction that the nascent nation's future was

God's hand working history—that through diligent commitment, a "manifest destiny" would issue from the unique virtue of the "American experiment." Like ancient Rome before her, and whose course they had diligently studied, her Founders were convinced that she was created for a special mission. America was to be "God's Crucible," the great melting pot wherein, from the God-given abilities of peoples from every corner of the earth, a new governance would be forged.

Their faith issued from a belief in the notion of "exceptionalism"—the thought that God, in forging this new nation, had somehow set it apart from the ranks of others through endowing it with its commitment to democratic capitalistic ideals—and upon the foundations of this mandate, it would stand as an exemplar to the world.[1] In the words of its second president, John Adams: "I always consider the settlement of America with reverence and wonder, as the opening of a grand scene and design in Providence for the illumination of the ignorant and the emancipation of the slavish part of mankind all over the earth."[2]

"America's story" is indeed exceptional—the first revolution of a people breaking off from a colonial power to establish a free nation—and on the residual strength of her historic values, she aspires to the mantle of global leadership. But how long can she hold on? Today, she is a nation at peril. At a time when her hard-won status of global preeminence is threatened, the issues at stake, as political scientist Samuel Huntington has aptly asserted, are who she is and what type of nation she aspires to be.[3]

This is indeed the message of Huntington's compelling close to his *Clash of Civilizations*—that change is already underway and that it is inevitable. To wit: "All empires decline. America is an empire. Therefore, she must decline." Such contentions come as corollaries to Paul Kennedy's concept of "imperial overstretch"—to wit: that the United States is where Great Britain was at the onset of the twentieth century, a condition wherein her commitments have outrun her ability to confront them, causing many to now ask: "Will this be America's fate as well?"

Answering such cogent questions transforms this inquiry into one of why great civilizations perish, assessing first contemporary trends, both social and economic, within America that match classic patterns of decline, then exploring potential remedies to reverse the evident decay. For as analysis reveals, those societies that have disintegrated from *within*, absent invasion or other *force majeure*, have generally imploded in a three-stage process incorporating

- deteriorating cultural values, resulting in
- increasing civic alienation, producing
- mounting complexity and cost of governance.

Alternately put, those polities that are in the dying process are usually first plagued with cultural dissonance bred of diversity, leading to increasing disregard for patriotism and the rule of law. In the process, historic civic foundations are weakened, education is undermined, and longstanding traditions are abandoned.

It is at this stage, then, that, because of the evolving complexities of administration needed to manage the resulting chaos, government begins to prey upon its citizens through the increased taxation and regulation required to fund the resultant bureaucratic overburden, all latter-stage signs of evolving societal disorder that are the early harbingers of ultimate demise.[4]

Indeed, it is precisely the coalescing of such factors that comes to forge the subsuming welfare state and the associated exorbitant public sector costs that precipitate its eventual downfall—looming socioeconomic challenges that must be expeditiously addressed if America is to successfully confront the realities of her present and succeed in her quest for a secure, more buoyant future.

The progression of cultural decline thus is an incremental process. Best described as the "Durkheim constant," as defined by French sociologist Émile Durkheim, it posits that there is a finite limit to the amount of deviant behavior that any society can "afford to recognize." As behavior worsens, the postulate holds, society gradually accommodates it by readjusting its preexisting standards downward so that conduct once considered to be reprehensible eventually becomes the norm. Absent its clinical nomenclature, the late Senator Daniel Moynihan (D-NY) simply called the process "defining deviancy down."[5] And thus it is that a civilization sinks ever deeper into the morass of an enveloping Dark Age.

Foreboding within the context of their pathological symptoms—as her social values become ever more corrupted by the rise of counterculturalism, as her civic values are diminished through unassimilated immigration and a concomitant decline in patriotism, and as her social welfare burden grows accordingly as a consequence of such developments—these are survival issues replete with peril that America has not faced before.[6]

Assessing the challenges through the Founders' conceptual prism, this inquiry therefore looks both retrospectively *and* introspectively for prudent policy guidance—an analytic exegesis vividly confirmed by the lessons of socioeconomic history. As to date, there has been a lamentable historiographic tendency to portray the death of nations as a consequence of invasion from *without*. But while that methodology may be appropriate respecting *nations*, great *civilizations*, as in the case of ancient Rome as well as her successors, almost invariably die from cultural decay and attendant cultural alienation metastasizing from *within*.

That is why, as Winston Churchill has astutely counseled, if one truly desires to draft what is intended to be an objective analytic history as a basis for gleaning lessons learned, it is best that it be written clearly, carefully, and circumspectly—and with precise hands-on attention. For as George Orwell presciently observed: "He who controls the past controls the future."

Deciphering history's cogent socioeconomic lessons is this inquiry's quest—with the demise of ancient Rome, the first civilization to embark upon inexorable decline in the full light of written history, presenting a classic study of the likely outcome of incorporating within a heterogeneous domain ideologically disparate elements who abjure the traditional values that are its social glue, and become instead proponents of a countercultural revolution antithetical to its bedrock values. For Rome ultimately did not die because her armies weakened, but because her citizens forgot what being "Roman" meant.[7]

Each nation has its defining moment. When Caesar crossed the Rubicon in 49 A.D., his action signaled the death of the Republic and the onset of the Empire. "By crossing it," British historian Thomas Holland asserts, "Julius Caesar engulfed the world in war and . . . helped to bring the ruin of Rome's vaunted freedoms, and the establishment of a monarchy." De facto, then, the new government became a bureaucratic autocracy masked in the guise of a republic.[8]

America too now faces her own Rubicon—her tectonic watershed—as the parallels between her course and that of late imperial Rome—in the forms of declining cultural values, increasing civic alienation, and attendant mounting administrative complexity, and their associated bureaucratic transaction costs—are striking.[9]

Accordingly, she has become a nation foundering on the quicksand of her erstwhile faith and fervor. Her traditional values are increasingly under attack by those who would undermine her cultural underpinnings. Civic alienation is mounting as she is increasingly peopled by those who "do not love Rome" but are only here to exploit her for her welfare largesse. In the macrocosm of time, the clock is ticking on what some have called "the American hour."[10]

In February 1941, Henry Luce, in a celebrated editorial in *Life Magazine*, proclaimed "the American Century." "As America enters upon the world scene," he wrote, "we need most of all to seek to bring forth a vision of America as a world power that is authentically American," for only such a vision "can guide us to an authentic creation of the twentieth century, our Century."[11]

But things are very different now—some seven decades removed from the prescience of Henry Luce. Clearly, the nation is at one of its most decisive moments, as its present course cannot prevail if the twenty-first century is to again be "the American Century." Profound midcourse correction is invoked. To this end, inquiry focuses upon those incipient processes of decay that are corroding the nation's cultural core values and, indeed, the very essence of its civilization.

In the process, analysis explores the socioeconomic context wherein the "politically correct" radical counterculture that has been metastasizing throughout America over the past half century and the "politics of victimization" that has attended it, have evolved, commencing with an assessment of the societal impacts of the "multicultural" movement—a dogma that, in the words of historian Diane Ravitch, "traces its roots to the ideology of ethnic separatism and the black nationalist movement."[12] This phenomenon would prove to be a ready recourse in the quest for redemption in race relations for those wallowing in the mire of "white liberal guilt."

Yet the task of projecting a movement's course by merely retracing it back to its roots cannot be reduced to such simplistic terms. For atavistic "multiculturalism," as it is today preached and practiced, is a multiheaded hydra. As defined in one acclaimed analysis, it is

> a leftist political ideology that sees all cultures, their mores and their institutions, as essentially equal. No culture is considered superior or inferior to any other; it is merely different. Criticism of other cultures, especially non-Western minority cultures, is labeled "insensitive" or bigoted. There is one major exception, however. Euro-American culture, with its Judeo-Christian underpinnings, is not only criticized, but often condemned, accused of racism, sexism, and classism.[13]

Succinctly put, multiculturalists view Euro-American culture as not having been of abiding benefit to non-Western and minority cultures; hence, its values and truths must be discarded as specious and irrelevant. As social commentator Dinesh D'Souza has aptly observed: "It [multiculturalism] represents a denial of all Western claims to truth."[14]

Under the guise of multiculturalism, then, immigrants and other minorities have been encouraged to retain their unique cultural and ethnic identities by deliberately not assimilating the majority norms and mores—as acquiescing to such assimilation is deemed tantamount to succumbing to cultural imperialism.

In promoting this agenda, moreover, government itself is concurrently expected to assume a countercultural role in fostering diversity rather than promoting patriotism; in promoting historical revisionism; and in legislating multilingual education in the nation's schools at the expense of English, the uncontested language of jobs and commerce. Indeed, even the word "foreign" is deemed politically inappropriate, as it does not conform to the expressed political values and ideologies of the omniscient multiculturalists.[15]

Consequently, Americans are being sold a specious bill of goods by self-proclaimed "do-gooders" avidly marketing counterculturalism in an ethereal quest for power under the banner of "diversity." But what they offer as "diversity" is not "diversity" at all—in the sense of that rich leaven that the Founding Fathers fondly contemplated in promoting multicultural immigration.[16]

It is instead a pernicious form of "reverse bigotry" peddled on a one-way trip down "leftist lane"—with the omnibus denouncing of Western civilization as hopelessly nativist, racist, sexist, elitist, and patriarchal; the replacing of classic college curricula with "new wave" countercultural counterparts; the blatant recasting of history to soothe wounded ethnic feelings; the ongoing efforts by college administrators to enforce speech codes on campus; and the endless crusade of the establishment media to inculcate the nation with 1960s "flower child" values—in the process, dangerously undermining the erstwhile bedrock core of American society.[17]

It is a perceptibly deceptive, and particularly insidious, campaign. For in its workings, while political elevation of the precept of "difference" may superficially seem like a noble prescription for plurality and tolerance, in reality, it is not—having instead fostered a "1984" Orwellian environment wherein "diversity" mandates rigid ideological conformity, and "tolerance" is afforded only to those who submit to its perspectives—as the driving force that propels the multiculturalist agenda, in a crass perversion of classic Churchillian historiography, is its blatant attempt to reshape history by rewriting it.[18]

That the multiculturalists have had a profound impact upon American society cannot be denied. Yet the question, as always, must concurrently be asked: "If America is indeed so oppressive and perverse, why do countless millions continue to come here viewing this nation, in Abraham Lincoln's immortal words, as 'the last, best hope on earth'?"[19]

The French philosopher Ernest Renan observed that "a nation is a soul, a spiritual principle," and that two elements constitute that soul. "One is its common possession of a rich legacy of memories; the other is its 'present consensus,' the desire to live together, the will to continue to value the heritage that has been received undivided."[20] Neither aspiration is accommodated by multiculturalist cant.

In the nineteenth century, Georges Clemenceau accused the United States of having passed from barbarism to decadence without the normal interlude of civilization. But such is really not the case. To the contrary, the "American experiment" was built upon the firm foundations of a durable social system that survived for nearly two centuries before its legacy of treasured cultural values became increasingly renounced in favor of that evolving decadence that is barbarism's inevitable precursor.[21]

In the wake of the countercultural revolution engulfing the nation, and its academic base in particular, therefore, the imperative for a "counter-counter revolution" to restore its historic legacy is urgently invoked. To these ends, the quest for a comprehensive cure that constitutes the focus of this analysis concludes with an agenda redressing those ongoing assaults on the America's traditional values—civil, civic, and economic—now advanced in the guise of "diversity" and "political correctness."

This inquiry is, in essence, not only an exploration of the process by which great civilizations deteriorate and die, but concurrently an exposé of how 1960s "hippy groupies," gaining little from college experiences that might have prepared them for meaningful, productive private-sector jobs, elected instead to remain in place to become tenured professors and administrators—thereby providing a platform for launching their present reign of ideological terror through a regimen of censorship and ideological intimidation that has now spread beyond the campus confines to corrupt the American values system at large.

It is concurrently a litany of how self-serving politicians—through the politics of "victimization and dependency"—first-recourse tools in their disingenuous arsenal of "prevailing through perceived oppression"—and the attendant spending, tax, and regulatory excess required to underwrite it—are increasingly undermining the economic foundations of the nation's private infrastructure. It is, in sum, at once a cultural biopsy of a metastasizing, ideologically driven social cancer as well as response to the question increasingly globally being asked: What happened to the America that we once knew and admired?

Seeking answers to that quintessential question, the analysis that follows is a detailed documentary of the decline of America as an admired moral and economic exemplar through the loss of cherished values that once empowered her to become the mightiest and most emulated nation on earth—and the attendant financial costs rising from those developments that now threaten her demise. It proceeds mindful that while midway through the eighteenth century, the French philosopher Voltaire wrote: "It is dangerous to be right when your government is wrong"—it is equally dangerous to be silent, muted by indifference.[22]

Indeed, a far greater danger, as the McCarthyism of the 1950s made clear, is that of being paralyzed by inertia into lethargy and inaction. For in the present instance, the country is not wrong in precept, but is instead being misled by those who, in pursuit of self-serving political dogmas and agendas, would subvert her historic mission.

McCarthyism—now a synonym for sinister authority and political repression—was in the 1950s an insidious tool of the political far right. Today, however, it has been possessed by the body snatchers of the radical left. But whether issuing from the right or left, it is equally wrong. Of late, such multiculturalists—indulging in the politics of "McCarthyism"—have sought to make their values system paramount and unequivocal, leaving America in the throes of a cultural and moral crisis—standing at the juncture of that crucial crossroad of determining just what type of nation that she wishes to be.

Two centuries ago, at the close of the U.S. Constitutional Convention in 1787, when asked, "What kind of government will we have?" Benjamin Franklin responded, "A Republic if we can keep it," an answer doubtless reflecting equally his knowledge of the underlying causes precipitating demise of the Roman republic and the contemporary thinking of his French friend Voltaire who believed that all republics eventually end in tyranny.[23] To which Thomas Jefferson assessed somewhat more optimistically: "I believe that our government will remain virtuous."[24] In this spirit, Thomas Paine would concurrently assess: "We have it in our power to begin the world over again."[25]

Throughout her history, America has met great challenges. She won a war of independence against near-insurmountable odds. Her Founders forged a unifying constitution at a time when her original thirteen colonies lacked both political and economic cohesiveness. She prevailed in a bitter and divisive civil war. She survived the Great Depression and two great world wars. She endured the social chaos of the 1960s and won the Cold War in the 1980s.

Today, because of the corrosive undermining of her cohesive historic values by rabid counterculturalists, she is again called upon to rally her resolve and resources. The course will not be easy. For as Albert Einstein cogently asserted, "The problems that exist in the world today cannot be solved by the levels of thinking that created them."[26]

But the time to act is now. World War II naval hero Admiral Bill "Bull" Halsey once observed: "There are no great men, just great challenges that ordinary men, out of necessity, are called by circumstance to meet"—an apt insight worthy of the equally cogent counter-corollary attributed to the eighteenth-century British parliamentarian-philosopher Edmund Burke that: "All that is needed for the triumph of evil is that good men do nothing."[27]

Part I

WHY CIVILIZATIONS DECLINE

On Ozymandius

I met a traveler from an antique land who said:
"Two cast and trunkless legs of stone
Stand in the desert. Near them, on the sand,
Half-sunk, a shattered visage lies, whose frown,

And wrinkled lip and sneer of cold command,
Tell that its sculptor well those passions read,
Which yet survive stamped on these lifeless things,
The hand that mocked them and the heart that fed;
And on the pedestal, these words appear:

'My name is Ozymandius, king of kings;
Look on my works, ye Mighty; and despair!'

Nothing beside remains round the decay
Of that colossal wreck, boundless and bare,
Save the lone and level sands stretched far away."

"Ozymandius," by Percy Byshe Shelley, 1817

1

Historic Causes of Collapse

There is the moral of all human tales;
Tis but the same rehearsal of the past.
First freedom, and then glory—and when that fails.
Wealth, vice, corruption—barbarism at last!

—Lord Byron, in *Childe Harold's Pilgrimage*,
in contemplating the residual ruins of imperial Rome

ON THE COLLAPSE OF CIVILIZATIONS

Why do great nations die? Or more precisely, how do great civilizations die? The distinction is crucial inasmuch as nations and civilizations may, at times, perish for different reasons. In the case study of Rome considered, for instance, it is critical to ascertain whether her collapse meant that her great traditions were no longer practiced, or whether her society was in acute dysfunction and on the threshold of ceasing to function, or whether the formal state itself had fragmented.

Civilizations may die while the skeletal remains of their national support infrastructures struggle on—and conversely. But while the deaths of nations may result from either external or internal causes or both, causes of the deaths of civilizations, though they may be influenced by external factors, almost invariably, and almost by definition, are internal.

It is here, then, that precise analysis becomes essential in seeking to discern between forests and trees, and, in turn, between trees and their tenuous twigs. The distinctions are critical, as they can spell a defining difference between conclusions that are hair-splitting or hair-raising in determining the death of empires, states, and civilizations.[1]

It is the answer to the latter question, why *civilizations* die, that is the crucial focus of this inquiry. For history is littered with tattered remains of ancient empires—of a vast multitude of societies that have risen and fallen on this planet within the past ten millennia. They have disappeared in a multitude of ways.

Some, like that of Rome, collapsed in the full light of history. Others, like the Mayans of Central America, simply disappeared—leaving behind a legacy of ruined temples, palaces, and entire cities hidden abandoned in the jungle. The Mayans, in the words of sociologist Robert Netting, are "a people whose greatest mystery is their abrupt departure from the stage of history."[2]

The nature of civilizational death likewise can play out in many complex ways. Externally, they can be absorbed by empires as Greece was by imperial Rome in ancient times and as Armenia was liquidated by Turkey early in the twentieth century. They can also be overwhelmed and deconstructed, as was the case with the Mongol invasion of Central Asia and the Ottoman capture of Constantinople in 1453.

Internally, they can undergo ideological conversion, as did Arabia with Prophet Muhammad and Ireland with St. Patrick. Or they can simply dissolve and disintegrate, as did imperial Islam in the Middle Ages and the Soviet Union and Yugoslavia in the late 1980s and early 1990s.[3] In the words of Samuel Huntington, "Civilizations are dynamic. They rise and fall; they divide and merge. And as any student of history knows, civilizations disappear and are buried in the sands of time."[4]

Often, the causes of collapse can commence with good intentions. Some powers inadvertently bring their declines upon themselves. The Greeks asked the Romans, the Romans the Visigoths, and the Celtic Brits the Anglo-Saxons each for military help in warding off their enemies, yet in each case, the benevolent ally eventually became the occupying enemy—supplanting the beseecher as the ruler.

Sometimes, the requisite help is economic and not military. The Romans, after they had won their empire, imported vast populations of foreigners into Italy as artisans, merchants, slaves, and soldiers—and as a result, over time, the native Romans, and their culture, were gradually, but inexorably, subsumed and marginalized to the point of extinction. Irrespective of the explicit cause of demise, however, the end results of societal collapse have been invariably the same—cultural destruction followed by economic disintegration followed by political extinction.[5]

The many, varied reasons for the deaths of civilizations have been a cause of contemplation dating back to first appearance of historian E. A. Gibbon's conspicuously dated 1776 epic—*The Decline and Fall of the Roman Empire*—which is the classic case study to which much of modern "doomsday literature" turns.

Speaking to this topic, British historian Thomas Holland writes: "Enthusiasts for empire argued that Rome had a civilizing mission; that because her values and institutions were self-evidently superior to those of the barbarians, she had a duty to propagate them; that only once the whole globe had been subjected to her rule that could there be a true universal peace."[6] Instead, he counters, Julius Caesar "engulf[ed] the world in war . . . [and] helped to bring about the ruin of Rome's ancient freedoms, and the establishment, upon their wreckage, of a monarchy."[7]

The downward spiral thus continued, and, as a result, historian Christopher Scarre writes, by the time of Emperor Constantine's death in 337 A.D., "Rome had lost her preeminence, the old gods had gone, civic values and political values had been transformed."[8] Constantine's legacy was, in fact, a theocratic-autocratic state. On the consequent civilizational devolution, writer Gore Vidal, in his biography of Emperor Julian, observes:

> The world Julian sought to preserve is gone . . . the barbarians are at the gate. Yet when they breach the wall, they will find nothing of value to seize, only empty relics. The spirit of what we were has fled. . . . With Julian, the light thus went out, and now nothing remains but to let the darkness come, and hope for a new sun and another day, born of time's mystery and man's historic love of light.[9]

However poignant, and more tragic still, the regression would inexorably continue to unfold. As under classic Rome's immediate successor, the Holy Roman Empire, Anthony Gottleib, in his review of Charles Freeman's *The Closing of the Western Mind*, asserts, by the year 1000: "All branches of science, indeed all kinds of theoretical knowledge except theology had pretty much disintegrated. Most classical literature was largely unknown. The most educated people . . . knew strikingly less than had many Greeks 800 years earlier."[10]

Small wonder, then, that writing early in the fourth Christian century, the Christian chronicler Lactantius despaired: "What purpose now does knowledge serve. . . . What blessing is there for me if I should know when and where the Nile rises and falls, or whatever it is that under the heavens the 'scientists' rave about."[11]

Because America's present socioeconomic course evinces symptoms strikingly parallel to those of empires past, and to that of imperial Rome in particular, the causes of the ultimate demise of civilizations merit special consideration.

THE DIMINISHING PRODUCTIVITY OF COMPLEXITY

What causes such abject decline? Is it mere happenstance? Like ancient Ozymandius, is it the sheer intellectual arrogance of a political leadership glaring defiantly to the heavens—basking in unconstrained ambition—while missing entirely the somber litany of the epitaph even then being sculpted onto the sarcophagi of civilized existence that underpin their realm?[12]

Ultimately, as analysis will show, on the fiscal plane, most civilizations throughout history that have been destroyed from within have collapsed when the bureaucracies that supported them became too costly—in physical and financial resources—to sustain them. Indeed, often physical and financial resources have impacted as reciprocals of each other in precipitating such decline.

Certainly, such was the case of imperial Rome as well as that of the medieval Islamic empire, and may well be true of America today. Those civilizations died when they became too bureaucratically complex to govern—or more precisely, because of the resultant exorbitant cost, in the forms of taxation and regulation, required to financially underwrite their complexities. But in seeking remedy to the underlying policy dilemma, a quintessential question becomes: What caused them to become bureaucratically complicated in the first place? Examination of that phenomenon is illuminating.

James Howard Kuntsler, in his 2005 work, *The Long Emergency*, advances a compelling thesis that as all civilizations mature, they, of necessity, become ever more administratively and socioeconomically complex until they finally directly collide with growing shortfalls in the resource base needed to provide the financing required to sustain them.[13]

Geographer Jared Diamond likewise argues that most civilizational crises are caused by declining resources. Evaluating the decision making of those ruling on Easter Island, the Mayans of Central America, and the Norse in Greenland, he paints pictures of leaders so fixed in their values and so set in their ways that they refused to alter them, even if they knew that course meant eventual societal destruction.[14]

Of those residents on Easter Island, he maintains that, without regard to consequence, they cut down the trees that were their sustaining lifeblood, not only to create agricultural plantations but also to obtain logs to transport and erect those giant stone idols that were the objects of their veneration—propensities that ultimately resulted in total deforestation, leading to war, the overthrow of their elites, and, ironically, to a demise in their famed stone statue building itself, thereafter ending in a massive population die-off. On these downwardly spiraling events, Diamond speculates:

> I have often asked myself: "What did that last Easter Islander who cut down the last palm tree say while he was doing it?" Like modern loggers, did he shout: "Jobs, not trees?" Or: "Technology will solve our problems, never fear, we'll find a substitute for wood?" Or: "We don't have a roof, or that there must be palm trees somewhere else on Easter Island. We need more research; a ban on logging is premature and driven by fear-mongering."[15]

Diamond's contentions, though likewise compelling, are nonetheless not without their logic shortcomings. Foremost among them is the inconvenient reality that some countries with great resources and large populations, such as Mexico, are poor; whereas others with few resources and relatively small populations, such as Switzerland, are rich. Still others, with fairly large, creative populations, can become extremely rich, as Japan has proved. The case for continuing to search further still for the prospective causes of civilizational collapse thus is compelling.[16]

To this end, political scientist C. Northcote Parkinson openly indicts overly centralized government, top-heavy administrative systems, attendant rising bureaucracies and regulation, a loss of economic discipline through political urges to overspend, a decline in the quality and relevance of education, a concomitant rise of "liberal opinion," and a resultant inordinate growth in taxation—in short, the popularization of policies evolved more from political pandering than from sound moral judgment.[17]

American historian Joseph Tainter, in turn, advances a corollary predicated on the premise that while the magnitudes of political problems grow geometrically, the analytic abilities needed to solve them grow only arithmetically—contending that in the process of attempting to adjust to the on-the-ground realities of their resource endowments, all civilizations eventually collapse from the sheer deadweight burden of the bureaucracies created to solve their crescendoing socioeconomic complexities, together with the attendant repressive taxation and regulation required to underwrite them. Accordingly, then, if this hypothesis is correct, societal collapse is in-built into the civilization process itself.[18]

Alternately put, whereas civilization-building involves the processing of ever-greater quantities of information and energy, the formation of ever-larger settlements, the development of more complex technologies, and an attendant increasing class differentiation and stratification—*civilizational collapse*, which involves a progressive weakening of society's political and administrative controls, is the reverse of that process and is a recurring fact of history. As an institutional phenomenon, it posits that as complexity takes its toll on societal output, it initially courses a graphic curve of increasing marginal productivity; then slowly diminishes over time as bureaucratic complexity increases—with the outcome that the civilization commensurately dies.[19]

The setting in of what might be charitably called bureaucratic elephantiasis, therefore, is cumulative—to wit, public taxes rarely, if ever, go down, only up; the processing of information becomes more dense and difficult; standing armies grow larger still; and the underpinning bureaucracies expand rather than shrink—with the result an unending spiral of increasing complexity and correspondingly higher sustainment costs, thereby producing diminishing marginal economic returns.[20]

Eventually, then, as the center of gravity of this bureaucratic spiral becomes too elevated, the benefits per unit of investment begin to drop off, setting on a course of diminishing returns—making ultimate collapse not only inevitable but useful. As it is here that, though the effects usually are not pleasant, collapse becomes an economizing process, the most rational adaptation under the circumstance.[21]

Tainter's contentions are compelling. As analysis will show, there is indeed a relative ratio of bureaucratic overburden to productive activity that any economy can effectively sustain before stress fractures in its socioeconomic infrastructure start setting in. For though bureaucratic process adds nothing to productive enterprise, when the former overwhelms the latter, society sets upon its inexorable decline.

Tainter further steadfastly maintains that whether in the case of agricultural and other resource production, science and technology, or overall economic productivity, this law of diminishing returns evolving in tandem with protracted exploitation and development is axiomatic. The declining productivity of medicine, for instance, is that inexpensive diseases and ailments tend be conquered first, leaving those remaining to be cured more difficult and costly to resolve.

The decline in *scientific* productivity is similar. As R&D becomes more specialized, it becomes more expensive because it has exhausted the stock of less costly research. It is at that point, then, that the output of R&D experiences mounting diminishing returns, creating economic weakness. Were 4 to 5 percent of GDP in R&D expenditures to become necessary to increase a society's productivity by 2 percent, then, ultimately, everyone within it would perforce become a scientist.[22]

Per-capita rates of economic growth likewise decline with increasing GDP, so that as the economy of a society expands, its rate of growth concurrently slows down. The same trend holds true for the phenomena of sociopolitical specialization and control, wherein the reasons why investments in public sector complexity yield declining marginal returns relate to (1) the increasing sizes of bureaucracies themselves, (2) their growing specializations, (3) the cumulative nature of their requisite public sector solutions, and (4) the aggregate costs of their operation and maintenance.[23] The rationale for civilizational decline, leading to collapse, as explained by Tainter, thus is basic:

1. human societies are problem-solving organizations;
2. sociopolitical systems require human focus for their maintenance;
3. increased complexity carries with it increased per capita costs; and
4. investments in sociopolitical administration as a problem-solving system thereby often reach a point of declining marginal productivity returns.[24]

The reason advanced for such sequencing is that bureaucratically organized solutions are cumulative. Once developed, as noted, their operational features are seldom abandoned. Welfare costs seldom go down. Standing armies seldom get smaller. Tax rates, therefore, most often go up rather than down. Hence, to sustain mounting complexity, bureaucratic hierarchies must perforce raise taxes. Yet at some point, by exhausting the economy, even these levies will yield declining returns, as the course of economic history leaves no doubt.[25]

As a society increases in complexity, moreover, so do its social systems. For as interlinked societal parts adopt a growth direction, others must adjust accordingly. If, for instance, the regulation of production increases, attendant investments must be made in the production facilities hierarchy, bureaucracy, and security as well, thereby increasing infrastructural complexity. Growth in benefits relative to costs will then perforce experience diminishing returns over time consistent with the marginalizing product curve of complexity.[26]

Complexity, in sum, is a "problem-solving process," reflecting the reality that the challenges that any society confronts are, for all practical purposes, infinite in number and endless in their variety. As problems rise, new institutional and economic solutions must be developed, typically focused upon increasing costs and declining marginal returns. But over time, the marginal returns on such investments continue to deteriorate until they reach the point at which the socioeconomy becomes increasingly vulnerable to collapse.[27]

Accordingly, as the marginal return on complexity declines, its virtues as a strategy yield comparatively lower benefits at ever higher costs—producing stress fractures within its civil infrastructure. A society that cannot effectively counter these disparate trends thus becomes ever more vulnerable until finally, in weakness and impoverishment, its ultimate collapse becomes a probability.[28]

Yet not all societies are preordained to collapse. Some have successfully coped with the challenges of finite resources and remained intact without reaching a production limit for declining strategic resources that portends disaster. If a society recognizes its problems in time, aggressively addresses them, and is willing to change its causal habits in a quest for ultimate survival, therefore, it may be able to persevere in the near term and prevail over time.

It is insightful, then, to again reflect upon why civilizations decay, decline, and fall. Again, the critical question thus becomes: What caused the bureaucracies of these civilizations to become so complex that the resource costs of administering them became impossible to meet? In aggregate, from cultural cause to fiscal close, it may be said that the root causes of such internally-induced collapse may be traced back to three prime factors:

1. an undermining of traditional culture produced by evolving ethnic and social diversity and alienation from within, as they transition

from the core ethnicities that empowered their incipient dynamism into balkanized, multicultural societies;

2. a subsequent resultant decline in adherence to the traditional civic and social values that had been initially established by those core ethnicities by other ethnic and racial groupings now espousing new and differing sets of cultural values; which in turn, have initiated

3. attendant rapidly mounting bureaucratic costs of adapting to the new cultural realities, including the social welfare costs of managing increasingly diverse societies and requisite demands upon the underlying resource bases required to sustain them.

In this process, then, cost and complexity are merely symptomatic of the death throes of a civilization—the by-product of preceding declines in social and civic values that caused its bureaucracy over time to become complex and costly, in a three-stage sequential process devolving initially in the forms of

- deteriorating cultural values; resulting in
- increasing civic alienation; producing
- mounting complexity and cost of governance.

More succinctly put in formulaic format:

Deteriorating Cultural & Social Values	+	Increasing Civic Alienation	—>	Crescendoing Complexity & Cost	=	Core Causes of Civilizational Collapse

What do these ominous trends posit for contemporary America? Jane Jacobs, in her seminal work *Dark Age Ahead* effectively consigns Western civilization to a new "post-Roman" epoch of medieval chaos and despair brought on by the collapse of nuclear families, combined with attempted governmental usurpation of the family's erstwhile role as a bulwark of societal stability, and the surging tax costs associated with such usurpations. "The collapse of one sustaining institution enfeebles others," she contends, and "with each collapse, still further ruin becomes more likely."[29]

SOCIOECONOMIC FACTORS CONTRIBUTING TO MOUNTING COMPLEXITY AND COST

Cultural Alienation: The Case of Rome

Rome is a historic civilization appropriate for analyzing decline and collapse—and for exploring what her message from the past portends for

America in particular—because unlike most other such civilizations, in addition to the normal residual archaeological evidence available for such analysis, the course of her regression is illuminated in the contemporary written sources of the era.

Thus, historians of antiquity, papyri, coins, monuments, and other artifacts conspire in concert to provide graphic details of her gradual dissolution that are largely absent from the evidence of other ancient civilizations. In the words of T. S. Eliot: "We are, insofar as we inherit the civilization of Europe, all still citizens of Rome."[30]

In a less abstract, more cogent sense, the propriety of studying the decline of Rome as a measure of America's current course is linked to the reality that she was, at her inception, forged in a Roman polity mold. As at the onset, the Founders, many deeply steeped in ancient history, viewed themselves as the embodiment of the Roman republican ideal. Equating their perceptions of the pre-republic Roman monarchy with that of contemporary Britain, which they equated with tyranny, they pursued the dream of an "American republic"—and with the reformed Roman systems of checks and balances in mind, they crafted the nascent nation's governance.[31]

Thus, the Founders aspired to an America framed within the distinct model of the Republica Romana. Indeed, the writings of Adams, Jefferson, Franklin, Hamilton, and Jay are filled with allusions and invocations of the republican virtues espoused by Cicero, Virgil, and Cato. George Washington was deemed a "modern Cincinnatus." Their vision for a Senate was modeled on its Roman counterpart, and their symbols of state and architecture echoed the glory of ancient Rome.[32]

Their aspirations stand on their merits, as the economic, intellectual, and territorial achievements of imperial Rome need no great elaboration here. Monuments residual throughout the Mediterranean basin stand in mute testimony to the architectural magnificence of her once-widespread classic civilization. Indeed, at her imperial zenith, her total land mass was the largest until then ever assembled under a single administration.

Her ascension was perceived as part and parcel of a divine mandate, a "manifest destiny" as it were, as reflected in Virgil's *Aeneid*, cited with reverence by the Emperor Augustus: "Your task, Roman, is this: to rule the peoples. This is your special genius: to enforce the habits of peace, to spare the conquered, to subdue the proud."[33]

Yet the grandeur that was ancient Rome eventually came undone—at human hands—by the gradual collapse of her social values, by an attendant loss of a popular sense of what it meant to be "Roman," by a burgeoning bureaucracy required to preside over the resulting cultural diversity, and by the exorbitant regulatory and tax costs required to sustain it. The evolution, or devolution, of this process provides keen insights for would-be modern public policy makers and analysts.

"Civilizations die from suicide, not murder," proclaimed historian Arnold Toynbee, and that certainly was among the foremost factors in the recorded decline of many ancient ones. They can die from corrupt and incompetent governance. They can perish from the deepening decay of decadence. Or they can simply be overwhelmed by demographic changes forged by influxes of foreign migrants alien to their historic cultures, as was the case of classic Rome.

Nominally, the Western Roman Empire drew its last breath when a rag-tag military force led by the tribal chief Odoacer, half Hun and half Scirian, subdued an imperial army of which he and his barbarian hoards themselves a few months before had been a part, killing its commander under whom he had previously served. This thus was no invasion. It was instead, at best, a petty civil war, and in reality, little more than a minor mutiny culminating in a coup d'état.[34]

Entering the city of Ravenna, which then served as an imperial capital, in 476 A.D., Odoacer deposed the youth Romulus Augustus who had served as emperor for but a year. But though this was a significant change of power from a lineage standpoint, the usurper was scarcely less worthy of authority than those whose throne he had usurped. Already, he had annexed his military to that of Rome in the 460s A.D., was schooled in Roman ways, and was a Christian, as were most Romans by that time.[35]

Yet unlike the fall of Carthage six centuries before—when the Romans slaughtered the inhabitants and razed the city—there was now no rape or pillage, there was no devastation, there was no social implosion. Rome didn't burn in a day. The imperial city itself, in fact, largely went untouched, as life for the empire's citizens appeared scarcely different than the year before. Accordingly, few likely woke up on January 1, 477, and exclaimed: "Good God, it's the Dark Ages!"[36]

Thus it was that of the fall of Rome, historian Will Durant observed: "Rome was conquered not by barbarian invasion from without, but by barbarian multiplication from within." For the reality was that when Rome fell, it did so, in large part, because no one remembered how things used to be, and thus no one stood up for her traditional values. This view, endorsed by Russian classics historian Rostovtzeff, was the inevitable outcome of a process set into motion by the Emperor Claudius, who first formulated the sweeping policy of bringing in foreigners as a means of both manually strengthening the regime and winning a broad base of support for it.[37]

Initially, the method worked to the degree that midway through the fourth century, after an auspicious victory in 357 A.D., the Emperor Julian would boast that he had just added ten thousand foreign military prisoners to induct into the military and civil service of Rome. But the remedy of Claudius was a palliative, not a cure—and would, in fact, become a cause of the catastrophe to come. For it was now that, given alternatives to productive work afforded by the influx of the barbarian cheap labor, Rome's once-legendary appreciation for the virtues of work and "commitment to commitment" would increasingly attenuate the traditional sources of her civic strength.[38]

A degeneration of cultural values characterized by *luxuria* ("luxury") and *licentia* ("licentiousness"), accompanied by a decline in work ethic that the contemporary historian Sallust maintained had set in as early as the age of the general Sulla—a military officer who had conquered Athens in 86 B.C. and prevailed in a subsequent civil war, from which he emerged as dictator—thus now proceeded to perniciously infect Rome's citizens, precipitating mounting welfare burdens requiring a growing civil service to administer, adding to already heavy public revenue demands upon the imperial fiscus.[39]

Rome's system of social services was pervasive—a program initiated by Caesar Augustus (Octavian) as an opiate to assuage the populace as it transitioned from republic to autocracy at the time of Christ—but would become increasing more expansive as the empire sank ever deeper into decadence and economic disarray over subsequent centuries.[40] Among the benefactions employed were massive *gratis* handouts of bread, oil, and wine and incessant public entertainment—a welfare program that was eventually extended to more than a quarter of a million residents of Rome who consumed the equivalent of six million free sacks of grain per year.[41]

Concurrent with such "entitlements" was entertainment, as gladiators engaged in combat with feral animals and with each other, and chariot races, which were major betting events, staged at the central amphitheater called the Circus Maximus and similar local facilities that were showcased as issuing from the benevolence of the emperor himself. Indeed, it is estimated that a total of more two hundred thousand gladiators met their deaths in the Coliseum and that nine thousand animals were slain as a result of such activities at the festival celebrating its opening in 80 A.D. alone.[42]

Overall, there were about twenty-six such annual festivals, and by the fourth century, 177 days per year—a state holiday practically every other day was devoted to the games at the circus. In the poignant words of the poet Juvénal, in lamenting the loss of the republic by the citizens: "With no vote to sell, their motto became 'couldn't care less.' The time was when their plebiscite elected generals, heads of state, commanders of legions. But now they have retrenched and the only two things that concern the people who conquered the world are bread and circuses."[43]

Thus, the contemporary fourth-century historian Augustine would lament the prevalence of "people who want to ruin themselves by funding actors, theatrical performers, performers in wild beast spectacles, and chariot drivers. How much they give! How much they spend! They pour forth their resources, not only their ancestral properties but their very souls."[44]

As a consequence, Rome's degenerate social state, as succinctly assessed by historian Thomas Holland, became such that "the Roman people . . . in the end, grew tired of their antique virtues, preferring the comforts of easy slavery and peace."[45]

Concurrently, to support such tax-supported largesse, the state civil service payroll, which had totaled four million *sesterces* under Augustus, doubled under Domitian and quintupled by the rule of Septimus Severus. The great cost of the imperial court, the public works administration, the postal service, and other bureaucratic apparatus further added to the taxpayers' burden. At times, citizens living proximate to tax-collecting postal stations went so far as to abandon their homes altogether to escape the postal service's incessant revenue levies. In the words of one contemporary chronicler, those living off of the treasury were now more numerous than those who were paying into it.[46]

For now, *nothing* escaped the ubiquitous grasp of the omnipresent Roman tax collector, as new taxes, tolls, and in-kind confiscations of every kind soon multiplied to meet the revenue demands of the ever-expanding military and bureaucracy. Indeed, no levy was too costly in the quest to sustain the army and the welfare burden. To quote the sentiments of a contemporary rabbi, "The Romans built marketplaces for their whores, baths for them to wallow in, and new bridges for the purpose of exacting tolls."[47]

As a consequence, most emperors, upon their accessions, came to power with insolvent governments that were seldom able to accumulate ample reserves for emergencies. Yet with each new conquest would come the need for even greater bureaucratic complexity—for a still bigger military to defend the empire, for a larger civil service to administer the realm, for enhanced public works, for increased welfare benefits for citizens—and with the mounting complexity, gradual declines in marginal rates of return on productivity.

Whereas in earlier days the military had maintained order, moreover, in the dark days of Rome's collapse the corrupt appetites of her influential citizens undermined her social structure, so that by the fourth century, there was an utter free-fall deterioration of moral and social constraints. In the words of the contemporary Roman poet Livy: "When men had fewer possessions, they were also more modest in their desires. Lately, riches have brought only avarice and abundant pleasures, and the desire to carry luxury and lust to the point of ruin."[48]

The collapse of the rule of law was concurrent and equally critical, and there are many vivid historical examples of the outcomes. Over time, then, Rome herself fell prey to the very licentiousness that she had exploited to divide and conquer other nations—as in her latter days, her own laws became pragmatically ineffective. Indeed, even the imposition of tyranny in her latter years had little effect and could not reverse the collapse of social structure. And when the "Roman Peace" became no longer possible, her empire fell as well—and the Dark Ages, which spread over Christian Europe for a thousand years, issued from the resultant loss of civic order and balance in the heretofore civilized ancient world.[49]

To illustrate the potentially devastating impact of massive alien immigration on societal preservation, Rome's example once again commends itself—as her gradual infiltration by elements alien to her culture not surprisingly resulted in a concomitant decline in popular attachment to her once vaunted civic values; as over time, the early decision by Emperor Claudius to import foreign labor would prove to be disastrous.

Yet at its inception, from both economic and martial standpoints, it was a policy that worked well. Barbarian forces were stationed as auxiliaries at the empire's borders, and they eventually came to play increasingly more prominent roles in their maintenance. Indeed, late in the fourth century, when alien troops were formally incorporated into the Roman military commencing in 376 A.D., Ammianus Marcellinus, a soldier and minor official functionary who fancied himself as a historian, writes that the Emperor "Valens was overjoyed at the prospect of so many recruits. He reasoned that if the Goths were inducted into his army, it would give him an overwhelming force."[50]

Indeed, after Valens and two-thirds of his forces were slain on the battlefield at Adrianople in 378 A.D., the process of incorporating alien elements into the military would accelerate further still, as the Romans had no choice but to reconstitute their legions in any way they could. Thus, while barbarians had, for centuries, been ingested into the military in large but assimilable numbers, now, for the first time, as a condition of settlement on lands claimed as part of the Roman domain, they were invited *en masse* to fight under the imperial banner—and allowed to stay intact as peoples occupying territories within the realm led by their own leaders.[51]

Accordingly, as with the modern U.S. military, Rome's army, in its time, became a central institution of social integration. Inducted immigrants learned to speak Latin. They adopted Roman arms and uniforms—and they married Roman women upon retirement. Indeed, although various units of the army bore ethnic names, immigrants often appeared beside Roman provincials in mixed units.[52] A major benefit of the immigrants, according to Ammianus Marcellinus, was not that they were better soldiers, but because "in place of a levy of soldiers in the provinces, the Treasury would gain huge sums of gold instead," as native Romans were "all too glad to contribute gold in lieu of service to spare their own lives" from military conscription.[53]

Hence, initially, the immigration policy did not appear as ominous as it would ultimately become. For again like America today, Rome, in her early formation, was extremely adept in assimilating newcomers. Unabashedly syncretic, the Romans borrowed heavily from others. They had come into their own while part of a world in which certain foreign peoples—Greeks,

Phoenicians, and Egyptians among them—were, by most cultural measures, more advanced than they. As she expanded, then, Rome took such groups under her sway and incorporated the best of what they had to offer—enlisting them not only in the military and as manual labor but as an integral part of her formal civil service.[54]

Indeed, until America, she was history's most successful multiethnic state. But eventually, the influx of Huns sweeping down from Eurasia became too massive to meld within Rome's "melting pot," and the empire became instead a polyglot of disparate and restive alien groupings who would gradually greatly undermine the culture that it had worked so hard to build.[55] Of these developments, the near-contemporary historian Cassio Dio writes: "The barbarians were adapting themselves to Roman ways, were becoming accustomed to hold markets, and were meeting in peaceful assemblages. They had not, however, forgotten their ancestral habits, their native manners, or their old life of independence."[56]

Over time, such cultural dissonance would grow ever more prominent. When Alaric, fighting as a commander of the allied border forces under the Emperor Theodosius, and his Visigothic contingents turned on the very empire that they served and sacked Rome in 410 A.D., historian Ramsay Mac-Mullen writes, "he and his men *were* the Roman army and had been for decades."[57]

His was, then, a two-decades-long mutiny, not an invasion, executed by professing Christians, who, once inside the sacred city, treated Rome's holiest places with then greatest of deference and respect. Nonetheless, unbeknownst to then contemporary native-born Romans, this violation of the territorial sanctity of Rome was an early harbinger of the end of civilization as they knew it—and what followed was, in fact, the "Dark Ages."[58]

Commenting on this phenomenon in his contention that "a nation need not be overrun by a foreign enemy to be utterly destroyed," classics scholar Victor David Hanson maintains that Rome's final collapse "was a result not of imperial overstretch on the outside but of something that was happening from within that was not unlike what we ourselves [the West] are now witnessing," asserting: "Earlier Romans knew what it was to be Roman, why it was at least better than the alternative, and why their culture had to be defended. Later, in their ignorance, they forgot what they knew, in pride, mocked who they were, and in consequence, disappeared."[59]

At first, as clearly noted, the system had worked as planned—providing bonded troops to serve with the Roman legions. Indeed, from Ammianus Marcellinus's picture of the fourth-century army in action, there is little evidence that its standards of discipline had fallen in any substantial way, or that the barbarians in the ranks were less inclined to obey orders or more likely to make common cause with the enemy.[60]

But though these bonded border guards were initially committed to accept Rome's sovereignty and as such, were incorporated voluntarily as would-be loyal allies, many often did not stay particularly loyal for long—as they were not peoples who had come for patriotic reasons. Nor were they particularly devoted to a given sovereign, but in the empire's declining years would instead become pawns in incessant jockeying for position among Rome's power elite. As Tacitus indelicately put it: "May the tribes ever retain, if not love for us, at least a hatred for each other!" A review of these devolving developments is illuminating.[61]

The barbarian immigrants, as stated, had initially been rapid learners who had come not to destroy what Rome had to offer but rather to win a share of it for themselves in the forms of employment, land, and status. Starting at the borderlands, and then even further inside, they were given jobs that the native Romans didn't want or could not fill—in the fields, in the mines, and in the forts—including jobs as seasonal workers. Their leaders, in turn, would be trained at the imperial court and then sent back as "Romans" to maintain order at the borders of the empire.[62]

Whatever the incipient economic benefits, however, the ultimate outcome of this immigration process would culminate in crisis. Financially, it meant ceding the tax revenues from wherever the barbarians settled in Gaul, Spain, and Africa. Concurrently, civically, it brought within the realm new ethnic blocs that were, in effect, second-class citizens, but who, nonetheless, because they fielded armies, became major players in its already contentious politics.[63]

Indeed, over time, the semiautonomous regions that they created within Rome's imperial borders would devolve into de facto petty kingdoms so powerful that they often perceived no real need to maintain the pretense of participating in an artificially forged imperium, and when this happened, Rome collapsed. In the masterful understatement of historian Walter Goffart: "What we call the 'Fall of the Western Empire' was actually an imaginative experiment that got a little out-of-hand."[64]

Accordingly, as time progressed, due to the pernicious multiculturalism evolving within her midst, Rome's tasks of governance became more difficult than her initial conquests, as her domains became a fractious *potpourri* of crowd, creed, and culture. Undoubtedly, the Germanic tribesmen who took over the western Empire's outlying provinces had initially *professed* a commitment to her. They saw themselves as Rome's heirs and protectors and wanted to preserve her achievements. Nonetheless, under their later rule, the fabric of Roman society slowly dissolved, and within two centuries, Roman law, administration, public works, literature, and even literacy itself had vanished.[65]

Together with the collapse of her culture, Rome concurrently endured a societal decline in her desire for conquest and for things martial. As with the decay of her early republican values, the vaunted Roman legions became more and more a reserve army of non-Romans, half-Romanized barbarian mercenaries, and servants sent in the stead of freemen who did not want to be bothered by the noisome vulgarities of waging war. Indeed, in the empire's last days, the histories relate, male citizens commonly mutilated themselves to escape military service, though such a crime was—at least in theory—punishable by death.[66]

Concurrently, military conscription teams that were sent to the great estates would meet resistance to such extent that influential landowners were frequently allowed to send money in lieu of men. Recruitment problems of the army further multiplied as native-born soldiers were often allowed to "buy" leave from their superiors through military furloughs—and then disperse into the civilian populace while being kept on the official rosters, often never to return. For the penalties for being away without official leave were lenient—a ten-person demotion for an unauthorized leave of a year, and mere expulsion from the service after four years of such absence.[67]

Consequently, by the fifth century A.D., unit commanders were routinely sending inflated rosters of the native-born to their headquarters for payment on a fictitious head count basis, while keeping the cash differences for themselves. To compensate for the manpower shortfall, therefore, when barbarians were accepted in the empire as allies, they were even more increasingly required to provide troops in exchange.[68]

The problem so multiplied, in fact, that in 409 A.D., faced with an essentially undefended frontier, Emperor Constantine III announced the unthinkable: henceforth, slaves would be permitted, even encouraged, to enlist, and for their service, each would receive a bounty and his freedom. With this dramatic development, then, it soon became often difficult to tell the native Romans from the barbarians, particularly along the frontiers.[69]

But as these alien peoples had no *inherent* love for Rome, her culture, and her traditions, their loyalties were inevitably malleable. Indeed, in 476 A.D., as indicated, the Germanic barbarian Odoacer—in an internal disagreement over land allotments for his troops and without significant resistance to what was, in effect, no more than a petty mutiny—came to govern in condominium with the Senate in the emperor's stead.

Thus, as Rome had conquered the barbarians, so now the barbarians conquered Rome. As assessed by Will Durant:

> If Rome had not engulfed so many men of alien blood in so brief a time, if she had pressed all of those newcomers to her schools instead of to her wretched slums, if she had only occasionally closed her gates to let assimilation catch up with infiltration, she might have gained a new racial and literary vitality from the infusion, and might have remained Roman Rome.[70]

Yet Rome did not, and thus she died—as history's cogent lessons leave no doubt that there are implicit dangers in permitting balkanized alien amalgams within any culture. In the twentieth century, by way of stunning modern example, Indians were initially imported to the island nation of Fiji to work as merchants and civil servants, yet within a few decades, they had taken majority control away from the native Fijians.[71]

That is not to deny that immigrants who bring particular skills, or "human capital," cannot be of immense help in building a society. But as economist Thomas Sowell asserts—in his master work, *Migrations and Cultures*, addressing the large-scale immigrations of peoples who are distinct from the host populations that they join—such immigrations "can profoundly affect the fabric of a society and even dissolve the ties that hold a nation together."[72]

Resulting Fiscal Collapse: The Case of Rome

Conventional histories tend to assess the decline and fall of Rome as a devolution in which an empire's reach became greater than its grasp—an imperial *elephantiasis* wherein the body grew faster than its head. But while this is a logical conclusion based on superficial manifestations, it is also a simplistic one that analyzes symptoms rather than root causes.

Undeniably, the largest, most important line item in the federal budget of the realm was the exorbitant cost of its ever-expanding army, upon which its strategic goal of imperial conquest was dependent. To quote a contemporary Roman general officer, "Stability amongst the tribes cannot be maintained without armies, nor armies without pay, nor pay without taxation."[73]

Undeniably also, the burden of maintaining armies was an enormous one. Ironically, it may be said that those very factors of strength that initially had sparked Rome's spectacular rise in the end became factors of weakness that prompted her precipitous decline. Her initial sweeping territorial expansion was indeed due, in no small part, to her magnificently disciplined military. As the empire expanded geographically, therefore, it became necessary for its forces to correspondingly increase.

The actual size of the Roman army over time remains a topic of scholarly debate. It is generally believed that its paper strength under the Severan emperors early in the third century consisted of thirty legions of 5,000-plus men each, and an equal number of auxiliaries, making an aggregate total of around 300,000 soldiers. By the accession of Diocletian at the onset of the fourth century, the best estimates concur that it had increased to about 390,000 soldiers and 45,000 sailors, for a total of about 435,000 troops. For its time, this was a sizable military force.[74]

But the assertions of Victor David Hanson notwithstanding, in a classic case of what Professor Paul Kennedy would later call "imperial overstretch," the requisite logistics expansion to support the forces needed to preserve military security took place at a pace far more rapid than the growth of the revenue base required to sustain it. Diocletian's early fourth-century reforms alone resulted in a doubling of the cadres within the army, whose size ultimately came to exceed a half-million men—in short, massive forces with ever-increasing salary demands. Classic historian Michael Grant describes the resulting escalating fiscal crisis thusly:

> Under Augustus, the pay of a legionary soldier amounted to 225 silver coins. By the end of the first century A.D., Domitian had brought this figure up to 300. Septimus raised it again to 500 and increased the pay of his reconstituted praetorian guard from 1,250 *denarii* up to 1,700. His son, Caracalla, introduced a further 50 percent pay raise. In so doing, he reportedly said: "Nobody but I ought to have money, and I must give it to my soldiers!"[75]

Indeed, Domitian's 83 A.D. pay increase alone had raised the cost of Rome's military budget by a third, and it would continue to spiral thereafter. The pay increase of Carracula at the onset of the third century added another massive seventy million *denarii* to the price of sustaining the Roman legions. Yet those costs would grow geometrically further still, if some primary sources are to be believed in their assessment that the ranks were quadrupled to a million men by the close of the fourth century.[76]

Thus, a fiscally devastating "closed loop" paradox evolved. As described by Tainter, the Romans established an empire paid for by the monetary subsidies of subsequent conquests—ascending to her imperial greatness when she learned that she could increase her energy supply by conquering and commandeering the labor of her neighbors to serve her immediate power needs. Indeed, it was a system that long worked well, empowering Rome to become the most powerful force on the planet.[77]

But there were serious span-of-control limits to such geometric expansion—realities that gradually set in over the three centuries ranging from the rise of Augustus in 27 B.C. to the accession of Diocletian in 284 A.D.—compelling the empire, particularly after a series of successive losses to Germanic barbarians, to consolidate its domains, stabilize its prosperity, and maintain what was to become thereafter essentially a defensive army.[78]

Secondly, though perhaps of equal import, while the captive peoples initially financed the empire's subsequent conquests, a point eventually was reached wherein they ceased to be profitable due to the fiscal realities that (1) the more the conquered provinces became part of Rome, the less they could be leached for their financial productivities, and (2) the attendant extravagant administrative and garrison costs required to sustain them eventually became overwhelming. In the somber epitaph of famed early twenti-eth-century Belgian historian Henri Pirenne:

> The Empire alas was ruined. Its exhausted finances no longer enabled it to maintain on its frontiers the compact armies that might have contained at any point, the sharp German thrust driven by Atilla, whose hoards were still advancing triumphantly toward the West, overthrowing, as they came, people after people. Stilicho had saved Italy only by leaving undefended all the trans-alpine provinces. The result could not be long delayed.[79]

Indeed, chroniclers at the time were aware of this dire reality as well. Empires commence to decline, Thucydides keenly observed, when they cease to expand. For a time, Rome had been able to effectively organize the world according to her own convenience. But there now came a point when doing so became at first difficult, and then impossible. And with the end of her geographic expansion, there was a corresponding decline in her bounty proceeds of conquest as well. Hence, from Augustus to Diocletian, most emperors were confronted with serious shortfalls in public sector revenues to pay administrative costs, which included not only the massive military and civil service, but also the postal service, public works, education, and welfare stipends.[80]

As a consequence, as windfall proceeds from new subjugations ceased to pour into the treasury, the administration and defense of the empire had to be paid for primarily from agricultural production. But this recourse, of necessity, meant ever-rising taxes on farmers until they reached the point where fertile lands were increasingly abandoned due to the onerous revenue levies of the central government—to the degree that by the fourth century, peasants were left with so little of their produce that many were unable to provide for their own families' survivals.[81]

Thus, as a consequence of such excessive taxation and economic malfeasance, and despite incessant official efforts to bind the farmers to their lands through legal fiat, vast tracts of farmland throughout the empire were summarily abandoned, with the productive capacity of the support population deteriorating dramatically.[82]

Political economist Guglielmo Ferraro indicts ultra-urbanization as a concurrent cause of Rome's collapse. In his view, a rapid rise in commerce led to the evolution of prosperous citizens who then migrated into cities to participate in their extravagances. As the countryside was taxed to sustain urban living, they were joined by the incoming peasantry now fleeing their farms as well, causing massive rural depopulation. But the greater the depopulation, the further the need for expenditures on cities and the more burdensome the taxation of agriculture—until ultimately the tax levy system spiraled beyond the limits of its financial tolerance and collapsed.[83]

This was, in fact, also explicitly the assessment of the fourth-century Roman chronicler Ammianus Marcellinus who attributed Rome's decline to excessive bureaucracy and the onerous taxation needed to sustain it—as all of the burgeoning bureaucratic requirements invoked the need for greater financial resources, either by raising taxes or by devaluing the currency.[84]

In the precisely tailored words of financial analyst Stephen Leeb: "Taxes grew so exorbitant that landowners abandoned their farms, causing food production to fall. In time, the cost of conquering territories exceeded the rewards. Eventually, even defending existing territories against the barbarian invasions became too expensive. Rome, the predator, had itself become the prey."[85]

Whenever the heavier taxation failed to cover imperial expenses, moreover, Rome turned to inflation; as throughout the third century, her currency was continuously debased. The empire had inherited from the monetary policy of Caesar Augustus a magnificent argentiferous coinage of unparalleled quality whose nominal value was equal to its intrinsic value. When Trajan introduced new silver *denarii* worth but 85 percent of face value, he set a dangerous precedent, but the damage was not yet done.[86]

For under his successors, Rome's once-vaunted monetary system collapsed entirely. The values of Septimus Severus's currency issues averaged 43 percent of silver, whereas those of Aurelian contained no more than 5 percent. Indeed, the sundry issues of a number of their successors grew progressively worse until some of the coins were reduced to as low as 2 percent of par value.[87]

As the empire's monetary base became increasingly more unstable, moreover, its sovereignty fragmented as well, as cities and provinces increasingly took to issuing their own coinage. As a result, business people incessantly lamented that loans contracted at a fixed cash value were, at their redemptions, being repaid in nominal coinage worth but a fraction of the originally stipulated amounts.[88]

Yet such cries were only met with even greater currency debasement, still higher taxes, reintensified tax collection efforts, and systematic confiscation of still more private property. Outlying provinces, in consequence, in still greater numbers, resented and resisted their mounting exploitation to satisfy the seemingly insatiable revenue appetite of the Roman fiscus.

Hence, unable to generate fair returns on investments, the landed gentry increasingly committed their own surplus capital to the most sumptuous of luxuries. The work ethic of the laboring classes concomitantly diminished toward extinction as they too focused on the hedonistic pursuit of "bread and circuses."[89]

When shortfalls in the Roman treasury made it impossible to pay her legions adequately and on time, moreover, elite guard units often took into their own hands the license of empowering new emperors of their choosing in the hopes of securing their own financial well-beings. But such actions merely made shambles of orderly governmental successions and policies, including even the process of establishing budgets to support the legions themselves—a chaos that, over time, would grow only worse, not better.[90]

Accordingly, in the half century from 235 A.D. to 284 A.D., Rome had twenty-six separate army-proclaimed emperors who, with but a sole exception, succumbed to public assassination or private murder. In this sinister accession and deposition process, moreover, Rome's other institutions, including even the Senate and the diplomatic corps, were often implicated.

Unfortunately, then as now, the collapse of one sustaining institution merely enfeebled others, making it more likely that they too would give way. Indeed, it would take the rise of a powerful and indefatigable emperor, Diocletian, a tough old soldier of peasant stock from Croatia, to put an end to all of that.[91]

By promising in advance to abdicate voluntarily after twenty years of rule, a commitment that he, in fact, kept, Diocletian thus came to power with a commitment to pursue aggressive administrative reform. His famed "Edict of 301"—the "law of maximum"—sought by royal decree to curb rampant inflation and promote commercial sales by fixing ceiling prices for producers and maximum wages for all goods and services throughout the realm at rates denominated in his newly reformed currency. He concurrently established a process whereby tax rates in a given year were explicitly geared to anticipated expenditures, in effect creating the semblance of a balanced public budget.[92]

But though his fiscal reforms were sweeping, their impacts were instantaneously disastrous—as with a single act, Rome declared the death knell for most forms of free market exchange within her borders with a punctuation seldom equaled before or since; and, in so doing, sealed the empire's fate. For to governmentally impose a new wage and price control regime upon a private sector industrial base already reeling from inordinate taxation—a failed approach quite remarkably later replicated by Franklin Roosevelt in his frenetic quest to end the Great Depression of the 1930s, and with similar results, as analysis will show—was economically devastating.[93]

Thus, Diocletian's reforms were ultimately as unsuccessful as they were initially momentous. The steady precipitous decline in the value of money, wages, and prices continued in defiance of the law. Contemporary historian Lactantius reports that many merchants now withdrew their goods from the open market rather than to sell them at the publicly-established prices, and that a flourishing black market soon ensued. Finally, as prices rose even more and blood flowed in the streets, the emperor was compelled to withdraw his edict altogether.[94]

Diocletian's successor, Constantine I, also sought to achieve monetary stability and moderate ever-rising prices by reducing the legal value of circulating gold and silver currencies. But his efforts also met with predictable failure, for they too were regulatory palliatives, not economic cures.[95] Public outrage, civil disorder, and eventual anarchy were the inexorable outcome, as the exorbitant costs of preserving the "Pax Romana" throughout the third and fourth Christian centuries came to eradicate all vestiges of personal freedom in the realm's desperate quest for survival.[96]

Meanwhile, other critical expenditures of state continued to increase. Augmentation of the bureaucratic apparatus needed to implement Diocletian's fiscal reforms appears to have been massive. Lactantius reports that the foremost beneficiaries of public expenditures—army officers and their soldiers, tax collectors, and other officials—were now more numerous than the taxpayers, as the farming of taxes to military commanders became even more commonplace.[97]

As a consequence, the faster the state's expenditures grew, the more rigorous the tax collection became. But the more onerous the tax collection, the greater was the recourse to tax fraud and evasion. As a result, quite predictably, tax yields ceased to rise as a function of tax effort.

Indeed, many people now abandoned their productive properties altogether to escape tax repression. Lactantius, in discussing a new tax register implemented to administer the constantly rising tax levies, describes the overall frustration of the tax collection process thusly:

> After all men were listed, then so much money was laid upon every person's head, as if it had been to pay so much for his life. Yet this matter was not trusted to the first tax men but to follow-on new sets of them as well. One after another were sent about so that new men might find new matters to work on; and though they could not really discover anything, yet they increased the numbers so that it might not be said that they had been sent for no purpose. By means of such oppressions, the stock of cattle was diminished, and many men died. *But taxes continued to be levied, even on the dead* (!)[98]

The extent of the tax-collector problem is suggested in a petition from a contemporary patriot to the emperor circa 370 A.D. seeking revenue collection processes reform: "They are the more oppressive because their wickedness flows from the very source that should afford relief. As if their own injustice were not enough, each one sends out their own collectors to spread ruin of the same sort, and drain off taxpayer resources through various devices of plunder."[99]

Eventually, therefore, as a direct result of this rapidly spiraling escalation/collection/evasion tax cycle, those market-driven motivational incentives needed to sustain production based upon the expectation of a just reward for diligent effort predictably gradually declined and were ultimately extinguished by the repressiveness of governance. Public revenue yields concomitantly contracted, and a debilitating financial paralysis now set in throughout the entire state bureaucracy.[100]

The dissipation of private profit motive and an attendant disintegration of industrial production thus were the inevitable results—as in rapidly spiraling fashion, Rome's economy spun utterly out of control. Over time, in fact, the marginal returns on investments within Rome would sink so low that the costs of her bureaucratic excesses made rule by barbarian interlopers preferable to that of her native-born citizens.[101]

Accordingly, over time, that vaunted entrepreneurial spirit that had heralded Rome's spectacular rise—private investment capital committed on the expectation of a fair monetary return—was inexorably suffocated, and the level of economic surplus needed to underwrite civilized progress dried up with it as well. Turning a blind eye to the financial conditions that ultimately would destroy them, the Romans thus set into place the preconditions for Europe's prolonged "Dark Ages."

Modern Lessons from the Fall of Rome

With Rome having never been formally driven from the field, and with her official religion likewise that of her occupiers, then, the critical question that must be asked is this: While imperial Rome did, over time, disappear as a formal legal construct, did she really fall or did her essence merely fade away and mutate into a different kind of civilization through cultural osmosis?[102]

That question's answer is pregnant with profound implications in seeking analogies to modern circumstance. For in large part, as noted at the onset, changes in ordinary life were not significantly perceptible. Landlords continued to manage their properties, peasants worked their lands, and members of the imperial bureaucracy continued to fulfill their functions—only now in the service of barbarian chieftains rather than in that of the erstwhile Roman emperors. Indeed, a Senate composed of bureaucrats would continue to convene a full century after Rome's supposed fifth-century fall.[103]

Yet while for reasons emanating more from inertia than resilience, the Roman corpse was initially able to sustain itself a while longer, the twilight of the empire's once-vast hegemony had set in. For as the empire's heralded, once unparalleled, political and economic infrastructures deteriorated further still throughout the course of the fourth to sixth centuries A.D., Rome's educational and cultural institutions concomitantly deteriorated with them.[104]

In this process, savants now increasingly withdrew from active creative thought to become mere commentators on the monumental works of more illustrious predecessors. Scientific experimentation was reduced to the rote task of aggregating technical fables. Philosophic inquiry degenerated into the formulation of sophomoric "moral maxims." Great literary composi- tions of the past now became little more than anecdotal recollections—and Rome's renowned dynamic art forms soon lost their erstwhile creativity to become crude stereotypes of their former selves.[105]

Charles Freeman, in his epic *The Closing of the Western Mind*, describes in poignant terms how Rome's fourth- and fifth-century rulers closed famous libraries like that in Alexandria, discarded the scientific works of Aristotle and Ptolemy, and limited the availability of scholarly books. From the last recorded astronomical observation in 475 A.D. he observes, "it would be over a thousand years—with publication of Copernicus' *De Revolutionibus* in 1543—before these studies again began to move ahead."[106] The Dark Ages thus could not be far behind.

Hence, just as the rise of Rome can be explained by her superior eco- nomic, industrial, and trade techniques, so her subsequent economic and political disintegration in the third to sixth centuries can equally be ex- plained by her unfortunate social, civil, immigration, and tax policies—and the attendant destructions of personal profit motive and private economic surplus that those policies engendered.

When the empire's political authority and the administrative infrastruc- tures upon which it had been founded utterly collapsed, moreover, the out- lying "Roman world," with the noteworthy exception of Byzantium, lost its socioeconomic vitality as well—to the degree that by the seventh century's onset, the ancient "Western Empire" was in the final stages of its political and economic demise.

It is not surprising, then, that all that today remains of Rome's once- vaunted imperial grandeur are the remnants of her once-grand physical stat- uary—massive monuments standing in mute testimony to the folly of her profligate public policies. As due to declining cultural values, civic alien- ation, attendant mounting social welfare costs, and the absence of a fair and equitable tax structure, a mighty empire fell.[107]

Accordingly, E. A. Gibbon assesses the demise of imperial Rome thusly: "Instead of now inquiring why the Roman Empire was destroyed, we should rather be surprised that it subsisted for so long."[108] To which, an- cient European scholar M. P. Charlesworth appends, "The marvel is not that the Empire was in so poor a state in the Fourth Century, but that it was in any state at all."[109]

What lessons, then, can America learn from history's legacy of precipitous decline? Among them that, as analysis will show, harbingers of America's demise now parallel those of ancient Rome. Her civilizing forces have been corrupted. Her work ethic has declined. She has turned to alien labor to per- form those tasks that her people no longer wish to do themselves—entrusting them to peoples who do not "love Rome." And the attendant welfare burden required to sustain the latter, in turn, has invoked the need for spiraling taxation and regulation that has set her on an unsustainable fiscal course.

Accordingly, the nation now confronts imposing bureaucratic challenges—including those of managing the ever-increasing administrative complexities documented in subsequent chapters. It must not allow itself, therefore, to be lulled into inactivity through the vain promises of pandering political leaders on the campaign stump, as governments only make profound sustaining changes when compelled to do so.

Indeed, to summarily ignore the problems now impacting its well-being will ensure that, precisely like empires of old, it will be destroyed equally from within, through the decline of its social values, and from without, through the attenuation of its erstwhile industrial vitality within the ever-more-global economy, together with an attendant deterioration of the premier defensive forces that it now sustains to keep it free.[110]

Succinctly put, reminiscent of the somber admonition of ancient Ozymandius, historian and philosopher of religion Os Guinness, in his masterwork *The American Hour*, issues the ominous but timely warning that: "A generation that fails to heed the signs of the times may later be forced to read them on the wall."[111]

America today stands at that crossroad. The choices that she makes will determine whether the twenty-first century will again be the "American Century"—or whether she will instead follow Carthage, Greece, imperial Rome, Islam, Spain, and Great Britain into irreversible decline. The parallels are significant and the issues at stake are great. She cannot afford to fail.[112]

2

Contemporary Causes of Collapse

Your Republic will be fearfully plundered and laid waste by barbarians in the twentieth century just as the Roman Empire was in the fifth; with this difference: that the Huns and Vandals will have been engendered within your own country, by your own institutions.

—Lord Thomas Macaulay, to an American friend, 1857

CIVIC CHALLENGES: THE CULT OF COUNTERCULTURALISM

The American Creed

So again, focused analysis reverts to the question: Why do great civilizations die?" In many cases, such as that of Rome, as shown, the principal cause is cultural attenuation, civic alienation, and resultant fiscal deterioration through sustaining the social services burdens attendant to a decline in work ethic among the native-born, combined with a corresponding influx of "barbarians"—alien workers—allowed to infiltrate to fill the resulting workplace void.[1]

Evidence is strong that identical patterns are unfolding within America today—but why? Why are there so many seemingly determined to undermine her long-standing, cherished, nearly universally envied traditional values through an activist countercultural revolution? And precisely what are those historic values that multiculturalists work so tenaciously to upend?

Generally, it may be said that within America, as in any great civilization, the innate values system consists of three core components that comprise the essence of her citizenship: cultural values, civic values, and socioeconomic values.

29

Thus it is that the tripartite civilizational deconstruction formula of (1) evolving ethnic and social diversity, causing (2) mounting cultural alienation and disaffection, producing (3) burgeoning public-sector social welfare costs to sustain the disaffected—phenomena explored in chapter 1— now plays out in grand array throughout contemporary America. Its implications are profound and sobering.

Richard Nixon, in his capstone masterpiece, *Seize the Moment,* written over a decade and a half ago in 1992, observed that the "apogee of civilization," the pinnacle of scientific and technological progress, has moved ever westward—from the Ming Dynasty in ancient China and the invention of paper and gunpowder—to the Islamic East in the Middle Ages and the pioneering of astronomy and many of the principles of modern mathematics, physics, and medicine—to Christian Europe in the Renaissance and the revival of an appreciation for the classic arts and letters.[2]

Then onward to the Industrial Revolution—to the application of scientific process to mechanical production—which led to the passing of the baton of global preeminence to the United States at the close of the nineteenth century, making the twentieth century, in the words of President Nixon, as well as renowned publisher Henry Luce, "the American Century." Nixon then presciently predicted that in the twenty-first century, the "apogee of civilization" would commence moving back to eastern Asia, making it the "Age of the Pacific Rim."

Like Nixon, many observers have today proclaimed that the world has entered the "Pacific Century." In their view, Europe dominated the nineteenth century, the United States became preeminent in the twentieth century, and the Pacific Rim will take center stage in years ahead. Indeed, they perceive this ever-westward shift in history's focal point precisely as the dynamic economies of East Asia are coming to power the world engine of economic growth.[3]

Seemingly, they are right. Eight years into the twenty-first century, with the ongoing emergence of China, Korea, Indonesia, Vietnam, and Singapore as high-tech industrial powers, and with the looming economic recrudescence of Japan, few would question the prescience of the Nixon prediction.

Concurrently, the manifest challenges to America's preservation and sustained global preeminence are many—both internal and external, and with both interrelated—critical challenges that must be decisively addressed. For the relevance of her response will determine whether the twenty-first century will again be the "American Century," or whether she will transition into the ranks of second-rate global powers.

America, though bounded by two oceans, was nonetheless born with a global vision. Throughout her history, she has been a beacon summoning immigrants arriving at her hospitable shores from differing ethnic, racial, cultural, and religious traditions, nearly a million strong each year. The genius of her existence, in turn, historically has been her unique ability to forge a single nation assimilated from those incoming peoples of diverse ethnic, racial, and religious backgrounds.

Her creed—a belief in freedom, justice, and democracy—contemplates a country of self-determining individuals acting in concert, not one founded upon the static friction of the inviolable interactions of intractable ethnic communities. Her essence has been based on individual rights, not group rights. In return for statutory guarantees of equality and just treatment before the law, she has insisted upon respect for her prevailing standards, her values, and her customs.[4]

America's creed, in the words of political sociologist Samuel Huntington, is a belief in liberal democracy and its associated practices. It involves the rule of law, the virtues of democracy, and the importance of justice, equality, and freedom.[5] It is, as conceived, thus a consensus between the governed and their governance—a set of constitutional safeguards offered in exchange for shared commitment—in effect, a quest for a common culture and a national identity that is at once multicultural. Within it, people are free to live as they choose—ethnically, racially, religiously, and otherwise.[6]

They thus are free to take pride in their individualities as they rejoice in their commonalities to which all have contributed. Her culture is the product of that commitment—building upon the aspired ideals of those intrepid Europeans commencing four centuries ago who left behind a difficult past yearning for a more promising future as Americans. It is a bond uniquely fashioned. In the words of twentieth-century English philosopher G. K. Chesterton: "America is the only country ever founded on a creed."[7]

Underpinning that creed, therefore, is a binding social contract derivative of the political ideology of eighteenth-century British philosopher John Locke, an early contemporary of America's Founding Fathers—as ably articulated in John Adams' definitive preamble to the Massachusetts Constitution: "The body politic is formed by a voluntary association of individuals. It is a social compact by which the whole people covenants with each citizen, and each citizen with the whole people, that all should be governed by certain laws for the common good."[8]

The cohesiveness of such a contract, it is clear, directly hinges upon the solidarity of a society's "national identity"—a concept perhaps best defined as a psychological attachment to one's homeland community, its institutions and practices, its constituent members, the intrinsic psyche of its way of life, and the ideals for which it stands.

There has always been something magnificently special about America's absorptive ability to take in the "wretched refuse of the teeming shores," as beckoned by her Statue of Liberty, and meld them into the mightiest and most magnanimous nation on earth—a premise founded upon an implicit, heartfelt willingness by would-be citizen-immigrants not only to abide by the nation's written laws, but also by its "unwritten laws" and cherished traditions.[10]

Such precepts incorporate those principles that make up the invisible, albeit vital, fabric of American civilization: respect for the individual as citizen-sovereign, a balance of freedom and responsibility, equality before the law, independence and self-reliance, a powerful work ethic operating within a realm of unlimited economic opportunity—and above all, a willingness to join with fellow citizens in sustaining those values that make the nation special and unique.[11]

Because all polities are varying interlacings of ethnicity, race, and culture, then, "national identity" frames explicit structural dimensions both for a country and for its people—a reality that has now taken on new dimensions in the post-9/11 world. As in its aftermath, the crucial issues at stake center upon how the nation's psyche, its culture and values, and its formal institutions fit together.

Deconstructing the American Creed

Indeed, were those precepts to be solemnly observed, current threats that now jeopardize the nation's social well-being would not loom so ominously. In reality, however, as former U.S. Solicitor General Robert Bork has observed, its greatest and openly avowed threat, "militant multiculturalism," has been conjured up to serve as a "societal battering ram" designed to bring society down.

Multiculturalism's doctrine is a demand for radical change. It claims that perceived slow progress in the quest to ensure equality for all, as it defines it, and toward more civilized, enlightened attitudes, as it defines them, is unacceptable. Though racism does not define its trajectory per se, hyperbolic racial thinking does explain why it functions in its peculiarly unidimensional way.[12]

Regrettably, the composite outcome has been one of both confused citizens and convoluted public policy—as perceptions of multiculturalism and illicit immigration have now been inverted to such extent that a deepening erosion of the historic sense of "national community," the logical presumption that all residents stand equal as Americans regardless of their differences, has become a national security challenge as well as one of mounting civic dissonance.[13]

The net result then has been that, instead of being unified by its diversity, American society has become ever more segregated and balkanized, with each cohort of so-called victims striving to carve out its preferential niche. In the sobering assessment of political economist Paul Craig Roberts, "Americans may now have become so politically correct and racially sensitive as to be unable to deal with the inherent problems at all."[14]

Accordingly, while an appreciation of, commitment to, and responsibility for the United States and her institutions should be foundational prerequisites for citizenship, rising questions of extent of fealty to an "American identity"—given her combination of internal diversity and external dangers—have become a matter of critical concern. In an age of ever-present threats of terrorism and the security needed to deter it, in fact, it is perhaps the most serious policy issue facing the nation today.[15]

Security challenges and civic concerns—each a derivative of the other—are thus integrally intertwined. For despite her historic commitment to an open society of individuals interacting in mutual respect, America's global preeminence, founded her bedrock social values, today founders on numerous rising threats, with many more internal than external.

As a consequence, her long-standing social strengths, sustained by powerful ideological and cultural sinews that have permitted her to prevail in an often challenging and complex world, now stand in jeopardy—making it not tautological to say that her principal socioeconomic threats are equally social *and* economic.

As within the past half century, the national attachments of those recently arrived and those here to greet them have been subjected to the fires of a flaming demographic cauldron. Their manifest flames—social conflict and civic disconnectedness—have concurrently been fanned by the rise of a radical cult of anti-American, liberal elitists engaged in a debilitating cultural confrontation called by some the United States' "Second Civil War."[16]

In the process, great battles are being waged over everything from the nature of families in America; to the proper role of religion in society; to the subversive content of countercultural civics, history, and linguistic curricula in educational institutions that have served to weaken patriotic respect for the nation's primary social and political ones.

Concurrently, multiculturalism has successfully championed the primacy of parochial cultural, ethnic, racial, and linguistic identities over historic national attachments while applying the epithet of "nativist," intended to be pejorative, to those who would aspire to preserve traditional legacies and values, with one of its big lies being that it always portrays societal issues in black and white terms.

In the process, the very term "multicultural" has degenerated from a descriptor of the virtues of strength through the blending of ethnic diversity into a code word for "cultural dry rot"—for the notion that everything in American society is bad, and that of every other group, whether civilized or not, is good! Yet regrettably, the reality is that as a civilization that is made to feel guilt for everything it does will, over time, come to lack the conviction to defend itself—and as a consequence, will die.[17]

This, thus, is a civilizational war. But unlike the first Civil War of the 1860s, which pitted North versus South, commerce against agriculture, and urban vis-à-vis rural interests and tradition, America's "Second Civil War," commencing in the 1960s, has been launched on multiple vectors moving outward everywhere throughout the nation.

Unlike its more physical predecessor, moreover, refuge from it cannot be sought in the country's primary institutions—its rich religious, cultural, martial, and political organizations, and its families—for that is precisely where, and against which, this war is being waged—on school, history, language, religion, antimilitary, and family fronts.[18]

Such countercultural conflict, and its strategic battering ram—the tactics of "political correctness" run amok—thus share deep and tangled roots, borrowing heavily upon the social theories of Sigmund Freud while tracing their origins to breakaway Marxist movements evolving in the 1930s that sought to defeat democratic capitalism not by directly challenging the economic system that nurtured it but rather by undermining the traditional culture that supported it and lent it its enduring strength.[19]

Among its earliest champions were neo-Marxists—radical scholars who commenced their proselytizing at the Frankfurt School of Social Research, and then went on to comprise the dogmatic vanguard that laid the ideological foundations for America's 1960s "ivory tower" socialist intellectual revolution. In a remarkable confluence of cresting ideological currents, their arrival coincided with the rise of the radical anti–Vietnam War movement on U.S. campuses, creating a synergy that lent momentum to both agendas.[20]

Foremost among the neo-Marxists was the apostle of libidinal utopia, Herbert Marcuse, a Columbia University professor often credited—if "credit" is the proper word—as being the "father of the New Left," who would lead antiestablishment rallies on politically active campuses throughout the United States, commencing in the mid-1960s.[21] Indeed, he taught the cult children of Woodstock and Haight-Ashbury the very language of revolution.[22]

Advancing an incendiary countercultural ideological didactic forged by Marcuse, the so-called New Left dogma thus took root, as articulated in his masterwork, *Counter-Revolution and Revolt*, which proclaimed: "If the New Left emphasizes the struggle for a restoration of nature, if it demands a new sexual morality . . . then it fights against those material conditions imposed by the capitalist system and their reproduction."[23]

Indeed, in the "Political Preface" to a 1966 screed titled *Eros and Civilization*, Marcuse openly called for all-out revolution against the "political machine, the corporate machine, and the cultural and educational machine . . . of affluent Western society"; in so doing, invoking a revolt against the very civic, social, and intellectual traditions that have historically defined American values.[24]

In this quest—in a jewel of opacity labeled "liberating tolerance," a precursor to the "politics of meaning" that would later become the social mantra of the Clinton administration—he demanded not just equal, but "extra-equal" primacy for the "New Left," and sinisterly called for the use of "extra-legal means if legal ones have proved to be inadequate."[25]

The movement's targeted recruits were radical youth, black militants, feminists, Third World revolutionaries, homosexuals, and the antisocial and alienated—self-determined, self-proclaimed angry victimized voices deemed persecuted by "the West." Central to its campaign—in a manner not unlike Adolf Hitler in the 1930s seeking to revive the spirit of a fallen people by finding suitable scapegoats upon which to blame their fall—it launched its effort to make innate patriotism and traditional values its first victims, and to demonize those who support them as "politically incorrect" and ideologically beyond the pale.[26]

Adopting "Make love, not war!" "It is forbidden to forbid!" and "Sex, Drugs, and Rock and Roll!" as its working slogans, the New Left thus became a prime motivating force of late 1960s U.S. college students for shouting down defenders of the U.S. war effort in Vietnam—in the process, welcoming antiwar activists denigrating those who did fight as "baby killers," "genocidal," and "racist" while shouting "Hey, Hey, LBJ! How many kids did you kill today" and burning American flags as they waved North Vietnamese counterparts.[27]

What Herbert Marcuse offered, in fact—under the guise of an imposed Sovietization of intellectual life wherein values are determined not by their innate qualities but by the degree to which they hue to the official party line—was "intellectual cover for cowardice, inconvenience, and indifference," a way for war protestors to dodge the draft while arrogating to themselves an aura of moral superiority over those who nobly served.

Theirs was a watershed in America's cultural evolution—as "Vietnam" became a conveniently powerful metaphor for their conviction that "Amerika's" polity, economy, society, and culture were inherently corrupt. Oblivious, or perhaps wedded, to the nihilistic political realities that their objectives would invoke, their protests largely involved their self-perceived greater wisdom vis-à-vis the corresponding shortcomings of their home countrymen.[28]

Ultimately, these new liberal leftists were able to penetrate to the very highest levels of U.S. government—with Michael Lerner, Clinton social policy advisor and architect of its signature byline, "the politics of meaning," who was later to become editor of *Tikkun*, explaining the "New Left's" affinity for the inspiration of the Marcusian didactic thusly: "Marcuse remained an inspiration to many of us because he unashamedly embraced the need for utopian vision and a revolutionary metaphysics that could recognize human needs that transcend economic security, individual rights, or the struggle for inclusion and non-discrimination within an oppressive social reality."[29]

Continuing this thesis, Lerner explained that "the freedom obtained through free market economies increasingly feels empty, and people in fact become trapped and dominated by a subtler but equally coercive power now operating by shaping their consent rather than opposing it."[30]

The message that Lerner and fellow statists thus conveyed was to offer to citizens the sense that "you must trust us as your rulers to impose more meaning in your lives"—ostensibly on the presumption that the more intolerant life becomes, the more "meaningful" it will be. As forced equality is itself punitive policy, the more equality that government purports to impose, the more the political order is poisoned by its resulting arbitrary powers.[31]

Leftist legal philosopher Ronald Dworkin, who is on record with the homily that "We must take care not to use the Equal Protection Clause to cheat ourselves out of equality," defines it unabashedly: "A more equal society is a better society even if its citizenry prefer inequality."[32] Or, as alternately put by fellow-traveling Cornell political scientist Andrew Hacker: "Citizens should be given the blessings of equality whether they want them or not."[33]

As this torqued "communistic" ideological influence gradually evolved within the ranks of the American "academic Left," moreover, it eventually flowed out into the nation's popular culture as well, finding an army of willing foot solders in the nation's universities in the late 1960s and 1970s—a socialist sanctuary where many at the forefront of the mid-1960s cultural deconstructionist movement now serve as tenured faculty. That such an ivory tower ideological evolution—the spread of antisocial psyche—should perhaps be not entirely unexpected, however, is manifest in the keen insight of philosopher Samuel Butler that "academicians . . . often live in such a rare, uncommon atmosphere that common sense can rarely reach them."[34]

This was nonetheless a development within American society largely unforeseen by many, as historically the country's campuses were its foremost bastions of liberty and free thought—the place where creative ideas evolved and were smelted and refined in the forge of Socratic method. As assessed by literary scholar John Ellis, writing in the 1990s: "Twenty years ago, no one would have believed it possible that professors, of all people, would argue that the universities would one day have an overtly political function."[35]

How did such a bizarre reversal happen? How could a group expected to behave one way do exactly the opposite? One factor is certain: the campus radicals of a half-century ago have now come of age. They today have tenure, academic chairs, and whole departments—they have moved the entire campus culture radically to the left—with the by-product being that society no longer influences the campus but the exact reverse: the radicalism of the campus, with the liberal media as its prime conduit, is now seeping out into society at large.[36]

Indeed, it is as if the countercultural hippies of the mid-1960s never left. For the reality is that when the "flower children" of that era shunned the free-market world to receive instead their *in situ* professorships and deanships, they did not abandon their dreams of radical cultural transformation. Rather, they expanded and proceeded to implement them using the university as a staging ground for political indoctrination and insurrection.[37]

Hence, today, rather than disrupting classes, they are now actually teaching them—establishing their contents while administering their curricula. Instead of attempting to destroy America's structural institutions externally, they are subverting them internally, as the left-wing ambitions of erstwhile campus renegades have become the academic agenda of the in-house intellectual power elite.[38]

As a consequence, efforts to dismantle academia's traditional curricula, once vociferously demanded by campus activists on the streets, are today routinely implemented via orders from the dean's office and the faculty senate. As Henry Gates, chairman of Harvard University's Afro-American Studies Department—in a dazzling display of the patently obvious proffered as a triumphant revelation—has asserted: "Ours was the generation that took over buildings in the late 1960s and demanded the creation of Women's and Black Studies programs, and now . . . we have come back to challenge the traditional curriculum."[39]

Identifying a "rainbow coalition of blacks, leftists, feminists, deconstructionists, and Marxists" that had infiltrated academia and were "ready to take power," he presciently predicted: "As the old guard retires, we will be in control. Then, of course, the universities will become more liberal politically."[40]

Gates' assertions—proof positive that rabidly militant antimilitary socialists who ardently oppose capitalism tend to stay within the university system because they can't function outside of it—is resoundingly echoed by campus activist and Middlebury College Professor Jay Perini who states: "After the Vietnam War, a lot of us didn't crawl back into our literary cubicles. With the war over, our visibility was lost, and it seemed for a while—to the unobservant—that we had disappeared. Now we have tenure and the work of reshaping the universities has begun in earnest."[41]

In like manner, Annette Kolodney, dean of humanities at the University of Arizona, allowing that she was ideologically shaped as a leader of the 1960s University of California-Berkeley protests and as a worker for César Chávez's United Farm Workers, openly concedes that "I see my scholarship as an extension of my political activism."[42] As described by former

U.S. Solicitor General Robert Bork, America's ongoing countercultural revolution thus was, in fact, precipitated by

> the Sixties Decade, the decade not only of burning law books but of regulatory nihilism, occupied and terrorized universities, and the Establishment's surrender. The Sixties may be seen as a mini-French Revolution that seemed to fail; but ultimately did not. The radicals were not defeated by any conservative or traditionally liberal opposition but by their own graduation from universities. And theirs was merely a temporary defeat. They and their ideology are all around us now.[43]

However, it is not just that the contemporary peddlers of politicized "New Left" polemic are, in many cases, among the most celebrated academics in the nation—holding distinguished tenured chairs at such venerated academic institutions as Harvard, Princeton, Duke, Penn, and Michigan—it is equally that department chairs now sit on hiring and promotion committees and are actively engaged in developing and implementing radical curricular change at the nation's higher learning institutions.

Thus it is that throughout many sectors of American academia today, professors are unlikely to get hired unless they embrace *in toto* the socialistically prescribed package of "politically correct" campus *isms*—multiculturalism, postmodernism, radical feminism, and sexism.[44]

Today, therefore, the 1960s radicals are still around. But now, they don't just paralyze the universities, they run them. But they did not merely take over academia. For though, by training, they were never likely to go into business or the skilled professions, they went instead into education, journalism, politics, church bureaucracies, foundations, and Hollywood—and anywhere else where public attitudes could be influenced—and influence them, they did.[45]

The 1960s thus were a trying time for America. As assessed by social scientist Robert Nisbet: "I think it would be difficult to find a single decade in the history of Western culture wherein so much barbarism—so much calculated onslaught against culture and convention in any form, and so much degradation of culture and the individual—passed into print, into music, into art, and onto the American stage as in the Nineteen Sixties."[46]

Indeed, the decade produced, in the words of historian David Potter, "perhaps the most aggressive rejection of dominant values that any society has ever permitted without seriously attempting to curb the attack and without really defending the values being assaulted"[47]—an assessment to which noted sociologist Alan Bloom has appended: "Enlightenment in America came close to breathing its last in the Sixties."[48]

As New Left ideas have spread beyond the campus, moreover, even old-style liberals have become no longer safe from their "politically correct" reach—to the degree that in the early 1990s, the late, noted Kennedyesque lion of liberalism Arthur Schlesinger would warn that this "cult of ethnicity," as he labeled it, "could destroy the nation."[49]

"Multiculuralism," in its essence, then, is incontrovertibly opposed to European civilization, and by virtue of the extension of its derivatives, to traditional American values. Needing "big government" for its empowerment, within the past half century, its access to reins of power has impacted dramatically, and ominously, upon each of the American societal values analyzed in detail in three separate, sequential chapters of this inquiry—education, media, and citizenship—as well as on the socioeconomic realm evaluated in follow-on analyses.

It manifests itself in many forms—with cultural relativism, promoting within the nation's schools and institutions of higher learning the notion that the values of Western civilization are biased and destructive, and historical revisionism, endless working to rewrite the past to portray a more secular, "subcultural" message, both being subsets of the same liberal elitist agenda.[50]

Underpinning this radical countercultural agenda, of course, is the fundamental premise that patriotism to one's adopted residence must be subordinated to loyalty to one's ethnic or racial group, which is the prime source of his or her identity. In short, domestic multiculturalism seeks to transcend traditional national identity by deconstructing it into constituent social subunits.[51]

Alternately stated, the counterculturalists view most nationalistic and social group attachments as antithetical rather than compatible, and they urge individuals to resolve this conflict by valuing, and lending priority to, ethnic and racial attachments over more patriotic civic and community responsibilities and ties.

In so doing, they create "wedge issues" that then empower them to exploit their "politics of victimization by virtue of difference." And thus it is that an "anti–Vietnam War" movement initially precipitated by 1960s hippy flower children lacking the courage to serve their nation has now been transubstantiated into a full-blown "anti-America" countercultural crusade.[52]

Indeed, this crusade is one that, within the past half century, has steadily traced a dramatic downward course—with reverence for national values and traditions built throughout the 1800s and the first half of the twentieth century peaking in the outburst of patriotism that attended post–Pearl Harbor World War II. It would culminate symbolically with President Kennedy's clarion call in his 1961 inaugural address, "Ask not what your country can do for you—ask what you can do for your country."[53]

Yet such a consistent devolution should again come as no surprise. For though at mid-twentieth century, America largely remained a multiethnic, multiracial society with an Anglo-Protestant primary culture encompassing a multitude of subcultures and a common political creed clearly rooted in that mainstream culture, that noble era wherein national identity was paramount and Americans were unabashedly patriotic began to wane throughout the 1960s.[54]

Since the second half of that century, moreover, primarily as a result of the adoption of the new doctrines of multicultural diversity popular among influential elements operating among the nation's intellectual and political elites—combined with the subsequent supporting of governmental policies on affirmative action and bilingual education that those doctrines espoused—the nation has faced the very real prospect of devolving into a "sexually liberated," culturally bifurcated society with Spanish vying with English as the national language.[55]

This demise in national identity has had several causes: (1) the ascendancy of the "didactics of diversity" among the nation's liberal elitists who believe that racial, ethnic, gender, and other subnational identities enjoy higher priority claims to civic loyalty than does national identity; (2) the weakening of social factors that previously promoted immigrant assimilation; (3) the concurrent increase of a tendency among immigrants to maintain dual identities, loyalties, and citizenship; and, finally, (4) a growing desire and dominance of the proponents of "Hispanization" and their grand design to transform America into a bilingual, bicultural society.[56]

With their intent transcending mere cognitive dissonance, then, their consequences have been cosmic—as the malignancy of multiculturalism reflexively reacting against "Euro-centrism" has today mutated into an ethnocentrism of its own. Having emerged both as an ideology and a mystique, many of its disciples bring with them a genuine hatred of the West, which they blame for what they perceive to be generations of imperialism, racism, colonialism, condescension, and exploitation.[57]

The rapid rise of this radical cult has, in fact, impacted dramatically upon American social values—and its prospects for further success are not inconsequential. For while ethno-ancestral identities are inherited, cultural values are fungible and can be molded through indoctrination. The cult's crowning achievement—which has been as politically impressive as it has been socially disastrous—has been its successful deconstruction of "reality," targeting the socioeconomic fabric of America by assaulting long-held values tightly woven over time into the tapestry of her culture.

In this fervid quest, these radicals stop at nothing. As in their intellectual rampage, traditional expressions of faith have been banished from the public square, and in the resultant absence of commonly held absolutes—those homogenizing moral values that have historically epitomized "decency" within American society—everything that the nation has historically stood for has been reduced to a state of relative moral abstraction.[58]

Traditional ethical standards are thus today called arbitrary and authoritarian. Values such as "right and wrong" are deemed "absolutist"—and hence fascist—as a new twilight zone of ideological reality has become the social norm within the leftist crowd who now serve as the nation's ethics police.[59]

Their exploitation of public education has been particularly egregious and devastating. Historically, schools were the conduit through which immigrant children were integrated into America's society and inculcated with her values. The goal of the militant multiculturalists, on the other hand, is to achieve the exact opposite—to replace English as a teaching tool with ethnic tongues while lending priority to the cultures of subnational groupings.[60]

Several factors underlie this transformation. Since the 1960s, in a sea of social ferment, powerful movements have arisen to challenge the salience, substance, and utility of traditional concepts of Americanism. For them, the nation is not a community of individuals sharing a common history, culture, and creed, but instead an aggregate of races and subcultures whereby they should be defined.

They interpret the inscription on the Great Seal of the United States and on all U.S. coinage—*e pluribus unum*—not by its literal translation—"out of many, one"—but rather as predictably articulated in reverse by Al Gore—"out of one, many"—a cause captioned by Bill Clinton's proclamation in June 1998 hailing the prospective "liberation" of Americans from their dominant European culture by mid-twenty-first century—while adding that the prime reason that she is in danger of being attacked is because of her history of slavery and treatment of Native Americans.[61]

This, despite the reality that for two centuries, American schoolchildren have been taught to take seriously the opening three words of the preamble to the U.S. Constitution: "We the people . . ." and the nation accepted literally the concept of *e pluribus unum*—initially borrowed as its slogan by Jefferson from the famed Roman poet Virgil's *Moretum*. Thus, it was indelibly impressed on the country's conscience as the motto of the "melting pot."[62]

But then came the counterculturalists of the past half century. Despising societal assimilation, they aspire instead to *e pluribus plures*: "preserving the many as many." For to them, *e pluribus unum* is no less than social oppression by the vested majority over the underprivileged minority. They thus promote deliberate "balkanization" so that each racial and immigrant ethnic group can retain its cultural identity, to wit: the iconography of "one nation, under God, indivisible" now sacrificed on the altar of "multicultural diversity."[63]

Supplanting traditional left-wing sympathizers and their socialist ideologies of the early to mid-twentieth century, the modern countercultural deconstructionsts—now prevalent in academia, Hollywood, and the media, and among "minority rights" groups, ubiquitously abetted by pandering politicians—are, in general, therefore, antilegacy, antihistory, antitradition, and antimilitary. In promoting programs that emphasize sexual, racial, ethnic, and cultural subidentities to the detriment of a national one, they thus denounce efforts to "Americanize" them as "un-American"—notwithstanding that such multiculturalism reduces a nation to being little more than a demographic holding pen.[64]

What the proponents of this "new diversity" aspire to, then, is reverse assimilation—seeking for American society to adapt to values of other cultures. The left-wing analogue to 1950s McCarthyites, they view traditional Western societal contributions as no less than a litany of crimes. In support of their ends, they rewrite history syllabi and texts to substitute the history of subnational groups for that of America. They rhapsodize over César Chávez while denigrating Thomas Jefferson, extolling Malcolm X while maligning the motives of Abraham Lincoln, revering "Kwanzaa" all the while deprecating Christmas.[65]

Succinctly put, if those minorities today being admitted to academia under special standards are having difficulty comprehending Plato, Shakespeare, Milton, Locke, and Madison, then the reason must perforce be because they were all white male chauvinists—with the ready remedy a recourse to the teachings of H. Rap Brown, Angela Davis, Maya Angelou, and Gloria Steinem in their stead.

THE COUNTERCULTURAL AGENDA

What America confronts today, then, with the gradual but steady evolution of the multicultural movement, is no less than the destruction of those fundamental precepts that underlie the nation's historic concepts both of liberal education and of a liberal democratic being. Such values include color-blind justice and respect for the rule of law; promotion pursuant to merit, not in accordance with predetermined cultural and ethnic quotas; and above all, the right to unbridled expression—Western concepts that constitute the bedrock core of America's political and economic systems.[66]

Indeed, there is no escaping that free speech is quintessential to a free society. The First Amendment has served the American republic well as the cornerstone of her bedrock core. Compromising its safeguards in a quixotic ethereal quest for a convoluted liberal notion of "social justice" puts her liberties at risk. For as the social philosopher Alexis de Tocqueville wrote of her: "It is by the enjoyment of a dangerous freedom that Americans learn the art of rendering the dangers to freedom less formidable."[67]

Writing in *The Closing of the American Mind*, Alan Bloom postulates that the tendency of academics to discard two millennia of learning codified in the great works of Western civilization constitutes an intellectual suicide tantamount to that which precipitated the Dark Ages. If the American empire is to survive, he argues, it will be because her people choose to recognize their heritage and traditions and reject those who would denigrate and deconstruct them.[68]

Bloom's words are paralleled in the writings of modern philosopher Susan Haack's *Manifesto of a Passionate Moderate*, wherein she argues that though the goals of the multiculturalists may well be laudable, they "seem to have encouraged the idea that truth, evidence, and reason are tools of oppression, an idea as tragic as it is bizarre."[69]

Her assessment is profound. For a principal argument articulated by those who advocate their countercultural cause is that it is philosophically "democratic" in its essence. Ever-emphatic in their assertions, they are convinced that Americans are sufficiently sanguine about the sanctity of the concept of democracy that they will accept anything so labeled unequivocally.[70]

Yet nothing could be further from the truth. For in abjuring the preamble of the U.S. Constitution—"We the people"—they adhere to a wholly nonassimilationistic "we the *peoples*" doctrine, while proceeding oblivious to the reality that while America's greatness may have been forged on the foundations of a multiethnic society, the secret to her success has been her "monocultural—not multicultural—aspirations and her extraordinary ability to homogenize and assimilate diversity."[71]

Indeed, rejecting Jefferson's classic prescription for nation-building patriotism—"out of many, one"—to champion the rights of "peoples," as multiculturalism does in its "what's in it for me as a victimized minority" dogma—is itself contrary to the foundations of those traditional democratic freedoms that have their roots in "individual rights," not group rights.[72]

There can be no doubt that the suppression of individual rights throughout history—as in the cases of Nazi Germany and the erstwhile Soviet Union—brought with it them death of democracy and freedom in their wake. Hence, the inherent error of the multiculturalist rhetoric: for once individual rights are subordinated to those of the "group," democracy becomes an empty shell.[73]

Accordingly, while global communism may well be dead, the teachings of Karl Marx live on in the ideology and politics of modern-day counterculturalism. Indeed, a foremost Marxist concept is the belief that all inequalities, including social inequality, are inherently evil. Thus, as seen through the prism of the proletarian protagonists, all cultures are to be valued equally—and to believe that some are superior to others is sociological heresy.[74]

Marx viewed such inequality within the context of economics, and for him, there too, it was the greatest of all evils. Extrapolating the concept of inequality to contemporary society, in turn, the multiculturalists argue that it is the product of cultural imperialism, "imperialism" being a Marxian-despised attribute.

Accordingly, they believe that it must be uprooted by teaching in all phases of education that all cultures must be equally valued to appease the culturally oppressed, "oppression" being another paramount Marxist/neo-Marxist concern and propagandistic tool. And thus it is that today, just as most of the nations of the world are abandoning communism in droves, the counterculturalists want to take this nation there.[75]

Yet throughout America, wherever the multiculturalists have, in fact, prevailed, the consequences have been catastrophic—with the first and foremost casualties including the long-standing Western conviction that truth and ideas, as absolutes, transcend the vagaries of more ephemeral race, class, and sex considerations, and the conviction that the truths embedded in the classics are the foundations upon which the quest for ultimate truth should commence.[76]

But this is an aspiration utterly disputed by Marxist followers who, in rejecting the fundamentals of Cartesian logic—"I think, therefore, I am"—argue instead that all ideas of truth are relative and class-bound. To wit: "It is not the consciousness of men that determines their existence; to the contrary, their social existence determines their consciousness." It is classic values, therefore, that are the target of their frontline assault.[77]

Notwithstanding, identifying such parallels within the "Marxist-multiculturalist symbiosis" is itself a path that must be pursued equally with methodological trepidation and objective determination, as there are clear pitfalls in any such démarche. It must be approached with caution, of course, lest one be accused, or even actually be guilty, of neo-McCarthyism. It must be pursued with conviction, nonetheless, because the threat that counterculturalism poses to the historic American way of life is very real.

The prospective outcome is not inconsequential. For as assessed by historian Diane Ravitch, multiculturalists and their allied race/ethnic/sexist sympathizers "celebrate everything that is non-white, non-Western, and non-male, while criticizing everything that isn't"[78]—an accusation echoed by social scientist Dwight Murphey in his assertion that teaching multiculturalism in the nation's schools "is far more than a mere academic exercise; it is a struggle for hearts and souls—for our collective memories and self-perceptions."[79]

Indeed, as the analyses of chapters 3 through 5 make clear, pursuant to their agenda, the counterculturalists would, and do, seek to do:

- Censor First Amendment–guaranteed "free speech" as a violation of political correctness doctrine;
- Rewrite history texts to discredit traditional American heroes and replace them with countercultural ones;

- Decry capitalism as evil;
- Downplay the significance of IQ tests and meritocracy while promoting racial and ethnic quotas;
- Ban the Ten Commandments from all institutions of higher learning, courts, and other public places;
- Legally compel Boy Scouts to accept atheists and homosexuals within their ranks;
- Promote same-sex marriages;
- Discredit "WASPs" while indiscriminately bashing all white males;
- Forbid voluntary prayer in schools;
- Condemn Christopher Columbus as an Indian murderer and exploiter
- Portray traditional Judeo-Christian values as obstacles to "diversity"; and
- Encourage American flag-burning in support of their parochial causes.[80]

Indeed, it is the incessant spate of such pernicious countercultural claptrap engaged in by the residual radical roots of the 1960s "Free Love," anticapitalist, antiwar movement that moved French social commentator Jean-François Revel to describe them thusly:

> To say that a system that had done more than any other to spread well-being and social justice deserved to die, as did the young rebels commencing in the sixties, was to reveal a profound and thorough gap between reality and the concepts needed to comprehend reality.
> To recall how stupendously large this gulf was, bear in mind that the revolt against democratic capitalism was led by young people in the best universities who had access to all of the information that they could ask for.
> Yet they chose as their political role models men like Fidel Castro, Mao Zedong, and Ché Guevera whose deeds were not in the area of good government but mass terrorism, not social justice but economic incompetence, not expansion of liberty but criminality.[81]

This, then, is the fractious and invidious state of the intellectual reign of terror being waged by the campus-housed *cognoscenti* under the rubric of "political correctness" throughout much of American academia today. In the words of historian Victor David Hanson, "The radical Left is courting disaster and threatens to destroy the credibility of true liberals who appear fearful of condemning the madness in their midst."[82]

Another regrettable, albeit likely paradoxically inadvertent, ramification of pursuing such a disparate diversity agenda, however, is the suggestion that the highest achievements of Western civilization are somehow technologically off-limits or inaccessible to certain groups because they are not of an appropriate ethnic background, race, sex, or intellect to comprehend them.

It is as if the teachings of Socrates, because he was a white Mediterranean male, are somehow unapproachable by, or unintelligible to, a black male or Chinese female. The racial and sexist implications of such assumptions are as patently ironic as they are ludicrous, as what they are advocating is nothing less than a concession of intellectual inferiority—and with it, intellectual entropy inseminated through institutional means.[83]

Does this, then, make the counterculturalist ideologies intrinsically evil? Here again, the great English philosopher-politician Edmund Burke may offer insight in contending that, "I revere men in functions that belong to them, but not beyond," and in conceding that they "may do the worst of things without being the worst of men," nonetheless concluding that "it is no excuse for presumptuous ignorance that it is driven by insolent passion."[84]

IS "POLITICAL CORRECTNESS" ITSELF POLITICALLY CORRECT?

Nonetheless, proceeding without prejudice to its perceived mandate and irrespective of its intent, such so-called political correctness is merely the flagship of the multiculturalists' anti-Americanist armada—a force whose outright assault on citizenship denigrates the value of the national birthright.

Indeed, all of their disparate subversive initiatives, historiographic reconstruction and bilingualism by legislative fiat foremost among them, are no less than battles deliberately waged in an all-out war on the U.S. identity—an assault on societal homeland values possibly unprecedented in human history. In sum, they are in conflict with every aspect of American culture as they have been understood and revered for the past two centuries.[85]

For "political correctness"—neutralization through intimidation—is, as openly proclaimed, one of the foremost Marcusian inventions for the destruction of capitalism—instilling fear within those responsible, inhibiting enlightening discussion, bashing those who believe otherwise, and destroying the classic values that the nation cherishes. In its modern understanding, then, doctrinaire insistence on its use is no more than the imposition of censorship on any and all traditional ideas to which one is opposed.[86]

Indeed, the very notion of "political correctness"—whose so-called corrective program, as noted, is focused particularly upon the nation's media and educational systems—is itself a direct frontal assault upon the First Amendment doctrine of unfettered free speech. For what began as a polite means to counter communicational incivility has now instead mutated into a tool for controlling society—a didactic that betrays cherished historic legacy, replacing that long-standing tradition of assimilation that is the nation's social glue with deliberate cultural, ethnic, and racial fragmentation.[87]

During the past couple of decades, Americans have, in fact, gained fairly good insight into what political correctness really means; to wit: no more than compelling people to conform to dogmas advanced by advocates of the multiculturalist agenda. For when individuals, higher education students, for instance, do not comply, they are usually disciplined and sometimes even expelled in a classic totalitarian example of reverse bigotry practiced in the guise of eliminating bigotry.[88]

Their goal is thereby to manufacture seeming virtue out of deliberately fostered guilt, reflecting a curious symmetry that today exists at both ends of the political spectrum—the fact that the fanatics on the Left are mirror images of the zealots on the Right—but with one defining difference. While the Right seeks to zealously preserve democratic capitalism, the Left seeks to decimate it and replace it with their tortured vision of a utopian socialistic totalitarian state.[89]

The Leftists' agenda thus is an approach reflective of a revolutionary demonology wherein America is depicted as not only dominating the Third World, but, in so doing, causing its radical leaders to act immorally. It is their need to bridge the vast chasm between their socialistic dream and the abject barrenness of socialist reality, however, that produces both their skewed political ideology and their totalitarian mandate. Thus, they endlessly endeavor to transform a failed past into a redemptive future. Turning Santayana's famous warning inside out, they refuse to learn from their past precisely because they want to repeat it.[90]

Their approach enjoys powerful historic precedent. The communists of the former Soviet Union and the fascists of Hitler's Germany, among others, aggressively employed just such political correctness long before the current crop of multiculturalists ideologically stumbled onto it, thereby propelling themselves prominently onto the political scene—with speech or action not in line with socialist or fascist doctrine subject to severe and certain punishment.[91]

Today, while the multiculturalists may not actually send the politically incorrect to Siberia or Buchenwald, they nonetheless impose draconian punishments on those who do not march in goose step conformity with their dogmas and rigidly enforced norms. Alternately put, political correctness is to culture what Marxism is to economics. To again quote social theorist Alan Bloom, "Our universities today have become the battleground of a struggle between liberal democracy and radical, or one might say, even totalitarian egalitarianism."[92]

More ominous still, the ongoing multicultural revolution has infected America's judicial system as well. As is the case in their quest for absolute political correctness, the courts have subordinated the rule of law to social biases in favor of "lifestyle" determinants that celebrate group identity and radical personal autonomy in basic moral matters. Consequently, there is today a fundamental disconnect between America's jurisprudential corner-stone, its system of constitutional law, and the traditional values by which Americans have lived and wish to continue to live—those foundational institutions that have undergirded American moral life for four centuries and that of the West for two millennia.[93]

Indeed, the effect of the judicial interventions since the 1950s onset of the so-called "Warren Court" has been overwhelmingly to undermine or overthrow traditional American beliefs and practices on basic issues of domestic social policy. Yet in its sanctimonious arbitrariness, there is no oversight respecting its decisions; it is not only above the law, its decisions, it insists, are the law. As future Chief Justice Charles Evan Hughes candidly remarked in 1907: "The Constitution is what judges say it is."[94] To which Justice Robert Jackson later famously appended: "We are not final because we are infallible, but we are infallible because we are final."[95]

Such sentiments regrettably are not new, as such authoritarian propensities already were a prime matter of concern in the time of Thomas Jefferson when he warned of those who "consider the judges as the ultimate arbiters of all constitutional questions; a very dangerous doctrine indeed and one which would put us under the despotism of an oligarchy."[96]

Societal values undeniably are not immutable. They inevitably change— sometimes for the better—to adjust to evolving social circumstance. Those mores that guided a parochial, essentially agrarian nineteenth-century society arguably may not be entirely appropriate for a more global twenty-first-century one. But the pace of that change, and the role of law in effecting it, are questions of primary importance to the type of society that America aspires to be—and should develop as a function of their own volition and not as a litany of whimsical edicts of a liberal court system.[97]

Such questions, moreover, evolving within the framework for change contemplated by a democratic form of government, are intended to be resolved by the nation's private institutions—families, communities, schools, and churches—and seldom, if ever, by elections and laws that seek to impose a top-down legal and moral consensus—and certainly not within a crucible wherein natural moral evolution is preempted by minority moral preference arbitrarily enforced by judicial fiat.[98]

It is indelibly clear from the *Federalist* writings that the Founders contemplated the Constitution to be just that—a "constitution"—binding law—and not a mere list of "helpful suggestions" for would-be-lawmaker-judges who seek to transform their traditional role as law interpreter into that of legislator.

Now however, in an age when judicial activism has replaced constitutional constructionism as the cornerstone of law, the Constitution, intended by the Founders as the guarantor of basic rights, is instead steadily being reshaped into a tool for depriving mainstream citizens of their most fundamental right, the right to self-governance.

In the process, under the tortured interpretations of the Supreme Court, flag desecration and nude dancing have been proclaimed as protected free speech, whereas prayer in school is not; and racial discrimination, in the form of arbitrary quotas, has been sanctioned as a preferred basis for public sector decision making respecting the apportionment of rights and privileges.[99]

Concurrently, "separation of church and state"—a phrase that appears nowhere in the Constitution, Declaration of Independence, *Federalist Papers*, or other official Founding documents—has become the "constitutional" basis for framing the role of religion in American society. As what the cultural left calls the "mainstream" values has instead become a polluted political cesspool that has grossly overflowed its banks and continues to wreak devastating havoc upon upon the landscape of the nation's traditional morality and cherished precepts.[100]

Indeed, some of the judicial efforts at legislating morality would be outright laughable were they not so socially devastating. There has been a time in the nation's recent history, for instance, when the assignment of children by race to public schools was constitutionally permissible, another when it was constitutionally prohibited, and yet another, as now, when it is sometimes constitutionally required—the overarching legal mandate seemingly fluctuating with the circumstance, with the court, and with the whimsy of the judge.[101]

In each of these determinations, the nation's courts have overturned the constitutionality of policy choices reflecting historic values made in the ordinary political process, only to substitute radical policies to further the social agenda of the political left. Decisions of any comparable importance reversing that course, on the other hand, are conspicuous by their absence—as in the guise of enforcing the Constitution, the courts have instead enacted the agenda of the multicultural revolution.[102]

Notwithstanding, there are perforce beliefs that bind together any great society—values that its people deem precious and hold dear—and must be held inviolate. Absent them, as the great nineteenth-century champion of the philosophy of liberty, John Stuart Mill, explicitly warned, the potential for societal devolution is accentuated:

> In all political societies which have a durable existence, there has been some fixed point; something upon which men agreed in holding sacred; which might or might not be lawful to contest in theory, but which no one could either fear or hope to be shaken in practice. . . .

> But when the questioning of these fundamental principles is the habitual
> condition of the body politic . . . the state is virtually in a position of civil war
> against itself and can no longer remain free from it in act or fact.[103]

The latter is, in fact, the state of judicially forged society-building that actively afflicts America today. Yet the framing of constitutional law—absent
the Constitution—policy-making for the nation as a whole by a mere majority of nine unelected lawyers—is the antithesis of a constitutional system
whose principles of federalism, separation of powers, and representative
self-governance were the basis for its founding.[104]

As Texas law professor Lino Graglia has asserted: "The thing to know to
fully comprehend contemporary constitutional law is that, almost without
exception, the effect of rulings of unconstitutionality over the past four
decades has been to enact policy preferences of the cultural elite on the far
left of the political spectrum."[105]

To which his university colleague Stanford Levinson appends: "The death
of constitutionalism may be the central event of our time, just as the death
of God was that of the past century."[106] In this spirit, Justice Antonin Scalia—
contending that the Constitution is precisely that, a "constitution," and as
such, immutable, and not a "living document" that evolves over time, always
in the direction of expanded federal power—in cogent inquiry asks:

> What secret knowledge, one must wonder, is breathed into lawyers when they
> become Justices of this Court that enables them to discern that a practice which
> the text of the Constitution does not clearly prescribe, and which our people
> have regarded as constitutional for 200 years, is unconstitutional? . . . Day by
> day, case by case, [the Court] is busily designing a Constitution for a country
> that I do not recognize.[107]

Alexis de Tocqueville clearly understood these consummate dangers
when—in noting that "scarcely any political question arises in the United
States that is not resolved, sooner or later, into a judicial question"—he
wrote in his 1834 published treatise, *Democracy in America*:

> The President, who exercises a limited power, may err without causing great
> mischief in the state. Congress may decide amiss without utterly destroying the
> Union, because the electoral body in which the Congress originated may cause
> it to be retracted by changing its members. But if the Supreme Court is ever
> composed of imprudent or bad men, the Union may be plunged into anarchy
> or civil war.[108]

The judicial bottom line, then, remains that the essence of democratic
governance is the right of the people to engage in public deliberation over
what is right and what is wrong and to decide how those rights and wrongs
are translated into what is legal or illegal. Conversely, the elevation of

juridically-created notions of "right and wrong" to trump collective moral judgments made by the people as citizens undermines constitutionalism as conceived by the Founding Fathers and as was practiced by America for most of its first two centuries.[109]

For in favoring "group rights" over "individual rights" and the "rule of the enlightened" over "the will of the people," its logic makes no concessions to historic standards of decency and traditional concepts of right and wrong. It has instead produced a bizarre twilight of judicial reality unprecedented in human history—producing a civilization whose intellectual culture is at odds with its very ideals of civilization. It is a démarche inimical to the rule of law, contrary to the nation's self-proclaimed political raison d'être—and it directly defies America's long-standing legacy of normative traditions respecting interpersonal civility and common courtesy.[110]

DECONSTRUCTING THE DECONSTRUCTIONISTS

Paradoxically, though, the handiwork of the countercultural militants—however powerfully persuasive to their own minds—has unfolded exactly opposite to their intent. They have contended that a main objective of public education must be the celebration, perpetuation, and strengthening of ethnic origins and identities. Yet though their objectives were legally sanctioned with the Ethnic Heritage Studies Program Act of 1974, to their consummate chagrin, such separatism has merely nourished prejudices, magnified differences, and stirred antagonisms further still.[111]

Indeed, their consummate successes in exploiting civil, voting, and immigration rights for minorities—ironically largely initiated by the more orthodox political establishment in their quest to achieve social equality in the mid-1960s—have resulted in a reappearance and reinforcement of subcultural and subnational identities instead. As today, rather than promoting equal opportunity and common access, they seek privileged opportunity while operating from isolated ideological enclaves defined by sexual preference, ethnicity, and reverse racism.[112]

As soon as the Civil Rights Act of 1964 was passed, in fact, liberal elitists and minority leaders stopped demanding those inherent rights common to all citizens and rather began to demand special government programs for racial and ethnic groups in order to achieve "social and economic equality" as they, from their ivory towers, perceived it.

Whereas President Kennedy, in March 1961, signed Executive Order 10925 ordering governmental contractors to hire and treat employees "without regard to race, creed, color, or national origin," an order subsequently affirmed by President Johnson, for example, the U.S. Labor Department in 1968 began issuing orders requiring governmental contractors hiring new employees to take into account racial proportion within their geographic areas of operation.[113]

In like manner, the Voting Rights Act of 1965, designed to ensure equal access to the democratic process by forbidding jurisdictions from denying, restricting, or hindering the rights of minorities to vote, was soon transformed by judicial interpretation, and through a process of racial and ethnic legislative district gerrymandering, into initiatives to ensure the election of minorities to "safe seats."[114]

Never mind that the consequences of such "beneficence" can be, and often are, socially destabilizing—sometimes even to the degree that the so-called beneficiaries themselves find such propositions preposterous. In polls conducted in 1987 and 1990, for instance, the Gallup poll asked whether people supported or opposed the following concept: "We should make every effort to improve the position of blacks and other minorities even if it means giving them preferential treatment."[115]

Collectively, in both polls, 72 percent of the public at large opposed this proposition, whereas 24 percent supported it, with blacks voting 66 percent in opposition and 32 percent in favor.[116] In a similar 1995 poll querying whether "hiring, promotion, and college admissions should be based strictly on merit or on qualifications other than race or ethnicity," 86 percent of whites, 78 percent of Hispanics, 74 percent of Asians, and 68 percent of blacks agreed to the proposition of strict merit-based decision making.[117]

Yet, unabashedly, the multiculturalists proceed. This despite the fact that among the cultures that they aggrandize and adore, the Aztecs massacred their prisoners of war as human sacrifices, then turned their flesh into a ceremonial stew, and were likewise not adverse to ripping out the hearts of virgins and children in supplication to their gods; that the Kukuku culture of New Guinea likewise cannibalized its prisoners of war; that the Toltecs of Mexico engaged in human sacrifice; that the Inca Indians of Peru also engaged in cannibalism and child sacrifice; and that the Auca Indians of East Ecuador put chronically crying babies into purpose-built holes wherein they were trampled to death.[118]

Even today, sanctioned wife beatings throughout much of southwest Asia are not uncommon; Indian subcontinent widows, through the practice of *sati*, in fact, are often burned alive on the funeral pyres of their deceased husbands' cremations; and many young African women, particularly in East Africa, are subjected to female clitoridectomies. These are precepts opposed by the West, not locals.

As the nineteenth-century British Governor General of Sind, Sir Charles Napier, famously affirmed in elegant multicultural fashion to assembled local dignitaries: "You say that it is your custom to burn widows. Very well. We also have a custom. When men burn a woman alive, we tie a rope around their necks and hang them until dead. You build your funeral pyre; and beside it, my carpenters will build a gallows. You follow your custom, and then we will follow ours."[119]

Can anyone objectively argue, then, that these barbaric practices were Euro-American culture formulations? Can anyone seriously deny that the forced genital mutilation of women is a traditional African practice and not some arcane custom introduced by Western colonialism? Some role models to feel good about, exult, and emulate![120]

This also despite the fact that it was native Africans who sold fellow Africans, at times, even their own tribesmen, to predatory slave merchants; that slavery lasted at least a century longer in Africa and Asia than it did in Europe and America, being abolished in Ethiopia in 1942, in Saudi Arabia in 1962, in India in 1976, in Mauritania in the 1980s, and may still continue to be practiced in many parts of the Sudan.[121]

This, too, despite the reality that closer to home in North and Central America, slavery was practiced by Indian tribes long before the white man arrived; that the Pima Indians of Arizona enslaved members of the Apache and Yuma tribes; that the Illinois Indians at times bartered their slaves with the Ottawa and Iroquois Indians; that the Mohawk tribe derived its tribal name from its practice of eating human flesh; that the Mayans engaged in human sacrifice; and that myriad other cannibalisms, human sacrifices, and scalpings perpetrated by peoples admired by the multiculturalists concurrently took place. Of this, of course, their litanies say nothing.[122]

Never mind either that countervailing Western values are neither whimsical nor happenstance—they have instead been the world's unique source of the noble precepts of individual liberty, human rights, democratic self-determination, equality before the law, and religious and cultural freedom. These are Euro-American ideas—and not Asian, not African, nor Middle Eastern, except infrequently by emulation—precepts that remain the planet's most precious cultural legacy and to which the entire globe today aspires.[123]

It was America, in fact, not non-Western cultures, that in 1865, first abolished slavery—and that over the stiff resistance of Middle East and African slave traffickers who were selling their own brothers into involuntary servitude. It is likewise Anglo-Saxon democracy that today attracts the peoples of all creeds and continents—and inspires them with dreams of self-determination.

When Chinese students died vainly seeking democracy in Tiananmen Square in 1989, as Arthur Schlesinger has noted, they were not bearing representations of Confucius or Lenin or Chairman Mao but rather replicas of the Statue of Liberty—doubtlessly aware that though America didn't murder one hundred million of her innocent citizens, Joseph Stalin did; and that Chairman Mao murdered thirty million of his own as well.[124]

Critics of the U.S. system also must explain the religious freedom safeguard of the First Amendment; the nineteenth-century policies that established free public schools for all; the post–Civil War reaffirmations of liberty and full equality before the law embedded in the Thirteenth, Fourteenth, and Fifteenth Amendments; the universal political suffrage established by the Nineteenth Amendment; and the McCarran-Warren Act of 1952 that permitted all legal immigrants to become naturalized citizens.[125]

It was likewise the "old-guard Washington establishment" that initiated the Civil Rights Act of 1964—strongly supported by 80 percent of all Republicans and 61 percent of Democrats in the House, and 82 percent of all Republicans and 69 percent of Democrats in the Senate—led by Senate Minority Leader Republican Everett McKinley Dirksen, while concurrently vigorously opposed only by such ranking Southern Democratic senators as Albert Gore of Tennessee, Richard Russell of Georgia, and Robert Byrd of West Virginia—initiatives enacted well before the multiculturalist movement began to gain its momentum in the mid-to-late 1960s—all inconvenient realities that America's liberal media does not deem worthy to recollect.[126]

Critics of the system likewise are obligated to explain why Asian Americans—who are neither white nor overwhelmingly Protestant—account for a higher percentage of college graduates than do non-Asian Americans, why they then proceed to generate annual incomes within their first years of graduation, on average, $4,000 higher than the national average, or why in the aftermath of the passage of the California Civil Rights Act of 1996, which mandated college admissions on merit-based factors alone, absent quotas, over 40 percent of admissions to the University of California-Berkeley each year are now from the nation's minuscule Asian-American community— free citizens who were not directly targeted beneficiaries of the multiculturalists' self-presumed "benevolence."[127]

Indeed, though today, whole libraries are being rewritten in the quest to prove that a free-market system characterized by its openness and tolerance is actually a regimen of oppression, they are being formulated by the same crowd that four decades ago was assuring society that one communistic government after another was a "workers' paradise"—at the very time that the would-be worker beneficiaries themselves were doing their utmost to escape their so-called utopias, often losing their lives in their desperate attempts.[128]

In all of this pedagogic finger-pointing, it likewise is critical to bear in mind that there is no one within the present generation who can be blamed for those injustices suffered by America's Indians more than a century ago. Nor are there any Euro-Americans alive today who were responsibly for the enslavement of blacks in the United States in the eighteenth and nineteenth centuries, however odious the practice may now appear in retrospect.[129]

Apart from possible achievement-based scholarships for minority high school students who perform well on their Scholastic Aptitude Tests, therefore, there is no case for reparations here—as it is one thing to tolerate something, and quite another to accept that which is being tolerated.

To force people alive today to assume the ownership of alleged ancestral injustices is, in fact, not only judicially irrelevant, it is culturally counterproductive to the cause of collegiality as well as the precept of equality before the law—and does not, in any way, resolve the status claims of the minorities involved.[130]

There is, in fact, something morbidly ironic in the New Left multiculturalists' use of ethnocentrism to flog the West for chauvinism, since both the idea and the modern application of the concept of egalitarianism have been distinctly Western. Indeed, as her immigration record shows, there has not been a society since ancient Rome more open to other cultures than that of America—nor has there ever been a place on the planet wherein minorities, be they racial or ethnic, or women or homosexuals, for that matter, have enjoyed greater freedoms than in the United States.[131]

The system's naysayers likewise are at a loss to explain why peoples from all over the world, legally or illegally, seek to immigrate here. They do so not because they believe that America is perfect, but because they are convinced that Western democratic capitalism offers greater individual freedom, personal dignity, and economic opportunity than anywhere else on the planet.

They do so because they understand that their choice is not between multiculturalist nirvana and societal repression but instead between the rich rewards of a proven benevolent culture and the degeneracy of a communal barbarism that is reduced to attempting to promote equality at the bottom of the social ladder because it is doctrinally incapable of offering economic opportunities to ascend to its top.[132]

In short, only through blatant historical revisionism and raucous politicking has a small liberal lunatic fringe been able arrogate to itself the right to redefine and dictate, indeed "dumb down," the values of America in seeking victory in a cultural war that cannot be won through other, more noble, egalitarian means.

They are, in fact, precisely the types of secular elitists that British historian Lord Thomas Macaulay doubtless had in mind when he presciently predicted in a letter to an American friend in 1857: "Your Republic will be fearfully plundered and laid waste by barbarians in the twentieth century just as the Roman Empire was in the fifth; with this difference: that the Huns and Vandals will have been engendered within your own country, by your own institutions."[133]

The cogency of Lord Macaulay's warning lies in just how accurate it was. For just as civilizations rise, so they die—a stark reminder of which is encapsulated in the poignant observation of early twentieth-century American journalist and social commentator Walter Lippman, "We should remember that when Shakespeare was alive, there were no Americans; when Virgil was alive, there were no Englishmen; and when Homer was alive, there were no Romans. *Sic transit gloria!*"[134]

In the 1930s, European philosopher José Ortega y Gassett wrote: "Civilization is, above all, the will to live in common. . . . Barbarism is the tendency to disassociation. Accordingly, all barbarous epics have been times of human scatterings, separate from and hostile to, one another." Multiculturalism is no less than barbarism so defined, and as subsequent analysis will show, it has now brought America to the threshold of a more barbarous age.[135]

THE PLIGHT OF ROME IN MODERN CONTEXT

This analysis constitutes, then, the story of how a radical antimilitary counter-cultural movement that festered and grew on U.S. college campuses during the turbulent 1960s Vietnam war era, then seeped from academia, via a the conduit of a liberally-biased media that it had trained, out into the mainstream to corrupt American society at large. The net result is that America is fostering an educational system that is really not about education and a press that is really not about reportage of the news—with deterioration of non-civic cohesiveness the inexorable result.

When he spoke at Westminster College in Missouri in March 1946, addressing the advance of global communism, Winston Churchill proclaimed: "From Stettin in the Baltic to Trieste in the Adriatic, an iron curtain has descended across the continent of Europe."[136]

Well-known words, but in that same famed "Iron Curtain" speech, Britain's then ex–prime minister uttered other lesser known, but equal cogent, admonitions as well—among them the time-tested truism that "freedom of speech and thought should reign; and that courts of justice, independent of the executive, unbiased in any part, should administer laws which have received the broad assent of large majorities or are consecrated by time or custom."[137]

The precepts that Churchill espoused were not unfamiliar to his audience. Indeed, they were those classic American values championed by her Founding Fathers who had dutifully cast them into concrete in their Declaration of Independence and Constitution—cherished beliefs that vividly distinguish American and Western civilization from the barbarism of both atavistic communism and totalitarian fascism.[138]

Today, six decades later, with much of the nation's history now unlearned and forgotten, those noble traditions cannot be blithely taken for granted. For a new iron curtain has descended, this time not on Eastern Europe but instead on U.S. college campuses nationwide—as unfettered debate on social issues is no longer fostered, and, ideologically, much of the reigning faculty is as resolutely radical leftist as it is anti-American. Indeed the Republic is now passing through a profound academically-led countercultural revolution—unleashing a radicalized social transformation for which it is not prepared.[139]

In one of the most memorable speeches of his long, illustrious career, distinguished conservative philosopher Russell Kirk in 1992, in the immediate wake of the fall of the Berlin Wall, queried: "America has now overcome the ideological culture of the Union of Soviet Socialist Republics. But in the decade of this victory, are Americans to forswear the beneficent culture that they inherited? For a civilization to arise and flower, many centuries are required; but the indifference or hostility of a single generation may suffice to work that civilization's ruin."[140]

How unfortunate it now is, therefore, that out of thousands of years of suffering and oppression, a beacon that had come to burn so brightly for nearly two and a half centuries, espousing the revolutionary idea that America could be free—master of her own governance, free to worship her own God, dazzling the entire world not only with her power and progress, but also with her innate goodness—should now be threatened with extinction by "new wave" intellectual proponents of those identical discredited socialist ideologies that precipitated the planet's long-standing massive outpouring of suffering and oppression in the first place.[141]

For as subsequent analysis will show, the great "melting pot" has today been callously corrupted by self-serving neo-Marxist disciples, oblivious to the reality that every country needs its cause, a distinguishing ideology, a creed that embodies those precepts in which it profoundly believes, as the monumental remnants of that internal cultural alienation that brought about the demise of ancient Egypt, Greece, Carthage, and Rome leave little residual doubt. The United States is today, therefore, a polity at risk—a nation intellectually held hostage by flame-throwing, socialist ideologues that must now be taken back.[142]

In 84 B.C., the Roman general Sulla asked: "Now that the universe offers us no more enemies, what will be the fate of the Republic?" His answer came a few decades later when it collapsed into the autocracy of Caesarism. When global communism lost its doctrinal appeal in the late 1980s, ending the Cold War, the Soviet Union concurrently lost its collective identity and fragmented into sixteen separate states, each claiming an identity of its own as defined by its unique, rediscovered culture and history. Will this be America's fate as well?[143]

Part II

DECLINING CULTURAL VALUES

The liberties of our country, the freedom of our civil constitution, are worthy of defending at all hazards; and it is our duty to defend them against all attacks. We have received them as a fair inheritance from our worthy ancestors; they have purchased them for us with toil and danger and expense of treasure and blood, and transmitted them to us with care and diligence. It will bring an ever-lasting mark of infamy upon our present generation, enlightened as it is, if we should suffer them to be wrestled from us by violence or without a struggle, or to be cheated out of them by artifices of false and designing men.

—Samuel Adams, Publisher, Politician-Patriot, 1771

3

The Excesses of Education

To conform the principles, morals, and manners of our citizens to our republican forms of government, it is absolutely necessary that knowledge of every kind should be disseminated throughout every part of the United States.

—Founder Benjamin Rush, signer of the
U.S. Declaration of Independence

EDUCATION AND THE FOUNDING FATHERS

"The government should be capable of offering greater education and better instruction to people than they would demand from it," opined nineteenth-century British economic philosopher John Stuart Mill. "Education, therefore, is one of those things that a government should provide for its people." This was a position adopted by America's Founders, and was a clear aspiration in their attempts to forge national education policy—building upon long-standing and long-recognized tradition.[1]

"Education," in the words of historians Will and Ariel Durant, "is the transmission of civilization."[2] H. G. Wells, in his *Outline of History*, declared that "history is a race between education and catastrophe."[3] Franklin Roosevelt, echoing Plato, called learning the "foundation of democracy."[4] As Henry David Thoreau put it: "I know of no fact more encouraging than that of man's ability to elevate his life through conscious endeavor."[5]

Given academia's foremost role of preserving and transmitting knowledge—of being a civilization's conservator of tradition and cultural values—it is distressing to contemplate the base, self-serving propagandistic role to which it has been reduced in the humanities departments of many of even the finest colleges and universities throughout America today. But though it was in higher education that the country's cultural decay first set root a half century ago, it was not always so.

Indeed, America's early educational infrastructure was expressly built upon the nation's irrevocable commitment to imparting knowledge and preserving a panoply of freedoms—political, personal, and religious freedoms foremost among them—in its quest to build a "Biblical commonwealth" and to then pass the torch of that knowledge on to forthcoming generations.[6]

Her initial settlers, many of whom had suffered persecution for their religious beliefs in Europe, believed that it was biblical illiteracy—and the attendant inability to distinguish right from wrong—in fact, that was the incipient cause of civic abuse. The nation's earliest efforts at public education, therefore, were attempts to preempt those perceived abuses of power that can be inflicted upon a *biblically* illiterate people.

To further such early attempts at education, books would be brought in from England, often by incoming immigrants a few volumes at a time, throughout the eighteenth century. Various manuals to provide guidance for education within the colonies—such as John Brinsley's *A Consolation for Our Grammar Schooles*, produced in 1622—were designed to preserve the purity of the English language of a people dwelling in such a faraway land, explicitly referring to Virginia. It took as its express goal to improve the "country grammar schooles" and to "expand the Kingdom of Christ, especially among the heathen Indians." A few books, such as the Bay Psalm Book of 1640, likewise were printed in America herself.[7]

The Protestants who predominantly settled the English colonies greatly valued the school, of course, because it taught their children to read the Bible, which was deemed the seminal document guiding early colonial life and education. Beside it in the classroom was the so-called horn-book, a small, wooden paddle-shaped instrument upon which was inscribed the Lord's Prayer, the alphabet, basic numerals, and sundry other reading materials, which were covered by transparent horn that lent the instrument its name.[8]

At the onset of the Republic, therefore, public education dedicated to service of God was among its foremost distinguishing features—with its purview and administration largely a requirement and function of the individual states. For the federal Constitution did not explicitly address education, though its subsequent influence upon the discipline has been manifold and profound. Instead, relying upon the doctrine of reserved powers delineated in the Tenth Amendment, the prime responsibility for education was not only delegated to the states, but the federal government was concurrently precluded from interference in its execution.[9]

Nonetheless, the Founding Fathers retained a sincere and abiding interest in fostering learning. The foremost goal of public education in the early United States, as they perceived it, was succinctly articulated by George Washington on May 12, 1779, to chiefs of the Delaware Indian tribe: "You do well to wish to learn our arts and way of life, and above all, the religion of Jesus Christ. This will make you a happier people than you are. Congress will do its utmost to assist you in this wise intention."[10]

In his famed Farewell Address, in turn, Washington reiterated the familiar words: "Promote, therefore, as an object of primary importance, institutions for the general diffusion of knowledge. For in proportion as the structure of government gives force to public opinion, it is essential that the public option should be so enlightened."[11]

Writing from his official ambassadorial posting to Paris in 1786, Thomas Jefferson similarly asserted that only through education could peoples preserve their freedoms and ensure their individual happiness. Education, therefore, he proclaimed, "is the business of the state to provide, and that through a general plan." In like manner, the nation's first chief justice, John Jay, considered "knowledge to be the soul of the republic," whereas its fourth president, James Madison, declared that "knowledge will forever govern ignorance; and a people who mean to be their own governors must arm themselves with the power that knowledge gives."[12]

The Founders, it must be noted, themselves were not illiterate men. To the contrary, they were extraordinarily erudite. George Washington, in preparing to lead the Continental Army, claimed to have read five seminal works—all military. John Adams—who wrote that "except for my Wife and Children, I want to see my books"—reportedly as a child was seldom seen without a copy of Cicero's *Orations*. He also often quoted Polybius and once sailed to Europe with Molière's *Amphitryon* as his companion. Among more modern philosophers, Machiavelli and Montesquieu were his favorites. Jefferson, in turn, referred to his books as "mental furniture" and would complain when the "enormities of the times" would take him away from "the delightful pursuit of knowledge."[13]

James Madison, who succeeded Jefferson as president, was well acquainted with Aristotle and Demosthenes, John Locke and David Hume, John Milton and Jonathan Swift; whereas Alexander Hamilton read the philosophies of Cicero, Bacon, Hobbes, Montaigne, and Hume, and had a keen affinity for Greek, Prussian, and French history. At age fourteen, Benjamin Franklin reportedly was reading books by John Bunyan, Daniel Defoe, John Locke, and Xenophon. At sixteen, he was publishing his own newspaper. At nineteen, he opened his own press.[14] He was said to have been so well read, and found reading stimulating to such an extent that he was determined to instill the same spirit in others, organizing America's first subscription library in Philadelphia.[15]

Hence, John Adams, reflecting the product of an expansive liberal education, in 1776 would rejoice: "It has been the will of Heaven that we should be thrown into existence at a period when the greatest philosophers and law givers of antiquity would have wished to live. . . . How few of the human race have ever had the opportunity of choosing a system of government for themselves and for their children!"[16]

Endowed with this rich intellectual legacy, then, it came as no surprise that Article III of the Northwest Ordinance, enacted in 1789, stipulated that "religion, morality, and knowledge, being necessary to good government and the happiness of mankind, schools and the means of education shall be forever encouraged." This statement vividly makes clear that it was the intent of the First Congress that a prime responsibility of the nation's public school system was to instill religious and cultural values within the citizens of the realm.[17]

While this provision at its inception applied only to the original territories of the United States as of 1789—Indiana, Illinois, Michigan, Minnesota, Ohio, and Wisconsin—it was also gradually extended to other territories as they were incorporated into the United States, including Mississippi, Alabama, Missouri, Arkansas, Kansas, and Nebraska—all of which replicated the language of the Northwest Ordinance respecting the establishment of public education.[18]

Thus it was that America's public schools became what Jefferson called "the keepers of the vestal flame" and grew to be the principal institution entrusted not only with imparting knowledge but with preserving and then passing on the nation's identity and mission from generation to generation, inculcating an impassioned reverence for faith, unity, civility, and American ideals that were their reason for being.[19]

Indeed, until the mid-twentieth century, the nation's public school system was the central institution charged with building patriotism and adherence to civic values through its cultural assimilation processes. Its creation in the mid-nineteenth century was, in fact, in large part shaped by a perceived need for the "Americanization" of citizens, particularly immigrants, as the nation looked to education as the optimal way to transmit Anglo-American values and preserve civic institutions.[20]

To these ends, also, the local schools offered civics classes that stressed American principles, history, and ideals. In the words of social analyst Stephen Steinberg: "More than any other single factor, the public school system undermined the capacity of immigrant groups to transmit their native cultures to their American-born children." Critical undertakings all, as articulated in the simple eloquence of Ronald Reagan: "If we ever forget what we did, then we won't know who we are."[21]

ON THE CAUSES OF DISINTEGRATION OF AMERICAN EDUCATION AT THE COLLEGE LEVEL TODAY

The Evolution of the "Marcusian Dialectic"

Today, in many ways, America has largely forgotten that legacy of learning that is her intellectual endowment—and thus it is that her education system—both at its higher and secondary levels—stands in acute crisis. The challenges involve equally the qualitative aspects of the curricula taught and the blatant judicio-political biases that have crept into the processes of teaching them. In the latter case, controversy centers on interpreting the First Amendment of the Bill of Rights not only for education, but also for the role of media responsibility within society.

Such precepts have, in fact, been a source of controversy equally within the domains of education and the media, as subsequent chapters of this inquiry strikingly reveal. Indeed, in education, it has been a source of outright political confrontation. On the left, there is a hope that academia, through education, is dealing with the social problems of inequitable distribution of power and injustice more explicitly and progressively than in the past.[22]

On the right, in turn, are those who believe that mounting leftist domination of whole academic disciplines have transformed the classroom into a partisan pulpit from which alleged sectarian, racial, and sexual oppression is propagandized—with opposing viewpoints being suppressed—and with students thereby being forcibly immersed into the "politics of victimization." And on both sides of the political divide, there are also genuine concerns that ongoing on-campus intellectual indoctrination and posturing may be supplanting critical classroom imperatives in the dissemination of knowledge.[23]

At the crux of the problem, in the wake of the post-1960s "New Left Intellectual Revolution," moreover, has been an arrogation to itself by academia of the role of *loco parentis*—the university assuming the function of parents—by self-appointed "progressive" counterculturalists who concurrently presume the right to propagandize their intellectual charges at their will and sufferance.[24]

The net result of this unwarranted "ivory tower" ideological intrusion into the traditional central role of the nuclear family has been an intellectual tyranny more dangerous than America has confronted in her past—one that seeks absolute control over the thoughts and individualities of students. It is, in essence, a tyranny that seeks to trump the essence of liberty itself—a danger made more evident when reflecting upon the cogent counsel of renowned jurist Learned Hand that "liberty lies in the hearts of men and women; when it dies, no constitution, no court, no law, can save it."[25]

Though it may seem surprising to some that the most lethal and wide-ranging assault on the First Amendment's core precept of free speech has come not from politicians or bureaucratic agencies, but instead from academia—whose legacy of intellectual freedom has historically invoked liberty and tolerance—this evolution of events has clearly been no accident.[26]

Indeed, much of the present disarray and misfocus within American higher education, as previous discourse has described, directly traces its roots to the New Left movement introduced onto college and university campuses by the Frankfurt School of Social Research and the late Columbia University–affiliated neo-Marxist social and political philosopher Herbert Marcuse and his disciples described in chapter 2—Rabelaisian ideologues committed to bringing down capitalism by undermining its cultural underpinnings.[27]

Building upon the works of Rousseau and Marx to create a torqued concept of liberty distinctly at odds with historic First Amendment doctrines, this alternate analytic framework, though employing traditional terms of reference, has frequently assigned to them radically different meanings, thereby challenging the essence of conventional free speech while, in the process, laying the foundations for many of today's chilling, and patently unconstitutional, academic "speech codes."[28]

In a 1965 essay titled "Repressive Tolerance," for instance, Marcuse concluded that the "neutral tolerance" for ideas supposedly prevailing in America in the 1960s was, in reality, a highly selective tolerance that benefited only the rich and powerful. Such an approach, he said, served to the express advantage of the affluent and well positioned and to the detriment of those lacking such facilities, thereby directly serving the "cause of oppression" and the "established machinery of discrimination."[29]

For Marcuse, then, so long as society was held captive by pervasive institutionalized economic and social inequality—so long as the holders of power maintained their control through manipulation and indoctrination of the masses—which he characterized as "regressive practices"—"indiscriminate tolerance" would serve what he deemed to be parochial, highly discriminatory interests of regression.[30]

In contravention, he contended, reopening channels of tolerance and liberation presently blocked by "organized repression and indoctrination" must, at times, be forcibly accomplished by "apparently undemocratic means." In a cosmic spasm of arcane sophistry, he suggested that such means could include "withdrawal of toleration of speech and assembly from groups and movements which promote aggressive policies, armament, chauvinism, or discrimination on the grounds of race or religion"— all "reactionary" ideas.[31]

"Liberating tolerance," Marcuse wrote, in contrast to "indiscriminate tolerance," would be a new double standard of "intolerance against movements from the Right and tolerance of movements from the Left." This duality, moreover, would "extend to the stage of action as well as of the discussion of propaganda, of deed as well as of word," because, for him, words had consequences, and if their consequences were to be avoided, then the words themselves must perforce be silenced.[32]

The Marcusian premise—one that separated his political philosophy from the until-then accrued body of First Amendment jurisprudence—was that liberty, as it had evolved, was, in effect, a "zero-sum game." To wit: an "exercise of civil rights by those who don't have them presupposes their withdrawal by those who prevent their exercise." For Marcuse, therefore, the application of such undemocratic, albeit necessary, actions would foster a society distinguished by universal tolerance and freedom—as to forge a society of *universal tolerance*, one could not tolerate reactionary ideas.[33]

Marcuse concentrated upon the education of youth: "The restoration of freedom of thought may necessitate new and rigid restrictions on teachings and practices in the educational institutions which, by their methods and concepts, serve to enclose the mind within the established universe of discourse and behavior," he claimed.[34]

Because incoming college students were deeply indoctrinated in ideals that traditional established powers, such as the family, school, and church, had ordained, then, extraordinary steps were, of necessity, needed to rescue them from the "autonomous thinking" and regressive channels wherein society had molded their minds. To these ends, he argued: "The preempting of the mind vitiates impartiality and objectivity. . . . Unless the student learns to think in the opposite direction, he will be inclined to place the facts into the predominant framework of [historic] values."[35]

Hence, to more fully free the students' minds, Marcuse prescribed that they not be exposed to conventional "spurious neutrality," which he deemed to be imbedded within the perceived problem of indoctrination, because "it serves to reproduce acceptance of the dominion of the victors in the consciousness of man." To this end, for example, history must be taught so that the student understands "the frightening extent to which history was made and recorded by the victors, that is, the extent to which history itself has been the unfolding of oppression."[36]

Accordingly, to produce the requisite conditions whereby "Marcusian freedom" could flourish first on campus, then throughout society at large, reeducation in progressive universities was necessary. "Revolutionary thinking" could then break the ideological stranglehold of the powerful on the minds of students and citizens—and thereby, this reeducation, in itself, could create a "progressive society" wherein true freedom and democracy would reign.[37]

In this initial dogmatic "thought reversal" process, Marcuse conceded, the censorship of ideas was essential because ubiquitous regressive notions were dangerously susceptible to being rapidly translated into practice. Indeed, for Marcuse, censorship, though temporal, must nonetheless be pervasive. But once its incipient objective had been achieved, there would be no further need for such "antidemocratic" expedients, which were, in the last analysis, designed to redress present imbalances between the "oppressor" and the "oppressed." The ultimate result, he promised, would be to re-create genuine freedom so that the words "freedom" and "liberty" could reassert their true meanings.[38]

These Marcusian prescriptions, then, form the didactical underpinnings of modern multiculturalism as well as the foundations of the model for the assault on free speech ongoing on academic campuses throughout America today. That they have, in fact, now succeeded is captured in Thomas Sowell's somber assessment that "Marxism . . . now continues to flourish on American college campuses as perhaps nowhere else in the world."[39]

Indeed, these prescriptions for socialist revolution have been fervently taken up as a cause by countless left-wing academics who are openly hostile to the "neutral content before the law" doctrine upon which First Amendment jurisprudence has traditionally relied. The outcomes of their carefully crafted juridical handiwork now threaten free speech as it has been practiced in America for the past two centuries.[40]

That their countercultural craftsmanship was quite unforeseen is remarkable for several reasons. First, it runs contrary to U.S. academic history, which has traditionally sought to inculcate America's values rather than to champion the ideological values of those who would oppose her—who, in the first half of the twentieth century at least, were deemed to be the planet's fascists and communists. Universities, it was said, should teach the virtues of the American way of life and should not employ, or extol the values, of Marxists who, according to then-prevalent belief, were working openly to bring it down.[41]

To fulfill this profound commitment, the overwhelming majority of America's tenured professors argued, the proper role of the university was to serve in a nonpartisan way; the outside world could call upon them for expert knowledge, but to make this use realistic, they had to remain objectively neutral. Alternately put, direct involvement of academicians in the mundane dimensions to everyday life was to be avoided so that they could observe it, reflect upon it, and dissect it from the broader perspective of participatory distance. Requiring them to preach a political position, conversely, would undermine this inquiring spirit.[42]

Accordingly, three decades ago, no one would have believed it possible that educators, of all people, would lead their universities in an overtly political function, work directly for social and political change, and seek to inculcate a particular political position, let alone a countercultural neo-Marxist one, within their students.

Yet the bizarre and unpredictable is now reality. It is the professors who aspire to political power. A new, entirely different concept of academic life has evolved wherein the faculty no longer is content with merely reflecting and analyzing but instead wants academe directly involved in the day-to-day dynamic of real-world decision making seeking to transform it.[43]

This transformation of conviction, in turn, has impacted directly upon how curricula in general—and the humanities in particular—are taught—as in a relatively short period, academic analytic processes have been dramatically reshaped. Consequently, many now regard social activism as the prime purpose of scholarly criticism, and not mere social activism but one of a specific kind—addressing the perceived issue of "oppression" by virtue of race, ethnicity, gender, and class. In the process, they have also come to view the very concept of a classic "canon of great works" reflecting traditional values as an elitist notion that needs to be dispelled.[44]

The regrettable outcome has been the evolution of an institutionally entrenched new orthodoxy armed with a didactic of deconstruction of the established order, empowered by an unyielding imposition of political correctness whereby dissenters are not only criticized but are denounced as bigoted moral outcasts—racists, sexists, nativists, and a host of other "ists and isms" now intrinsic to their nomenclatures—and, in the requisite zealous pursuit of this agenda, it is permissible that revolutionary, often even wholly fabricated, dogmas be enforced through totalitarian means.[45]

The cruel paradox of the "politically correct" process, however, is that it is invariably destructive. For just as Marxism proved to be inoperable in the economic sphere, so neo-Marxist rhetoric enforced through political correctness has proven to be so within the cultural sphere. Marxism promised an economic utopia to be shared by all, if only the existing economic order could be dismantled. But in the end, it could achieve only the dismantling, not the subsequent effective reconstruction, with the result that erstwhile socialist countries targeted by the experiment today face a long economic rebuilding process.[46]

In like manner, the cultural neo-Marxists now promise social abundance for everyone in a new egalitarian environment if only they utterly reject their "elitist" Western culture—with the ultimate result just as predictable—and with all ending up culturally poorer for the process. As again, the reality of destruction proceeds, but the promised state of cultural nirvana never regenerates to replace it.[47]

America's people generally recognize this reality, and that is why, as patriots, they reject it. They realize that their Western cultural inheritance, though not perfect, has raised society from barbarism to the highest level of social order that civilization has yet achieved—and that if deconstructionist envy and resentment are permitted to prevail, to destroy the good in a perverse quest to create a perceived ethereal "perfect," as with communism as a form of economics, the would-be beneficiaries will again endure the societal destruction without ever experiencing the promised resulting social benefits.[48]

Given such realities, it comes as no surprise that 58 percent of Americans polled in July 2007 believed leftist professorial political bias to be a serious problem—and that 65 percent are convinced that non-tenured professors do a better job of teaching than do tenured ones—and likewise that, in response, legislation has been introduced in more than a dozen states across the country to counter political pressure and the proselytizing of students in college classrooms. Such concerns are well founded. For in the ominous warning of University of Pennsylvania legal scholar Alan Kors: "For the first time in the history of American education, the barbarians are now running the institution."[49]

The Political Import of the "Marcusian Didactic"

The modus operandi of counterculturalist academia, as cited, is thus predicated on the premise that to empower true freedom on campus, wherein "disadvantaged" students share equally with more "advantaged" ones, certain restrictions must be imposed by the powers-that-be upon individual rights and prerogatives. In other words, while the concept of freedom is highly valued in precept, in order to ensure equal access to it, it must first be destroyed in practice.[50]

This confounded ideological handiwork, in turn, is firmly founded on the double standard that some rights and values are more equal than others—a discriminatory didactic that denies the freedom of self-definition, a betrayal that extends to dictating speech and inner conscience—a latter-day analogue of the early twentieth-century *Comintern* "thought re habilitation" process that commences with the twin frauds of so-called diversity and political correctness being perniciously perpetrated by pedagogic ideologues.[51]

By way of example of their brazen convoluted logic, when, for sheer lack of funding, parents were recently forced to abandon their attempts to legally block the ACLU's blatant efforts to impose top-down politically correct dogma in the California K–12 educational system, ACLU staff attorney Julia Harumi arbitrarily assessed: "The plaintiffs' decision to walk away from this stage of the case . . . sends a message throughout the state that schools have the authority to require mandatory attendance in tolerance-building and diversity education programs."[52]

In fairness, it must be observed that there are indeed valid alternate distinct meanings to the concepts of "diversity" (a wide variety of persons), and "multiculturalism" (the social interactions of individuals from diverse backgrounds). On most campuses, however, those terms, and the political agendas that foster them, respect neither the differences nor the individualism that lie at their essence.[53]

Instead, academic notions of the twin concepts are distinguished, almost invariably, by dogmatic and partisan countercultural models that incorporate specific racial, ethnic, or sexual objectives. Despite spates of empty talk about "celebrating diversity," for instance, academia doesn't usually really mean a profound analysis of fundamentalist Protestant culture, nor of traditionalist Catholic culture, nor of Orthodox Jewish or Sunni or Shi'i culture, nor of black American Pentecostal culture, nor of its counterpart white Southern Baptist culture. For such sundry cultures, within their strained definition, are not really deemed by the multiculturalists to be "multicultural" at all.[54]

They likewise do not mean the study of Samoan culture, west African Benin culture, Confucian culture, or Eskimo culture. For all that the social engineers of the liberal left really mean in employing the term "diversity" is an appreciation for, and celebration and study of, peoples who think exactly as they do about the nature and incipient sources of "oppression," wherever they are to be found—and then seconded, through a hate-inducing agenda of race, ethnicity, gender, and sexual preference to their cause via the arcane, insidious lure of the "politics of victimization."

At its essence, then, this tortured approach is no more than one of allowing one's personal hang-ups and obsessions to become the essence of a core curriculum.[55] In the process, such once vividly clear academic terms as "diversity" and "multiculturalism" have instead become perversions of their English language meanings wholly unworthy of those precepts of objectivity that have historically characterized the process of genuine academic inquiry.

More ironic still, by their actions, they have turned Martin Luther King's cherished dream that children "not be judged by the color of their skin but by the content of their character" into a countercultural nightmare—to wit, the converse: "judge me by the color of my skin, for therein lies my identity."[56]

Indeed, this approach—the study not of others, but of oneself—is, in itself, a base perversion of the educational cross-cultural transfer process, for one of the primary ways a society improves is by borrowing from others. European culture, by way of example, was vastly enriched by borrowing astronomy and much of mathematics from the Arabs. But the essence of multiculturalism is to the contrary—to wit; the deliberate isolation of groups so that they do not borrow from one another—with the end result being cultural impoverishment and the societal shortchanging of all.[57]

Yet as noted radio commentator Dennis Prager has asserted: "If we continue to teach about tolerance and intolerance instead of good and evil, we will end up instead with the tolerance of evil."[58] As executive director of the

National Association of Scholars, Bradford Wilson has similarly contended: "There is a deeper, far greater threat to freedom of speech, and even of thought, on campus. It is an orthodoxy that, in the name of multicultural-ism, has elevated sensitivity over truth, political consensus over disinter-ested inquiry, and intolerance of disagreement and contempt for 'Western civilization' over political and intellectual pluralism."[59]

In their defense, the nation's colleges and universities justify their cultural phobias and subordination of individual identities to "group identities" by claiming that they have inherited the unconscionable injustices of Ameri-can history. Yet here reality intervenes—incontrovertibly and in a manner aptly affirmed by John Adams: "Facts are stubborn things, and whatever may be our wishes, inclinations, or the dictates of our passions, they can-not alter the state of evidence."[60] Or as put more succinctly still by Mark Twain: "Truth is our most prized possession. We must not economize it."[61]

Yet denial of truth is the centerpiece of the counterculturalist cabal's dogma—as in their ideological machinations, they enforce deliberate deci-sions that themselves betray history, notwithstanding the cogent reality ex-pressed in the eloquence of Supreme Court Justice Robert Jackson a half century ago, "individual freedom in the sphere of intellect and spirit is in-separable from the highest values of American liberty and possibility."[62]

The propagandistic devices employed by multiculturalists to ensure that their indoctrination approach is effected, as noted, are so-called campus speech codes lifted directly from their toolkits of "political repression." In-deed, over two-thirds of the nation's colleges and universities have now adopted speech codes that censor free speech to explicitly suppress opin-ions deemed "politically incorrect"—enforceable on the penalty of arrest, fines, required attendance at "sensitivity retraining sessions," or even out-right suspension from the learning institution.[63]

Institutions of higher learning often justify the operation of such "group-think" indoctrination codes on academic grounds. Unless "harassing" speech is banned, they contend, it will be difficult for students in "histori-cally disadvantaged" categories to benefit from the educational opportuni-ties presented.[64]

But instruments that operate at the beckoning of so-called anti-harassment policy enforcement gestapos must clearly be seen for what they are—the out-ward manifestations of an all-out "New Left" assault on campus liberties: the denial of controversial ideas; the banning of terms offensive to those vested with self-anointed "special rights"; and the outlawing of discourse that, in the view of the pontifical new orthodoxy, can create an hostile academic environment—even to the extent of banning listening to conservative talk radio programs in the dormitories of the Bucknell University campus.[65]

Their dicta are preposterous. The Rutgers University speech code mani-festo proclaims that it will punish "students whose words offend on the basis of race, religion, color, ancestry, handicap, marital status or sexual orientation." Occidental College in California, in turn, has extended its conformity code to prohibit "unwelcome jokes, comments, invitations, and looks"—while even permitting third parties to file complaints. Indeed, at least three hundred American institutions of higher learning punish free speech "either through specific speech codes or as integral parts of their overall rules of conduct."[66]

However well intended toward assimilation, though, the net result instead has been a balkanization of campus cultures subdivided into multiplicities of ideologically warring camps—while leaving the world at large to ponder whether America, and her academia in particular, is degenerating into the status of a totalitarian state—developments lending more than a modicum of credence to social commentator Camille Paglia's description of the "political correctness" movement as a "fascism from the left."[67]

The indoctrination process starts from the first day on campus—as at many colleges and universities, special "diversity training" courses are required for incoming fresh*men* (itself a sexist term in the feminist lexicon) and those students seeking special jobs such as dorm counselors. Such sessions are normally run by memberships of groups that feel that sensitivity toward their group is lacking—black student unions, feminist and gay and lesbian rights organizations, and the like.[68]

Thus it was that when at the University of Pennsylvania, an institution of higher learning founded by that great questioner of orthodoxies, Benjamin Franklin, a student member of an "educational diversity" panel expressed in writing her "deep regard for the individual . . . and desire to protect the freedoms of all members of society," a university administrator, in a dazzling display of deconstructionist legerdemain, circled her ostensibly "inflammatory" testimonial, underlining the word "individual" and annotating the comment:

> This is a red flag phrase today, which is considered by many to be racist. For arguments that champion the individual over the group ultimately privilege those individuals belonging to the largest or dominant group.[69]

Indeed, in the administrative conduct guide *Multicultural Experiences at Penn: What You Can Do*, incoming students are admonished not only to behave well, but that if they are even "perceived" to harbor impure thoughts, they are, *ipso facto*, guilty of "an attitude of intolerance." To wit: "If you are *perceived* [emphasis added] to be racist, sexist, heterosexist, or ethnocentric, or biased against religions different from your own, you must unconditionally acquiesce to examining and changing that behavior."[70]

The proceeds of such convoluted thinking can be mind-boggling. In a seminar on "Racism on the Campus" convened for nine universities in central and western Pennsylvania, participants were given a "Glossary of Terms" which queried—who is a racist?—and then answered: "All white individuals in our society are racists. Even if whites are free from all conscious racial prejudices, they remain racists." Another glossary answer, offered under the rubric of "White Racism—Power + Prejudice = Racism," stipulated: "In the United States at present, only whites can be racists." "Personal Racism," in turn, was termed "a lack of support for ethnic minorities who take risks to change organizations."[71]

In like manner, Colby College in Maine restricts behavior that "causes loss of self esteem," and the University of Connecticut bans "inappropriately directed laughter."[72] In the enforced imposition of such "values," moreover, campus disciplinary bodies often function not unlike "star chambers"—wherein no verbatim records are made of proceedings, the accused are automatically presumed guilty, and violators are denied legal counsel and even the right to call witnesses or otherwise introduce exculpatory evidence.[73]

Academia remains, in fact, the only major sector within American civil life wherein not only does arbitrariness reign rampant but where legal process and conventional fact-finding procedures—indeed, individuals' full body of constitutionally-bestowed First Amendment rights—are actually, with disturbing frequency, precluded by regulation, even in state-supported institutions, notwithstanding the clear stipulation of the Ninth Amendment of the Bill of Rights that no state "shall deprive any person of life, liberty, or property without due process of law."[74]

Not infrequently, moreover, the penalties imposed for convicted offenders of "normative multicultural mores" are equally arbitrary and capricious, as suggested in the following "sentence" assessed on an unwitting University of Pennsylvania student in April 1992:

> You are to participate in a comprehensive program on sexual harassment except for the time you are attending classes . . . or [at] employment. Said program shall include . . . assignments . . . each week in which classes are in session through the Spring, 1992 term. You [must] present written evidence of completion of assignments, and a satisfactory performance must be documented by Elena DiLapi, Director of the Women's Center, or her representative, before your transcript can be released.[75]

At the University of Michigan, a student who belittled homosexual acts in a classroom likewise was compelled by the school's administration, as a condition of continued enrollment, to write a public apology titled "Learned My Lesson" for publication in the school newspaper, the *Michigan Daily*, and to attend "Gay Rap Sessions."[76]

Yet such arcane agendas, procedures, and verdicts—coming at the direct expense, in terms of time, of a fuller immersion into mathematics, physics, engineering, and those other hard disciplines for which the individual is paying tuition that would empower him or her to lead an economically more productive life and thereby contribute to the greatness of America—merely cater to the latent, even loony, "political correctness" whimsies of the "New Left" ivory-tower "professoriat."

A further exacerbating factor is that, within academia, efforts to establish the ground rules of political correctness are based on a pernicious double standard—with "sensitivity" being in the eye of the beholder. For, as noted in the case of Pennsylvania, only white heterosexual males are capable of committing insensitive acts—whereas racial minorities, homosexuals, or women—however egregious their conduct—are deemed incapable of insensitivity.[77]

There is, moreover, yet another annoying, but nonetheless important, issue that is invoked—the vexing question of whether such anti-harassment policies violate the right to free speech guaranteed by the First Amendment. As one student government leader freely, but aptly, admitted: "What we propose is not completely in line with the First Amendment. But I am not sure that it should be. We at Stanford are trying to establish a different standard than society at large is trying to accomplish (!)"[78]

It comes as a consummate and sobering irony, then, that what began in the mid-1960s as a "New Left" appeal for "free speech" at the University of California-Berkeley should now end in a fervent appeal at Stanford to impose on-campus censorship of political thought.[79] Or as University of Pennsylvania legal scholar Alan Kors has asserted:

> "Harassment policies" at growing numbers of universities have used the very real need to protect their students and employees from sexual and racial abuse as a partisan pretext for . . . "privileging" one particular ideological agenda and for controlling speech deemed offensive by those designated as victims of American society. . . . In short, Penn is a tolerant and diverse community, and if you don't agree with our particular notions of tolerance and diversity, we will gradually reeducate you.[80]

Academia nonetheless generally justifies such patently biased rule-making—albeit prejudicial to the constitutional rights of the accused and ill-designed for the process of actually discovering truth—on "educational" grounds. Their rationale is that the student disciplinary process is meant to teach, not punish. Hence, such legally prescribed niceties as procedural fairness, rational fact-finding, the First and Ninth Amendments, and due process of law are not required or even deemed to be germane to its enforcement.[81]

Vague statutes—selective enforcement—no rules of guiding precedent—no right to legal counsel—often no right to call defense witnesses—the admission of unsworn, hearsay evidence—no subpoena power—no right to confront and cross-examine one's accusers and their witnesses—judgment by a biased panel in a hostile environment—no right to discuss the judicial proceedings outside of the court room, *ad infinitum*—on the other hand, are.[82]

The politics of "political correctness" have thus come to be arbitrarily administered by academics who, not unlike the stereotypic Southern rural sheriffs of the 1950s, are fervently convinced that "rules of evidence" and "standard courtroom procedure" merely interfere with the realization of their more important social goals. Some introduction they offer to the workings of constitutional democracy in America on the nation's presumed foremost bastions of liberty and freedom, universities.[83]

In fairness, it may be said that part of the inequity may issue from conviction, the remainder from intimidation, as the prime goal of most modern academic administrators is to buy "peace in our time" and to preserve the illusion of "competence in our tenures"—factors essential to enhancing and extending their careers—as the zeal of the student radicals of the 1960s has now become internalized in their new roles of responsibility as deans and faculty chairs within academia.[84]

Their rationale is both logical and simple—the foot soldiers of the "New Left" possess the most latent potential to radically disrupt the otherwise tranquil ascendancies of their career trajectories. Moderate Republicans, Catholics, Lutherans, and law-abiding minorities don't threaten that course. But counterculturalists do—and thus it is that administrative attention is focused on the grievances of militants who might destabilize the campus, occupy buildings, and attract the media—with the imperative being to appease radical leaders of potentially disruptive groups.[85]

Hence, the march of multiculturalism moves forward—with some of its perverse double-standard absurdities, and the moral decay attendant thereto, quite classic. At the University of Pennsylvania in 1986, a fraternity was censured for a "show-off-your tan" poster that depicted a coed whose bikini bottom revealed a discrete tan line after vehement protests by feminists groups—organizations that had at the same university just a short time before, in protest to Catholic anti-abortion sentiments, carried posters reading "Keep Your Rosaries Off Our Ovaries" and "Spreading Our Legs For Jesus"—without the slightest official approbation.[86]

At Penn State, in turn, there was no punishment for the unlawful seizure of over eight thousand copies of the conservative newspaper, the *Lionhearted*, by student protestors who objected to its caricature of a bikini-clad female carrying a sign that read: "Feminist at Work!"[87] It is in this spirit of academic enlightenment, then, that the University of California-Davis "style sheet" has instituted the practice of using the feminine pronoun in all articles and publications save for those instances referring to a criminal defendant, whereupon the male pronoun is to be preferred![88]

Whither the absurdity—the suppression of free speech in a surreal environ wherein the exercise of "free speech" applies only to the "politically correct"? Whither the operation of the guarantees of universal free speech constitutionally guaranteed by the First Amendment? What if other American institutions also came to believe what her universities today believe and practice—that they don't have to tolerate that which offends either their personal or commonly shared values, and, the Constitution notwithstanding, that they may legally dispense freedoms and justice unequally apportioned in accordance with their particular sense of decent and indecent belief?[89]

The consummate irony, however, is that a foremost concern of the 1960s campus protestors—the leaders of the so-called free speech movement who have today morphed into academia's tenured faculty—as noted, actually once was freedom of speech. But today, in support of many of those same goals, the issue is merely how speech can best be shaped and convoluted to serve politically correct social ends.[90]

This is not robust scholarly inquiry in the highest traditions of academe. It is instead its antithesis—in full compliance with the Marcusian notion of "withdrawal of tolerance of speech" from those ideologically opposed, though in direct contravention of John Stuart Mill's argument that even offensive speech serves the purpose of illuminating error.[91]

Indeed, it is a "McCarthyism of the Left" that imposes a chilling effect not only upon free speech but on academic freedom itself. For repression of expression denies individuals what they need most for intellectual fulfillment: knowledge, unfettered inquiry, candor, and plain-spoken critical thought. As described by Donald Kagan, former Yale dean of arts and sciences: "It takes real courage to oppose the campus orthodoxy. To tell you the truth, I was a student during the days of McCarthy, and there is less intellectual freedom now than there was then."[92]

Hence, though America's academic infrastructure should now be blazing new frontiers in the social realms of boundless educational inquiry and open freedom of expression, today it is not—proceeding oblivious to the oxymoronic reality that freedoms cannot be saved by destroying them. Liberty is the exception, not the rule, in human history, and once lost, either in belief or practice, it is difficult to resurrect. Nevertheless, the manifest problems grow only worse, not better, as the revelations that follow reveal.[93]

MANIFESTATIONS OF THE DISINTEGRATION OF AMERICAN EDUCATION AT THE COLLEGE LEVEL TODAY

On the Pedantics of Ivory Tower Pedagogical Propaganda

"Cultivated intellect, a delicate taste for learning, a candid, equitable, dispassionate mind, a stable and courteous bearing in the conduct of life,"

Cardinal John Newman wrote more than a century and a half ago, "these are the objects of a university!"[94]

How the mighty have fallen—as the modern drive for rampant multiculturalism has disastrously undermined the cherished aura of the idyllic "ivory tower." For within the past half century, an age of intellectual inquiry—man's last, best bastion in the quest for truth—has fallen, gradually yet systematically and decisively, to those who have co-opted it for self-serving ideological purposes.

The great "molder of the melting pot"—the conservator of culture and transmitter of tradition—has thus degenerated into a pitch pit for partisan polemic and countercultural propaganda. In its wake, legacy prerequisites for human enrichment such as civics, history, classical art and literature, foreign languages, and math and science that were standard academic fare until the 1960s have now become Jurassic relics of a nobler educational past.[95]

History is being rewritten, English is losing its status as America's national language, and a drastic new agenda—a new dialectic auguring for dramatic social change—"diversity" in the stead of civic excellence—has replaced the historic role of academia as the repository for the best that mankind, in its sojourn on the planet, has produced.

The reason?—ready acquiescence to parochial ethnic, racial, sex, and gender demands of a new tenured liberal faculty that has taken upon itself to be the nation's principal agent for social change—and the ideological multiplier effects of that movement's intense activities now percolating throughout the nation's academic and media infrastructures and from there, out into society at large.[96]

The net result is a balkanization of academia wherein cultural egocentricity, in replacing traditional cosmopolitan values, has spawned a multiplicity of parochial special interests each vying with the other for ascendancy and privileged position—as an incessant quest for political power under the rubric of diversity has developed its own set of peculiar partisan prejudices.[97] In the opinion of one studied analyst of the contemporary campus scene, Dinesh D'Souza:

> One reason for the increasing radicalism is that, with the collapse of Marxism and socialism around the world, activist energies previously channeled into championship of the proletariat are now seeking to "come home," so to speak, and investing in a domestic liberation agenda.[98]

Alternately put, in pursuit of the countercultural mandate, the term "diversity" has lost its procedural meaning—no longer referring to a rational range of views on diverse issues, but rather to the process of enlisting in multifaceted ideological causes that take as their collective rallying cry the notion of being "for diversity" as an abstract. As assessed by Oberlin College President S. Frederick Starr: "Diversity should not be the prerogative of any particular political group. But it now means subscribing to a particular set of political views."[99]

Accordingly, while there once was a time when the prime purpose of higher education was to train students in the tools of examining and understanding the accumulation of knowledge past and present, today the process of education is being radically redefined by those who view themselves as missionaries sent to earth by alien gods to convert their students to disparate, newly found, radical polemics.[100]

There is no question as to the provenance of the agenda. Its countercultural posture and intent derives almost exclusively from the Marxist *weltanschauung* that permeates so much of the thinking of the far left and, in particular, of its apostles of socialist dogma and disciples of ideology who today dominate the nation's campuses.

For Marx argued that it was not enough to merely understand the world, it must also be changed. That determination has now become the multiculturalist gospel—and that is why it becomes critical that its would-be converts not be enamored with the merits of a more traditional past and its more conventional values system. In this reindoctrination process, far too many tenured professors have thus become the goose-stepping gestapo of the revolution, and deans and department chairs their all-too-willing consorts in their quest to transform a traditional classical curriculum into a revolutionary Third World regimen.[101]

This is precisely why Yale University recently turned down a $20 million grant from its billionaire Bass brother alumni of Ft. Worth when it learned that a course offering in Western civilization was a condition of the grant—with its faculty, in essence, saying: How dare you ask us to dedicate twenty million dollars to a program that teaches the history of our own culture?

And that is why the University of Michigan's Department of Near Eastern Studies similarly turned down a $20-million contract from the Department of Defense to teach Arabic —because it didn't want to be *tainted* with military money. It is ironic, but not probably surprising, then, that the only higher education institutions in the nation wherein a course in constitutional law is a prerequisite to graduation are the Army, Navy, and Air Force academies where a modicum of patriotism still prevails.[102]

The opponents of such learning opportunities are, in fact, little more than ideological drones—remnants of the "peace at any price" countercultural hippie infrastructure that led campus revolutions in the 1960s—the intellectual antimilitary fraternity brothers of that anthropology professor at Brown who opined that the war on terror "can end only to the extent that we relinquish our roles as world leader," of the New Mexico history professor who told his students in the immediate wake of 9/11 that "anyone who can blow up the Pentagon gets my vote," and of the physics professor at the

University of Massachusetts-Amherst who proclaimed that "the American flag is a symbol of terrorism, death, fear, destruction, and oppression."[103]

Or the University of Hawaii professor who asked: "Why should we support the United States whose hands in history are soaked with blood?" Or the Columbia professor who said that he "would like to see a million Mogadiscus," referring to the deaths of American soldiers in a humanitarian mission, or the administrators at Central Michigan University where students were ordered to remove allegedly *offensive* and *nontolerable* patriotic posters and American flags from their dorm rooms in the aftermath of 9/11. Such diatribes, it bears reiteration, are not the handiwork of hate-spewing anti-American Pakistani *madrassas*, but rather of their liberal elitist U.S. academic counterparts.[104]

In tandem, administrators at Duke University closed down a faculty member's website calling for a military response to terrorist attacks on America. At Johns Hopkins, a professor likewise was removed from his post at the Central Asian Institute for stating that a military response to 9/11 was appropriate.[105] At the University of Massachusetts, students were given permits for an on-campus rally against President Bush and the "War on Terror," but pro-Bush supporters were denied the same privilege.[106]

And at Holy Cross, a department secretary was forced to remove an American flag from her desk that she put there in memory of Todd Beamer, the American hero on doomed United Airlines Flight 93 en route over Pennsylvania to destroy the White House, who is now known for his famous call to patriotic resistance: "Let's roll!"[107]

Thus it is that Boston University history professor emeritus Howard Zinn, in a vitriolic piece titled "Putting Away the Flag," prepared for Independence Day, July 4, 2007, argued that the nation's story is one of decadence, greed, oppression, and deceit:

> On this July 4, we would do well to renounce nationalism and all of its symbols: its flags, its pledges of allegiance, its anthems, its insistence in song that God single out America to be blessed. [For isn't devotion to the flag] one of the great evils of our time, along with racism . . . ?
>
> We need to refute the idea that our nation is different from, or morally superior to, the other imperial powers of world history. We need to assert our allegiance to the human race, and not to any one nation.[108]

Such diatribes aren't education, and they certainly aren't patriotism. They instead reflect the reality that within the ranks of the New Left, antimilitarism and bitterness toward America run deep—and come replete with echoes of the Marcusian didactic seeking to bring down American capitalism by undermining the core values that support it. As a result, then, only at the margin is the regimen of higher education over which they now preside in any way related to the actual education process—and might instead more properly be called the "higher indoctrination process," as subsequent analysis will show.[109]

Part of the problem, of course, is that much of the senior faculty has written off classroom duties in favor of research, writing, and other career-enhancing non-teaching activities. A greater dimension to the problem, however, is that American higher education, in large part, has today devolved into a mere pretext for aggregating large numbers of poorly prepared, unsuspecting would-be students into convenient concentrations, not unlike Maoist reeducation compounds or Orwellian boot camps, wherein they are mentally manipulated by radical left-wing faculty for purely ideological reasons.[110]

As today, throughout much of academia, the once-vaunted freshman orientation process instead serves as an educational rehabilitation center featuring introductions to cross-cultural living, feminist concepts of "new wave political correctness," "Homosexual Coming Out Week," and other centerpieces of countercultural inanity explicitly aimed at the emotional manipulation of incoming students on a host of "politically correct" concerns.[111]

In this process, at a time when more than two-thirds of the nation's institutions of higher education no longer require a survey course in the history of Western civilization—featuring Socrates, Da Vinci, Dante, Shakespeare, Milton, Thomas Jefferson, or Tolstoy—they have supplanted them with the teachings of Malcolm X, Ché Guevara, Chairman Mao, Herbert Marcuse, and Betty Friedan.[112]

It is in this petri dish of radical ideological ferment, then, that in March 1988, amid controversy, Stanford University's Faculty Senate voted 39–4 to drop its mandatory year-long course in Western civilization in favor of a new prerequisite called in the official syllabi "Culture, Ideas, and Values"— CIV, as the course is known in campus vernacular—a compromise ostensibly designed to preserve an illusion of normative civilization in its acronym but without incorporating the offending adjective "Western"—whose content is instead devoted to the glorification of the irrepressible "multicultural trinity" of race, ethnicity, and sex.[113]

At 75 percent of the country's universities, in fact, an undergraduate degree can be earned without having to study European history, and 86 percent no longer require students to know anything about the classics or Graeco-Roman civilization. At Cornell, for instance, students are required to take at least one course in a non-Western culture, but they can graduate without taking a single course in Western culture or civilization; at universities such as Florida State, every student must take a mandatory course in "multiculturalism."[114]

At the University of Wisconsin, in turn, the *only* required undergraduate course is a multicultural one focused primarily upon minorities. At the University of California–Berkeley, the analogous course is called the "American

Cultures Breadth Requirement." In sum, the vast majority of the nation's academic institutions have totally lost touch with what a "higher education" used to be.[115]

Too often now, moreover, even when what appears to be a history of Western civilization course appears on the horizon, it turns out to be no more than a chimera. Certainly, when students at the University of California-Berkeley take their one-time mandatory "American culture" class as a prerequisite to graduation, they hardly realize what they have actually gotten into, as the content of the class fails to live up to its stated objective—with the concept of *e pluribus unum*, many peoples coming together as one, nowhere on the Berkeley radar horizon.

In characterizing the course's content, even the campus newspaper, the *California Patriot*, assesses of it: "Too often students learn only that 'American culture' consists solely of white racism and oppression, liberal social policies, and the rejection and ridicule of any ideas that challenge these notions."[116]

Indeed, at Maine's Bowdoin College, where there is no U.S. history or Shakespeare prerequisite, there is, contrarily, a "non-Eurocentric studies" requirement—a mandate to elect at least two classes that are not based on Western culture. When the National Association of Scholars recently examined the curricula at what it deemed to be the top fifty U.S. universities, it found that only one-third still require freshman English, just 12 percent require math, merely 34 percent have a science requirement, and but one college among the fifty offers a mandatory course in American history.[117]

Small wonder, then, that the nation's college students no longer have a concept of exactly who they are. Small wonder either that students are being taught by educators employed by some of the nation's most prestigious institutions of higher learning that all of the classic accomplishments of ancient Greece and Rome were stolen from the Africans![118]

In sum, the multicultural iconoclasts of Western historiography have today established at least three formidably solid, heavily defended bridgeheads within American academia: (1) prevailing in the notion that Western culture isn't worthy of study; (2) that even if it were, it is not important that students be exposed to it; and (3) that if students do not elect to study Western culture, they will then hopefully have no interest in defending it from the onslaughts of still further future multiculturalist attacks—all predicated on the premise that people usually will not defend that which they do not understand.[119]

Yet if America's next generation is forced to conform to their mentors' perverse vision of political correctness rather than uphold what is constitutional and that which has historically been deemed to be morally correct, how can they preserve that legacy of liberties that their forefathers so faithfully fashioned? How will they ever know that it was not just any culture, but American culture, that formulated the greatest precepts and practices of liberty ever to be forged in human history—freedom, democracy, equality of opportunity, and an unshakable observance of the rule of law?[120]

Regrettably, this litany of "reverse discrimination" against traditional Western values does not end there, but goes on further still. Seattle University canceled the appointment of a former CIA agent to serve as a visiting professor for 1991 amid multiculturalist protests that permitting students to learn from an ex-CIA employee would conflict with their leftist agenda of "diversity."[121]

California State University, for the same reasons, rejected scholarships from the Sons of Italy, an Italian-American philanthropic organization that earmarks some of its monies for needy American students of Italian descent—claiming that it only accepts socially or ethnically directed scholarships that benefit African Americans, Native Americans, and Hispanics.[122]

The speaking engagement of Linda Chavez, a Hispanic American who personally believes that all Hispanic immigrants to the United States should learn English as soon as possible, was similarly canceled by Arizona State University, whose cancellation letter openly and proudly proclaimed: "The Minority Coalition has recommended that we cancel this engagement and bring other speakers whose views are more in line with their policies."[123]

This breathtakingly regnant campus culture mentality also explains why Columbia University, which bans ROTC on the pretext that the military bars professed homosexuals from service, nonetheless welcomed with open arms as guest speaker, in September 2007, Iran's President Mahmoud Ahmadinejad, whose government publicly executes them. It also explains why Hofstra's law school invited to speak on "legal ethics" one Lynn Stewart, a lawyer convicted and sentenced to twenty-eight months in jail for aiding and abetting a terrorist.[124]

The only common denominator in each action?—the fact that academic multicultural diversity is being promoted only to the extent that it is at odds with traditional Western, capitalistic, or Judeo-Christian values—and that it avidly supports a leftist "diversity of ideas" curriculum harboring no tolerance whatsoever for more conservative or traditional norms and beliefs.

Ignored in all of this politically correct invective, then, is the critical question: Will merely adopting the outward semblance of another culture—which usually means wearing some foreign attire, replacing one's own name with a foreign one, imitating some foreign rituals, and professing to aspire to some set of foreign beliefs—contribute to making an individual a more intelligent, more productive, most prosperous, and more well-rounded citizen—which is explicitly what a higher education is supposed to do?

To the contrary, whereas academia once prided itself in offering healthy doses of core curricular content focused upon America's stellar achievements in fostering democracy, culture, science, and industry, today—awash in the muddy groundswells of a rampant Nietzschean nihilistic skepticism made possible only within academia—it focuses upon her alleged failures—slavery, chauvinism, cultural imperialism, misogyny, and sexual repression.

The premise of the proposition being, of course, that America has fostered a degenerate civilization that is the creation of aristocratic white males, and that the less that is known about it, save that it is racist, chauvinistic, and wicked, the better—thereby enabling it to offer to unsuspecting incoming freshmen such intellectually enlightening "alternate lifestyle" cultural enrichment courses as the following:[125]

- The University of California–Berkeley's "Politics and Poetics of the Palestinian Resistance," whose course description counsels that "conservative thinkers are encouraged to take other sections"; The University of Michigan's "English 317: How to Be Gay: Male Homosexuality and Initiation"; Dartmouth's "Queer Theory, Queer Texts"; Yale's "Introduction to Lesbian and Gay Studies"; the University of Maryland's "Select Topics in Lesbian, Gay, and Bisexual Literature"; and Brown's "Unnatural Acts: Introduction to Lesbian and Gay Literature."
- The University of Chicago's "Fetishism, Gender, Sexuality and Capitalism," plus "Third Wave Feminism and Girl Culture"; the University of Wisconsin's "Goddesses and Feminine Powers"; and Stanford's more omnibus "Homosexuals, Heretics, Witches, and Werewolves."
- Wesleyan's "Pornography Writing of Prostitutes"; Swarthmore's "Lesbian Novels since World War II"; the University of Pennsylvania's "Feminist Critique of Christianity"; and Oberlin's "Feminist Criticism of Shakespeare"; not to mention Harvard's "Feminist Biblical Interpretation."
- The University of North Carolina's classic "Magic, Ritual, and Belief"; Bowdoin's "Witchcraft within the Modern World"; Columbia's "Sorcery and Magic"; Bucknell's "Witchcraft and Politics"; the University of California-Santa Barbara's "Black Marxism."
- And, of course, the University of Indiana's "Star Trek and Religion"; the University of Massachusetts' "Rock and Roll"; and the University of Iowa's "Elvis as Anthology."

Thus it is that in this prurient spirit of modern intellectual inquiry, the University of Oregon likewise mandates that all students take two courses to meet their "Race, Gender, Non-European-American" requirement; that the University of Massachusetts–Amherst offers a potluck of courses in "Lesbian/Gay/Bisexual Oppression," "Oppression of the Disabled," and "Erroneous Beliefs" (!); and that Northeastern University accords gays and lesbians preferential treatment in hiring.[126]

At Bowdoin College, in turn, the music appreciation curriculum includes a class to analyze Beethoven's Ninth Symphony as a metaphor for a rapist at work; at Duke, the inquiring mind can gain from a botanist whose specialty is ferns offering crucial insights into the symbiosis of "Feminism and Botany"; at Syracuse, no longer encouraged to study Shakespeare and Dante, an academic inmate can enjoy a summer-semester Caribbean cruise perusing gay and lesbian literature.[127]

At Cornell University, however, he or she can instead elect to remain on campus to pursue a less exotic, but perhaps more erotic, minor in "homosexual and bisexual studies"; at UCLA, nascent scholars can pursue such studies while living in purpose-built lesbian and homosexual fraternity houses; and at Texas, students can sign up for "Race and Sport in African-American Life," a regimen that explicitly seeks to examine "how sports have been used to justify racist notions of blackness."[128]

And at the University of Virginia, for those students who may have missed entirely the collapse of global communism in the late 1980s, the opportunity exists to study "Marxism: What Can Be Learned from It?"—with its course catalog description confidently proclaiming Marxism as "the standard against which all subsequent social thought must be judged."[129]

These, then, are the intellectual offerings today held out as moral exemplars for guiding America's forthcoming generations. Yet, these are not the offerings of those aspiring to quality higher education. They are instead the handiwork of sophists from East Wackistan. As even Robert Berdahl, chancellor of the ultra-liberal University of California-Berkeley, asserts: "It is imperative that our classrooms be free of indoctrination—for indoctrination is not education."[130]

Harvard graduate and former Reagan presidential advisor Hugh Hewitt puts it this way: "Even the most casual observers of elite academia know of the thorough decay now ongoing within its ranks, with its attachments to absurd theories and utter rejection of anything like traditional core curricula. For a quarter of a century, undergraduates have been fed an academic diet based on intellectual junk food that will eventually cripple the eater."[131]

As with the aforesaid lamentation of Lactantius on the decline of ancient Rome before her, America's arts and letters have become parodies of their former selves—and when Rome fell into such a state of scholarly ennui, the intellectual abyss that was to become the Dark Ages could not be far behind.

Small wonder that Alan Kors and Harvey Silverglate append in their master work, *The Shadow University*, that the academy "will have to answer for its betrayal of the nation's and its own traditions."[132] The results of this "multiculturalism gone mad" thus are rich and variegated, and include the following:

• Questionable course content combined with exceedingly low academic standards;

- Educational aimlessness, as there are seldom formal syllabi to govern course conduct;
- Propagandistic indoctrination through trivialized and politicized course content; and
- All made compulsorily available at parents' and taxpayers' expense.[133]

For now, as Professor E. Christian Kopff from the University of Colorado has incisively observed, the term "multiculturalism" doesn't have anything to do with foreign languages or particular cultures—but is instead a code word for lightweight courses presented by faculty offering a leftist view of particular cultures—it is do-gooder politics gone awry."[134]

Whatever the merits of sexism, ethnocentrism, and analogous self-esteem promoting curricula, however, they not only mis-educate, they divert resources away from genuine education in an era in which America, though it today spends far more on the imparting of knowledge than do other Western industrialized nations, gets far less learning in return. This misguided educational policy course is not only harmful to individuals and to U.S. global trade competitiveness, it likewise is a source of social unrest and racial, ethnic, and sexual antagonism.[135]

This, then, is no less than "larceny by tuition"—for given that hard-earned dollars are required to enroll in such courses, it is unconscionable that students should be asked to pay for the dubious privilege of having leftist professors mold them in their own ideological images. Nor should parents be asked to underwrite such a litany of nonsensical multiculturalism, nor should tax-funded federal funds be provided to academic institutions, public or private, audacious enough to offer them in the guise of higher education.

Succinctly put, it is manifestly unjust that institutions that receive hundreds of millions of dollars in U.S. citizen-taxpayer-funded subsidies represent but one predominant political "worldview"—that of the anti-American, pro-socialist ultra-left. For what is now being mentally done to college undergraduates, hidden behind the ivy-covered walls that protect their propagandistic platforms, is "something truly chilling," as Professors Alan Kors and Harvey Silverglate of the University of Pennsylvania, contend.[136]

It is a hidden, systematic assault on liberty, individualism, dignity, due process, and equality before the law, . . . as the nation's colleges and universities, "have become the enemies of a free society. For while their tenured staffs profess to stand for "diversity" and "tolerance" the reality is that they are more ideologically monolithic than culturally diverse and incredibly intolerant in their indoctrination methods.[137]

Reaping the Intellectual Whirlwind

Regrettably, but not surprisingly, the efforts clearly show in the results. In a test commissioned by the American Council of Trustees and Alumni examining high-school-level history knowledge among seniors at the nation's top fifty liberal arts colleges, a full 81 percent received grades of D or F—with, in stunning tribute to the extent to which the Marcusian didactic has penetrated the American educational system, a full 35 percent guessing that the phrase "from each according to his ability, to each according to his needs" came from the American Constitution rather than the *Communist Manifesto*.[138]

Over 40 percent of the students, moreover, could not place the U.S. Civil War in its correct half century; only 30 percent knew that Reconstruction was related to it; just 42 percent knew that the accolade "first in war, first in peace, and first in the hearts of his countrymen" was coined about America's first president, George Washington; just 25 percent could identify James Madison as the father of the Constitution; and only 22 percent knew that the phrase "government of the people, by the people, and for the people" came from Lincoln's Gettysburg Address.[139]

No one should be surprised either that a Department of Education "History Report Card" reveals that 57 percent of the high school seniors tested flunked even a basic knowledge of American history—being taught instead

> that the colonization of America was accomplished by genocide; that the Founding Fathers were classist, racist, sexist, and homophobic Euro-focused bigots; that the winning of the American West was an act of capitalistic pillage; and that the so-called "Robber Barons" of the nineteenth century forced widows and children into homeless lifestyles in the streets *en masse*.[140]

The crucial question to be asked thus is this: How do such didactics differ from Japanese textbooks downplaying the Nanjing Massacre, Palestinian textbooks containing maps deleting the State of Israel, or Russian schoolbooks extolling the socioeconomic virtues of Stalinism?

Indeed, a 2007 test by the Intercollegiate Studies Institute of fourteen thousand college freshmen and seniors at fifty U.S. colleges and universities in four U.S. subject areas—history, government, foreign policy, and the market economy—found that seniors collectively scored just 1.5 percent higher than freshmen. And at sixteen institutions of higher learning, the seniors scored lower than the freshmen, meaning that they not only learned absolutely nothing about civic process in four years of college, but were probably actually worse off for the experience—as seniors at twenty-two of the fifty colleges were, on average, correct on less than 50 percent of the multiple-choice questions, a failing grade by any standard on a college course exam.[141]

Yet, nostalgically, there was a time not long ago when American students knew about the glories of the Revolutionary War and the tragedies of the Civil War. They read the *Federalist Papers* and could quote passages from the Founding Fathers. They were cognizant of the intellectual disputes between

Thomas Jefferson and John Adams—of the patriotism of Samuel Adams and Paul Revere—and the legendary exploits of Davy Crockett and his fellow heroes at the Alamo. But not today—as they are rather being taught that Americans should be ashamed of their nation, that other cultures are superior to it and indeed have suffered because of it.[142]

Indeed, the true magnitude of the historical inversion that has taken place is reflected in the reality that it was Jefferson, holder of the title "Father of the University of Virginia," who persuasively argued that America's youth—"without regard to wealth, birth, or other accidental condition or circumstance"—should be educated at public expense. A liberal education in "reading, writing, and arithmatick," he wrote, followed by the reading of "Graecian, Roman, English, and American history," would render them "worthy to receive and guard the sacred deposit of the rights and liberties of their fellow citizens."[143]

Not only did such noted Founders as Jefferson, Madison, Franklin, Benjamin Rush, and Noah Webster expect the nascent nation's public schools to provide instruction in Greek, Latin, geography, and mathematics, therefore, they expected them to concurrently instill within their minds "the first elements of morality"—foremost among them, love of a country they believed to be good and just.[144]

Thus, it was no accident that de Tocqueville a half century later would conclude that "it cannot be doubted that in the United States, the instruction of the people powerfully contributes to the support of the democratic republic, and that will be the case, I think, where the instruction that enlightens the mind is not separated from the education responsible for moral manners."[145]

Contrast that spirit with the modern *zeitgeist* wherein a prevailing cancerous anti-Americanism pervades the country's campuses—and where countercultural moral relativism, if actually taken seriously, renders it difficult, if not impossible, for educators to do what they were originally commissioned and traditionally expected to do, namely, to build public-spirited citizens. For how can they teach students to love their country and make sacrifices for it while simultaneously instructing them that their culture is not only not special among others but indeed is a foremost exploiter of them?[146]

The defining difference lies in the aspiration. For it is noteworthy that the Founders in *Federalist Papers* 10, 24, 41, and elsewhere spoke of "civilized nations," as opposed to "savage tribes," and did so because they believed the distinction between civilization and barbarism to be significant in their ambitions for America. But no such distinction can be made within "politically correct" academia today; for while teachers may speak of cultural differences, they may make no distinction that implies a moral judgment—as "diversity is today the virtue taught, with judgmentalism the corresponding vice."[147]

Thus it is that the nation finds itself in the throes of its own Chinese Communist Cultural Revolution, wherein everything is political and no contrary thinking is allowed—wherein nothing must be permitted that impedes the will of the entrenched doctrinal elite, a mindset very much in sync with the worldview of George Orwell's *1984*—which, for its prescience in its time, was objectively on target, as evidenced by the blanket censoring of contrarian thought imposed by the draconian speech and thought codes now pervading the country's campuses.[148]

Indeed, in such a stifling intellectual environment, students are likely actually better off not being subjected to the notion of history at all. In the germane words of educational analyst and author Martin Gross:

> The dumbing down of the American college serves the motives of the New Establishment which now finds it easy to indoctrinate its undergraduate students into its biases and bigotries. Since college graduates, especially those from the prestigious Ivy League, inevitably wind up as the nation's leaders, what does this say about the present and future of American culture—its politics, economics, literature, journalism, films, and especially its philosophical direction?[149]

This, then, is the seminal performance question pervading academia today—not just that the nation's higher education system is cranking out graduates whose diplomas are little more than certificates of attendance, but more specifically involving the educational caliber and moral fitness of those whom it produces and who will lead this nation in coming years. For imperial Rome, it bears repeating, died not from invasion from without, but from cultural disintegration from within—not because its leaders did not want to lead, but because they didn't know how.[150]

How did it come down to this? The academic cloisters, ridiculed for generations as places in which nothing of substance ever happened, have today instead become a foremost battleground for the soul of America, presiding over a free-fall collapse of educational standards and debasing of morality among the nation's knowledge-aspiring young adults that is unprecedented in human history.[151]

As a consequence, throughout America today, higher education—and the study of the humanities in particular—is in a state of crisis, as proponents of cultural deconstruction, radical sexism, reverse racism, and other politically motivated challenges to traditional tenets of humanistic study have become dominant voices on the campuses of many of the nation's foremost universities.[152]

Indeed, often the prominence of their presence becomes self-perpetuating by virtue of carefully constructed ethnic, racial, and gender quota admissions standards deliberately designed by faculty to make incoming student classes "look more like them"—a condescending regimen enforced to the degree that it has been often recently said that a white male has to be truly exceptional to be considered—and that under today's "politically correct" admission rules, Albert Einstein probably wouldn't ideologically make the cut as an incoming freshman aspirant.[153]

In the cogent insight of the noted linguist John McWhorter, author of *Losing the Race: Self-Sabotage in Black America*, speaking of the sociopolitical milieu that pervades the faculty of the University of California-Berkeley: "What is truly alarming is that one can now sit through full two-hour meetings of concerned Berkeley faculty and administrators without the slightest acknowledgment of class, merit, or fairness. Instead, the agenda is implicitly restricted to mere speculation on how to reinstate racial preferences in other guises."[154]

Again, to what end this course of parceling out preferential college admissions benefits based on ethnicity, race, and gender? If equity means to be "fair," and "fair" means equal opportunity to gain access, why not just make the admissions process a lottery instead of cloning admissions offices to serve as sub-units of the Equal Rights Division of the Department of Justice merely to give leftist-leaning faculty a student body more susceptible to their monolithic monologues of incantation and indoctrination?

That this is a carefully formulated conspiracy there can be no doubt. For while there may be slight differences at the margin among the objectives of the sundry politically activist groups today at work, when viewed through the prism of the traditional values that they are seeking to subvert, they exhibit a quite remarkable unity of purpose—no less than the destruction of the mores, methods, and motivations of the country's historic cultural base.[155]

Their end goal is perhaps best encapsulated in the rally slogans of the Reverend Jesse Jackson in leading campus marches in the 1980s—among them, the one at Stanford protesting its now infamous Western civilization course because Aristotle, Machiavelli, Rousseau, Shakespeare, and Locke turned out to be white males: "Hey, hey, ho, ho! Western culture's gotta go!" And in Stanford's case, it did![156]

The insinuation of radical political agendas into the historic higher education mandate manifests itself in other, subtler, ways as well. At many institutions of higher learning, traditional methods and goals of humanistic study have been cast aside as hopelessly outdated. Heuristic *reading* is no longer viewed as a productive activity worthy of pursuit as a constructive means for gleaning meaning from books and ideas, but instead is advanced as an elaborate interpretative game designed to expose the impossibility of meaning.[157]

In like manner, *writing*, in the new scholarship, no longer means the quest to express oneself clearly and precisely. To the contrary, it is to be pursued with consummate deliberation as training in the techniques of preparing and promoting doctrines that support subversive activities carefully constructed to challenge conventional bourgeois faith in clarity, intelligibility, and communication.[158]

The academic institutionalization of the Marcusian "New Left" radical ethos has, in fact, brought with it not only an increased polarization of the curricula of the humanities, but also an increasing ignorance of the human legacy. For now, instead of studying the great classics of the past—in the sciences, arts, history, and literature, students watch movies and peruse third-rate propagandistic pedagogic works held dear by their favored ideological cohort.[159]

Rather than reading widely in the major primary texts, moreover, today, they merely absorb abstruse commentaries on them, reverting to the originals only by reference to cite illustrations for pet critical social theories—as much of the great American college experience has gradually, but inexorably, been reduced to the base level of *Cliff's Notes* and *Classics Illustrated* comic magazines.[160]

In the attendant reindoctrination process, therefore, all of the historic arts and humanities, as well as the social sciences, are undergoing fundamental redefinition to conform more closely to a modern code of moral relativism. In their place is offered a radiant vision of a new world order—a new "age of enlightenment" to be governed by a rebellious new political system eager to be born.[161]

The Politics of Ivory Tower Political Propaganda

The political polling numbers make clear the reason. In a Luntz Research survey, conducted on behalf of the Center for the Study of Popular Culture, of the ideological orientations of the faculties at Ivy League universities:

- 64 percent self-identified as liberals, 23 percent moderates, and 6 percent conservatives;
- 53 percent identified themselves as Democrats and just 3 percent as Republicans;
- 61 percent believed that the federal government—and not individuals, communities, or private enterprise—should do more to solve the nation's problems; and
- a whopping 80 percent disagreed with the premise that "if the federal government has a budget surplus, the balance should be returned to taxpayers in the form of a tax cut."[162]

In short, the number of faculty identifying themselves as conservatives, let alone Republicans, is shown to be in the single digits. But this propensity comes as no surprise, as a similar survey found that self-professing liberal faculty members outnumbered their conservative counterparts by 166:6 at Cornell, 116:5 at the University of Colorado, 141:9 at UCLA, 151:17 at Stanford, 141:1 at the University of California–Santa Barbara, 80:11 at San Diego State, 18:1 at Brown, and 6:1 at Penn.[163]

Likewise, among all thirty-two colleges surveyed in a poll of prevailing opinion of some others of the nation's finest *vendors of liberal education*, in both connotations of the phrase, there were 1,397 registered Democrats whereas just 134 professors admitted to being Republican, and reported political donations similarly went 90:1 for Democrats at Georgetown, 19:1 at Yale, and 8:1 at Michigan.[164]

In the 2004 presidential election, the ratio of Kerry donations to Bush donations likewise ran 302:1 at Princeton, 43:1 at MIT, 25:1 at Harvard, 20:1 at Yale, and 15:1 at Georgetown. A more recent September 2007 poll, in fact, found that employees of Yale and its affiliates preferred the Democratic presidential field to that of the Republicans by a ratio of 120:1—with Yale faculty itself contributing a total of $44,500 to Democratic candidates but only $1,000 for their Republican counterparts—as tenured liberal professors have obviously clearly determined where their ideological bread is buttered.[165]

Indicative, then, of the not-surprising handiwork of this left-leaning cabal are such banal race-gender-sex ruminations as those on the discipline of geography highlighted in a work titled: *Feminism and Geography: The Limits of Geographical Knowledge*—a tome that purports itself to be "a sustained examination of the 'masculinism' of contemporary geographic discourse":

> I maintain that to think geography—to think within the parameters of the discipline—is to occupy a masculine subject position. Geography is masculinist. In examining many of the founding texts of philosophy, science, political theory, and history, feminists have argued that the notion of reason, as it developed from the seventeenth century onward, is not gender neutral. On the contrary, it works in tandem with white, bourgeois, heterosexual masculinity.[166]

And those of Howard University political science professor Alvin Thornton, who organized campus protests to force the resignation of Republican strategist Lee Atwater from the university's Board of Trustees, ostensibly over his role in developing controversial political ads in the 1988 presidential campaign—all the while openly conceding that he was more concerned over the prospects of Atwater recruiting more affluent tax-paying blacks to the Republican Party. "The last thing that we now need as a people is to have our most fortunate separated from our least fortunate," he said.[167]

Or Cornell classics professor Martin Bernal's quixotic quest to "lessen European cultural arrogance" by conclusively proving that many of ancient Egypt's pharaohs were "usefully black."[168] Or black feminist poet Maya Angelou's assertion that "I *know* for certain that William Shakespeare was a black woman."[169]

Or radical academic Susan Sontag characterizing the "male-dominated white race" as the "cancer of human history."[170] Such is the status of scholarly inquiry on display throughout much of American academia today—with traditional values now recast as fraudulent by a self-serving ivory tower patriarchy and its newly evolving parallel matriarchy.[171]

Thus it is that the nation's great achievements are billed instead as colossal myths and its former glories depicted as among history's most conspicuous lies. Their patent biases are manifest in their academic agendas, wherein generic Western civilization courses are portrayed as no more than unvarnished cultural imperialism designed to stamp an imprimatur of European mores and traditions upon American society at the expense of non-Western ones.[172]

In the resulting inquisition and historiographic reinvention process, long-standing curricula have today been reduced from year-long courses to mere multiparagraphed sections citing Jefferson, Jackson, the Constitution, the Civil War, and Reconstruction if such content is presented at all. As the canons of great literature are increasingly sacrificed on the altar of counterculturalism, moreover, the once-unifying force of democratic ideals is concurrently being dismissed as Anglo-Eurocentric chauvinism—Columbus and the Founders are recast as imperialists while the nation's earliest leaders are reduced to depictions as environment-despoiling exploiters of slaves.[173]

Such demagogic pedagoguery would be risible were it not so educationally tragic and, in fact, so demonstrably wrong. In the case of Columbus, for instance, his discovery of the Caribbean, in the new histories, is characterized as an "invasion" that introduced slavery and genocide into the islands—with their native populations declining appreciably as a result.[174]

What the histories fail to mention, however, is that the islands upon which Columbus actually landed in 1492, then occupied by the Taino tribe, were concurrently under attack by Carib tribesmen who were cannibals. Thus, the possibility cannot be discounted that the decline in populace attributed to a hypothesized policy of genocide attributed to Columbus for which there is no documentation is instead no more than the by-product of the countercultural culinary habits of local peoples.[175]

Accordingly, the challenges of preserving traditional cultural values become acute. For because conventional American history is portrayed as one of abuse and exploitation, in pursuit of such historiographic nonsense, students can lose respect for their heritage of freedom. They rather come to believe that Western civilization does not merit preservation, electing more revolutionary ideologies instead. And because their knowledge has thus been corrupted, the cultural elitists who are their teachers become their role models, making them easy targets for subversively liberal ideologies.[176]

Here again, reminiscent of the "mind-speak" of the novel *1984*, the counsel of education professor Charles Pierce at Harvard instantaneously becomes germane:

> Every child in America entering school at the age of five is mentally ill because he comes to school with certain allegiances toward the founding fathers, toward elected officials, toward his parents, toward a belief in a supernatural being, toward the sovereignty of this nation as a separate entity. It is up to teachers to make sick children well by creating the international children of the future.[177]

Yet to what end? Why is there no outcry among respected scholars when students are taught that William Shakespeare was a black woman; that black Egyptian pilots were flying gliders around Africa in ancient times; that blacks invented democracy, philosophy, and science, which were then stolen from them by the Greeks; or that black astrologers had discovered the distant star Sirius B millennia before the telescope needed to view it had even been invented?[178]

The supposed logic behind such convoluted contentions flows as follows. Though the first philosopher in Eurocentric eyes was Thales, who lived circa 600 B.C., the first in Afrocentric view was a black Egyptian named Ptahotep, who antedated him. This interpretation continues by maintaining that Thales studied in Africa, as did Socrates, Homer, Pythagoras, Xenophon, and Plato, who then stole the rich legacy of local philosophy—as well as learned measurement, astronomy, geometry, arithmetic, writing, the calendar, medicine, architecture, law, and all else worthy of note—from the Egyptians.[179]

The source of such unique argumentation, in turn, derives from the reality that Egypt is deemed to be to African civilization what Greece is to the West. Ancient Egypt, then, is the summation of all African civilization that preceded it, and the source of all that succeeded it—including all things good. As apparently within the tribal confederation that today is academia, there is a law that holds that, irrespective of the facts, any member of any given tribe can write its history exactly as he or she wishes it to have transpired and be perceived: "My history, right or wrong, my history!" Hence, the ongoing reforging of history into the mold that all things African are good, whereas all things Western are bad.[180]

No doubt, the West has perpetrated terrible deeds, not the least of which were to itself. But what civilization has not? E. A. Gibbon characterized history as little more than a register of the crimes, follies, and misfortunes of mankind. But whatever the sins of the West, they are no worse than those of Africa or Asia, and generally pale in the comparison.[181]

For the Founding Fathers, it bears reiterating, were not an aggregate of unlearned and unwashed barbaric Indian-murdering, river-polluting, plantation-possessing slave owners. Indeed, in the Constitution's framing, they drew heavily upon Greek and Roman models—making, among other things, their careful choice of the word "Senate"—a Roman designation—to describe the nation's new legislative upper house—no accident. Thus, John Adams would observe: "We shall learn to prize the checks and balances of free government if we recall the miseries of Greece which arose from its ignorance of them."[182]

For theirs was a worldview eclectic and diverse—being conversant in Aristotle, Herodotus, Plutarch, Thucydides, and Virgil—as well as with the Greek version of the New Testament. Indeed, the cover title on Jefferson's commentary on the Bible, euphemistically called the *Jefferson Bible*, makes clear that he extracted it "from the Gospels in Greek, Latin, French, and English."[183]

The didactic of the multiculturalists thus is not true history. It is instead a disastrous impoverishment of history. For at its strategic essence, history is a liberating teacher for receptive minds—ideas have consequences, and taken in the aggregate, their lessons leaven the human experience. Its great utility, in the view of Thomas Jefferson, is that "apprising people of the past will enable them to judge . . . the future. It will avail them of the experience of other times and other nations; it will qualify them as judges of the actions and designs of men." To which John Quincy Adams incisively appended: "To a man of liberal education, the study of history is not only useful, it is indispensable."[184]

On the other hand, bad history—history biased for its propaganda value—is worse than no history at all—for "history as a weapon" is an abuse of history, which must perforce not be a quest for vindication of self but instead for objective knowledge. Hence, once parochial ethnic pride or racial prejudice drives the curriculum, objectivity goes by the boards.

As such, "feel good" history designed merely to promote individual or collective self-esteem is a corruption of sound scholarship, and its use as therapy is a perversion of the historiographic process—a superficial academic accommodation that does injustice to the portrayal of all of civilization. For "history is an early warning system," said Norman Cousins. "Nations ignore their histories at their perils."[185] Political historian Arthur Schlesinger, in commentary lamenting that "the melting pot has now yielded to the Tower of Babel," likewise asserts:

> The prime purpose of history is to promote not group self-esteem but an understanding of the world and the past, dispassionate analysis, judgment, and perspective, respect for divergent cultures and traditions, and an unflinching protection of the unifying ideas of tolerance, democracy, and human rights that make all free historical inquiry possible.[186]

Equally, if not more damaging, however, is the disservice that such teaching does to the would-be minority "beneficiaries" of such bogus claims of social achievement themselves—the notions that an unjust system is out to "get them," that all rules are unjust, that justice is simply the will of the stronger party, that "individual rights" are no more than a code term signaling social privilege that should be subordinated to the claims of group interest, that double standards are acceptable so long as they are enforced for the benefit of "minority victims," and that social justice cannot be achieved by neutral rules but only through a forced rationing of power among separatist minority groups.[187]

In addition, further to these ends, they hold that knowledge should be pursued not as a virtue in its own right but for the pursuit of political power, that conventional indices of intellectual progress are no more than establishment norms, and that hard work will achieve for those who elect to make the effort very little under the current culturally biased system.

Accordingly, those who aspire to victim status now do so not because they want to be oppressed but rather because of the political utility of the moral capital of "victimhood." But would they not be infinitely better off in seeking to build productive economic futures were they instead encouraged to improve their academic performances instead of conceding outright that "the system" is rigged against them?[188]

This is a point clearly recognized by NAACP Director Roy Wilkins as early as four decades ago when he accused college administrators of trying to "buy peace at any price" by setting up insular on-campus black studies centers for "racial breast-beating" purposes—at a time when black activist Bayard Rustin was concurrently warning that "black studies should not be used to enable black students to escape the challenges of the university by setting up 'soul courses' that they can just play with and pass." The case against social engineering predicated upon the politics of class warfare and victimization has seldom been so eloquently yet simply framed.[189]

The net result of the ongoing intellectual inquisition of the modern multiculturalists—the *Torquemadas* of tradition—however, is that Americans today, and immigrant Americans in particular, no longer enjoy, nor are they afforded the opportunity to acquire, those levels of basic information and understanding needed to effectively participate in a democratic-republican form of government. Indeed, such deficiencies extend from the average student to even the best and brightest—raising serious questions about whether young Americans are being provided the tools needed to shoulder the responsibilities of informed citizens functioning in a highly competitive and turbulent twenty-first-century world.[190]

Such handiwork is, in fact, worse than a national scandal, it is a threat to national survival. When the government began to expand its network of public schools at the onset of the twentieth century, its imperative was that freedom depended upon an educated citizenry. In its curriculum, then, civics and history weren't electives, they were capstone courses. Yet today, in many curricula, they don't even appear as elective options.[191]

In sum, too many America's colleges and universities are now so radically to the left of mainstream that they have disappeared from rational view. Just about the only place in the world where one can find bona fide Marxist ideologues anymore, in fact, is on Western college campuses where, as tenured professors, they are insulated from the realities of productive economic life.

This, despite the fact that the ideal of a socialistic nirvana lies in shambles practically everywhere across the planet, except perhaps in isolated outposts of left-leaning academia where "intellectuals"—famously defined by the late Bishop Fulton J. Sheen as "those educated beyond the limits of their intelligence"—still cling to a failed notion that communistic governance is wiser than the rationales of the free-market democratic process.[192]

Yet as ably rejoined by modern social philosopher John Searle: "The idea that curricula should be converted to partisan purpose is a perversion of the ideal of a university. The object of converting the curriculum into an instrument of social transformation (be it leftist, rightist, centrist, or whatever) is the very opposite of higher education."[193] More bluntly put by Margaret Thatcher in a 1997 U.S. speech:

> When a Stanford University English professor describes Milton as an ass, and when Shakespeare is on the syllabus of Duke University in the words of yet another professor only to illustrate the way that seventeenth century society mistreated women, the working class, and minorities . . . we should be duly warned.
>
> A society needs but one generation to abandon the task of learning and transmitting its culture for it to become an alien, lifeless, irrelevance. A powerful radical left wing cabal is bent on destroying what every generation past would have understood to be the central purpose of an education—that is, again in the words of Edmund Burke, allowing individuals "to avail themselves of the general bank and capital of nations and of the ages."[194]

With education providing that priceless bank of knowledge, informed citizens and their constitutionally guaranteed rights thereby become the very cornerstones of the democratic process. For in the words of British sociologist David Martin: "Democracy is built on citizen participation, and its ideal is the meaningful participation of an informed citizenry. This presupposes a level of devotion to the enterprise to approach public issues as a unified community."[195]

If citizens are denied the opportunity to learn their nation's history or to comprehend the profound policy dilemmas that it faces, therefore, a critical linchpin of informed governance is lost. Such historical ignorance or amnesia become the more dangerous, moreover, at a time when the nation and its citizens must confront the potentially catastrophic security threats of international terrorism in tandem with the internal dangers of civic disaffection and cultural alienation.[196]

To these ends, now more than ever, it is quintessential that informed citizens operating within a democracy understand the historic ideals of personal, religious, political, and economic freedoms that motivated those who founded the country and forged its national identity. It would concurrently be constructive were they to be familiar with the courage, determination, and pragmatism that accompanied those motivations. Such knowledge would, in fact, be particularly useful to new immigrants in their struggles to join those of their predecessors who successfully found their productive places in the American way of life.[197]

But this time-proven venue to upward mobility the multiculturalists reject—in so doing, consigning their would-be beneficiaries to the inevitability of a lesser economic state. For their salvation lies not through group solutions, but through individual initiative and self-determination. To quote John Stuart Mill: "Whatever crushes individuality is despotism!" Thus, to teach the nation's minority poor and disadvantaged that they can ignore with impunity those social standards and modes of competitive behavior that have always contributed to upward mobility in the quest for success in American life is more than mere silliness. It is a devastating economically counter-productive lie.[198]

The critical question thus becomes this: Can America, and her majority and minority communities alike, withstand the growing numbers of reformers and activists who would today dismantle her prized and cherished values systems, and her *economic* values systems in particular? The answer must be soon in coming, for at the political bottom line, unless this course is soon decisively corrected, subsequent generations of American children may never know the legacy that they have lost.

Indeed, with the ongoing, prolonged decline in the quality of the nation's education system, in a few short decades will there be anyone left who cares?—as the ultimate losers then will be those students, who, in their diminished intellectual state, won't have the slightest notion of the cherished values that they are now being taught to disparage.[199]

To reiterate classics scholar Victor David Hanson's epitaph to the fall of imperial Rome: "Earlier Romans knew what it was to be Roman, why it was at least better than the alternative, and why their culture had to be defended. Later, in their ignorance, they forgot what they once knew, in pride mocked who they were, and in consequence, disappeared."[200]

As Alexis de Tocqueville similarly assessed nearly two centuries ago:

> Because Roman civilization perished through barbarian invasion, we are perhaps too much inclined to think that is the only way that a nation can die. For if the lights that guide us ever go out, they will fade little by little, as if of their

own accord. . . . We therefore should not console ourselves into thinking that the barbarians are a long way off. Some peoples may let the torch be snatched from their hands, but others may stamp it out themselves.[201]

Such determinations quite obviously offer somber admonitions, but the warnings that they convey are, in essence, precisely what modern leftist academicians are now accomplishing in their ongoing quests to transform traditional American culture and values into banal "new wave" serendipity—building their didactic upon foundations of abject ignorance, naive misinterpretation, and unreal expectations.

In sum, there is today a dissonant disconnect between what American universities are mandated to teach and what they practice, as they proceed blithely through their administrative processes oblivious to the need for civic instruction and the operation of due process and other decencies of constitutional law.

Their scofflaw approach to academic management—pursued solely to satisfy their idyllic, ill-conceived, self-serving ivory tower "political correctness" goals—thus clearly must be stopped. For while universities may be enclaves, they are not sovereign nations. Ultimately, they must be compelled to answer for their defiance of the workings of America's legal system and their perversions of her values and traditions.[202]

As under the watchful eye of the heirs of Herbert Marcuse, the theory of "repressive tolerance" and the practice of "progressive intolerance" now still largely govern the extracurricular lives of the nation's higher education students—with many of the 1960s Marcusian "flower children"—professionally untrained, and therefore unable to compete in the profit-driven private sector arena—remaining instead on campus to become its tenured professors, counselors, and administrators—and hence, its governors.

It is thus appalling, but nonetheless true, that the academic world now perforce must itself be taught a lesson in intellectual freedom from society at large.[203] For if the American experiment in human liberty is to survive, her citizens must fervently endeavor to keep alive the pursuit of critical truth and the free exchange of ideas, values, and convictions, and to preserve the due process rights of all citizens to equality before the law, cognizant that the alternative has a single, somber name—and that is tyranny.

When in the 1950s, America was threatened with the demagoguery of McCarthyism, as sociologist Sidney Hook has noted, learned men of reason courageously stood up to put down that demagogic menace. With the threat of countercultural Marcusian demagoguery now looming ominously foreboding, a call to arms of citizens of equal stature is once again invoked.

For in the socially deviant world where multiculturalism prevails, there is no Aristotelian search for ultimate truth, but merely vitiating pedantry that subscribes to nineteenth-century French philosopher Louis Veuillot's description of the modus operandi of those who pursue the perfidious practice of political didactics. To wit:

> When I am the weaker, I beseech you for my freedom, because that is your principle. But when I am the stronger, I take away your freedom, because that is my principle.[204]

In the last analysis, then, the decisive question again becomes: Is America bold enough to right its now-capsized educational system? This is a quintessential query, for ultimately education is not just about the institution, its accumulated knowledge and research, or even about its vital role of initiating young people into the "life of mind."

To the contrary, it is equally about preserving the intellectual, social, cultural, and moral legacy that it inherits—and then, as faithful stewards of the public trust, passing it down to subsequent generations to enable them to likewise faithfully adhere to those civic values that empower them to inherit and assume the full responsibilities of productive citizenship.[205]

The challenge doubtless is daunting, for as sociologist Robert Conquest has asserted, while "New Left" intellectuals may say they believe in social justice and freedom of thought, they instead rely upon dogmatism, social oppression, and Marxist-style thought control to maintain their power base[206]—a phenomenon that caused then Yale President Benno Smith in 1991 to observe:

> The most serious problems of freedom of expression in our society exist on our campuses. The assumption seems to be that the purpose of education is to induce correct opinion rather than to search for wisdom and thus liberate the mind.[207]

This, then, is the paradoxic, pedagogic puzzle that pervades academia and, by extension, America today. For unfortunately, little has changed in the seventeen years since Smith uttered those words—as retrograde liberals remain in charge of the ivy-covered halls—fulfilling George Santayana's keen observation that "fanaticism consists of redoubling your efforts when you have lost your aim."

In the meantime, student prospects for a truly "liberal" education continue to decline—and unless this course is soon reversed, intellectual freedom in America will have been lost, and Herbert Marcuse, the Frankfurt School, and Karl Marx will have won.[208]

4

The Manipulation of the Media

Enlighten me now, O Muses, tenants of Olympian homes, for you are goddesses, inside on everything, know everything. But we mortals hear only the news, and know nothing at all.

—From the *Iliad* by Homer

THE MEDIA AND THE FOUNDING FATHERS

The long-standing American tenet holding that the media serves as the fourth branch of government is predicated on the premise that the media bears an obligation, in its mandate, to be faithful to its public trust. Today, due to a corrosive deterioration of objectivity within its ranks, serious questions have arisen as to the anti-traditionalist countercultural role that it arrogates to itself in news coverage. As subsequent to the leftist seizure of academia described in chapter 3, it was but logical that the wave of those ideals should spill over into other disciplines, and that the nation's media should wallow in its ideological wake.

It was not always so. Indeed, early on, the media played an integral role in establishing a mantra of objective responsibility—as it came to be a foremost catalyst in strengthening the nation's intended democratic, capitalistic architecture—a function that provided powerful political proponency at the founding of the Republic.

"The basis of government being the opinion of the people," Thomas Jefferson wrote, "the very first object should be to keep that right; and were it left to me to decide whether we should have a government without newspapers, or newspapers without a government, I should not hesitate a moment to prefer the latter."[1]

Today, Jefferson might have serious second thoughts—and indeed, as analysis will show, he later did—which perhaps should also come as no surprise. For though the nation's media began, and continues to be, political in its focus, nowhere in America are the clear manifestations of internal societal and cultural decay more manifest than in the flagrantly countercultural prejudices of her contemporary mainstream press.

Such proclivities are evident equally in its advocacy of a leftist social agenda that contradicts her legacy of patriotic national values, its deliberate attempts to deconstruct the underpinnings of her democratic, capitalistic core, and its all-pervasive, antimilitary bias—in effect, precisely those central elements advanced as key determinants for victory in that "winning strategy" articulated in the 1960s neo-Marxist "Marcusian doctrine" previously described.

Again, it was not always so: as early on, the aspired precept of a vibrant press determined to develop that informed constituency prerequisite to the successful functioning of a democracy rose to enjoy an auspicious status in the early civic life of colonial America, even in her infancy.

For though in England, the newspaper was still young when the initial New World settlements were established, the first successful U.S. newspaper, the Boston *Newsletter*, made its inaugural appearance in 1704—and during the remaining seven-decades-plus of her colonial status, the media would develop into an institution that would play a major role both in her struggle for independence and in the development of her indigenous educational system.[2]

For the evolution of the school and press in America were integrally linked. While the schools taught the essentials of reading, the newspapers provided prime content to read, thereby not only furthering education in academic subjects and other general interest topics but further disseminating the crucial information that the schools sought to promote regarding their curricula, teaching terms, and dates of opening.[3]

The right to free and open discourse was thus central to the core values of the nation from its very founding. Indeed, even as the last embers of a successful "revolutionary war" were sparking, the nascent nation's architects were contemplating the formation of a new republic characterized by its commitment to unfettered speech as a social glue binding society—a conviction articulated a century and a half later in the assertion of Justice Oliver Wendell Holmes that "the best test of truth is the power of thought to get itself accepted in the competition of the marketplace."[4]

In addition to its educational function, the early America media played a catalytic *political* role as well—not just through its editorializing but through opinion sharing, including "letters to the editor." In this process, rudimentary newspapers came to play a primary role in the dynamic political debate that led to the nation's liberation. Indeed, increasing in number from the appearance of the first colonial broadsheet in 1704 to over fifty fledgling newspapers by 1776, most assumed an aggressively "pro-independence" stance, while staunch in their support of George Washington's Revolutionary Army.[5]

Their convictions would also reverberate throughout the rhetoric of America's 1787 Constitutional Convention—an assembly whose deliberations would culminate in the First Amendment's ironclad guarantee to the nation's press and populace of unequivocal and unbridled free speech. To wit: "Congress shall make no law . . . abridging the freedom of speech or of the press."[6]

One of the most critical mistakes made by the British, in fact, was their attempt to levy a "stamp tax" on the colonies that applied to legal documents and newspapers, thereby incurring the ire of two of the most vocal proponent groups in the colonies—the lawyers and the media owners. In the words of U.S. education historian H. G. Good: "Only a tax on sermons would have been more ill-advised."[7]

It was no doubt a dangerous strategy—as some of America's most prominent political leaders, Benjamin Franklin, Samuel Adams, and Thomas Paine foremost among them, had earned their prominence as founders and owner-operators of the nation's earliest newspapers. Indeed, at the time of the American Revolution and for several decades thereafter, it was unconditionally taken for granted that newspapers were the mouthpieces of politicians and political parties.[8]

As such, it was generally well-known and accepted that the *Philadelphia Aurora* was the voice of Thomas Jefferson and his so-called Republicans, the forebears of today's Democrats; whereas the *Gazette* of the United States was a steadfast supporter of Alexander Hamilton, Jefferson's great rival, and a strong proponent of the latter's Federalist Party platform for the new nation. When the First Amendment to the Constitution, outlawing any restrictions on the freedom of the press, was drafted, therefore, the assumption was that the press would perforce be partisan.[9]

It was not until the mid-nineteenth century, around the onset of the Civil War, in fact, that newspaper publishers and editors began to proclaim an independence from organized professional political parties. At the onset, it was the *New York Herald*, founded by James Gordon Bennett in the 1830s, and the *New York Tribune*, established by Horace Greeley in the early 1840s, that first attempted to portray a less parochial perspective on public affairs.[10]

And then for a full century thereafter, until the onset of the multicultural revolution in the mid- to late 1960s, the nation's media—though often accused, and indeed, often guilty, of favoritism and partisanship—nonetheless aspired to an avowed goal of providing coherence and meaning to the news without representing any particular political persuasion—a conviction of the national need for unencumbered dialogue on critical issues.[11]

Throughout her history, then, the United States has generally pursued a steadfast commitment to the value of unfettered speech, limiting its proscriptions to specific and unique circumstances, usually in times of war.[12] As such, it has sought to censor speech and constrain movement only infrequently, as with the following:

- the Sedition Act of 1798;
- President Abraham Lincoln's suspension of the right of *habeas corpus* during the Civil War;
- the prosecution of some 2,000 persons in World War I for opposing the war and draft under the Espionage Act of 1917 and the Sedition Act of 1918;
- the internment of 120,000 persons of Japanese descent during World War II;
- the outbreak of the Cold War, which led to the investigations of the House Un-American Activities Committee and Senator Joe McCarthy in the 1950s;
- the efforts of the federal government to ban publication of the "Pentagon Papers" and prosecute antiwar protestors for burning draft cards in the volatile 1960s; and
- the Patriot Act in the wake of 9/11.[13]

Over the years, American presidents have thus responded in varying ways to political crises and the First Amendment, often in ways differing from those of their predecessors. President Lincoln did not propose a sedition act as had occurred during the administration of John Adams; President Wilson rejected calls to suspend the right to *habeas corpus*, in contrast to Lincoln; and President George W. Bush has not demanded loyalty oaths from Muslims nor interred them in concentration camps, as did Franklin Roosevelt with the Japanese in World War II.[14]

But even the Sedition Act of 1798, enacted because war with France was imminent, draconian as it was, expired after three years in March 1801—and when it did, one of the first official acts of incoming President Jefferson was to pardon all those convicted under it, noting that it was "a nullity as absolute and palpable as if the Congress had ordered us to fall down and worship a golden image."[15]

Indeed, forty years later, on July 4, 1840, Congress repaid all the fines that had been levied under the 1798 law with interest, again declaring that it had been passed under a "mistaken exercise" of power and that it was "null and void." The patent unconstitutionality of the act, the Congressional report proclaimed, had now been "conclusively settled."[16]

More than a century later, moreover, the Supreme Court, in its landmark *New York Times v. Sullivan* decision, concluded that "although the Sedition Act was never tested in this Court, the attack upon its validity has carried the day in the court of history."[17]

The Court's decision, as stipulated in its own words, thus celebrated America's "profound national commitment to the principle that public debate should be uninhibited, robust, and transparent." What has evolved since then, however, in the course of the multicultural revolution, and the suppressing cloud of censorship under the pretext of so-called political correctness that it has engendered, is the focus of this chapter.

PUBLIC RESPONSIBILITY AND THE FOURTH ESTATE

Though evolving somewhat surprisingly, then, the ascendancy of an irresponsible U.S. partisan political press has arisen in parallel to, and coincidental with, the demise of the nation's civic values documented in preceding analysis—with the result blatantly manifest in the prevalence of an ever-more-unabashed media bias.

For today, masquerading behind a facade of journalistic impartiality, de facto political activists posing as dispassionate reporters employ the same seductive marketing techniques that have long been the commercial hucksters' recourse. As a consequence, what was once a vaunted "free press" has degenerated, in large part, into little more than an ultraliberal public relations establishment whose express goal is to advance political and social agendas and ideologies openly hostile to traditional American values.[18]

The problem, at its most basic, is one of particular political perception— the prism through which one views the world. As America's far-left media— which perpetually portrays itself as "mainstream"—views conservatives as rabid right-wing radicals and itself as "middle of the road." As such, it blithely proceeds with a paradoxic abiding faith in the civilian bureaucracy yet a deep suspicion of the U.S. military, while maintaining an unwavering commitment to such socially divisive issues as cultural diversity, affirmative action, and the politics of victimhood to the detriment of social assimilation, patriotism, and traditional values.[19]

Imbued with this preconceived mindset, then, it approaches its reportage mission with a reflexive tendency to blame America first for whatever is wrong with the world; with an enthusiastic attachment to public sector cures for every private sector problem; with a profound dedication not to equality of opportunity but instead to equality of outcome; and a commitment to the statutory use of legal mandates and numeric quotas when the workings of democracy, in their view, prove to be inadequate to that end. Consequently, that pernicious brand of bigoted, biased political press coverage that a century ago caused it to be castigated as "yellow journalism" today is simply called "journalism."

The political paradox manifests itself in many ways. The media is convinced that most problems with minority communities are largely attributable to bigotry and racial discrimination—but there is no attendant acknowledgment of the correlation between family dysfunction—particularly fatherless families—and the proliferation of crime. Consequently, in in its publication decision-making process, the determined 1960s motto of "we shall overcome" has been transformed into a more desultory "we shall overlook!"—with the century-old slogan "all the news that's fit to print" degenerating into "all the news that fits, we print."[20]

Yet those who support affirmative action enforced by legislative fiat are nonetheless left to confront inescapable crucial questions, among them: Is affirmative action appropriate policy? Why are so many minority children—far more than in the days when racism was rampant—now born out of wedlock? Is white racism holding black Americans back, or is the real reason something more complex such as the dissolution of the black family and the low priority placed on the value of education within it?[21]

The responses to such questions are critical. For restoring integrity in reporting is a quintessential prerequisite to sound governance—as ideas have consequences and each word makes a difference. "Facts are stubborn things," said John Adams, which was amended by Daniel Moynihan to hold: "Everyone is entitled to his own opinions but not to his own facts." Both are sound maxims that are too often utterly ignored by the American media today.[22]

The hypocrisies and overt biases in reportage—more discretely called "advocacy journalism"—are readily evident. Despite the fact that the ranks of those who avowedly call themselves "liberals" today have shrunk to less than one-quarter of the nation's populace, for example, conservatives remain "right wing" whereas liberals deem themselves "mainstream." The media called Lee Atwater's 1980s Republican "Southern Strategy" immoral, but were, for a century, curiously profoundly silent when Northern Democrats, without significant media approbation, bedded down with segregationists.

When Ronald Reagan died in June 2004, the media joined most Americans swept up in the pageantry of a weeklong memorial pregnant with poignancy and praise, eulogy and processions. With "Hail to the Chief" punctuating the background, they memorialized the fallen president's role in winning the Cold War, rescuing the nation's economy from the throes of Jimmy Carter's "chronic malaise," and rekindling American's faith in their country and its enduring values.[23]

In the ensuing outpouring of nostalgia, such familiar and evocative phrases as "a shining city on a hill," "morning in America," and "Mr. Gorbachev, tear down this wall" were invoked for one last time by media commentators whose musings reflected the deep sentiments of the vast majority of the American people.

Yet would that those "media talking heads" had been so kind to Reagan when he was still alive, as he was often subject to visceral attack by the nation's left-wing press—with CBS News reporter Leslie Stahl asserting: "I predict that historians are going to be totally baffled by how the American people fell in love with [Ronald Reagan] and followed him the way we did."[24]

In the process of historical and cultural revision, then, double standards pose no problem in the course of press coverage—with the mainstream media condemning the Catholic Church for allowing predatory homosexual priests to destroy the lives of young boys, while simultaneously condemning the Boy Scouts of America for seeking to avoid precisely the same occurrence within their own organization—all enigmatic developments that are foci of the analyses that follow.[25]

THE PRESS, POLITICIANS, AND THE PARTISAN SYMBIOSIS

Despite the auspicious beginnings of a vibrant political press in America, therefore, that ongoing constructive democratic debate contemplated by the Founding Fathers is, in the course of the first decade of the new millennium, deafening in its silence beyond the campaign clutter that customarily characterizes modern American political campaigns—subdued by massive daily menus of radically biased press propaganda.

Examples are legion. Recurring media speculation in 2006 was that though bereft of focus and ever-waffling in message, the Democrats would nonetheless receive a resounding Congressional victory of the magnitude of the Republican fifty-four House seat pickup of 1994. Yet that outcome didn't happen. Instead, quite to the media's bafflement, the outcome of the 2006 election was predictably routine—replicating almost exactly the prototypic loss of six Senate and twenty-nine House seats that for nearly a century has characterized the "sixth year of presidential incumbency off-year" elections, standing in stark contrast to Reagan's loss of eight Senate seats in 1986 and Roosevelt's loss of seventy-one House seats in 1938.[26]

Notwithstanding this outcome, the media portrayed the results as a massive repudiation of George W. Bush. The question becomes why—as there were distinct and defining differences between the two elections. In 1994, Newt Gingrich articulated a vision of fiscal responsibility resonant throughout America—balanced budgets, tax moderation, line-item vetoes—the "Contract with America." Yet, ironically, in a poll of 139 Washington journalists, 59 percent deemed the "Contract" to be no more than an "election-year campaign ploy," whereas only 3 percent considered it to be "a serious reform proposal."[27]

By contrast, the Democrats in 2006 offered no such clear defining message. Indeed, had perceptible media pressure compelled them to project the actual volume of revenue dollars required to meet their campaign commitments to their pet constituencies—their need to dramatically raise taxes to fulfill special interest mandates of the Pelosi-Jackson-Schumer-Kennedy-Sharpton crowd—the end-product would instead have been a "Contract on America"—and they would have lost fifty-four House seats!

Yet such disparities were not explored—as the press ignored entirely a dynamic economic recovery then underway. Nor did it exert tangible effort to compel the Democrats to clearly articulate what they claimed to be their alternate, superior vision. That there were no serious media demands that the Democrats more precisely define themselves, however, should again come as no surprise. For "the old argument that the networks and other 'media elites' have a liberal bias is so blatantly true that it's hardly worth discussing anymore"—wrote correspondent Bernard Goldberg in a 1996 *Wall Street Journal* op-ed—"No, we don't sit around in dark corners planning how we will slant the news. It just comes naturally to most reporters."[28]

The resultant recurring reporting is all too familiar. When gasoline prices trend up toward $4.00 per gallon, Bush administration policies are blamed. When they revert downward toward $2.00 per gallon, the focus shifts to Iraq, where Bush administration policies are again blamed. When good news issues from Iraq, media focus shifts to "l'affaire Mark Foley," or its Larry Craig counterpart, with the media virtually accusing Republicans of breaking the Democrats' historic lock on fostering pedophilia and pederasty. Why, though, is homosexuality OK, and wholly non-newsworthy for more than one Democratic member of Congress from Massachusetts, but verboten, and a source of histrionic headlines, for a Republican member of Congress from Florida?

A media that knew for years, but didn't disclose, reports of John Kennedy's insatiable appetite for women, and Paula Jones' early 1990s allegations that Bill Clinton had exposed himself to her in a hotel room, is nonetheless all too quick to jump on the bandwagon of banner headlines when allegations of sexual impropriety arise respecting Republican senators from Louisiana and Idaho in 2007.[29]

The media is appalled when a Republican candidate for Senate from Virginia makes what possibly could have been an obscure ethnic slur, while once again endorsing for reelection for the fiftieth time in neighboring West Virginia the Democratic "dean of the Senate," Robert Byrd, who openly admits to having been a kleagle for the KKK and opposed the Civil Rights Act of 1964.

Republican Senator Trent Lott is politically crucified for noting a modicum of merit in the career of Strom Thurmond, while Democrat Senator

Chris Dodd is lauded for praising the pork barrel legacy of Byrd. Newt Gingrich's $400,000 book deal while in Congress invokes media outrage, while Hillary Clinton's $8 million book deal under similar circumstances elicits media praise. *Ad infinitum.* As *Washington Weekly* columnist Peter Mulhern has blithely yet accurately asserted: "Most journalists have a tribal attachment to the Democrat Party that transcends ideology."[30]

Indeed, so out of touch is the establishment media with everyday existence—at least that on the partisan "right side" of Main Street, America—that on November 6, 1994, just two days before the Congressional elections that would sweep Republicans into control of both legislative branches after a hiatus of half a century, in a *Washington Post* survey of fourteen prominent Beltway pundits and journalists polling how many Congressional seats each party would win, only three guessed that the Republicans would take control, and one was paid Bush campaign strategist Mary Matalin![31]

Indeed, of those three, the average predicted Republican House winning margin was seven seats; with the other eleven prognosticators predicting that the Democrats would hold the House by an average of at least seventeen votes. Though the actual Republican margin was a pick-up of fifty-four seats for a twenty-two-vote controlling margin, just two days before the election, most of the country's most admired and attuned "inside-the-Beltway" political analysts professed absolutely no clue as to what was about to happen.[32]

How, then, did the nation's media get from "there" to "here"? That is an evolution that has endured a long and sometimes fractious gestation. Theodore White doubtless precisely documented the process setting into motion—deeply changing the face and focus of political journalism—with his book *The Making of the President 1960.* Joe McGinness, a decade later, however, in his book, *The Selling of the President, 1968,* forever changed the parameters of how politics is journalistically covered—regrettably to the detriment of that informed consensus that empowers a democracy to function, as Charles Lewis's *The Selling of the President, 2004* would later incontestably prove.[33]

The net result is that *noncounterculturally-based* political and socioeconomic achievements, however positive their social impact, are rarely the immediate focus of modern media curiosity or inquiry. As today it is predictable to the point of being tautological to conclude that any objective review of ongoing news coverage by the nation's so-called establishment press—its traditional TV networks and its largest newspapers—will inevitably conclude, complete with compelling documentation, the full depth and breadth of a distinctly, overtly partisan leftist-leaning propensity that might appropriately be called the "Democratic-journalistic symbiosis."

Indeed, nowhere was this partisan symbiosis more vividly evident than in the immediate aftermath of the aforesaid watershed 1994 Congressional election. For as Republicans assumed control of the U.S. House of Representatives and Senate, thousands of Democratic Capitol Hill staffers, who thought they had earned jobs for life, now found themselves thrown precipitously out of work.[34]

They were the people whom the Washington press corps had come to intimately know—as neighbors, college classmates, friends from the Rotary, and so on. But though from a national electoral perspective, this loss of a few hundred political patronage jobs was natural, and indeed inconsequential, the Beltway media took the defeat personally, showing a concern for this loss of jobs far greater than it had ever felt for the millions of private-sector jobs lost through downsizing or outsourcing.[35]

Thus, the ultra-leftist radical media revolution marches on, with NBC's Lisa Myers rhapsodizing about Bill Clinton (though not of his political foe Bush the Elder) in the course of the 1992 election, "Throughout his life, Clinton has been committed to public service and doing good."[36] Yet conversely: "It's tough to lead when you don't know where you want to go. Call it a vision; George Bush doesn't seem to have one."[37] *Newsweek's* Howard Fineman similarly describing President Bush's economic platform that year as: "On the big question—the economy—he has little more than gimmicks to offer, and his advisors know it."[38]

And National Public Radio and ABC News reporter Nina Totenberg notoriously proclaiming in response to conservative Senator Jesse Helms' claim that too much federal money was being devoted to AIDS research, "I think that he ought to be worried about what is going on in the good Lord's mind, because if there is retributive justice, he will get AIDS, or one of his grandchildren will get it."[39]

And *USA Today* columnist Julianne Malveaux similarly stating of conservative U.S. Supreme Court Justice Clarence Thomas: "The man is on the Court. You know, I hope his wife feeds him lots of eggs and butter and he dies early, like many black men do, of heart disease. That's how I feel. He is an absolutely reprehensible person."[40]

And *Time* reporter Nina Burleigh emoting: "Here was a woman [Hillary Clinton] who has kept her name! . . . I'll be voting for her just to be sure that Trent Lott doesn't get another foot soldier for his holy war"; as well as her epic (even for her): "I would be very happy to give him [Bill Clinton] a blow job just to thank him for keeping abortion legal!"[41]

What objectivity! One can only speculate how these messages might have been conveyed had not the messengers been employees of major news networks having an obligation for, and an ostensible commitment to, fair and decent balanced reporting.

All of which brings analysis to the media's treatment of right-turned-left-wing analyst David Brock who, when a conservative, was generally detested by most mainstream journalists. Yet when he later developed his leftist-leaning tilt, he was joyfully welcomed into their ranks with open arms as a redeemed lost soul—a "road-to-Damascus" ideological conversion that moved *Newsweek* editor Jonathan Alter to observe: "If David Brock, who helped to drive the truck into the muck, now wants help push it out, well, great!"[42]

This is also why Steve Forbes' "flat tax proposal" was called "wacky" and "an elixir" by veteran Washington correspondent Eric Engberg, but Hillary Clinton's "health care scheme" was not. This is also why, in the media's view, as Bernard Goldberg has observed, "homelessness" was a serious problem in the Reagan–Bush the Elder administrations, ceased to be so in that of Bill Clinton, but again became one as soon as Bush the Younger succeeded him in 2000.[43]

All this in an avowed media quest for consummate objectivity? Can there be any substance to such pretense? Are modern media efforts at ideological balance any more than a charade? Can there be any residual belief that *Countdown*'s hyperventilating Keith Olbermann—a legend in his own mind, whose daily cess dumps do for liberal causes what "Baghdad Bob" did for Saddam Hussein—or on the flip side, the paleolithically conservative Glenn Beck—aspire, in any way, to any semblance of an objective presentation of the news?

Small wonder that historian Will Durant longed for ages past when "medieval man could eat his breakfast without being disturbed by the industriously-collected calamities of the world; or when those that came to his ken were too complex for remedy."[44]

INCIPIENT SOURCES OF MEDIA BIAS

Today, of course, it is in the *zeitgeist* for the media to punctuate the point that, even though George W. Bush graduated from Yale with higher honors than did Al Gore and graduated from Harvard Business School, whereas Gore flunked out of a mid-level divinity school, Gore is the cerebral one, whereas Bush, like his father, is a man with limited talent and bereft of vision.[45]

Whither the provenance of such blatant media partisanship? While a logical assumption might be that politics and press are separate domains ambitiously coursing distinctly different trajectories, the reality is that they unavoidably interact within the same social environment—and therein lies the great ideological chasm that divides "media bias" from "marketplace reality" today.

When journalist Bernard Goldberg first elevated his warning addressed to the issue of "liberal media bias" in a February 13, 1996, *Wall Street Journal* op-ed, he was reviled by the publishing industry as a pariah. Notwithstanding, the mainstream media today continues to proudly take that same prejudicial approach as its mission mandate—and rejoices that this is political progress, constructive journalism by any standard, a material contribution to the "greater social good."[46]

Yet the issues at stake are not limited to just going easy on liberals but hard on conservatives. Rather, they extend to the way that press elites report what they perceive to be all major cultural and social issues of the age— from feminism and abortion to race and affirmative action, from gay rights to homelessness—all the while slapping "ultra-right-wing" labels on conservative organizations while seldom, if ever, painting analogous "left-wing" scarlet crosses on their liberal counterparts, as only conservative issues are deemed "partisan." The logic of the issues framed, syllogistically put in their atavistic partisan state, is this: "All philosophers who are mortal die. Socrates died. Therefore, all philosophers are Socrates."[47]

That is why when law-abiding Christians such as the Reverends Jerry Falwell and Pat Robertson enter politics, they are invariably branded as the "religious right"; but the term "religious left" is only rarely applied to the ilk of the Reverends Jesse Jackson and Al Sharpton, whose preaching engenders more appeal among America's leftist-leaning press.

All the while, the reprehensible hate-mongering of the Reverend Jeremiah Wright—a doctrine called by some the "black liberation theology"; but as a social gospel, comes off as more neo-Marxist than theological, more the secular agenda of the Democratic Party than the liberating calling of the Kingdom of God—is concurrently casually dismissed as "good message, bad technique."

In this instance, then, absent a genuine civil rights champion of the stature of a Martin Luther King, a fair question might logically be: If America's establishment media persists in labeling conservative Christians the "religious right," wouldn't the "fairness doctrine" to which liberals so assiduously aspire equally dictate that they call secular liberals the "heathen left"?[48]

Thus, media output today remains replete with controversial contradictions and profound political prejudices.[49] Several years ago, a Freedom Foundation–Roper Center survey of 139 Washington bureau chiefs and Congressional correspondents exploring that phenomenon learned that approximately 85 percent of the reporters covering the White House claimed to be Democrats; and indeed that in the 1992 presidential election, a higher percentage of Washington journalists had voted for Bill Clinton than did the voter category of "registered Democrats."[50]

Indeed, while America was electing Mr. Clinton over Mr. Bush by a 43 percent to 38 percent margin, America's press had voted for him by a margin of thirteen to one—doubtless reflecting the residual political preferences of a constituency that in 1972 voted 75 percent for George McGovern— perhaps the most liberal candidate that the twentieth century ever produced—in an election in which his opponent, Richard Nixon, carried every state in the Union except Massachusetts.[51]

Small wonder, then, that an October 2007 Gallup poll found that just 33 percent of all Republicans today deem "mainstream media" coverage of the news to be objective, in contrast with 66 percent of all Democrats.[52] As for the actual political and ideological affiliations of the journalists identified by the same poll:

- 50 percent professed to be Democrats; while
- just 4 percent said they were Republican
- 61 percent identified themselves as "moderate to liberal"; while
- only 9 percent stated that they were "moderate to conservative."[53]

Similarly, on social issues, recent polling has found that editors and elitist journalists overwhelmingly support liberal perspectives in comparison to American society at large—on affirmative action, 81 to 51 percent; on abortion, 51 to 33 percent; and on the morality of homosexuality, 83 to 41 percent—with similar polling numbers recorded in polling on religious conviction issues. It comes as no surprise, then, that a 2007 survey of journalists' political donations conducted by MSNBC Pulitzer Prize–winning investigative reporter Bill Dedman found that 125 had given to Democratic or liberal causes while just 15 gave to Republican or conservative ones.[54]

Such findings cause leading conservative author David Frumm to assess that the nation's media is simply out of touch with most of America—and to conclude: "Most reporters covering the rise of the religious right can make no human connections with these people. They think that they are dangerous."[55]

All the while, in this miasma of liberal messaging in which the Fox News Channel is the only medium where it is possible to hear political news that is other than direct press releases from the Democratic National Committee, Nancy Pelosi's Congress wants to legally circumscribe, and thereby suppress, the activities of "talk radio"—a phenomenon to which liberals react in much the same manner that Linda Blair reacts to "Holy Water"—because it is "too conservative!"

From the standpoint of the operation of democratic processes, therefore, what is now transpiring with the press is a dangerous devolution in objectivity that might compel an unbiased observer to ask: How can a street journalist report fairly on an issue such as affirmative action after the organization for which he or she works has already taken sides—not only taking a position, but declaring it to be the only moral, good, and fair one?[56]

How can such a person even pretend to represent the views of those millions of decent Americans who honestly believe—to the contrary, but with equal passion—that affirmative action is, in fact, nothing more than patent "reverse discrimination"?[57]

Such preferential media reporting, of course, would reach absurd levels when CBS anchorman Dan Rather stubbornly stuck by his efforts to derail the Bush campaign—and stonewall even the rest of the mainstream media—by arrogantly defending on *60 Minutes* what he represented to be the president's Vietnam-era military records, even though it was widely acknowledged that the documents were no more than multiple combinations of fabrication and adulteration.[58]

Does such blatant, crass, yet unimpeded, media bias result in objective issues and events coverage? Of course not! But reporters—usually better described as Democrats who don't have to face voters every two, four, or six years—have learned one essential fact. One doesn't win Pulitzer Prizes by merely standing idly by while conservative Republicans are enjoying unprecedented political success.[59]

For in the establishment media view, in the words of former CBS correspondent Bernard Goldberg: "Conservatives are from Mars; liberals are from San Francisco"—and this reality clearly plays out in contemporary political reportage—with the very term "conservative" deployed as an epithet not unlike the health warning on a pack of cigarettes.[60]

Thus it is that the Heritage Foundation is invariably described as a "conservative (or ultraconservative) think tank," while the Brookings Institution is seldom, if ever, labeled as a "liberal" one.[61] And thus it is that the "filibuster" becomes a sacrosanct "parliamentary maneuver" when engaged in by Democrats, but an "obstructionist tactic" when identically employed by Republicans, as suggested in the following distinctly contrasting *New York Times* editorials each opined by the same irrepressible publisher:[62]

Filibuster Employed by Republican Minority: (January 1, 1995)	*Filibuster Employed by Democratic Minority:* (March 6, 2005)
In this past session of Congress, the Republican minority invoked an endless string of filibusters to frustrate the will of the majority. This relentless abuse of a once time-honored Senate tradition so disgusted Senator Tom Harkin, a Democrat from Iowa, that he is now willing to forgo easy retribution and drastically limit the filibuster. Hooray for him. . . . Once a rarely used tactic reserved for issues on which senators held passionate views, the filibuster has become the tool of the sore loser . . . an archaic rule that frustrates democracy and serves no useful purpose.	The Republicans are claiming that 51 votes should be enough to win confirmation of the White House's judicial nominees. This flies in the face of Senate history. . . . To block nominees, the Democrats' weapon of choice has been the filibuster, a time-honored Senate procedure that prevents a bare majority of Senators from running roughshod. . . . The Bush administration likes to call itself "conservative," but there is nothing conservative about endangering one of the great institutions of American democracy, the United States Senate, for an ideological crusade.

It is not surprising, then, that attorney and media critic Bob Kohn—whose research into the political advocacy permeating the daily news content of the *New York Times* is documented in his landmark book *Journalistic Fraud*—

concludes that its "persistent publication of liberal views is still practiced with impunity." In the process, he demonstrates how that newspaper's toolbox of skewed editorial devices, including "loaded language" adjectival selection, subliminally colors the news, as arrayed in the following paradigm:[63]

Liberal:	Conservative:
Mainstream	Ultra-Right
Apolitical	Partisan
Staunch	Strident
Committed	Ideological
Dedicated	Unrepentant
Pragmatic	Extremist
Public Interest Group	Right-Wing Think Tank
Achieved	Engineered
Democratic-Sponsored	Republican-Backed

What a difference a word makes—often serving as the defining difference between news presentation and journalistic prostitution! This finding is, nonetheless, not groundbreaking, given that a 2001 textbook titled: *The Elements of Journalism*, coauthored by former *New York Times* Washington Bureau Chief Bill Kovach, unabashedly asserts: "It is worth restating the point to make it clear. Being impartial or neutral is not a core principle of journalism!" This new wave axiom quite obviously stands in stark contrast to those tenets of truth and objectivity upon which the ethics of the profession have historically been built.[64]

Nevertheless, the nation's mainstream media persists in marching in ideological lockstep with the *New York Times* on politically sensitive issues—hence, the shopworn journalistic joke: "Peter Jennings is not a 'yes man.' If the *Times* says 'no!'—Peter Jennings says 'no!'" Thus it is also that the nation has "right-wing Republicans," "right-wing Christian extremists," and "ultra-right-wing radio talk show hosts"—as if such adjectives defined the individuals thereby described with near-scientific accuracy. But, in the media's eyes, they have no leftist counterparts.[65]

Where, then, do Jesse Jackson and Al Sharpton and Hillary Clinton and Barack Obama stand on the political ideological spectrum? Are there no media-labeled "leftist Christians" left?[66] Perhaps not—as focusing through their leftist political prism, "mainstream broadcasters" would rather recite the Lord's Prayer openly in public school than apply the same partisan stereotyping standards to left-of-center politicians that they apply every day to right-of-center ones.

As pungently portrayed by one pundit: "There is a better chance that Peter Jennings . . . would identify Mother Teresa as 'that old broad who used to work in India' then there is that he would call a liberal Democrat . . . a 'liberal Democrat.'"[67]

Yet in engaging in such flagrant one-sided typecasting, the establishment political press disregards several inescapable realities—among them, that the workings of democracy directly depend upon objective reporting; that accurate, unadulterated information is essential to good governance; and that it is neither the calling nor the duty of the so-called Fourth Estate to bring down sitting administrations that it may disdain.

It is instead its duty to accurately report the news and let the chips fall where they may; as for objective reporting to serve the workings of democracy, there must be a clear distinction between "unbiased media," in a generic sense, and ideological mouthpieces posturing for parochial causes at the extreme.

MODERN MANIFESTATIONS OF "MAINSTREAM" MEDIA BIAS

"Rush Limbaugh Made Me Do It!"

The possibility cannot be dismissed, of course, that the major media moguls are not even aware of what they are doing, with their diversity drives often having had unintended, and unexpected, consequences on their financial bottom lines—as the subcultural focus so carefully constructed by media liberals has frequently not demonstrably materially contributed to an expanded, profit-producing readership base.

Among the examples, in the spring of 1999, *Newsday*'s parent company, Time Warner, closed that paper down after having lost a major portion of its subscribers because, as its erstwhile editorial writer James Sleeper observed, it had become the product of a company that "panders to cultural identity in a drive for elusive market share."[68] In the assessment of media expert William McGowan:

> Instead of raising the tone of public discourse, and making it more intellectually sophisticated, the diversity ethos has "dumbed it down," blunting the public's facilities for reasoned argument just when the edge has never needed to be sharper. Instead of expanding the boundaries of understanding, it has narrowed them; instead of offering "alternative pursuits," it has conveyed a restricted sense of the available policy options.[69]

Such realities are, of course, doubtless abetted by the possibility that much of the on-the-street media bias may not necessarily actually be intentional, as the nation's reportorial elite—those based in large cities and/or working for large news organizations in particular—often have outlooks and perspectives that radically differ from those held by average Americans.[70]

Polls have shown for years, for instance, that " top-scale reporters" tend to be less religious; more supportive of gun control, abortion, and homosexuality; more opposed to capital punishment; and in other various ways more "culturally liberal" than most of their fellow, more statistically representative American citizens.[71]

But considering from whence they come, this too is no surprise, as Bernard Goldberg articulates in his masterful, barrier-breaking work *Arrogance*, written in 2003:

> Today, every single network news reporter who[m] you see on ABC, NBC, or CBS is making over a hundred thousand dollars a year. A lot of them are making *way over* a hundred thousand dollars a year. Everyone on *60 Minutes* makes multi-millions of dollars a year. Network anchors make about ten million dollars a year, give or take a couple of million. . . .
>
> The problem is that the overwhelming majority of these reporters have *always* known privilege. I am not saying that they descend from the Rockefellers, just that many of them come from "comfortable" families and have degrees from prestigious colleges and probably haven't spent a lot of time with people outside their small, privileged realm.[72]

The bottom line, then, is that most upper-tier media professionals are political elitists who probably have expense accounts larger than the average U.S. breadwinner's annual income—and hence, have no idea what life is like for tens of millions of Americans seeking to earn a living wage. Given this reality, then, how can they possibly expect to be able to accurately digest and objectively cover typical middle-class political views, economic aspirations, and social values?[73]

As a consequence, too many decision-making newspeople—many of them based in such major metropolises as New York, Washington, and Los Angeles—are hopelessly out of touch with "Main Street America," have only liberal friends, and usually wind up talking primarily to people like themselves. Thus, over time, they come to believe that all civilized people think the exact same way that they do.[74]

This "inability to relate" phenomenon likely best explains the assertion of *Newsweek* Bureau Chief Evan Thomas on the Clinton–Paula Jones affair that: "Yes, the case is being fomented by right wing nuts, and yes, she is not a very credible witness, and it's really not a law case at all. But the president has got a problem here. He has a history of womanizing that most people believe is a problem. . . . . It leads to things like this, some sleazy woman with big hair coming out of the trailer parks."[75]

Or *Newsweek's* notorious Eleanor Clift, after Bill Clinton was impeached, saying: "That herd of managers from the House [of Representatives], all they were missing were white sheets."[76] That phenomenon likely likewise explains the frank admission of CBS News anchor Dan Rather of "biased coverage bred of street-level ignorance" in a Denver radio interview:

> I'm in the news all the time. Full power, tall tower. I want to break in when news breaks out. That's my agenda. Now respectfully, when you start talking about a liberal agenda and all of the quote "liberal bias" in the media, I quite frankly, and I say this respectfully but candidly to you, I don't know what you are talking about.[77]

That also is precisely why, in the opinion of veteran media analyst Bernard Goldberg, major media players not only simply disagree with conservatives, they view them as morally deficient: "What reasonable person, they wonder, could possibly be *against* affirmative action? Maybe some stupid people in the South or Midwest who wear polyester pants are against it. But what can you expect from *them* anyway?"[78]

Such insights, inadvertently bred of isolation, then, are no more than the handiwork of a patently liberal crowd who see themselves as the saviors of mankind and support affirmative action for the masses while parking their own kids in private prep schools and Ivy League universities. It is also why major media anchors—buying directly into the Democratic Party line while remaining utterly oblivious to fifteen centuries of Mideast history—can unblinkingly trace a straight line from 9/11 to Timothy McVeigh in Oklahoma City, to the Republican Party, to conservatives in general, to talk radio, and ultimately and more specifically, to Rush Limbaugh.[79]

Indeed, setting the bouncing ball of media blame into momentum in this regard, CBS legal analyst Andrew Cohen, in an April 19, 2003, *Court Watch* piece titled "Oklahoma City Bombing vs. Sept. 11," unabashedly proclaimed: "The Oklahoma City bombing can only be viewed through the prism of far more massive acts of terrorism—the attacks on the World Trade Center and the Pentagon."[80]

Cohen's assertions built upon a multitude of previous press speculation. CBS news anchorman Dan Rather was earlier on record as saying: "Even after Oklahoma City, you can still turn on your radio in any city and dial up hate talk: extremist, racist, and violent from the hosts and those who call it in."[81]

The late *Washington Post* columnist Carl Rowan, in turn, opined: "Unless Gingrich, Dole, and the Republicans ask: 'Am I inflaming a bunch of nuts?'—you know that we are going to have even more major events. I am absolutely certain that the harsh rhetoric of the Gingrichs and the Doles creates a climate of violence in America."[82]

Time senior correspondent Richard Lacayo—in seeking to establish linkages between terrorism, partisan politics, and talk radio—framed it this way: "In a nation that has entertained and appalled itself for years with hot radio talk on the campaign trail, the inflamed rhetoric of the '90s is suddenly an unindicted co-conspirator in the [Oklahoma City] blast."[83]

Nina Easton of the *Los Angeles Times*, in turn, wrote: "The Oklahoma City attack on federal workers alters the once-easy dynamic between charismatic talk show host and adoring audience. Hosts who routinely espouse the same anti-governmental themes now must walk a fine line between inspiring their audience—and inspiring the most radical among them."[84]

And in the final link of documentary evidence in proof that given two dots, it doesn't take a genius to connect them with a straight line—in this instance, establishing a linear connection between bin Laden, McVeigh, and Limbaugh—liberal, and at times, erudite, *Washington Post* columnist David Broder wrote:

> The bombing shows how dangerous it really is to inflame twisted minds with statements that suggest that political opponents are enemies. For two years, Rush Limbaugh described this nation as 'America held hostage' to the policies of liberal Democrats, as if the elected president and Congress were equivalent to the regime in Tehran.[85]

Q.E.D. *Cogito ergo sum!* Reality is clear: conservative talk radio, in league with conservative politicians, have created the antigovernmental attitudes that spawned 9/11 and the Oklahoma City bombings, and are therefore singularly responsible for the current wave of global terrorism highlighted by 9/11. All of which predictably lead Hollins College leftist philosophy professor Peter S. Fosl to extrapolate that Rush Limbaugh and fellow conservative commentators are "the Hutu broadcasters who urged on the Rwanda militias in their deadly missions."[86]

Such realities of relative cultural isolation and political illusion, of course, doubtlessly also explain why *New Yorker* film critic Pauline Kael was utterly baffled as to how Richard Nixon had won the presidency in 1972. "I can't believe it," she said. "I don't know a single person who voted for him!" Amazingly, even though Nixon had carried forty-nine of the nation's fifty states, she probably wasn't kidding.[87]

Accordingly, America's news coverage comes to be defined by agenda-pushing elitist journalists with no understanding whatsoever of the soul of the nation, and that is why her public policy is far too often interpreted, via a pandering press, through the prismatic insights of ideologically fellow-traveling cohorts like Jane Fonda, Barbra Streisand, Sean Penn, Al Franken, Michael Moore, and the Dixie Chicks.

And thus, the nation's media plods on in shaping the course of political opinion in a mid-American realm wherein the interpreters do not enjoy full insight, and by operating in a milieu wherein the would-be news consumers lack the transparency needed to discern the facts. In this manner, by inserting itself into judicial and entertainment realms, the nation's press has

come to exercise anti-American cultural, social, and legal impacts dispro-
portion to its corporate size.[88]

Indeed, noting the ivory tower elite media's profound, if often uniformed, influence on American public life, Vaclav Havel, president of the
Czech Republic, in a 1995 commencement speech at Harvard University,
courageously tried to balance the overall good and bad effects of the media
on everyday American life. On the good side, he observed, it allowed the nation's citizens to learn that their counterparts in many foreign countries
were suffering. On its bad side, he said, it distorted their views of their
neighbors and indeed of themselves.[89]

Already by 1831, in fact, America's French visitor Alexis de Tocqueville
was likewise observing that newspapers in the nascent nation were necessary to unite the many "wandering minds" that he was encountering in his
in-country travels. "The newspaper brought them together," he wrote, "and
the newspaper remains necessary to keep them together."[90]

How ironically lamentable it is, then, that the nation's press has now become both a culturally divisive flash point and a partisan ideological driver
in promoting a pernicious form of multicultural diversity that threatens to
tear asunder its long-standing, time-tested civic and social values. For objectivity's bottom line can be no less than this—that if any society founded
on democracy is to survive and thrive, it must enjoy access to the full news
story, and not just the part that fits a preconceived political script or adheres
to a narrowly held radical orthodoxy.[91]

As famed journalist Walter Lippman aptly observed as early as 1922:
"News and truth are not the same thing and must clearly be distinguished. . . . If they are to be sound, public opinions must be organized
for the press, not by the press, as is the case today. . . . For the most part,
we do not first see, and then define. We first define, and then see. . . . [with
the net effect of] making of mountains, molehills, and of molehills,
mountains."[92]

The Media and the Military

While many examples of blatant press bias are readily apparent, as
shown, the powerful operation of a countercultural agenda in America is
perhaps nowhere more evident than in the skewed nature of ongoing contemporary media battlefield action coverage—as the "peace at any price"
proclivities of her 1960s "flower children grown-up" now dominate the
portrayal of war news. Indeed, nowhere are the workings of modern journalism more inimical to the cause of democratic process than in its blatant
antimilitary bias.

As described by ABC chief White House correspondent Terry Moran:
"There is a deep antimilitary bias in the media: one that begins from the

premise that the military must be lying, and the American projection of power around the world must thus be wrong."[93]

As one noted media critic recently observed of the *New York Times* respecting the Iraqi occupation in particular—"It (the paper) has assumed the role of party of the opposition"—an all-too-regrettable reality that, in noting its concurrent zealous crusade to have women admitted to the all-male Augusta National Golf Club, moved political humorist Dennis Miller to observe that "were Saddam Hussein to open a golf club 'For Men Only' in Baghdad, the *Times* editors would doubtless readily do a 180-degree opinion reversal and support the war in Iraq!"[94]

Americans have a long-standing tradition of rallying to support war that preserves the cause of peace in the world. Today, irrespective of the initial merits of invading Iraq, the reality is that America is there. Lord Salisbury a century ago said: "England is, I believe, the only country in which, during a great war, eminent men write and speak publicly as if they belonged to the enemy."[95]

Now, as a result of the symbiosis between her leftist media and leftist politics, America can clearly be added to that list. The problem is twofold—established-media ownerships preponderantly imbued by liberal interests and lower-level widespread, albeit perfunctory and largely analysis-free, press coverage of military undertakings.

In the first instance, as the essayist and media critic A. J. Leibling famously said: "Freedom of the press is guaranteed only to those who own one."[96] In the second, it is because in war, press coverage is perforce cryptic in its nature, while substantive reflection on the defining merits of the undertaking's ideological underpinnings is rare—often rendering television, in particular, as relevant to war coverage as bumper stickers are to ideology.

It was not always thus—as there was a time when patriotism dictated that partisanship end at America's shoreline—an age before CNN efforts to undermine American will to win were joined in concert with a caviling opposition seeking to put partisan advantage above national interest through the pursuit of policies guaranteed to ensure "defeat at any cost." This latter development is clearly a post-1960s political phenomenon—the Lord moving in mysterious ways, let alone in Washington.

Throughout her history, America has been almost perpetually at war, whether hot or cold—from the Revolutionary War to the War of 1812, to the Mexican War, to the Civil War, through World War I and World War II, to Korea and Vietnam, and now into Iraq—protracted wars that Americans were willingly taxed and died for in a never-ending quest for equity and justice within the world. The nation has historically believed that there are things worth fighting for—and has always been willing to fight for—producing, quite ironically, perpetual war in quest of perpetual peace.[97]

And so it was with Iraq. Prewar planning anticipated a "Mesopotamian Stalingrad"—the loss of ten thousand to twenty thousand troops in intense door-to-door fighting for Baghdad alone. Yet as establishment media heralded the grim reality that the four-year Iraqi occupation had surpassed World War II in length in December 2006, fewer than three thousand American fatalities had occurred. Every human life, of course, is precious, and the loss of a single one is a human tragedy. But given the magnitude of the war effort, this casualty rate was remarkably low.

By contrast, in the American Civil War, nearly a half million lives were lost from a population of thirty million—a death rate that would translate to about five million persons today. Indeed, among its 23,000 mass casualties, there were 3,654 deaths in the Battle of Antietam alone in September 1862, making it the single bloodiest day in the nation's martial history. In World War I, 116,708 Americans died—and in the six-week-long Meuse Argonne offensive commanded by General John Pershing, between September 26 and November 11, 1918, there were 26,277 fatalities.[98]

In World War II, 407,316 Americans were killed—including over 19,000 dead and another 60,000 maimed or captured during the five weeks of the Battle of the Bulge; another 18,000 were killed at Okinawa and yet another 7,000 at Iwo Jima. Indeed, in a single day, D-day, June 6, 1944, she suffered 3,393 human losses—1,465 soldiers confirmed killed, and 1,928 missing and never found—more deaths than in the entire first four years of the Iraqi occupation. America likewise lost 33,651 soldiers in Korea, leaving that nation as divided as ever, and another 58,219 in Vietnam where she endured her first-ever defeat.[99]

The nation has also tragically lost citizens in catastrophes in orders of magnitude similar to Iraq when attacked on her own soil: 2,117 brave souls at Pearl Harbor, another 2,973 on 9/11. Indeed, there is no better case for preemptive war abroad than the nation's record of loss at home when it has not been prepared. Combat losses thus are not unique to America. What is unique is their newly found ability to deter her will to win.

Why is this reality the case? The defining difference—most probably the omnipresent intervention into American homes, via television, of Democrats who don't have to face the voters—also known as reporters—a media self-proclaimed to be 90 percent liberal that fervently believes that war at any cost is wrong and profits financially from histrionically hyping such convictions in its headlines.

What the nation daily sees on its TV screens, therefore, is an overtly antimilitary media acting in tandem with a calculating political opposition not above sacrificing national interest in the pursuit of pure partisan advantage— a conciliatory pacifist cabal ideologically preaching to an attention-challenged American public gullibly inclined to believe what it sees in the press—with the consequences for national security as ominous as they are obvious, reminiscent of Rome's latter days as described in chapter 1.

The net result is that America can no longer pursue a prolonged war, however just—be it in pursuit of relief from oppression, preserving self-determination, or ensuring democracy—and other well-meaning nations can no longer support her in pursuing protracted, albeit difficult, noble causes because the nation's domestic liberal opposition will invariably capitalize on the incredibly short and highly malleable shelf-life of America's "commitment to commitment" in favor of a course of "peace at any price," causing her precipitous and premature capitulation and withdrawal from the requisite war effort, thereby leaving all equally embroiled in a futile cause.

Already, the parallels between Vietnam and Iraq produced by partisan equivocation are tragically striking. As British counterinsurgency expert Sir Robert Thompson observed in similar circumstances in his after-action review of the U.S. military conduct four decades ago: "Perhaps the major lesson of the Vietnam War is: Do not rely upon the United States as an ally."[100] The reason? Like ancient Rome before her, America has lost her will to win.

Nowhere to be found in this highly charged political process, then, is evidence of the long-honored, time-proven precept that partisanship is best replaced by patriotism at the nation's borders. Nowhere are there manifestations of a political calculus to make the right choice in the national interest, or of America's historic determined public will to win "in spite of dungeon, fire, or sword" that conventionally characterized her confrontation of perils in the past.

The inherent dangers of such folly are made indelibly clear in the cogent lessons of martial history. As Harvard historian Niall Ferguson has calculated, the vaunted Roman Empire—created by Caesar Augustus (Octavian) in 27 B.C. and ending when Constantinople was established as a rival eastern empire four centuries later—lasted 422 years.[101]

The eastern empire of Byzantium, in turn, lasted until the sack of Constantinople by the Ottoman Turks in 1453—a 1,058-year total. The Holy Roman Empire, successor to imperial Rome, continued from its establishment by Charlemagne on Christmas Day 800, the day when he was crowned emperor, until the institution was abolished by Napoleon in 1806—some 1,006 years. The "typical" Roman empire thus lasted 829 years.[102]

Social scientist Michael Schermer, in researching the more than sixty civilizations that have risen and fallen on the planet within its written history, has similarly found that, in aggregate, they have lasted an average of 421 years—but that the average lifespan of the most recent twenty-eight, those that have risen since the fall of Rome, has been 305 years.[103]

By contrast, American public disillusionment began to set in with the 1960s Vietnamese War in August 1968, just three years after U.S. forces had arrived *en masse*. Indeed, it took American voters a mere eighteen months to start telling pollsters that the Iraq War was a mistake—making media-manipulated public opinion that drives national commitment a strategic factor that renders concerted, prolonged pursuit of modern "just war" ephemeral at best, as even benevolent empires do not survive for long absent popular consent.

What is the defining difference between recent modern conflicts and wars past? It is that now, while embedded journalists continue to diligently pursue information in accordance with precepts of access based on prevailing security considerations and the public's need to know, the liberal elites in their rearguard headquarters are succumbing to the ponderous weights of their long-standing parochial political biases. As a consequence, in the case of Iraq, with the war barely a week old, there was already incessant media fretting about whether the United States was "working itself into a quagmire."[104]

Indeed, while the frontline embedded troops were reporting just the opposite—great movement and progress—the Washington-embedded old guard anchors and commentators continued to gradually sink into the quicksand of their own preconceptions, dismayed at the prospect of American success and primarily worried about anarchy and looting in the aftermath of Saddam Hussein—replete with lamentations and prophecies of foreboding doom. Indeed, had the same parochial "peace in our time" crowd been covering Normandy in World War II, it is not difficult to contemplate them similarly engaged in public agony and angst over a potential destabilization of Germany in a post-Hitler world.[105]

When the details of the initial highly successful high-tech incursion were becoming clear, in fact, when the statue of Saddam Hussein came tumbling down in Baghdad's Firdaws Square, the event caused such gloominess in some news quarters that, in the words of one prominent political pundit, "a suicide watch had to be placed on Judy Woodruff."[106] Even so, the pessimists had achieved a significant achievement—lending comfort to the enemy by undermining the American public's confidence in their military's ongoing war effort.

All this despite the fact that the U.S. Army was demonstrating more capability, moving more military faster, and conquering more territory than ever before in the history of modern warfare. Small wonder that devoted *Times* readers often found it difficult to distinguish between the perceptions of the war's progress portrayed by the paper's publisher Arthur "Pinch" Sulzberger and those of Iraq's infamous Information Minister "Baghdad Bob."

Indeed, had there been a Pulitzer Prize for press bias, the former would have clearly found himself atop any ad hoc short list for his utter inability to distinguish between his deeply ingrained antimilitary sentiments and objective news reporting.[107]

This is precisely why America finds herself where she finds herself in Iraq today—with a belligerent, hostile, antimilitary media undermining that erstwhile indomitable public "will to win" that had characterized her national resolve from her inception through World War II.

It is a conciliatory "peace in our time" mindset now particularly most manifest in the incessant, ongoing efforts by a leftist-leaning Congress— abetted by its media surrogates—to legislatively mandate *battlefield* "pullout" deadlines, in so doing, flagrantly meddling in the U.S. military's traditional, time-tested role in the on-the-ground management of war, while concurrently transgressing its constitutionally granted power to declare, but not conduct, war.

With the current Congress so heavily invested in "cut and run" defeat, then, it comes as no surprise that Dr. Ayman al-Zawahiri, al-Qaeda's second in command and de facto chair of the "Caves of Wazirstan" chapter of "Democrats Abroad"—an organization now demonstrating a dangerously more than casual interest in the outcomes of ongoing U.S. electoral campaigns—soon after ratification of a House of Representatives resolution calling for all U.S. troops to be withdrawn from Iraq by April 1, 2008, would release a sixty-seven-minute tape in May 2007 proclaiming that recurring Democratic calls for troop withdrawal from Iraq are proof positive that the United States has already lost the war.[108]

To such depths, leftist "patriotism" has thus devolved—to levels where there is no honor left. On the eve of the Normandy invasion, General George S. Patton told his Third Army troops: "The very thought of losing is hateful to an American." Regrettably, to some today, the prospect of losing a foreign war is far preferable to the possibility of losing a domestic election; and indeed, the former is too often deemed a productively optimizing means to the latter.[109]

The dangers that the Congressional usurpation of power pose, and the spate of *jihadist* militant responses that have attended it, thus could not be more clear—nor more ominous. Al-Qaeda has already claimed credit for defeating one great global superpower, the Soviet Union, in the mountains of Afghanistan.

If they now succeed in driving the other, the United States, from the deserts of Iraq, not because of strategic military superiority or consummate guile, but because of partisan, press-abetted discord within Washington, they will have developed a religious validation replete with political resonance throughout the entire Islamic world—igniting an eclectic firestorm of retrograde Mideast elements who want nothing more than a direct frontal assault upon modern civilized progress as it is now conceived.

As the tragic events of 9/11 make clear, this is no idle threat. Hence, those who view Iraq as just "another Vietnam" must be made intently aware that in this case, there is a defining difference: while the Vietnamese wanted nothing more than national reunification, al-Qaeda seeks to destroy all of democratic free society in the name of a vengeful God—and particularly wants to achieve its victory not in Fallujah, Najaf, or Ramadi, but in Washington itself.

As the reality is, at the bottom line, that these are fanatic ideologues committed not only to bringing down moderate Muslim regimes throughout the Mideast but equally to attacking the "decadent" West and establishing a mutant global Islamic caliphate molded in the image of their deviant world view. To this end, they stop at nothing.

The stakes indeed are high. For if they succeed, word will again be out that the American "will to win" can be outlasted—with those who advocate precipitous withdrawal for partisan advantage coming to preside over a world in no way conducive to the enduring peace to which they may genuinely aspire. As amidst the echoes of Neville Chamberlain's cane on the cobblestones of Munich, the same Washington crowd—the "peacenik" leftists and their journalistic allies who snatched defeat from the jaws of victory in Vietnam—will have awarded this terrorist cabal its most noteworthy global success.

This outcome is not just an American tragedy, then, it is a global one— and an entirely avoidable one. For the lessons of history are indelibly clear. Military decisions must be left to military commanders. The record of Congress in running wars has not at all been good. When it tried to run the Revolutionary War, the outcome was a disaster—a disaster repeatedly replicated over time, and most indelibly, in its attempts to micromanage the Civil War and again that in Vietnam.

What is it in its abysmal track record of military oversight that compels the Congress to arrogate to itself the power to mismanage Iraq as well? War isn't pretty and it isn't expeditious. But to quote famed Revolutionary War–era pamphleteer Thomas Paine: "Those who expect to reap the blessings of liberty must undergo the fatigues of supporting it."[110]

It was not always thus. What a difference, in fact, a mere generation makes! When Japan attacked Pearl Harbor, college students stood beside farmers' sons and factory hands to enlist. Their collective experiences forged a national unity, later reinforced by the G.I. Bill, that welded the bonding of the nation and contributed to its greatness.

In World War II itself, the American public financed the war effort through federal bond purchases promoted in a series of nationwide tours in which patriotic members of Hollywood such as Jane Wyman participated. Indeed, while the Seventh Bond Tour alone—conducted from May 9 to July 4, 1945—targeted accruing $14 billion from a then-total U.S. population of 160 million people, many earning little more than a few thousand dollars a year, it actually raised nearly double that amount, $26.3 billion, a sum almost half of that year's entire federal budget of $56 billion. The statue of America's finest raising the flag of victory at Iwo Jima that stands majestically at Arlington National Cemetery today likewise was raised in that same era with private funds.[111]

Then, U.S. patriotism reigned righteous. Indeed, in the days following Pearl Harbor, America's youth flocked to military recruitment stations in droves. Contrast that with the 1960s when students at major U.S. universities were carrying Viet Cong flags—while burning American ones—and the days following the 9/11 World Trade Center massacre, when before a single cruise missile had been fired or a single soldier went into combat, antiwar rallies were already forming on campuses nationwide.

Thus, it comes equally with consummate irony and sanctimonious hypocrisy that those who would today indict America for failing in Iraq for want of troops are precisely those directly responsible for the military's deconstruction. For when the Congress and the media complain of lack of troops—of mothers needing to hold bake sales to financially underwrite the requisite body armor their sons and daughters need to survive—combined with the ongoing redispatch of troops back into combat without sufficient rest or time because of inadequate reserves, America must look directly to her disastrous force structure development policies of the 1990s for explicit cause.

As there the record could not be more clear. For more than a half century, the size and shape of U.S. armed forces were geared to fighting 2.5 medium-sized Iraqi or Afghani-type conflicts simultaneously. The militarily challenged Clinton administration—commencing with its early 1990s "bottom-up" force structure review—however, changed all that.

Relentlessly cutting the U.S. military nearly in half, they thus systematically destroyed that superb late 1980s American fighting force that Ronald Reagan had so effectively built that made possible the precision-like 1991 dispatch of Iraq in Desert Storm—while concurrently making it more than disingenuous when Democrats such as veteran Congressman John Murtha argue that America is now failing in Iraq for want of troops.

From 1990 to 1999, in fact, overall U.S. troop strength dropped steadily from 2.1 million to 1.4 million soldiers, sailors, marines, and aviators, where it has remained in recent years. Formal fixed force structure dropped even more, with active army divisions decreasing from eighteen to ten, and the actual army size slashed to a half million troops.

Since the 1990 Gulf War, the U.S. Air Force and U.S. Navy have also been cut in half. In 1990, the United States boasted a 600-ship navy. Today, the U.S. Navy is designing a 313-ship fleet, with contingency plans for a 200-ship navy by 2020. By the start of the 2003 second Iraqi war, the dynamically effective military infrastructure that enabled America in the 1980s to become the world's premier superpower, thus had, in effect, collapsed.[112]

Small wonder, then, the nation can no longer militarily prevail. For while through its sundry gender and sexual preference reforms, the Clintonites may have better socialized the U.S. military—to make it "look more like them," as they openly aspired—it is difficult to conclude that they strengthened it to win; as with manpower a clear-cut challenge to both militaries, the parallels to ancient Rome cited in chapter 1 again are striking.

There is little more despicable or disingenuous in American politics today, therefore, than the Democrats' incessant call to abandon the Iraqi people's right to self-determination on the pretext that the U.S. military is "over-extended."

The folly of their "swords to plowshares" approach is, in fact, deftly epitomized by CBS *Good Morning America* show host Charles Gibson in his pithy but unfortunate observation that: "My wife has a sign on her office wall that says: 'Won't it be a great when the Air Force has to hold bake sales and our schools have all of the money that they need?'"[113]

Yet they proceed onward, oblivious to the spirit of ancient Rome's martial maxim: *si vis pacem, pare bellum* ("If you desire peace, prepare for war!)—as well as to the time-tested Marine Corps axiom: "Nobody likes to fight, but when it becomes necessary, somebody better know how!"[114]

Preparedness must never be reduced to a discretionary option—as it must never be forgotten that John Kennedy's clarion call: "Ask not what your country can do for you" was preceded by his determined proclamation "We will pay any price, and bear any burden" to ensure the preservation of liberty in the world.

"Playing to Win" vis-à-vis Media-Orchestrated Political Opposition

The press also has given general short shrift to discrete alternate Iraq military strategies designed to enhance prospects for tangible success—a course that Washington's current cabal of antimilitary politicians again are apparently unwilling to abide—notwithstanding that there is a proven path to victory that America's long history of successful military engagement desperately now invokes.

For it is a time-tested infantry axiom that holds that winning wars involves much more than just prevailing in transitory opening battles—a military tenet that holds great relevance in Iraq today. As the U.S. strategy is not now falling short for want of troops and technologies prerequisite to capturing turf—it is instead failing for lack of forces available to occupy the territory that it is so capable of conquering.

Yet America cannot expect to win local hearts and minds in Fallujah if the indigenous enemy that the locals fear—an enemy that American troops can readily decimate in daylight hours—are then able to coalesce and reform behind the battle lines to threaten them once again at nightfall, as the active combat forces move on to prevail in tomorrow's battle at Ramadi.

The requisite military strategy, however, already is prescribed in existing U.S. battlefield operational manuals. Within them, the Petraeus Doctrine— so named after Iraq's current commander, David Petraeus—is about nation-building—an approach that requires physically occupying ground, notwithstanding that actually owning such territory inevitably requires ample highly trained forces.

Already at the close of 2007, with the recent 30,000-troop "surge," there are clear signs that the strategy is working whenever and wherever force deployment has been sufficient—but regrettably, given current force structure limitations, such scenarios remain too few and far between and they will continue to work only so long as commanders have sufficient troops to deploy to occupy ground.

Nevertheless, with decency an endangered species in the modern domain of political propaganda, this spate of inconvenient good news did not deter the notorious Democratic Party front group "MoveOn.Org" from funding in September 2007 a full-page *New York Times* advertisement condemning the surge captioned: "General Betray Us"—presenting yet another sterling example of that newspaper's policy of publishing "all the news that's fit to print . . . and then some."[115]

Such are ominous developments. For if the "surrender lobby" prevails with a U.S. defeat in Iraq, U.S. prestige will plummet across the planet. The Middle East will become a terrorist Wild West. Like the British and the French, the nation will be headed home from "East of Suez." And globally, what ally, in the future, will ever again rely on the United States for its security—as no nation can be a global hegemon if its enemies don't fear it and its friends don't trust it.

As a consequence, America may now well be lackadaisically, with active press acquiescence, witnessing how empires end—succumbing to a myopic policy of "peace in our time," notwithstanding all the while cognizant that the fall of imperial Rome to barbarians ushered in the Dark Ages.[116]

Again, war isn't pretty. It wasn't meant to be a media-orchestrated political event. Indeed, America didn't start losing wars until they became TV-choreographed "spectator sports"—politically correct, correspondent-embedded public spectacles subject to Neilson ratings and popular plebiscite. Succinctly put, a nation cannot win wars whose conduct is governed by personal journalistic perceptions of political correctness in martial conduct while concurrently immersed in doubts over the inherent virtue of the mission itself as an undertaking.

These stark realities particularly apply in situations wherein the political party in control of Congress—for sheer partisan advantage—isn't above pursuing defeat at any cost. Given its one-vote Senate control by virtue of razor-thin majorities in Virginia and Montana, the Democratic Party now lays claim to a popular mandate to pursue defeat in Iraq—notwithstanding that within its ranks, independent Senator Joe Lieberman, whose fifty-first vote is decisive in maintaining its Senate leadership control, won a solid victory in 2006 *with a pro–Iraq war message* in Connecticut, one of the most liberal of states.

This is, then, a specious extrapolation—as Americans, in their essence, are a good people who have historically tried to do the decent thing. Their mistake is that they tend to explicitly trust their media while lacking the transparency and analytic expertise to sort out its structural biases. It is equally a dangerous confluence of contemporary political realities. Indeed, had the first half of the twentieth century featured the current tenor of CNN reporting and the same caviling "cut and run" opposition that characterizes the present political landscape, German would likely now be the U.S. national language.

Concurrently, in their defense, it may well be that much of the established media isn't even aware of its in-built antimilitary bias—that in their fervent quest for peace at any price, they may even actually perceive themselves to be adhering to noble aspirations to patriotic ends.

But the pursuit of good intentions must not be conflated with outcomes of good results, as in the present instance, as analysis has shown, the consequences of their political handiwork have been unequivocally militarily disastrous—notwithstanding that America's stakes in southwest Asia are far too critical to remain a function of partisan political prejudice promoted by antimilitary bias.

The confluence of these realities nonetheless does not imply that the current war effort should proceed absent media scrutiny, as there are many dimensions to its conduct that may merit further deliberation. Among them is the endgame of the war effort itself. When can, in fact, a president, in this age of desultory wars, definitively proclaim: "mission accomplished"?

Today, America's performance as the world's last remaining superpower continues to baffle many. She is, among other things, unsuccessfully attempting to impose "top-down" democracy in Iraq using F-16s and M-1 tanks. Yet to hold together such a fractious hodgepodge of historically mutually hostile factions is not only immoral from a political self-determination standpoint, but requires the overwhelming use of force—a lesson that Saddam Hussein desperately sought to teach but America refused to learn.

But there is yet another, even more insidious folly inherent in such a precipitous approach—as all would-be democracies, advanced and maturing, are invariably vulnerable to demagoguery. Thus, prudence does not dictate mandating democratic elections in theological milieus wherein the victors concurrently proclaim eschatological hostility to the very precept.

For there is indeed a distinct, defining difference between a people's inherent right to self-determination and the attempts by another culture or nation to impose its own system of governance, even if it is called "democracy," upon another, top down, be it by moral suasion or by force.

For at the bottom line, nations cannot be "built." They must evolve. Institutions may be transplanted from one country to another, but the history and culture from which the attitudes and traditions evolved that empower those institutions to work cannot. They must be engendered from within.

It took millennia for modern democracy to evolve in the Western world. In the present instance, America cannot now create democracy in Iraq before establishing that security—the law and order—and those supporting social infrastructures that are prerequisite to viable government.[117]

Thus, it is far better to first foster the development of those institutions and cultural values that nurture democracies and empower them to survive—commencing by "leading by example" through a quest to regenerate them at home. Only then, from that higher moral pulpit, should they seek to export the democratic and social values of the America that the world once knew and admired—and such should, in fact, concurrently be legitimate issues of ongoing media concern.

How, Then, Are Partisan Politics and a Free Press Rationally Accommodated?

The answer is basic. The evidence makes clear that an objective, fair, and balanced media is essential to the effective functioning of a democracy. It is a prerequisite to an informed electorate and governance by the rule of law. Given the evidence presented, it is difficult to conclude that America enjoys the operation of a "fair and balanced" media today. Instead, her citizens are compelled to view their daily news through the kaleidoscopic prisms of a hopelessly prejudiced and unequivocally liberal press establishment.

What is the ultimate answer? Thomas Jefferson observed that "to compel men to pay money for the propagation of opinions which they disbelieve and abhor is sinful and tyrannical."[118] Later he would, in an 1807 letter to an acquaintance expressing pique at perceived media bias, add: "The man who reads nothing at all is better educated than the many who read nothing but the newspapers."[119]

In defense of Jefferson, and in his spirit, former correspondent and current media critic Bernard Goldberg would make biased reporting a punishable offense.[120] Yet such a course would clearly not comport with those First Amendment guarantees that prefaced this chapter.

Instead, to paraphrase Jefferson, the media themselves should be compelled to pay for their propagandistic propensities. As capitalistic moral suasion, directly tied to market-based solutions—striking at the press pocketbook by boycotting products of its media advertisers—would likely be a more productive course.

Whatever the answer, however, it must nonetheless be unequivocally decisive, and it must come now. For as the eminent political scientist and media expert Thomas Patterson, in his seminal tome, *Out of Order*, has admonished: "The press is not the only cause of our jaded and tattered institutions, but it is a prime contributor. America needs a press that is free and responsible. For an institution that asks so much of others, it has become remarkably derelict in the discharge of its public duty."[121]

Little wonder, then, that recent Pew Research Center polling has found that 53 percent of the nation's citizens consider its media to be "politically biased," and that more than one-half of its press professionals believe that "journalism is going in the wrong direction."[122]

Hence, America's media has devolved a long way from Theodore Roosevelt's lofty statement—

> The man who writes, the man who month in and month out, week in and week out, day in and day out, furnishes the material which is to shape the thoughts of our people is the man who, more than any other, determines the character of the people and the kind of government this people shall possess[123]

—to Harry Truman's:

> I look with great commiseration over the great body of my fellow citizens who, in reading newspapers, live and die in the belief that they have known something of what has been passing in the world in their time.[124]

The tragedy that it has come to this is underscored in the cogent admonition of nineteenth-century British parliamentarian-historian Lord Macauley: "I know but two ways by which society may be governed; one is by Public Opinion, the other by the Sword."[125]

In sum, "committing journalism" is no crime, but in a democracy, it must be perpetrated with objectivity. For it is civilization's first draft of history—the foundation upon which future posterity is built. Its present parochial biases, therefore, cannot be abided if a free American society is to prevail.[126]

5

The Crisis of Citizenship

I have always believed that there was a Divine Plan that caused people to uproot their lives to come to this continent to pursue their dreams in America.

—Ronald Reagan

CITIZENSHIP AND THE "AMERICAN EXPERIMENT"

"The course and effects of immigration," asserted historian Oscar Handlin, "involve no less a task than to set down the whole history of the United States."[1] Given the profound challenges to America's socioeconomic future posited by the sobering findings of this inquiry, it is illuminating to contemplate the current state of citizenship ostensibly operating within the rule of law as observed in America today—a phenomenon encapsulated in ongoing, increasingly divisive immigration political debate.

For amidst clear evidence of societal stress-fracturing produced by the migratory invasions now taking place at the nation's borders, diffident elected officials, despite swearing to defend the law, continue to treat with benign neglect threats that are both invidious and inexcusable—all the while callously calculating the number of votes that such migrations might bring in.

How else can one explain the cavalier, reckless opening of the nation's southern borders to massive immigration from Latin America and the Caribbean, and attendant massive voter registration drives conducted by the Clinton administration just prior to the 1996 presidential election? How else can one explain former New York Governor Elliot Spitzer's inane quest to issue driver's licenses, the ID of choice both at the polling place and of virulent terrorists seeking to get on airplanes, to illegal aliens? How else can one explain the Bush administration's "benign neglect" open borders policy?

Would that it were so simple—that the challenges could be solved by electing leaders of a stature more attuned to the nation's evolving socio-economic crises than to sheer self-serving parochial concerns! Yet that option must perforce become a critical first step in the quest for equitable remedy in the face of very real and imperiling demographic challenges that must be expeditiously addressed, with an estimated million-plus immigrants entering America each year, and perhaps an equal number more illegally.

Indeed, despite the unequivocal assertion of Article IV of the Constitution that "[t]he United States shall guarantee to every State in this Union a Republican Form of Government, *and protect each of them against Invasion*," America's politicians today proceed with tacit acquiescence to the ongoing massive influxes of aliens who defiantly initiate their stays by violating the nation's established rules for entry.

The violations, flagrant in their essence, thus invoke the crucial question: Why is "illegal" no longer deemed illegal? Why do those elected to serve the public interest so pander to certain ethnic groups at the expense of native-born Americans who are increasingly being asked to foot ever-larger shares of the resultant welfare bills?[2]

Why do they dismiss the reality that the assimilability of current newcomers is more challenging than that which characterized previous waves of immigrants? Why do they take no position on foreign governments' attempts to bind immigrants to their countries of origin? Why do they take no action on immigrants holding dual citizenship, possessing two passports, and voting in foreign elections?

Why likewise do they do so little to encourage immigrants to learn the country's language, English?[3] More basically, why do they treat immigration as some form of "bastardized civil right" arbitrarily extended to foreigners who have no regard for, let alone allegiance to, America's national interests?

Why do they ignore that current immigration is not just an economic challenge but a grim fiscal one involving massive transfer payments from American taxpayers to illicit infiltrators—vast monetary sums that are sucked out of the U.S. productive economy to the invaders' homelands in the form of repatriated incomes by those who knowingly flaunt the law? Why do they persist on a policy course wherein there is neither perceptible long-term U.S. economic benefit nor reasonable expectation of success?

Whither the days when immigration into the United States was deemed a privilege and not an assumed right afforded to one who can somehow manage to sneak across the border? The answers to such questions must be deliberate—and will determine whether the nation preserves its historic soul or slowly sinks into the enveloping morass of that clash of civilizations, lamented by political historians, that characterized the medieval Dark Ages.[4]

America's citizenship has historically been an awarded privilege based on a mutual social contract. As a nation, she has reached her premier state of economic, political, and social development by offering abundant personal freedoms and enormous economic opportunity. In return, she has asked of her immigrants that they learn the country's language, respect her social and civic values, and bring with them at least a modicum of commitment to her well-being and her future—in essence, becoming true Americans. Thus oriented, they would become part of the cultural and political life of their new home.[5]

Indeed, the nation has historically built its superb record of achievement in assimilation more through inspired socioeconomic values than through innate human resources—as in the latter, it started out with less than many—offering rich opportunity for those who came. The Statue of Liberty beckons the poor and disadvantaged to come to its shores to seek their aspired fortunes—and come they did.

America was founded on the strength and commitment of emigrés fleeing other lands. She was, in fact, created by seventeenth- and eighteenth-century settlers, the great preponderance of whom were political and religious protestors who came from Britain. Her aspiration, as articulated by her first president, George Washington, was: "I have always hoped that this land might become a safe and agreeable asylum to the virtuous and persecuted part of mankind, to whatever nation they might belong."[6]

The promotion of immigration likewise was a prime objective of Thomas Jefferson in forging the Declaration of Independence, in remarks that later inspired the drafters of the Constitution assembled in Philadelphia in the summer of 1787 to indict the emigration policies of British King George III, proclaiming: "He has endeavored to prevent the Population of these States; for that purpose obstructing the Laws for the Naturalization of Foreigners; refusing to give pass to others to encourage their migration hither; and raising conditions of new Appropriations of Lands."[7]

To these ends, Jefferson asserted that "the present desire of America is to produce a rapid population by as great an importation of foreigners as possible."[8] In his famed *Report on Manufactures*, Treasury Secretary Alexander Hamilton similarly noted that it was in the national interest "to open every possible avenue to emigrés from abroad."[9] To which James Madison concurred, arguing at the Constitutional Convention that immigration was part of America's grand national strategy, and that should any overcrowded nation such as Britain let its people go, those citizens "ought to be invited by a country greatly deficient in its population."[10]

That the goal of the Founding Fathers was to create one assimilated country dedicated to common cause likewise was articulated by America's first

Supreme Court Chief Justice, John Jay, in *Federalist No. 2*: "Providence has been pleased to give this one connected country to one united people . . . and it appears as if it was the design of Providence that an inheritance so proper and convenient for a band of brethren, united to each other by the strongest ties, should never be split into a number of unsocial, jealous, and alien sovereignties."[11]

It is no accident, then, that Article I of the Constitution mandated the Congress to "establish a uniform rule of naturalization." For from the onset, the Founders were aware that given the vast land and other physical resources to which they now had access, immigration was destined to play a dynamic role in their nascent nation's economic and political development.

Hence, they devoted significant attention to the formulation of policies and programs necessary to achieving their objectives. Because great inflows of newcomers were continuously required as human capital, therefore, considerable effort was devoted not only to developing selective, but liberal, open-door entry strategies to foreigners but also to relaxing prevailing European exit policies.[12]

Their concerns, as reflected in debate, centered upon the requisite qualifications for admission, including who possessed them and who was capable of being integrated into an American mold. Those discussing admission to their civic polity also contemplated safeguards to prevent the misuse of the country as a dumping ground for less desirables, including "felons, paupers, idiots, and the insane," as well as reflecting sundry racial, religious, and political considerations.[13]

Evidence is that they chose well. Indeed, the great legacy of those who heeded their calls to come is that the inherent strengths of their values, cultures, and institutions subsequently shaped those of America. Initially forging the nation's character in terms of ethnicity, culture, and religion, they later likewise found themselves forced to define it ideologically to justify their independence from their English birth land. The Declaration of Independence, *Federalist Papers*, and the Constitution are fortuitous end-products of that definition.[14]

America's core culture was distinctly shaped, therefore, by the global vision of these, the Founding Fathers. The central elements of her core culture included a rich admixture of Christian virtues, a powerful work ethic, limited government, the English language, British traditions of law and justice, and an appreciation for classic and European literature and philosophy.

These are the values that have forged the nation's special and unique character. Indeed, it would be a quite different country today had it been settled not largely by British Protestants but instead by the French, Spanish, or Portuguese—perhaps then becoming a Catholic nation more resembling Quebec, Mexico, or Brazil.

Instead, on strong and durable Anglo-Saxon foundations, what is today known as the "American creed" was built. Arthur Schlesinger assesses it thus: "The language of the new nation, its laws, its institutions, its political ideas, its literature, its customs, its precepts, and its prayers, primarily derived from Britain."[15]

As a result, America's citizens have historically been integrally a part of a "nation of immigrants" possessing distinct Anglo-Protestant values. Her Founding Fathers were largely English settlers—and the ancestors of her citizens, in one way or another, with the noteworthy exceptions of Rhode Island, Maryland, and Pennsylvania, initially came as predominantly European immigrants protesting perceived Catholic persecution at home.

For the same reason that Israel is Jewish and Pakistan is Muslim, then, in the words of the nineteenth-century Swiss-German visitor Phillip Schaff, "everything here had a Protestant beginning"—a phenomenon that would generally prevail for the first two centuries of the Republic.[16]

The nation's economic preeminence was built, in fact, upon the success of those intrepid souls who, imbued by the so-called Protestant ethic, came in equal status—entrepreneurs, factory workers, merchants, and farmers—all dedicated to the premise of diligent endeavor seeking a fair return.

As described by the aristocratic young French social philosopher Alexis de Tocqueville who arrived in America on May 11, 1831: "They were born equal, and didn't have to become so." Equally so, they were born Protestant, as recognized by the contemporary British parliamentarian-philosopher Edmund Burke:

> [The Americans] are Protestant, and of that kind which is the most averse to all implicit submission of mind and opinion. All forms of Protestantism, even at its most cold and passive, are a form of dissent. But the religion most prevalent in our northern colonies is no mere refinement on the principle of resistance; it is instead the dissidence of dissent, and the protestantism of the Protestant religion.

For all of these cogent reasons, then, pursuant to America's consecrated self-image as a land of hospitality and asylum, the Founders' contributions would move Franklin Roosevelt to counsel the Daughters of the American Revolution in 1938: "Remember, remember always, that all of us, you and I in particular, are descended from immigrants and revolutionists."[17]

Immigration has thus leavened and enriched the civilization that today is America. It has lent starch to her social fabric. As the late Senator Daniel Patrick Moynihan (D-NY) has articulately pointed out, the image portrayed by Emma Lazarus as the "wretched refuse" of the earth is an unfortunate myth. Instead, he contends, those who immigrated here were "extraordinary, enterprising, and self-sufficient folk who knew exactly what they were doing and did it quite their own way."[18]

Without such immigration, in fact, America's 2000 census would likely have reflected a population of about 130 million rather than 281 million.[19] She has opened her arms to immigrants, and her immigrants, yearning to be Americans, have welcomed her. In the process, she has produced the most racially, ethnically, and religiously diverse country on the planet. Indeed, each time new immigrant groups have come, her dominant social culture has been enriched by their presence—as evidenced by the number of foreign words that creep into her English vernacular each year.

In this process, her steadfast commitment to the precepts of free-market economics has produced unparalleled upward mobility and a concomitant commitment to individualism and innovation. Because she values merit, ambition, and achievement over legacy, inheritance, and tradition, therefore, new doors of opportunity have continuously opened to new talent and energy rising from the bottom—rendering her uniquely suited to today's rapidly changing, knowledge-based socioeconomy. Of this remarkable homogenization of values, F. J. Grund observed of America in 1837: "Protestantism, republicanism, and individualism are all one."[20]

In short, Anglo-Protestant culture has made Americans the most individualistic and enterprising people in the world. Indeed, the notion of the "self-made man"—implicit in the Constitution, the nation's social contract with its people, and made explicit in the writings of John Calvin—came strikingly to the fore in the presidency of Andrew Jackson, with Henry Clay being the first to employ that very phrase on the floor of the U.S. Senate in 1832. The cogency of the concept continues to this day, as observed by President Bill Clinton: "The American Dream upon which we were all raised is a simple but powerful one—if you work hard, and play by the rules, you should be given a chance to go as far as your God-given ability will take you."[21]

Today, in the United States, that dream has transcended from the ethereal into the realm of reality. Hence, her myriad suburban residents are the embodiment of her ongoing successful experiment in securing the "American Dream" via pursuit of a powerful work ethic operating within a free market. Her most recent immigrants are its aspirants.

The nation hasn't always imported the planet's "aristocratic elite." Indeed, she has more often received its "disenfranchised" citizens—peoples seeking refuge from perceived repression. Yet upon arriving, that great mosaic of humanity who did come—trusting the Constitution's failsafe guarantee of equal opportunity—have generally not been disappointed.

Once here, they have embraced her remarkable adaptation of capitalistic precepts embodied in unfettered democratic entrepreneurship—an ideology that has become the envy of the world. Once here, they have thrived in an economic system underpinned by the "rule of law"—the freedom to "contract" with guaranteed enforcement, protection of private property, equality before the courts, and, most importantly, a limitation of government that had, for long, and until the past half century, precluded the abject stifling of entrepreneurship through excessive taxation and regulation.[22]

Despite its short-term strains, immigration has always brought dynamic new peoples to the U.S. shores—952,000 Germans in the wake of that country's 1848 revolution; 800,000 Irish from 1845 to 1849 fleeing famine, another 914,000 Irish in the 1850s; and hundreds of thousands of enterprising Cubans, Vietnamese, and Chinese within the past half century fleeing communist repression.[23]

By coming here they have, in the cogent words of playwright Israel Zangwill, made America a true "melting pot"—and they, as committed loyal Americans, have often succeeded spectacularly upon arrival. Among them, Generals John Pershing (*Pfoersching* in German) and Dwight Eisenhower (*Eisenhauer* in German), teutonic products of the great melting pot, would become the supreme Allied commanders who led American forces—which also included thousands of American soldiers of German descent—to decisive victory over their ancestral homeland in World War I and World War II respectively.

In like manner, America's more recent occupation of Iraq has been, in large part, presided over by immigrant offspring—Norman Schwartzkopf, an American of German descent; John Abizaid, an American of Arab descent; and Richard Sanchez, an American of Hispanic descent—all outstanding military leaders in the finest tradition of the U.S. Army flag grade officer legacy.

No hyphenated American leaders these. No one referred to Generals Pershing, Eisenhower, or Schwartzkopf as German Americans. No one referred to former chairman of the Joint Chiefs of Staff John Shalikashvili as a Polish American. Why, then, do multiculturalists insist on referring to General Colin Powell as an African American? Certainly, he is as American as a Pershing or a Schwartzkopf, albeit, incidentally, originating from Jamaica and not Africa.[24]

Indeed, ethnically stereotyping Americans runs counter to long-standing national values and traditions. For hyphenating peoples does not bring them together, it divides them—segregating them into groups while qualifying the nature of their loyalties. That is why early in the twentieth century, President Theodore Roosevelt unequivocally opposed the practice, asserting:

> A hyphenated American is no American at all. This is just as true of the man who puts "native" before the hyphen as of the man who puts German or Irish or English or French before the hyphen. American is a matter of the spirit of the soul. Our allegiance must be to the United States.[25]

Assimilation works—its results having comprised the essence not only of America's amazing martial success but of her spectacular industrial prevalence.

For once here, the nation's newcomers have continuously spawned innovative ideas, new products, and emerging dynamic growth areas for her economy. Indeed, the U.S. economy today remains the strongest, most competitive in the world, in large part because of those hardworking immigrants who, for more than two centuries, have joined their predecessors in creating prosperous, job-creating enterprises.

The benefits bestowed, in turn, have clearly been mutual, as President John Kennedy, standing on that very shore in Ireland where his ancestor, Patrick Kennedy, embarked for America, poignantly observed on his sentimental journey to Ireland in June 1963: "When my great-grandfather left here to become a cooper in East Boston, he carried nothing with him except a strong religious faith and a strong desire for liberty. If he hadn't left, I would be working at the Albatross Company across the road."[26]

The American economic system thus spreads its blessings reciprocally—and the world knows it—and is today "voting with its feet." Double or quadruple whatever may be "politically wrong" with America—her would-be immigrants say—and we will still be far better off economically and socially in this country than in any other in the world.

America's entrepreneurial democratic free market is the defining catalyst that underwrites her greatness. Her unique commercial system—individuals seeking economic surplus won through wages and profits to finance their ambitions and their dreams—is why peoples from every nation and ethnic background have come to the United States to forge their destinies and win their fortunes on democratic capitalism's bountiful, hospitable shores.

If there is today a true mounting danger of America's free-market system spreading throughout the planet, as some have feared, therefore, then other nations should be so fortunate. For her capitalistic model gives peoples both liberty and a powerful incentive to innovate, produce, and trade—thereby generating prosperity for those who choose to compete.

CITIZENSHIP AND CIVIC RESPONSIBILITY

As analysis thus makes clear, perceptions of national identity frame distinct structural dimensions of unity both for a country and for its people. Indeed, today, in the post-9/11 era, engendering a powerful sense of national community—the presumption that all citizens are Americans regardless of their differences—has become a security issue as well as a matter of civic concern.

The issues at stake center on how the different ethnic, racial, and religious identities that constitute the core foundation of U.S. society fit together—relations confounded by such powerful, prevalent modern social trends as cultural conflict, civic disconnectedness, and counterculturalism. These are factors that become of transcendent importance within the context of increased U.S. threats of prospective catastrophic terrorism, circumstances wherein strong national attachment becomes a necessity, not an option, and immigration policy not a mere matter of sociology but of life and death.[27]

Because of America's successful efforts at it, many Americans hold an idealized view of immigration—perceiving the process through a hazy romanticized past and assuming that it is now like it was then. In many ways, however, it no longer is. Immigrants have traditionally come to the United States in order to escape a lack of opportunity and its tragic consequences—poverty, lack of freedom, and difficult lives offering little hope for a better future.

But whereas the nation's older waves of immigrants came from countries that they left behind to make a new life, not to replicate an old one, more recent ones often come with no expectations that they must, or will, diminish their emotional and financial ties to their home country, much less sever them altogether.[28]

Such arrivals often come early, in fact, bearing hopes of returning to their countries of origin at some point. Alternately put, they come to America for what she has to offer economically and in social welfare benefits, but with no intent of setting deep roots. They are, therefore, not true immigrants in the classic sense, but rather "sojourners"—parasitically in-country but not permanently as would-be patriots.

Their presence raises critical questions: What is their true sense of commitment and responsibility to America? Should they, in turn, be allowed to support parallel influxes of illegals of a similar homeland and nationality? Should they seek to foster their native languages in a country wherein English is the national tongue?[29]

The socioeconomic and political challenges that these realities pose thus are immense—as the United States today is, and has long been, a pluralistic nation, heeding the supplication indelibly engraved at the base of the Statue of Liberty:

> Give me your tired, your poor;
> Your huddled masses yearning to be free;
> The wretched refuse of your teeming shore;
> Send these, the tempest-tossed to me;
> I lift my lamp beside the golden door.

America remains a beacon for immigrants. Today, more than ever, she is heeding these poignant words penned a century and a quarter ago by the poet Emily Lazarus—as there are presently 38 million foreign-born documented within the United States, constituting about 12.6 percent of the U.S. populace, some 30 percent of them at minimum, and perhaps far more, estimated to be illegal.[30]

Indeed, there are more foreign-born in California—8.4 million—than there are people in New Jersey—and more foreign-born in New York State than there are people in South Carolina. Some two-thirds of Miami's residents are Hispanic, and Caucasians are now, in fact, a minority in more than 10 percent of the nation's counties.[31]

Over three million people inhabit Los Angeles County today, and 54 percent of them speak in their homes a language other than English, up from 45 percent in 1990. Over three-quarters of the students in the Los Angeles Unified School District are Hispanic, primarily Mexican—and over two-thirds of all births in Los Angeles County hospitals are to illegal immigrant mothers—leading some to charge that Southern California, "Mexifornia," is becoming a "Hispanic Quebec."[32]

In the 1990s, the 2000 census shows, immigrants and their children accounted for the entire population growth of the states of California, New York, New Jersey, Illinois, and Massachusetts—and over half of the growth in Florida, Texas, Michigan, and Maryland. Indeed, since 1990, over half of the U.S. states have more than doubled, and nine have tripled, their foreign-born populations. By mid-twenty-first century, the Hispanic portion of the U.S. population at large is expected to reach 102 million persons—and in New Mexico, the Hispanic proportion of its population has already reached 43 percent.[33]

Whereas Hispanics comprised two-thirds of U.S. population growth in the 1990s, moreover, they account for nearly all of it today. Such demographic phenomena—which stand in stark contrast to the nation's Anglo-Saxon heritage—have thus placed large parts of the nation in a distinct "dial 3 for English" mode—the coalescing of which moved incoming President George Bush in his January 20, 2001, Inaugural Address to note that "sometimes our differences are so deep that it seems we share a continent, but not a country."[34]

The "difference problem" rests not with legal Hispanic immigrants, of course, most of whom share traditional American values. Among them, family solidarity, work ethic, religion, and patriotism consistently rank high. Polls typically show that 90 percent of all Hispanic Americans believe that anyone living here should learn English as soon as possible. About 75 percent think that the nation already has far too many immigrants and that continued immigration suppresses wages. The problem lies not with them, therefore, but with internal and external phenomena both insidious and illegal.[35]

For while legal immigration has historically leavened the culture of America, there is a clear and present danger issuing from those who arrogate to themselves the right to break the law by infiltrating the country in pursuit of self-serving economic interests. For their actions are no less than the blue-collar equivalent of white-collar crime.

Indeed, it is estimated that there are as many as eight to twenty million illegal immigrants in America today—as amazingly, in a world where FED-EX can track millions of packages globally in real time every day, the U.S. federal government seems openly clueless about the whereabouts of some twelve to twenty million life-size aliens living illegally in the nation's midst.

America possesses more than 7,500 miles of border—5,525 miles to the north and 1,989 miles to the south. Each year, an estimated 20,000 illegal aliens cross her northern border with Canada and some 800,000 illegal aliens—about 2,200 per day—cross her nearly 2,000-mile southern border with Mexico. Indeed, at the Mexican border, they are aided by Mexican smugglers and often the Mexican border patrol itself—and once here, by liberal church, community, and ethnocentrist activist groups.[36]

At the core of the problem, and the overarching issue critically at stake, however, is not that the abstract precept of "immigration abetted by do-gooders" has suddenly gone bad—for the great influx of Mexican and other Hispanic emigrés who come, as noted, invariably enrich American society, both culturally and economically.

The overwhelming majority of the nation's Hispanic American citizens, in fact, respect its civic values and abide by its rule of law. They, like their earlier immigrant counterparts, have thus contributed immensely to America's greatness, immeasurably enriched her culture, and died to keep her free.

The problem is instead twofold: *domestically*, an ever-evolving, perversely contrarian, counterculturalist approach to assimilation; and *externally*, a kleptocratic Mexican government that has exploited that propensity for wholly self-serving political ends.

For since the late 1960s, the metastasizing concept of multiculturalism—which, as described, holds that Western civilization not only merits no special consideration inasmuch as all cultures are of equal merit, but also that it is the cause of much global exploitation of minorities—has proved to be the prime force multiplier of illegal immigration at the nation's southern border. The result has been catastrophic—turning traditional challenges of assimilation into a traumatic tragedy of social and cultural alienation stretching across both borders and generations.[37]

As a result, almost every well-intended gesture designed to assist immigrants within the past four decades—*de facto* open borders, bilingual education, supportive social welfare programs, affirmation of the merits of a hyphenated identity, and the like—has rather undermined the vital process of assimilation and associated efforts to promote economic parity between immigrants and native-born citizens, promoting instead isolationism, tribalism, statism, and balkanization.[38]

Indeed, almost every would-be uncompromising measure designed to welcome and support new immigrants to the United States—including language immersion and cultural outreach—has been either summarily dismissed by the newcomers or embraced only halfheartedly. At the core of the problem is a corrupt, calculating foreign government that seeks to export onto the United States economic problems precipitated, in large part, by its own socioeconomic shortcomings.[39]

Reconquista Through Immigration, Not Invasion

The reason for this unfortunate state of affairs is fundamental—as both the incipient controversy and attendant dissonance derive from the reality that haphazardly constructed and ill-enforced U.S. immigration policies have been shamelessly exploited as an instrument of foreign policy by the government of Mexico to shift its myriad social problems northward to capitalize on, and otherwise interfere in, the internal affairs of the United States.

Indeed, some view these activities in the more sinister context of a planned *reconquista* ultimately aimed at transforming the whole of previously Mexican-owned southwestern United States into a recrudescent "Atzlan," a formal province of Mexico. Deeming Mexicans now living throughout this region to be "America's Palestinians," the goal is to reclaim this territory through "immigrant invasion"—with a Zogby poll suggesting that 58 percent of Mexico's citizens support this objective.[40]

Indeed, a lead editorial issued in March 1995 in *Voz Fronteriza* ("Voice of the Frontierists"), a Hispanic publication operating on the University of California–San Diego campus, openly referred to all of America's Southwest—including California, Arizona, New Mexico, and west Texas—as "occupied Mexico," part of "Greater Atzlan"—and to Mexican-Americans as "Mexicans living on this side of the *frontera falsa* (false border)." The cover of this issue, incidentally but perhaps not coincidentally, depicted California Governor Pete Wilson in the crosshairs of a telescope sight.[41]

It then followed up with a May 1995 editorial that proclaimed: "The odds that the colonizers will give us our land are slim to none. Unless we are prepared for armed struggle, we will be kept at the level of servitude that we find ourselves today. The revolution has begun. Which side are you on?"[42]

To punctuate their point, armored Humvees, manned sometimes by as many as sixteen uniformed, armed Mexican border police, have been known to brazenly cross the demarcation line into the United States to aid illegal immigrants in their surreptitious entry, at times even exchanging gunfire with greatly underarmed U.S. patrol agents.[43]

Indeed, the same issue of *Voz Fronteriza* described Luis Santiago, a U.S. Immigration and Naturalization Service (INS) border agent killed in action pursuing illegal immigrants, as a "traitor to his race," asserting: "We are glad this pig died. He deserved to die . . . he is the worst kind of pig (one who chases his own kind.)"[44]

The magnitude of the problem evolving at the southern border of the United States is thus ever more self-evident. Tijuana is not Ellis Island; Brownsville is not an immigrant reception center; this is not a break-in, it is an invasion. Were the incessant waves of trespassers soldiers rather than civilians, they would most certainly be repelled by M-1 tanks and F-16s.

But usually not caught upon entry by the undermanned and under-equipped U.S. border patrol, they know that once here they will be warmly welcomed by family and friends and often have a waiting job. Alternately, they know that, if caught, in a worst-case scenario, they will be either re-leased into society with a pending court date or deported to their homes of origin. But their real hope is that, in coming in and overstaying, no one will take action.[45]

The total number of illegals, primarily Mexican, estimated to be residing in America, as noted, today remains speculative—with estimates ranging from eight to twenty million, and twelve million a commonly used sum—encumbering as many as ten to fifteen million U.S. jobs. The government of Mexico—a country of a hundred million people—openly encourages its citizens to enter the United States, legally or illegally, and work in areas wherein earning her minimum wage will provide them with twenty-five times more in daily earnings than they could make at home.[46]

Collectively, they then reportedly transmit more than $20 billion in American dollars in remittances back to Mexico each year. These billions of dollars in repatriated earnings—drained from the U.S. productive economy—are thus funds no longer available for prospective domestic reinvestments that could otherwise build homes and establish businesses that create high-quality jobs in America.[47]

That sum—combined with a massive influx of U.S. investment capital and an annual U.S. trade surplus of over $50 billion—explains why Mexican authorities do not try to curtail their illegal outmigration; indeed, they actively promote it. For unlike traditional European emigrés, for whom America was a terminus, for many Mexicans, it is little more than a financial rendezvous, a cornucopic ATM machine.[48]

Foremost among the illegal immigration advocates was Mexico's former president, Vicente Fox, who aggressively worked to export much of his crime and poverty to America in exchange for the billions of dollars in remittances sent back to Mexico each year. Seeking to govern a country over half of whose populace lives below the poverty line, he continuously artic-ulated this objective throughout his tenure in office, openly demanding an amnesty and work visa program for illegal Mexicans living in the United States.[49]

Describing himself as the president of 120 million Mexicans—100 million in Mexico and 20 million in the United States—he asserted: "Our proposal is to move to a second phase of NAFTA where in five to ten years, that border will be open to the free flows of people, workers transiting the border between our two countries, the same as we now do with products, services, and merchandise."[50]

His position was not surprising, as with the U.S. per capita GDP more than ten times that of Mexico, the cross-border income gap is the largest between any two contiguous countries in the world. That this approach is official policy was similarly articulated by Fox's presidential predecessor, Ernesto Zedillo, in a 1995 speech to Mexican American politicians in Dallas: "You are Mexicans—Mexicans who live north of the border." To which Zedillo later added: "I proudly affirm that the Mexican nation extends beyond the territory enclosed by its borders, and that Mexican migrants are a very important part of it."[51]

Lest there is lingering doubt that some form of *reconquista* is Mexico's intent, Fox's successor, Felipe Calderon—in his State of the Nation address in September 2007, likewise proclaimed to a wildly cheering audience: "Mexico does not end at its borders. Wherever there is a Mexican, there is Mexico."[52]

There thus is a pattern here. This is no happenstance. Indeed, a formal Office for Mexican Communities Abroad has been set up to provide the illegal aliens with instructions on how to avoid the U.S. border guards, to provide them with "survival kits" for their transit, and to offer information on how to obtain free social services once they reach their U.S. destinations.[53]

Of them, author and syndicated columnist Dr. Samuel Francis writes:

> The survival kits, however, are only part of the package. The kits are part of a larger program to instruct illegals in what to expect as they sneak into the United States alive. The pre-sneak training includes tips on maintaining self-esteem and on Asian meditation techniques designed to combat depression, stress, and anxiety in a country that they have entered illegally and without speaking its language.[54]

The Mexican Human Rights Commission, in turn, provides maps and detailed instruction on how to achieve successful surreptitious border crossings. Its official manual, *The Guide for the Mexican Migrant*, not only instructs the illegals on how to clandestinely enter the United States and live there without detection, it advises them of their legal rights and "entitlements," and prescribes procedures to take to get safely back home if caught.[55]

In support of such initiatives, moreover, Mexican consulates in the United States issue registration cards, the *matricula consular*, to their illegal aliens certifying that they are residents of the United States. Such registrations, it is critical to note, are often accepted by municipalities as identification for receiving governmental services, by police departments when detaining suspects, and by banks and other businesses to lure immigrant customers.

Once here, it is reported, these "consulates have been encouraging their nationals to naturalize as U.S. citizens, while concurrently keeping their nationalities as Mexicans"—thereby creating, in effect, an "*in*, but not *of*" status for their illegal aliens within America.[56]

To further promote these ends, Mexican officials openly meddle with impunity in the political affairs of the United States. They recruit Mexican Americans to advise the government on how to lobby U.S. policy makers on political and economic issues, and Mexican Americans are encouraged to run for the Mexican Congress.[57]

They sponsor get-out-the-vote drives for Mexican Americans in U.S. elections, including transporting them to the polls, replete with their presidential candidates openly campaigning in America's *barrios*. Every major Mexican political party has, in fact, opened offices in California—a state where César Chávez's birthday has joined the Fourth of July as a celebrated legal holiday.[58]

Indeed, Mexican diplomatic consuls actively campaigned against California's Proposition 187, which was designed to eliminate welfare benefits for illegal aliens, as well as against Proposition 227, which proposed to restrict bilingual education in public schools. They similarly worked for the defeat of Proposition 200 in Arizona, which would have required proof of citizenship before becoming eligible for welfare.[59]

Recently, the Mexican government hired an attorney to contest trespass charges against one of its illegal nationals in the United States lest his conviction "set a precedent." Concurrently, each one of Mexico's forty-seven U.S. consulates has a mandate to seek to introduce Spanish-language Mexican textbooks into American schools with significant Hispanic populations.[60]

Mid-range estimates suggest that upward of 20 percent of Mexico's citizenry has now been exported to the United States—over half of it perhaps illegally—albeit with official sanction and encouragement. Hence, Vicente Fox, while in office, often blasted proposals to build a 700-mile fence along the border between Mexico and the United States, describing it as "disgraceful and shameful" and in violation of the "rights" of illegal aliens. In his quest to preserve the status quo, moreover, he hired the noted Dallas PR firm Allyn and Company on retainer to fight immigration-reform initiatives whenever and wherever they would arise.[61]

This tragedy, then, is no less than tantamount to capitalizing upon cultural attachment to perpetrate a callous infringement of sovereignty. Japan, having been humiliated by the United States in World War II, rebounded to build an economic power of its own to compete with her conqueror without attendant constant lamentations about the shortcomings of its past. Mexico, on the other hand, seeks balm for her self-inflicted wounds rather than honestly confronting its failures of the present.[62]

While European countries have historically relinquished control of their emigrés once they arrived in the United States, moreover, Mexico deliberately exports its unwanted migrant workers north of the border, yet once they are safely settled on American soil, suddenly becomes their champion *in loco parentis* as much out of resentment toward her northern neighbor as concern for the well-being of the citizens so exported.[63]

At the heart of the problem, then, are race, politics, and economics. For, simply put, Mexico's ruling autocracy, to preserve its privileged status, relies on outmigration as an economic means of avoiding internal domestic reform. In so doing, the hope is, the country will never be forced to embrace free-market capitalism, constitutional government, and an independent judiciary so long as it enjoys the means to export its problems northward.[64]

Illegal immigration thus is a critical safety valve for a country that is a boiling demographic caldron with an indigenous populace of one hundred million souls and growing—and no way of providing jobs, health care, and social justice to a nation half of whom are under twenty-five years of age. Without an outlet to the north, the result might be internal political revolution or African-like famine, or both.[65]

Thus, under the pretext that "the American *gringos* stole our land," thereby forcing too many people onto all-too-little turf, a corrupt, elitist autocracy blames the United States for problems that are entirely of its own making. Its reward nonetheless is billions of dollars in repatriated incomes sent home by its expatriates in the United States in efforts to feed impoverished relatives who are denied a welfare safety net at home.[66]

The Domestic Socioeconomic Effects of Illicit Infiltration

America has thus become a nation of broken borders—with people entering the country seemingly at will and without regard for U.S. law—appropriating jobs, depressing wages, consuming vital social services and other finite resources, and jeopardizing national security. Compounding the problem is that while the fertility rates for native-born U.S. women have now fallen below the 2.1 child per capita natural replacement rate, rates for illegal Hispanic females approach 3.5 per woman, thereby altering the nation's ethnic mix further still.[67]

The net result is that illegal immigrants now represent nearly 5 percent of the U.S. workforce—people who are given jobs, medical care, and free schooling; pay few, if any, taxes; and are often provided services not available to the nation's legal middle class.

As a consequence, local social service infrastructure maintenance costs have risen dramatically, necessitating either tax increases on indigenous citizens or reduced service levels across the board. By some estimates, illegal immigration is costing the U.S. economy between $40 billion and $70 billion each year—with the educational expenses of 1.5 million illegal siblings alone costing the individual states some $12 billion of that amount.[68]

Unfortunately, the nation's lower middle class pays the price for such publicly funded largesse, not only as taxpayers but as working people, for immigration does not readily increase the size of the economic pie, only the way that it is split. As a result, over the past decade, more than two million lower-skilled Americans have been displaced from their jobs, and each 10 percent increase in the U.S. immigrant workforce depresses wages by an estimated 3.5 percent. Record teenage unemployment among the native-born is another consequence of the invaders' illicit presence.[69]

Indeed, social economist George Borjas estimates that between 1980 and 2000, immigration reduced the wages of native-born high school dropouts by over 9 percent. The question thus arises: Does America want a wage scale that competes with that of Mexico and China, mindful that she cannot maintain a First World infrastructure with a Third World economy and workforce?[70]

The answer to that question is critical to the nation's job and fiscal future equally. For under present immigration policies, illegal aliens now trade low-skilled labor for high-priced, tax-funded social services. Some estimates put overall wage loss due to immigration at over $200 billion annually. In the poignant admonition of eminent economist Milton Friedman, "It is obvious that you can't have free immigration and a welfare state."[71]

Every immigrant who arrives in the United States, whether legal or not, moreover, has access to its comprehensive public utilities and services infrastructure, including such basics as running water, sanitation, electricity, modern medical facilities, and free public education. Local public security also factors into the fiscal cost equation, making illegal immigration not a "victimless crime."

Such basic social services are, of course, underwritten by a tax-levying, services-providing infrastructure not participated in by illegals working off the books. But the hidden fiscal costs can be enormous—with estimates that illegal alien households use approximately $2,700 more in federal services than they annually pay in taxes, adding more than $10 billion to the national budget deficit each and every year.[72]

Indeed, analysts Robert Rector and Christine Kim, in a 2007 Heritage Foundation study, found that 4.5 million low-skill immigrant households, many of them illegal, receive nearly three dollars in taxpayer-funded services for each dollar that they pay in taxes. While low-skill immigrants paid an average of $10,573 in taxes in 2004, they received $30,160 in government benefits and services—for a $19,587 per household "fiscal deficit"—a total that added up to $564 billion that year. They also conclude that these individuals likely receive $2.5 trillion more in a smorgasbord of governmental "entitlements"—including Social Security, Medicare, Medicaid, public housing, and subsidized education—than they will pay in taxes in their lifetimes.[73]

Other respected analyses suggest that U.S. taxpayers are paying the 38 million immigrants now legally or illegally in the nation more than $9,000 per year per individual in tax-funded support benefits—in other words, more than $36,000 per each immigrant household of four.

For the reality is that most immigrants arrive much poorer and less educated than typical Americans and consume significantly more per capita in public services. Indeed, the poverty rate for immigrants has climbed 52 percent since 1990; today it is, at 27 percent, 47 percent higher than it is for the native-born—while 34 percent of Mexican immigrants use some form of welfare, more than double the rate of indigenous citizens; 31 percent never finish high school, a ratio nearly four times higher than that of those already here; and immigrant children account for one-fifth of all students in U.S. school systems, and nearly 100 percent of the increase in school enrollments over the past two decades.[74]

The presence of illegal immigrants is likewise a prime reason why national health care costs are continuing to spiral at a time when forty-three million residents, many of them illegal aliens, don't have adequate health insurance. Indeed, together with their skills and social services supplications, they have brought HIV/AIDS, tuberculosis, leprosy, polio, cholera, malaria, yellow fever, and hepatitis back to America's Southwest.[75]

Once here, moreover, though required to renounce previous national allegiances and attachments as part of their oaths of U.S. citizenship, millions of the immigrants, legal and illegal, make no effort to assimilate or seek upward mobility through traditional channels. As for them, America is not their home, Mexico is—and they wish to remain Mexicans.

Pursuing a process of "reverse acculturation," they thus have no desire to learn English. They create their own radio and television stations, newspapers, magazines, books, and films. They aren't interested in becoming citizens; they merely want to attach themselves to their adopted host and parasitically feed off its benevolence while maintaining their own identities and cultures. Lacking any sense of "community," they have no desire to contribute to society in return—asking what their newly adopted country can do for them, not what they can do for it.[76]

Their goal, in effect, is to deliberately forestall Hispanic assimilation into traditional American culture and instead create permanent, semiautonomous Spanish-speaking social *barrios* on U.S. soil. In that process, their goal is that America as a nation should no longer have a core Anglo-Protestant culture with multiple ethnic subcultures but instead two separate and dominant cultures, Anglo and Hispanic, replete with a bilingual *lingua franca*.[77]

The suspicion cannot be dismissed, therefore, that by not emphasizing and promoting traditional America education to young Latinos—courses in Western civilization, history, philosophy, literature, and the classics—Chicano leaders are deliberately ensuring the perpetuation of an enclave-isolated constituency that lacks the learning to question the mono-dimensionally torqued histories that they are attempting to force-feed them.[78]

Here, then, only to take American jobs and to capitalize on "free" U.S. education and social services, the illegal aliens are indeed sojourners rather than immigrants—creating a culture within a culture and a nation within a nation—notwithstanding that whenever their perceived "rights" as quasi-citizens are threatened, they take to the streets *en masse.*

In March and April 2006, in conjunction with a buying boycott and strike, in fact, two million Hispanics and their sympathizers marched in more than fifty cities spanning from Los Angeles to Atlanta to Chicago seeking amnesty—culminating in a "Grand March" in Los Angeles on May Day 2006 whose numbers exceeded a half million immigrants bearing Mexican flags while reportedly burning American ones. Not only were the illegals unapologetic for their illicit status, they were vehement in their demands for their "political agenda," which runs the gamut from open borders to free social services to driver's licenses to full amnesty.[79]

As a consequence of the dual citizenship anomaly, moreover, Mexican candidates for office now come to the United States to openly campaign for office and raise political funds—thereby giving parts of the nation the semblance of an "occupied country." It is the unfolding of such events in recent years that has led one *Los Angeles Times* reporter to conclude: "Playing in Los Angeles is no longer a home game for the United States!"[80]

This, then, is a cultural invasion unlike any other that has preceded it. The Irish, upon their arrival did not demand that Gaelic be taught in the schools that they attended, that American textbooks uniquely extol Irish contributions, or that the Irish be granted special civic or cultural rights such as legally mandated proportional representation within local political institutions or veto power over legislation that might affect their group.[81]

The current waves of illegal immigration now not only directly challenge the nation's vital health and social security systems, but the very foundations of its traditional culture as well. Recognizing the clear potentials for such a possibility as early as two centuries ago, James Madison wanted to exclude from entry "anyone unlikely to incorporate into our society."[82] Expressing a like concern, George Washington, in a letter to John Adams, while asserting that America "is open to the oppressed of all Nations and Religions," wrote:

The policy of (immigration's) taking place in a body (I mean settling them in a body) may be much questioned; for by so doing, they retain the language,

habits, and principles (good or bad) which they bring with them. Whereas by
an intermixture with our people, they, or their descendants, get assimilated to
our customs, measures, and laws; in a word, they soon become one people.[83]

The nation's first president thus believed that in order for immigrants to
become Americans, they must first embrace America's society, her language,
and her values. To that end, Thomas Jefferson also argued that they "should
distribute themselves sparsely among the natives for quicker amalgamation," for failing that, "it would be a miracle were they to stop precisely at
the point of temperate liberty"—whereas Benjamin Franklin believed that
it was necessary to "distribute them more equally, mix them with the English, and establish English schools where they are now too thickly settled."[84]

For Alexander Hamilton, too, success in nation-building depended upon
"preserving a national spirit and a national character"—a phenomenon
known in the early days of the Republic as "patriotism"—asserting: "The
United States have already experienced all the evils of incorporating a large
number of foreigners into their national mass; by promoting in different
classes different predilections in favor of particular foreign nations, and an-
tipathies against others, it has served much to divide the community and to
distract our councils."[85]

In aggregate, then, the Founding Fathers shared a common reservation
that unmonitored mass immigration had seious potential downside consequences. Addressing similar current concerns, news columnist Georgie Ann
Guyer maintains:

> What is happening with illegals—the occasional riots, the refusal to become
> American while demanding all of the rights of committed citizens, the desper-
> ate hanging on to their "Mexican-ness"—is not accidental. It is the result of
> careful, cynical plans on the part of the Mexican government to develop its
> own constituencies inside American society—and to keep it forever Mexican.[86]

In an era when native-born Americans are enduring dramatically increased security screening at airports, moreover, the nation's land borders
are becoming increasingly porous, with as many as a million or more persons illegally flooding across them each year. That sum includes not only
illegal aliens seeking jobs, education, and social services, but those actively
committed to doing the nation harm. On February 16, 2005, Deputy Secretary of Homeland Security Admiral James Loy testified at a Senate hear-
ing that:

> Recent information from our ongoing investigations, detentions, and emerging
> threat streams strongly suggest that *al-Qaeda* has at least considered using the
> southwest border to infiltrate the United States. Several *al-Qaeda* leaders be-

lieve that its operatives can pay their way into the country through Mexico, and believe that illegal entry is more advantageous than legal options for operational security reasons.[87]

Congressman Tom Tancredo (R-CO), in turn, contributes the following statistics: "In 2004, 1.15 million illegal aliens were apprehended crossing our borders, and more than 76,000 of them were non-Mexicans from countries with terrorist cells such as the Philippines, Indonesia, Morocco, Iran, Syria, Pakistan, and Iraq."[88] To which Stephen Camarota, research director at the Washington-based Center for Immigration Studies, adds: "If a Mexican day laborer can sneak across the border, so can *al-Qaeda* terrorists. We can't protect ourselves from terrorism without dealing with illegal immigration."[89]

Moreover, in the infiltration and insertion process, journalist Tom De-Weese charges, the Mexican government is presently using tactics similar to those used in the past by Fidel Castro to export his criminal elements:

> In 1978, Castro purged his prisons of murderers, thieves, and drug dealers by putting them into armadas of boats headed for America's shore. The resulting crime-wave flooded jails, overworked police and community budgets, and made living in Miami, Florida, almost unbearable for a time, and still afflicts the community's culture. Much the same is happening in Mexican border states, as crime rises and the quality of life diminishes.[90]

The imminent threat to American well-being, therefore, is not just the potential incursion of *al-Qaeda*, but of criminals and the criminally insane—presumably the "wretched refuse" contemplated by Emma Lazarus twelve decades ago. Once across the border, illegal trespassers then often openly threaten the physical security of the home and ranch owners with whom they come into contact in their transit—trespassing properties, jeopardizing their livestock and other property, and endangering their lives.[91]

In a post-9/11 world, safeguarding America's borders should not be a low priority—as the safety of her citizens must take precedence over the comfort and convenience of infiltrating illegal aliens. It should instead be considered quintessential to national security, reflecting poet laureate Robert Frost's sage admonition in his epic *Mending Wall* that "good fences make good neighbors."[92]

If the federal government cannot persuade its Mexican counterpart to become a partner in shutting down illegal immigration across her southern border, therefore, then that wall should go up now—cognizant of President George Washington's noteworthy warning in his farewell address: "Beware of entangling alliances." To which Congressman James Sensenbrenner (R-WI) appends: "It seems to me that you can't have homeland security without border security." The two concepts are synonymous.[93]

Hence, illegal immigration threatens not only national security, leaving the American people vulnerable, it threatens the very social fabric upon which the country has been founded. Bringing with it rampant crime, a buoyant narcotics trade, and a needless draw-down on social services, including welfare and education, it threatens the nation physically and financially as well. But these developments again come as no surprise. For why should it not be that illegals would bear greater loyalty to the land of their birth than to a foreign country that they illicitly broke into to find work?

As political commentator Peggy Noonan has opined: "What does it mean when your first act upon entering a country—your very first act on that soil—is the breaking of that country's laws?" The more fundamental question, though, is, if their violation carries no consequence, what message does that reality send them about contemporary respect for the rule of law? Is the value of citizenship not greatly diminished when those who infiltrate illegally are afforded the same benefits as citizens?[94]

The problem is compounded by the reality that the offspring of illegal aliens born in the United States—euphemistically called "anchor babies"— are awarded automatic citizenship and immediately qualify for social welfare benefits. Today, one-tenth of all U.S. births are such "anchor babies," citizens whose parents have legitimate claims on the public services of federal, state, and local governments—claims that come at the direct expense of indigenous taxpayers.[95]

Again, to what provident end? The added costs of schooling, health care, welfare, and prisons—plus additional draw-downs on land, power, and water resources—obviously exceed the dollar value of the taxes that the immigrants could possibly contribute—causing many to ask: "Does this risk justify jeopardizing the health and safety of citizens and the social cohesion and economic well-being of the country?" In the somber assessment of Congressman Elton Gallegly (R-CA): "The more we become a nation of illegal immigrants, the deeper we fall into anarchy!"[96]

There is, in fact, no precedent in human history for a sovereign country undergoing such a rapid and radical transformation of its ethnic character as is now ongoing in America. Heeding Euripedes' lamentation that "there is no greater sorrow than the loss of one's native land," Pat Buchanan warns that illegal immigration threatens to deconstruct traditional "American values"—and that unless it is curbed now, the United States will become "a people with not a thing in common: no history, no heroes, no language, culture, faith, nor ancestors . . . a country with nothing more than an economy."[97]

Harvard political sociologist Samuel Huntington casts the challenge more graphically still, similarly warning of the possibility of the United States dividing into "two peoples, two cultures, and two languages"—while predicting that the "American creed" will likely disappear if the United States loses her historic Anglo-Protestant roots, developing instead a "de facto splitting between a predominantly Spanish-speaking America and an English-speaking America," thereby creating a loss of national identity through a circumstance of deconstruction "quite possibly without precedent in human history."[98]

"If assimilation fails in this case," he asserts, "the United States will become a cleft country with all of the potentials for internal strife and disunion that such a course entails."[99] Thus, he contemplates a multicultural America that will in time become a multicreedal one consisting of groups with differing aspirations and espousing distinct political values and principles rooted in particular cultures. In such an instance, he grimly concludes: "If multiculturalism prevails and if the consensus on liberal democracy disintegrates, the United States could join the Soviet Union on the ash heap of history."[100]

Huntington's case is compelling. In noting that though an economy is not a nation, economic deconstruction has too often brought about the demise of nation states, Robert Samuelson documents the onerous tax and administrative burden placed upon the U.S. welfare system occasioned by its failure to halt the country's ongoing immigrant invasion:

> Since 1980, the number of Hispanics with incomes below the poverty level (about $19,300 in 2004 for a family of four) has risen 162 percent to a level one-third higher than the counterpart U.S.-born populace. Over the same period, the number of non-Hispanic whites in poverty rose 3 percent, and the number of non-Hispanic blacks rose 9.5 percent. What we have now—and would have with guest workers—is a conscious policy of creating poverty in the United States while relieving it in Mexico.[101]

Samuelson's economic data are eye-opening—as are the equally valid questions: What value-added does such immigration bring to the national social fabric? Is America economically or culturally richer for the experience? What expectations do such immigrants face? What skills do they bring to prospective employers? Do they face a future beyond exploiting the welfare generosity of U.S. taxpayers? Failing immigration reform, then, what are the policy options?

The Center for Immigration Studies reports that in 2005, there were 10.3 million school-age children of immigrants in the United States. In a recent survey of twenty countries, the mean literacy score for Americans was two points above that for all adults tested. Among the seventeen nations that disaggregated test scores among their native-born and immigrants, indigenous U.S. citizens scored eight points above the average of the other sixteen. But U.S. immigrants scored sixteen points below those in other nations, thereby significantly bringing U.S. test scores down.[102]

Such disparate trends are fraught with obvious dangers. Historically, the nation's immigrants have come in common cause seeking to be Americans—"one nation under God"—and to contribute to the legacy of America—not aspiring to build mini-satrapies of their departed homelands within their adopted country while concurrently working to change its national character and language. To again quote President Theodore Roosevelt:

> There can be no divided allegiance here. Anyone who says he is an American, but also something else, isn't an American at all. We have room for but one flag, the American flag. . . . We have room for but one language here, and that is the English language . . . and we have room for but one sole loyalty, and that is loyalty to the American people. . . . The one absolutely certain way of bringing this nation to ruin, of preventing all possibility of it being a nation at all, would be to permit it to become a tangle of squabbling nationalities.[103]

In Theodore Roosevelt's world, then, there was no room for hyphenated Americans—only assimilated ones—as evidenced in his assertion, "We are the children of the crucible,"[104] a thought echoed by President Woodrow Wilson in a 1915 speech to newly sworn-in citizens asserting:

> You cannot dedicate yourself to America unless you become in every respect and with every purpose of your will truly American. You cannot become thoroughly Americans if you think of yourselves in groups. A man who thinks of himself belonging to a particular national group in America has not yet become an American; and a man among you who trades upon your nationality is not worthy of the stars and stripes.[105]

Calvin Coolidge framed the challenge more bluntly still: "America must be kept American"—as did Franklin Roosevelt in asserting: "Americanism is not, and never was, a matter of ethnicity. The principle by which this country was founded and has been governed is that Americanism is a matter of the mind and heart. Americanism is not, and never was, a matter of race and ancestry. A good American is one who is loyal to this country and to our creed of liberty and democracy."[106]

All of this, then, stands in full affirmation of the proclamation of John Jay in *Federalist No. 2* that: "Providence has been pleased to give this one connected country to a united people . . . who through joint counsels, arms, and efforts, fighting side by side throughout a long and bloody war, have nobly established their liberty and independence."[107]

The lessons of history validate this proclamation. For once liberated, as shown, America's revolutionaries indeed became further bound together by common ideals as articulated in the Declaration of Independence, the Constitution, and Lincoln's Gettysburg Address—in short, they became "Americans," and patriots devoted to the national cause—a phenomenon ably captured by Arthur Schlesinger:

> The American Creed envisaged a nation composed of individuals making their own choices and accountable to themselves, not a nation based upon inviolable ethnic communities. For our values are not matters of whim or happenstance. History has given them to us. They are anchored in our national experience, in our great national documents, in our national heroes, in our folkways, our traditions, and our standards. Our values work for us, and for that reason, we live and die by them.[108]

In the view of many of the most prominent early Founders, then, America was not destined to be a nation of "mini-cultures." She was to be more than a mere polyglot boardinghouse. She is instead, and has forever constitutionally pledged to be, "one nation under God indivisible with liberty and justice for all."

The question thus becomes one of precisely what constitutes "illegal immigration." Doubtless in the view of the seventeenth-century American Indians, the Anglo-Saxons assembling on their east coast were "illegal immigrants"—making it doubly ironic that many today who bear their bloodlines are reciprocally viewed as "illegal immigrants" by America's still dominant Anglo-Saxon culture.

Notwithstanding, America, as currently configured, is a nation of laws safeguarding the rights of all—indeed, the very principle of self-governance to which her citizens have always aspired is underpinned by the rule of law—with such laws being absolute, not relative. Strict constitutionalist legal construct dictates, therefore, that the laws of the nation be unconditionally enforced.

For immigration laws are no different than any other—they cannot be subject to "selective enforcement." Accordingly, to these ends, all immigration policies must necessarily be strongly founded on national security considerations, and illegal immigrants, when apprehended, must be immediately deported to their countries of origin.

For it is unconscionable and immoral to subordinate the interests of legal immigrants who wait in line for years to get into the country via due process to those who have illegally cut into the queue ahead of them—in essence, rewarding lawbreakers while penalizing those who have elected to abide by the letter of the law.

Yet again, why? Illegal immigration is today destroying the nation's quality of life—and America herself—before her very eyes.[109] To quote Hamilton once more: "The current influx of foreigners . . . tends to produce an heterogeneous compound; to change and corrupt the national spirit . . . and to introduce foreign propensities." This phenomenon extends from a quest to change the nation's culture to one of seeking to change the nation's language.[110]

For concurrently, in recent years, the flood of Hispanic immigration has likewise lent the incessant quest for "bilingualism" new impetus. As with politicians ever-quick to move into the fray given an evocative demagogic cause, the Bilingual Education Act of 1968 provided the initial requisite blueprint and funding, while a subsequent 1974 Supreme Court ruling requiring school districts to provide special programs for students who don't know English set the misguided course.[111]

This mandate, while clear at its inception, has subsequently been interpreted by some to mean the mandatory teaching of two languages—one's native tongue together with adoptive English. Regrettably, but not surprisingly, the system has failed, as the "ethnicity odysseys" of elitist educators have invariably lent priority to the former to the detriment of the latter.

Yet even in the abstract, bilingual education does not work. It does not open bold new vistas of human understanding but instead closes them—undermining integration by nourishing self-ghetto-ization—in the process, fostering racism. And to what end? A billion people today speak English—it commercially reigns triumphant around the planet—it is the *lingua franca* of the twenty-first century.[112]

On this countercultural linguistic phenomenon, Dr. Samuel Francis writes: "Nothing is more basic to the assimilation of immigrants in a foreign culture than learning its language. But today, many Hispanics and other immigrants are not learning English, a strong sign that they haven't assimilated and don't intend to."[113]

The primary problem with widespread bilingual education is that it is culturally divisive. When imperial Rome afforded the Greek language equal status to that of its native Latin, the empire sowed the early seeds of that nation's ultimate dissolution. Multilingualism in erstwhile Yugoslavia contributed greatly to its ultimate break-up as well. Canada, too, in recent decades, has been struggling with issues of national unity after granting French equal legal status with that of the English spoken by two-thirds of the citizens of Quebec in 1982.[114]

When the U.S. Congress passed the Bilingual Education Act in 1968 as a pilot program not to provide for omnibus bilingual education but to meet "special educational needs" by temporarily helping Mexican immigrant children transition to English, Congressman James Scheuer of New York presciently lamented: "I think that we have just discarded the philosophy of the melting pot. . . . We have a new philosophy of enhancing, fortifying, and protecting differences."[115]

Time and reality would prove that Congressman Scheuer was unquestionably right. For as early as 1974, and again in 1978, the act was not only renewed but expanded—but now, not as a remedial measure at all, but instead "to encourage the establishment and operation, where appropriate, of educational programs employing bilingual practices."[116]

Notwithstanding President Theodore Roosevelt's sage guidance that "we believe that English and no other language is the one in which school exercises should be conducted," the multiculturalists had won—their so-called pilot program had been transformed into full-fledged native cultural and linguistic indoctrination, with perhaps a little make-weight English thrown in on the side to humor those who still believed that education in English is important, and that the act's original intent should, at least nominally, be honored.[117]

The challenge is further compounded by the fact that many of the student immigrants' parents didn't even come here to assimilate—and don't want their children to assimilate either. When German immigrants in the 1800s and early 1900s nobly preserved and spoke their native tongue throughout the nation's Midwest—as did the Italians and Irish in Boston and the Poles in Chicago and Buffalo—the U.S. government did not pander to the phenomenon, fund it, or mandate that it be perpetuated throughout the nation's K–12 system. Rather, it proudly acknowledged the process as part of the cultural leavening of the nation.[118]

Today, to the contrary, at the behest of abstract countercultural notions, the American government is spending finite tax dollars to perpetuate the foreign languages and cultures of new immigrants, thereby discouraging them from melding into society; and this, to their great social and economic detriment.

Indeed, if those who perpetuate this perverse process ultimately succeed in remolding America's four-centuries-old "melting pot," they will eventually transform it instead into an overheated "boiling pot"—thereby reducing that unanimity of purpose that once distinguished the *United* States downward to the status of a restive and fractious midcontinent Quebec.[119]

Rebuilding the Nation's Broken Borders

Such an outcome clearly runs counter to the Founders' intent, as institutionalized assimilation enjoys a lengthy history in America. "We must," John Jay said in 1797, "see our people more Americanized," a sentiment echoed by Thomas Jefferson. In 1919, Justice Louis Brandeis asserted that Americanization meant that the immigrant "must adopt the clothing, manners, and customs generally prevailing . . . substitute for his mother tongue the English language . . . [and ensure that] his interests and affections have become deeply rooted here."[120]

Traditionally, over time, both public and private institutions have abetted these efforts. Federally, the Bureau of Naturalization in the Labor Department and the Immigration and Naturalization Services (INS) established aggressive assimilation programs. At the state level, prime responsibility for inculcating American values was vested in the public school system, and the state of Connecticut even created its own "Department of Americanization."

Private institutions such as the YMCA and the Sons of the American Revolution likewise developed their own programs both in acculturation and in English training, as did churches and local communities; and private industry rapidly followed suit, with the Ford Motor Company, International Harvester, and U.S. Steel leading the way.[121]

As a result, historically, the incorporation of immigrants into her culture has been a great American success. She has been a nation of both immigration and subsequent assimilation, and that combination has produced "Americanization," a diverse cultural meld that has deeply enriched her society. She has embraced her immigrants, and her immigrants have embraced her—and that embrace is the essence of those values that have empowered her to become a globally-envied superpower.

For succinctly put, nationalism, patriotism, and freedom are inexorably intertwined. Hence, while indigenous job loss, worker displacement, and the ongoing costs to taxpayers caused by illegal immigration are undeniably critical, it is the loss of national identity that is most threatening of all. To again quote Schlesinger:

> The new ethnic gospel rejects the unifying vision of individuals from all nations melted into a new race. Its underlying philosophy is that America is not a nation of individuals at all but a nation of groups, that ethnicity is the defining experience for most Americans, that ethnic ties are permanent and indelible, and that division into ethnic communities establishes the structure of American society and the basic meaning of American history.[122]

Thus, things are very different now—immigrant attitudes are different, processes related to assimilation are different, and America is different—and these differences impact profoundly upon the nation's prospective future. For whether or not one agrees with the creeping coerciveness of government, no nation can ignore its laws with impunity and remain a free society. But such is the case of illegal immigration. Jump-started with the civil disobedience that attended the civil rights movements of the mid-twentieth century, illegal immigration from its onset was, and today remains, as the name implies, "illegal."[123]

America's current immigration challenges thus transcend a strict interpretation of the law and speak equally to the qualitative nature of its enforcement. For contrary to the contentions of its proponents, the Hart-Celler Immigration and Naturalization Act of 1965, which reallocated the national quota system—replacing the nation's four-decade-long experiment with national quotas with a more global one—did just the opposite.[124]

It, in fact, did little more than convert the threshold for admission from a ceiling to a floor—favoring family reunification over merit, while opening the floodgates of mass Third World immigration by redistributing visa allocations from the citizens of advanced industrialized countries who come to contribute to citizens from developing ones who instead come seeking contributions.[125]

At the time, the measure's prime sponsor, the venerable Senator Ted Kennedy (D-MA), solemnly promised, "This bill will not flood our cities with immigrants. It will not upset the ethnic mix of our society. It will not relax the standards of admission. It will not cause American workers to lose their jobs."[126]

But as Americans are now painfully aware, Senator Kennedy was, as usual, wrong on all counts—as the ill-conceived immigration measure produced, in effect, an outcome exactly opposite from the salutary results of strengthening the American socioeconomy that had been promised.

For whereas First World countries such as the United States have relatively equal income distributions, reinforced by income transfer payments from the rich to poor, Third World countries typically develop unequal income distributions, comparatively viewed. Hence, a skilled Third World worker has significantly less incentive to emigrate and integrate than his lesser-skilled fellow countryman.[127]

An ancillary adverse impact of the 1965 act's family reunification emphasis, moreover, has been to accelerate "chain immigration"—a devious process whereby an individual's accompanying immigration by spouses, children, parents, and siblings is sanctioned. Such newcomers, in turn, can then extend the same chain benefits to their own wives and spouses the same way—thereby producing a logarithmic effect whereby a single initial immigrant admission spirals geometrically in terms of the numbers of newcomers sanctioned.[128]

Rather than developing an omnibus policy of deporting the illegals and protecting the country from further alien invasions, as promised, and as Article IV, Section 4 of the Constitution requires it to do, however, the Congress merely compounded the problem by passing the Immigration Reform and Control Act of 1986—rewarding about three million more illegal immigrants, mostly Mexicans, with amnesty and a path to U.S. citizenship.[129]

Since then, moreover, the Congress has passed seven additional amnesties—awarding several million additional illegal aliens legal residence, thereby putting them and their relatives, through the "chain immigration" process, likewise on the path to legal residency and citizenship—while making a mockery of those law-abiding foreigners who patiently wait in line, in the prescribed legal manner, for their rightful turns to enter.[130]

It is the confluence of these income, demographic, and statutory anomalies that has opened up America's floodgates to the economically disparate.

As from a previous statutory limitation of 156,700 persons worldwide legally admitted annually, the amount soon ballooned to half a million and now to nearly a million legal entries, and entries today may well exceed another million each and every year.[131]

The cause? The federal government, for political reasons, has utterly abdicated its constitutional responsibility to protect the states from such invasion. Yet, as Milton Friedman asserted, no nation offering liberal welfare benefits can long afford an open immigration policy that beckons less-skilled workers if it hopes to preserve its fiscal integrity as well as the ambience of its living standards.

The bottom line, then: just acquiring more people, in itself, is not a society-worthy goal. In an ever-more-complex technological age, it is rather the valued talent of the people attracted—and the quality of the ideas that they bring with them—that ultimately matter. The challenge for prudent immigration, therefore, is that it must perforce be more qualitative than quantitative in its selection processes.

For post-1965 immigration is not only much larger than expected, but because its focus is largely on "family reunification" to the detriment of prospective economic contribution, it is also far less skilled than in the past, and is becoming even less so every year.[132]

Even worse, evidence is that the relative lack of skills among the present generations of immigrants is being passed along to their offspring, belying the Statue of Liberty's long dubious premise that peddler's sons are precisely posed to become rocket scientists. Some do. Most don't. But the bottom line is clear. By importing unskilled labor in such large quantities, the United States, as a practical matter, is dangerously downgrading the quality of its workforce.[133]

Already today, as noted, America admits about two million people each year—a "human tsunami" far greater than the number of aliens admitted by the rest of the world combined, and well above the aggregate 675,000 annual "flexibility cap" imposed by law in 1990.[134]

As a consequence, at current spiraling 3.5 child per Hispanic female fertility rates, comparable to those of the Islamic world, by 2050 America will largely have been transformed into a multiethnic, multicultural, multilingual conglomerate—a balkanized replica of the Roman Empire after the infiltration of the Goths and Vandals. Her total populace will consist of 420 million people—less than half of whom will be native Americans—with 102 million Hispanics performing menial labor, concentrated in the Southwest, the majority of whom having gained illegal entry.[135]

The problem will not be self-correcting. The Census Bureau—which indicates that 31 million of the 281 million citizens counted in the year 2000 were recent immigrants—now projects that by the 2100 census, the U.S.

population will increase by 50 percent, with 66 percent of the population increase consisting of post-2000 immigrants and their families.[136]

No nation, and certainly no democracy, can long endure such large numbers of citizens with shallow civic attachments. No country confronting divisive domestic issues, as America does, benefits from large-scale immigrations of interlopers with multiple loyalties. And no state, striving to sustain its citizens within a coherent civic and cultural identity, can afford to encourage its citizens to look abroad for their most fundamental national attachments.[137]

As Ronald Reagan lamented as early as 1983: "This country has lost control of its borders and no country can long sustain that position." More than Islamic terrorism, then, this is America's most immediate, most compelling, and most challenging crisis—making its urgent resolution a foremost imperative. For to again quote Toynbee, civilizations die when they fail to resolve the crisis of their age.[138]

But making illegal immigration "legal" by legislative sleight of hand, as the proposed, initially powerfully supported, but ultimately defeated 2007 Immigration Act would have done, does not solve America's socioeconomic problems either. It instead merely enfranchises them. Indeed, the proposal was perceived as such a farce that it generated widespread ridicule and condemnation.

Conversely, some have argued that illegal immigration—job leakage at America's southern border—is actually an economic asset because, as the Irish were in the 1850s and the Chinese were in responding to the surge in manpower demand to build mining infrastructure in California in that same decade, incoming aliens play an indispensable economic role.

Yet nothing could be further from the truth. Given more prudent public policy, the requisite workers exist within the nation's borders. Indeed, Americans already were performing those jobs until the government stopped enforcing laws against employers unscrupulously hiring illegal aliens at wage rates that demean the dignity of labor; and at the very same time that the states were continuing to expand the offerings within their market baskets of social service "entitlements" to the extent where drawing public assistance rather than working became, for many, a prudent business decision.

The policy requisite to get back to such a "work instead of welfare" approach, nonetheless, is simple and straightforward—and indeed is nothing more than what some have elected to call the "quick as hell" theory of full employment. Eliminate welfare and other social programs of the Great Society that today merely serve as excuses for not finding a job, they say, and America will restore full employment throughout the nation "quick as hell."[139]

Such an approach, then, is no more than time-proven common sense, as America historically was built not only on her steadfast commitment to a powerful work ethic, but also on her unique ability to attract the planet's "best and brightest." Indeed, they came in millions actively seeking a new life and to break their ties with the Old World. When they arrived, the centripetal socioeconomic forces of the age then melded them into a new amalgam, a social *melting pot*, to turn that much-used phrase.[140]

Today, due to illegal immigration, such clearly is not the case, as the melting pot itself is melting. Too many of those who come do so determined to maintain their own language, customs, and culture—to exploit the opportunities of America while giving back as little as possible in return.

Indeed, many now seek a kind of reverse cultural assimilation—for American society to incorporate and adapt to the values of the homeland from whence they came. Their ongoing quest to establish bilingualism as a national standard for governmental and commercial operations epitomizes their intent.[141]

Thus, the most fundamental of issues remains: Why is "illegal" no longer illegal? Is there not a certain logic that holds that when a government fails to enforce its immigration laws, it sends a message that its laws do not matter? Rather than sending a message that the rule of law is meaningless, should it not instead send the message that its edicts are nonnegotiable and at the heart of its system of governance? More fundamentally still, what is the qualitative difference in definition between "immigration" and "invasion"? When does a "melting pot" stop melding and dissolve into a " teeming cesspool"?

These are the quintessential demographic and socioeconomic questions of America's new century. Their answers will determine whether the nation sustains that unique heritage that has given her unparalleled prosperity and empowered her to ascend to the status of foremost global superpower—or disintegrates instead into a polyglot of disparate subcultures, an erstwhile Yugoslavia, a modern Lebanon, a latter-day late Rome.

For as the immigrant poor pour in, crowding K–12 schools while imposing constantly rising tax burdens on middle American taxpayers, their offspring continue to significantly pull down U.S. academic proficiency test scores, causing the nation's educational bureaucracy to evince ever greater alarm at the disparities in outcomes compared to international scores, and then to berate nation's taxpayers for not coming up with still more money to raise teachers' salaries.[142]

These, then, are profound social problems that need fixing. Perhaps America retains the luxury of continued profligate indifference to her now broken borders for a while longer. History will provide the final answer. But history generally judges harshly those who remain indifferent to their own security and survival. Misdirected priorities and half-hearted efforts are not the hallmarks of nations that survive adversity. They are instead usually the hymns of lamentation for lost glories sung by the heirs to once mighty, but subsequently dying, cultures.[143]

In sum, America is an ideal and a nation, not a market nor a continent. As such, the world today flocks to her as they once did to imperial Rome—cognizant that citizenship within her is one of the planet's most cherished possessions. Her abiding challenge thus is to be an empire in fact while remaining a democratic republic in spirit.

For citizenship within her is more than just a residence, more than a mere address. It is the basis for patriotism and national pride—making the issue at stake in addressing immigration more than abstract public policy; it is instead a defining determinant of whether she is going to preserve her civilizational existence.[144]

If she is to remain true to her history and her heritage, therefore, she must remain true to her identity and, in turn, to her destiny—true to a future not comprised of a vague aggregate of diverse, competing ethnic groups and creedal sects, but rather to the perpetuation of her status as a land of freedom and opportunity and as the world's last, best beacon of hope for the oppressed.

It is to an analysis of the fiscal impacts of these disparate social trends that analysis now turns.

Part III

MOUNTING COMPLEXITY AND COST

A democracy cannot stand as a permanent form of government and will survive only until its citizens discover that largesse can be voted from the Public Treasury. Thereafter, the majority will always vote for candidates promising the most benefits from the Treasury, with the result that a democracy will always collapse over loose fiscal policy, always followed by a dictatorship.

—Attributed to eighteenth-century British historian Alexander Tytler

6

The Burdens of Bureaucracy

> When a government becomes powerful, it is destructive, extravagant, and
> violent. It is a usurer that takes bread from innocent mouths and deprives
> honorable men of their substance for votes for which to perpetuate itself.
>
> —Cicero

COMPLEXITY: THE GROWTH OF GOVERNANCE

Bureaucracy and the Founding Fathers

Civilizations rise when people join in common cause to form a polity
that promises to fulfill their private ambitions individually and their social
goals collectively. They invariably rise with great expectations, often with
considerable promise, and at times with abundant natural and human resources to support those objectives.

As they grow, however, as chapter 1 described the multilayered strata of
government required to administer those ends becomes correspondingly
complex and costly until such point, having reached their hegemonic
apogees, they set inexorably downward into their declines. So again, the
quintessential questions must be asked: Why does this inevitable devolution
happen? And why, and at what point, do such civilizations decline and die?

As chapter 1 has also shown, each of the more than sixty separate civilizations that has risen and fallen on the face of this earth believed that they
were impervious to the prospect of perishing. Indeed, history teaches that
all societies believe that they are superior to their forebears and neighbors
and immune to the prospects of decline.

Few thus accept the possibility of imminent demise, just as few investors at the onset of the new millennium believed that the U.S. technology equities market could suddenly collapse. Evaluation of such phenomena is enlightening in the quest to reverse the seemingly inexorable course of civilizational demise.

For the civilizing process is itself a fragile undertaking—an enterprise fraught with uncommon dangers. Time-sequenced maps make clear that empires over time rise and fall with astonishing frequency. America is now in her 232nd year. Can she assume the ability to last longer than the three Roman empires, which collectively survived an average of nearly a millennium?

The fiscal numbers tell the story, whether the empire is the vaunted "Pax Romana" that ultimately fell because its mounting bureaucratic complexity required a tax base that eventually could no longer underwrite both the military required to defend it and the social services burden of the alien cultures invited in to accommodate an increasing unwillingness on the part of the decadent native-born to serve in the military

Or a "Pax Americana" that is today suffering for many of the same reasons, including a declining work ethic, an attrition of public staying power when at war, a diminishing desire to win at any cost, and a search by disparate elements to retreat from a role of hegemonic leadership.

The social and economic costs of cultural decay thus can be colossal. They were in the case of imperial Rome. They are becoming so in America today. Basic social welfare outlays alone at federal, state, and local levels now well exceed $1 trillion each year, approaching 5 percent of GDP.

Spending for the Department of Health and Human Services and Social Security Administration alone consumes 45 percent of the federal budget— expenditures for Medicare, Medicaid, and Social Security Insurance now encumber 40 percent of all governmental spending and 7 percent of GDP, and they are projected to exceed 50 percent of all U.S. outlays by 2030, equating to about 13 percent of projected GDP. The $9 trillion-plus federal debt itself now hovers at two-thirds of GDP.[1]

Whereas in 1963, prior to the onset of the "Great Society," "entitlements" accounted for just 22.7 percent of all federal spending—leaving 67.3 percent for discretionary purposes—they, together with interest on the national debt, now account for two-thirds of the federal budget, with income transfer payments its fastest-growing spending area.

Such costs are clearly not sustainable in the long term, as World War II baby boomers approach retirement age, and U.S. native-born fertility rates recede further below the 2.1 children needed to sustain zero population growth—while mushrooming to a 3.5 ratio among the nation's two fastest-growing immigrant groups—Muslims and Hispanics—half of the latter of whom may be in illegal status.

In the quest for requisite remedy, public policy matters. America faces tectonic watersheds. Her existence has spanned twenty-three decades. But just because a civilization has been around for two or three centuries is not prima facie proof that it will last forever. Indeed, as analysis has shown, she is positioned today where Great Britain was at the turn of the twentieth century.

While time remains, therefore, she faces a defining choice between righting her public policy course or following powers past—ancient, medieval, and more recent—into the trash bin of second-ranked global powers. Cognizant of these sobering precedents, learning the cogent policy lessons that the past provides can better position the nation to prepare for her strategic geopolitical future.

America was firmly founded on the precept of "democratic capitalism"— a somewhat improbable conjoining of terms inasmuch as the driving force of democracy is equality; of capitalism, inequality. The apparent incongruity is clearly echoed in the concerns of the Founding Fathers. Thomas Jefferson's idyllic world was one wherein democracy prevailed. In arguing for a "national bank," Alexander Hamilton conversely contemplated one where capital reigned supreme.

Yet the issue was effectively resolved with the establishment of an amalgamated system—one wherein the operations of capitalistic process are modulated and moderated by the corresponding workings of democratic process. The consummate success of this hybrid system of governance is reflected in many realities—among them, that even few of the most devout libertarians today would deny the utility of institutions such as Social Security or the Federal Deposit Insurance Corporation.

Early on, the issue was conjoined by federalist jurisprudence. For the Constitution didn't limit what citizens could do; it merely prescribed what was permissible for the federal government to do—stipulating that any act not expressly permitted for it was specifically forbidden to it.

The Tenth Amendment makes explicit, in fact, that those powers not sanctioned are denied. To wit: "Those powers not delegated to the United States by the Constitution nor prohibited by it to the States, are reserved to the States respectively, or to the people." Indeed, on the *precise limits* of federal economic jurisdiction, Article 1, Section 8, provides only that: "The Congress shall have the power . . . to regulate Commerce with foreign Nations, and among the several States, and with Indian Tribes."

Hence, the federal government was empowered to regulate the commerce of Indians, that between foreign governments, and that on an interstate basis only—and, in no way, to reign supreme over all things socioeconomic, to wit to "govern" the private sector. All other tasks—education, crime control, business regulation, ad infinitum—in turn, were specifically reserved for the states or for the people.

Such, however, is not now the reality—as the federal government has, over time, usurped the powers of the states and of the people—evolving into an hegemonic monolith administered by a massive sea of faceless bureaucrats. Today, it meddles in all aspects of human life—from birth, through education, through employment, through retirement, and ultimately, to death and, in the form of death taxes, at times, beyond.

In the process, it taxes citizens not only in their first years of income but throughout their lives—when they first commit their meager after-tax savings to those investments intended to secure their retirements, to the very estates that they have built as legacies to their children when they die. The result is not only a country that the Founders would not recognize, it is a malfeasance of economic governance, a denial of the lessons clearly offered by the planet's economic past.

Economic history portrays in vivid terms the dramatic elevation of society through time powered by the private pursuit of profit motive in an unfettered free marketplace, a steady evolution that now ranks among humankind's foremost monuments to progress—accomplishments forged directly from the Founders' blueprint.

Yet today, civilization's prized legacy of "democratic capitalism"—and with it, many of America's hard-won economic freedoms—stand gravely threatened from within, challenged by the wanton policy extravagances of her public sector and the exorbitant costs that they engender.

Such "bureaucratic transaction costs," a product of profligate public spending, matter because they vitiate that private profit motive that through history has been the primal force impelling progress—the fuel that powers the economic engine that drives the inexorable march of civilization. They matter because "big government"—regulation and other gratuitous public service—clearly has its price.

Its toll comes in the form of taxes and arcane, oppressive governmental regulatory processes that sap precious vigor from the productive private sector—while its financial multiplier effects erode the free economy in a variety of other ways. As described by Milton Friedman:

> None of this means that government doesn't have a very real function. Indeed, the tragedy is that because government is doing so many things that it shouldn't be doing, it performs the functions that it ought to be performing badly.
>
> The basic functions of government are to defend the nation against its foreign enemies, to prevent the coercion of some individuals by others within the country, to provide means for deciding on our rules, and to adjudicate disputes. . . .
>
> The net result has been that government has become a self-generating monstrosity. Abraham Lincoln talked at length about a government of the people, by the people, for the people. What we now have is a government of the people, by the bureaucrats, including legislators who have themselves become bureaucrats, and for the bureaucrats.[2]

Yet government cannot provide progress because it cannot create. It can only take and reallocate. It cannot produce anything, including jobs, that it did not arbitrarily seize in the first place. For fiscal policy is effectively little more than a "zero-sum" game wherein government cannot give in stimulus that which it did not first confiscate in taxes.

Because "bureaucratic transaction costs" systematically attenuate the earnings of private businesses, thereby undermining their global trade competitiveness, moreover, the afflicted jurisdiction, through downsizing and industrial out-migration, invariably continues to lose higher-paying production jobs that, as the "outsourcing" phenomenon makes clear, are, at times, often replaced with lower-paying service ones.

In seeking prospective remedy to the resulting deteriorating jobs and incomes situation, it is critical to bear in mind that the facts of life remain largely economic. Healthy macroeconomies produce robust private economic well-being, whereas deteriorating ones precipitate correspondingly adverse consequences. Unemployment is economic. Welfare is economic. Crime is economic. Unaffordable health care is economic. America's world, therefore, is one that is unequivocally economically-driven.

Americans, as good citizens who accept this reality, are willing to pay taxes—but they concurrently seek, and expect, value for their tax investments. In attempting to meet this reasonable expectation, the key policy question thus becomes: how does government within a democracy, faced with the need to win favor with voters by filling insatiable consumer demands, still preserve private property earned through the pursuit of profit motive while, at the same time, limiting the growth of government to control the public debt and deficit?

Mindful that the burgeoning public cost of mounting bureaucratic complexity is the internal undoing of most civilizations—a determination vividly sustained by the findings of this inquiry—defining the proper role of government within the lives of the citizens of the embryonic nation was indeed a clear concern of the nation's Founders. As articulated by her first president George Washington: "Government is not reason; it is not eloquence. It is force. Like a fire, it is a dangerous servant and a fearful master."[3]

John Adams, in 1772, similarly asserted that "the only maxim of a free government should be to trust no man living with the power to endanger liberty."[4] To these ends, James Madison, in *Federalist Paper No. 10*, compellingly warned against "that old trick of turning every contingency into a new resource for accumulating force within the government."[5] Whereas, the "First American Democrat," Thomas Jefferson, similarly wrote:

> The natural progress of things is for liberty to yield and government to gain. . . .
> The greatest calamity that could befall us would be submission to a government of unlimited powers. . . .

> The public debt is the greatest danger to be feared by a republican government. To preserve our independence, we must not let rulers load us with perpetual debt. We must make our choice between economy and liberty, or profusion and servitude.[6]

Somewhat later in his career, Jefferson would despairingly add: "Were we to be directed from Washington when to sow and when to reap, we would soon want for our bread!"[7]

Thus, the issues of government's proper role and the tax costs required to sustain it are long-standing. John Locke, the late seventeenth-century British philosopher-statesman whose conservative political ideas inspired the Founding Fathers, believed that not debt but the "preservation of private property" should be the ultimate end of government; whereas his slightly later eighteenth-century French counterpart, Montesquieu, in like manner, maintained that public taxes were no more than that part of any person's property relinquished in order to secure protection for that part which remained.[8]

Operating within this ideological framework of an overarching sense of public need to protect private possessions, then, the "republican" Alexander Hamilton espoused that "a national debt can be unto us a blessing," while the "democrat" Thomas Jefferson believed that "limiting the purpose and size of government" could best meet the private property needs of "workers, farmers, and small businessmen—the nation's citizens at large."[9]

Indeed, this was America's explicit "social contract" with her people, as delineated by Jefferson within the Declaration of Independence, the legally recognized principle that all were "created equal and endowed by their Creator with certain inalienable rights, among them, life, liberty, and the pursuit of happiness"—not happiness itself per se, but instead a level playing field in its pursuit.

That meant that the American people could not be bound by the sovereign will of the British king to pay taxes to sustain His Majesty's empire. For in the new United States, the people would reign sovereign, with the government reduced to the role of servant set up with a limited, carefully circumscribed mandate to fulfill with consent of the governed in the course of safeguarding their private rights.[10]

Today, however, the demarcation of the respective ideological roles among the parties has become less clear. For while Hamilton's Republican political heirs now preach, if not always practice, fiscal responsibility and balanced budgets, they instead preside over record federal deficits. Jefferson's Democrats, on the other hand, despite his aspirations to limited government, have come to believe that larger, more assertive government is necessary to achieve their income redistribution goals.

Yet ironically, the very programs that they espouse are today devastating Jefferson's aspired prime constituency—those "workers, farmers, and small businessmen" who are the nation's productive citizens—as their onerous tax costs undermine and destroy the people's abilities to help themselves.

Indeed, in a tragic spiral, as the tax burden occasioned by those costs grow increasingly more onerous, still more citizens are forced into the public-sector dependency cycle at the expense of those productive citizens who remain. Thus it is that, to paraphrase Tom Brokaw's epic documentary of the World War II era, *The Greatest Generation*, the lineal successors to that noble "generation that gave" have now been transformed into "the generation that took."[11]

Benjamin Franklin once averred that "nothing is certain except death and taxes"—the modern response to which is: "At least death never gets any worse!" But though such tax-consuming "big government" has long historic precedent, today its role is expanding in an unprecedented way—as business management expert Peter Drucker, in a seminal work, *The Age of Discontinuity*, concludes:

> There is mounting evidence that government is big rather than strong; that it is flabby rather than powerful; that it costs a great deal but doesn't achieve very much.
>
> There is mounting evidence also that citizens less and less believe in government and are becoming increasingly disenchanted with it. Government is sick—and at a time when we need strong, healthy government.[12]

The effects of such bloated government, which some have called "demosclerosis," can be devastating. Throughout the course of history, the world's great imperial powers—third-century Rome, ninth-century Baghdad, sixteenth-century Spain, and nineteenth-century Britain—empires whose ascendancies were all initially founded upon the inherent strengths of durable private economies that enabled them to be net exporters of capital—all eventually lost their global primacies due to the mounting taxes needed to cover burgeoning public debt produced by domestic fiscal excess.[13]

Such a danger clearly was a foremost concern at the time of the founding of the American Republic as well. Indeed, Jefferson, in many missives, argued to the effect that "loading up the nation with debt and leaving it for the following generation to pay is morally irresponsible. No nation has a right to contract debt for a period longer than the person contracting it can expect to live."[14]

Accordingly, upon reflection, he called upon the fledgling American democracy to

> Declare in the Constitution that they are forming that neither the legislature nor the nation can validly contract more debt than they can pay. . . .
>
> I wish it were possible to obtain a single amendment to our Constitution. I would be willing to depend upon that alone for reduction of administration of

government to the genuine principles of its Constitution. What I mean is an additional article taking from the federal government the power of borrowing.[15]

The Founding Fathers were thus attuned to the lessons of economic history as well as to the sage scriptural admonition that "a good man leaveth an inheritance to his children."[16]

Historically, in fact, America has long honored an implicit social contract to leave a productive legacy for her offspring. But today, a wantonly permissive public sector shortsightedness has set in that has left that contract in shambles. For in blithely passing off the burgeoning federal debt to her lineage, America stands in direct contravention of both historic warning and divine admonition—as generations yet unborn will bear the burden of the current budgetary process. In so doing, a group is unabashedly being taxed that has no vote—an act that precipitated the Founding Fathers' original political revolt: "taxation without representation," which they equated with tyranny.

Accordingly, the American Revolution of 1776 was, at its roots, a capitalistic revolution—a protest against the attempts by England's King George III to tyrannically impose his country's interventionist, anticapitalist system of mercantilism upon the colonies. As a consequence, foremost among the grievances in the Declaration of Independence were numerous economic ones.[17]

Complaining of the English king's tax collectors, Jefferson wrote: "He has erected a multitude of New Offices and sent hither swarms of Officers to harass our People and eat their substance." The Declaration also condemned the king for his protectionist trade policies: "For cutting off our Trade with all parts of the world."[18]

The king likewise was denounced for "imposing Taxes on us without our consent." Such protests came after a series of tax levies—the Navigation Acts, the Townshend Acts, the Stamp Act, and the Tea Act most noteworthy among them—imposed by imperial decree over the three decades leading up to 1776—significantly increased tariffs and taxation on the colonies.[19]

Hence, numerous specific safeguards were built into the Constitution of 1789. The Contracts Clause prohibited any laws abridging freedom of contract. The Commerce Clause outlawed protectionist tariffs in interstate commerce, thereby making the country a quasi-free-trade zone. The Due Process Clause protected private property by stipulating that no person "shall be deprived of life, liberty, or property without due process of law"; the Constitution likewise mandated that all taxation as then conceived be uniform in its levies.[20]

Consequently, the system of limited federal government contemplated by the Founding Fathers was framed by two provisions of the Constitution. As delineated in Article I, Section 8, Congress was specifically granted the powers to "lay and collect Taxes, Duties, Imposts, and Excises, to pay the Debts and provide for the common Defense and general Welfare of the United States; but all Duties, Imposts, and Excises shall be uniform throughout the United States."[21]

This power, however, was concurrently circumscribed by the Tenth Amendment, which, as noted, stipulates that those powers not expressly delegated to the federal government are forbidden to it.[22] Succinctly put, then, the federal government was empowered to, and limited to, provide for the "common Defense and general Welfare of the United States," which as defined by Article 1, Section 8, consists of seventeen discrete functions, cited in their order of appearance within the text of the amendment as follows:

1. contracting debt;
2. regulating foreign commerce;
3. establishing rules for naturalization;
4. collecting taxes and coining money;
5. establishing weights and measures;
6. punishing counterfeiting;
7. establishing a postal system and roads;
8. promoting science;
9. establishing a judicial system;
10. punishing pirates;
11. declaring war;
12. raising and supporting armies;
13. providing for a navy;
14. regulating naval and land forces;
15. calling forth the militia;
16. organizing the militia; and
17. administering the nation's capital

The Founders thus had a distinct, yet discrete, vision for America's administration framed as one of limited governance. Indeed, indicative of its circumscription, the fiscal model constructed below reflects how the FY 2007 federal budget would have looked had Congress incorporated within it just those seventeen functions that it can legally incorporate pursuant to the Article I, Section 8, "Duties and Responsibilities" prescriptions of the Constitution—while stripping out those functions expressly prohibited to it and reserved for the states and the people by the Tenth Amendment.

The regression, which employs estimated budgetary outlays, by function, for FY 2007 are presented in table 6.1.

"General welfare" functions, again cited as numerically delineated, are presented in table 6.2.

Table 6.1. "Common Defense" Functions, Cited as Categorically Delineated Within the Budget

Budget Category: Cost:	(U.S. $ Millions)
Common Defense:	
050 Total National Defense = —which includes: • punishing pirates • declaring war • raising & supporting armies • providing for a navy • regulating naval & land forces • calling forth the militia • organizing the militia	$571,869
700 Cost of Veterans Benefits =	$72,401
920 Homeland Security = —which includes: establishing rules for naturalization	$7,428
TOTAL =	$651,698

Source: *Budget of the United States, FY 2008*

The results produced by such a constitutionally prescribed and pro-scribed federal budget are thus extraordinary—revealing that by strict ad-herence to the Founding Fathers' fiscal mandate, the country could have eliminated all federal income taxation and still have produced a $431 bil-lion annual budget surplus in FY 2007 (see table 6.3).

Thus it may be shown that inordinate income taxation is the costly price that America pays for the "New Deal" and the "Great Society." The data fur-ther reveal that a succession of such annual budgetary surpluses using static revenue projections would enable the country to eliminate its present $9 trillion-plus federal debt—now standing at over at $30,000 for each and every citizen—in less than two decades. Alternately, assuming dynamic rev-enue scoring of the economic stimulus projected to be produced by elimi-nation of U.S. income taxation in its entirety, would result in the national debt being repaid within a decade.

Indeed, the results would be more remarkable still had just *those discrete portions* of the Department of Defense, Homeland Security, State Depart-ment, Justice Department, and Department of Transportation budgets that were the Founders' original intent been employed.

These budgets were nonetheless incorporated intact within the model both because they are integrally integrated national functions that the indi-vidual states cannot now be reasonably expected to unilaterally perform on

Table 6.2. "General Welfare" Functions, again Cited as Numerically Delineated

Budget Category: Cost:	(U.S. $ Millions)
B. General Welfare:	
900 Treasury Functions— which include: contracting debt; and collecting taxes and coining money = —Total Net Interest on Debt: $239,153 —Treasury Functions —IRS: $10,438 —U.S. Mint: $1,950	$251,541
50 Total International Affairs —which includes: regulating foreign commerce =	$35,071
372/400—which include: Establishing a postal system & roads = which includes: 372—Postal Service: −$5,715 (= off-budget revenue) 400—Total Transportation $74,607	$68,892
370—which includes: establishing weights and measures = which is the current responsibility of the: —National Institutes for Science & Technology	$558
250—which includes: promoting science which includes: —Total Federal Science & Technology =	$24,862
750—which includes: punishing counterfeiting; and establishing a judicial system = which include: —Total Administration of Justice which incorporates: —Federal Judicial Activities: $9,756 —Federal Law Enforcement: $24,846	$35,407
800 which includes: Administering the nation's capital = which includes: —Legislative Functions: $3,141 —Executive Functions: $517 —Payments to District of Columbia: $278	$3,936
TOTAL:	$420,267
AGGREGATE TOTAL FY 2007 FEDERAL BUDGET AS PRESCRIBED BY THE FOUNDING FATHERS:	$1,071,965

Source: *Budget of the United States, FY 2008*

Table 6.3.   Balancing the Federal Budget the Constitutional Way

Category:	(U.S. $ Millions)
• Total Estimated FY 2007 Federal Budgetary Outlays:	$2,784,267
• Total Estimated Actual Individual and Corporate Income Tax Collections FY 2007:	$1,510,900
Total FY 2007 Federal Budget If Constructed IAW the Founding Fathers' Constitutional Mandate:	$1,071,965
• Amount Available to Reduce the Federal Deficit after Achieving a Balanced Federal Budget While Also Eliminating All Federal U.S. Income Taxation:	$438,935

behalf of their residents and also to preclude equivocation over just what part of a given budget, say the defense budget, is actually "defense" and the like. Amazing what America could accomplish if she would just elect Congresses committed to the rule of law!

The Crescendoing of Complexity

Is constitutionally mandated federal budgeting an unreasonable aspiration? From economic and historic standpoints, certainly not. Nearly two and a half centuries ago Adam Smith defined the functions of government thusly:

> First, the duty of protecting the society from the violence and invasion of other independent societies; second, the duty of protecting, insofar as possible, every member of the society from the injustice and oppression of every other member of it . . . thirdly, the duty of erecting and maintaining certain public works and public institutions, which can never be for the interest of any individual, or small number of individuals, to erect and maintain.[23]

In sum, the concept that the Founding Fathers and their erudite contemporaries clearly had in mind in terms of limited governance and the monolithic behemoth into which the federal government has now evolved today stand at significant variance. The defining difference focuses on two points: (1) the Founders intended the federal government to provide for the *general* welfare of the people, not for *special interest* welfare; and (2) they did not contemplate Congressional usurpation of its constitutionally defined powers through such egregious acts as ripping off the sacrosanct "people's trust," the Social Security Trust Fund, to finance its self-serving political ends.

Because of such convictions firmly held by the nation's architects, then, prior to the Civil War, the national government was a minuscule, relatively weak, administrative institution. But, that posture would dramatically change with the war effort and its aftermath—as new departments were now added: Agriculture (1862), Justice (1870), Commerce (1903), and Labor (1913). New administrative agencies also soon naturally followed in their wake, as the federal government assumed control over immigration in the 1870s and established the Interstate Commerce Commission to regulate railroads in 1890, and so forth.[24]

This rapid mushrooming of government, and the attendant bureaucratic appetite that it engendered, continued its relentless escalation through the twentieth century—with World War I, the Great Depression, World War II, the "Great Society," and the Vietnam War prime contributors to the expansion— to the extent that today, government's "wants" have outrun its needs, in so doing, overriding the Constitution's limitation of its mandate.

As a consequence, federal, state, and local taxes now confiscate 47 percent of personal income—while regulation consumes another 10 percent—for a total of 57 percent—meaning that for every eight-hour day worked by an American, over 4.5 hours go to the costs of sustaining governance.

In this process of economic enervation, then, through bureaucracy funded by taxation, it punishes the many to reward the few. It decides which of those businesses—which provide the best goods and services at the lowest price—become too big or too successful as a result, and hence must be destroyed.

Pursuit of the "Great Society" has thus done nothing less than to destroy that sense of self-responsibility that made possible the freedoms that the nation's citizens once took for granted. How did a supposed democratic system allow such an egregious autocratic usurpation of political power and the public trust to happen on its watch?

The answer is forthright. Such proliferation of big government commenced innocuously a century and a half ago, largely in response to the Civil War. To confront internal resource challenges, conscription was introduced, a national income tax was levied, and the country was inundated with paper money—all violations of the Constitution.

Indeed, by 1865, the federal government's budget was twenty times larger than a mere half decade before. But though some of the draconian wartime impositions were subsequently repealed, the tax die was firmly cast, the precedent now set. A new world had evolved wherein bureaucratic needs superseded constitutional mandates, prescriptions, and proscriptions. In the noble process of freeing the slaves, government had usurped the role of master for itself.[25]

The pre–World War I so-called Progressive Era exacerbated the governmental mushrooming problem further still. Federal regulation, which had begun with oversight of the railroads in the late 1800s, was soon expanded to include "big oil," steel, and any other industry deemed critical to the national economic interest.

To cope with mounting public costs, the federal income tax was reintro-
duced in 1913, and that same year gave birth to the Federal Reserve System,
which, at its inception, was designed to keep the economy growing productively by regulating monetary supply, but soon presided over the nation's worst banking crisis in history and the "Great Depression" instead.[26]

Concurrently, the Federal Trade Commission and the Interstate Commerce Commission were contrived to regulate which products and services
consumers are allowed to buy. America's formal entry into World War I then
brought with it reintroduction of the draft, food rationing, and new maximum marginal income tax rates of 77 percent.[27]

The "New Deal"—set into motion by Herbert Hoover but formally forged
by Franklin Roosevelt—was another incredibly ill-contrived scheme to employ the Federal Reserve to put more money into the economy to address
perceived fiscal imbalances. When initially, however, the policy created
price inflation instead, the Federal Reserve reversed itself and took money
out of circulation, producing the stock market crash of 1929, in the process
precipitating a moderate recession.

In response, President Hoover tried to jump-start the economy with an
injection of massive federal spending, which in four years increased by
65 percent, and pressured private firms to keep prices artificially high—
producing massive unemployment and a glut of unsold products, thereby,
through proactive "governmental help," transforming what may have been
little more than the typical life cycle of a slightly more than routine recession into the onset of the Great Depression.[28]

Taking office in 1933, President Roosevelt built upon the misguided
Hoover policies, tripling the size of government within eight years. The net
result was that government now became a net intruder in practically every
aspect of U.S. economic activity—regulating life and business through new
taxes, price supports, and onerous rules, as the maximum marginal federal
income rate rose to 94 percent.[29]

Indeed, under Roosevelt, between 1933 and 1940, federal spending doubled while federal levies—in the forms of higher personal and corporate income taxes, higher excise taxes, higher estate and gift taxes, and the social
security payroll tax—rose as a percentage of GDP from 3.5 percent in 1933
to 6.9 percent in 1940. Concurrently, his disastrous National Industrial Recovery Act fixed arbitrary, artificial, above-market retail prices—as the federal government gradually mutated into a bureaucratic monster that replaced
the consumer as the prime governor of the market.[30]

The predictable resulting economic devastation, therefore, was no accident but was instead integral to Roosevelt's socialistic fiscal doctrine, which,
in an ominous message to Congress on April 27, 1942, proclaimed:"No
American citizen ought to have a net income, after he has paid his taxes, of
more than $25,000 per year."

To make sure that this point was not lost on his new legions of tax-collecting bureaucrats, he concurrently commenced federal income tax withholding from private paychecks, publicly promoted as a "pay as you go" tax scheme—a self-serving public-sector measure whose opportunity costs to American taxpayers today exceed $24 billion in interest payments each and every year.[31]

So antibusiness were FDR's "New Deal" public policies, in fact, that, in the express words of contemporary newspaper columnist Walter Lippman, the so-called reformers would:

> rather not have a recovery if revival of private initiative means a resumption of private control in the management of corporate business . . . as the essence of the New Deal is the reduction of private corporate control by collective bargaining and labor legislation on the one side, and by restrictive, competitive, and deterrent governmental action on the other.[32]

Though this great regulatory intrusion quite naturally and predictably profoundly altered America's structured economic life—dismantling the constitutional limits to federal power via a vast transference of economic power from the nation's private to public sector—it did not initially, at least, overarchingly undermine those dimensions to her national character comprised of citizens committed to self-responsibility for their own well-being.

Rather, it took Lyndon Johnson and his "Great Society" in the mid-1960s to do that, forever altering the linkage of reward to earning that had characterized, and indeed generated, the first two centuries of American prosperity. In its stead, and as a direct consequence of the resulting failed public benevolence, the so-called nanny state has come to shackle the past half century of the nation's poor to a regiment of bureaucratic servitude.[33]

Indeed, while as late as 1960 the federal government had little to do with welfare, education, and crime control, by 1975, it dominated them all, setting their rules while subsidizing their existence—with the nation paying a heavy price today in enduring an economy grievously attenuated by bureaucratic overburden.

In sum, the federal government in the twentieth century arrogated to itself massive monolithic powers not assumed in the nineteenth century and certainly never contemplated by the Founding Fathers. As sequentially, in an eroding downward spiral over the past century and a half:[34]

1. The Civil War era transformed the federal government into a polity superior to the states and to the people;
2. The Progressive Era established the precept that the federal government is responsible for the economy;

3. The New Deal established the notion that no area of life is off-limits to government; and
4. The Great Society destroyed that sense of self-responsibility that initially had made possible America's great prosperity and freedoms. As Ronald Reagan later famously lamented: "LBJ fought a big-government spending war on poverty, and poverty won."[35]

In aggregate, this liberal handiwork has thus left America's historic "democratic capitalistic social contract" with her people in chaos—and in a manner wholly oblivious to the cogent lessons of economic history—articulating a litany littered with the triage that occurs when bureaucrats can't keep their hands off a free-market economy.

The examples are legion. A century ago, exporting beef and wheat had helped make Argentina one of the world's wealthiest nations. But by the late 1940s, after dictator Juan Peron introduced pervasive economic controls, there were chronic beef shortages in what was once a land of plenty, forcing his people to subsist on bread.[36]

Russia likewise had been a major grain exporter, but the Bolshevik Revolution and decades of its "five-year plans" likewise brought shortages of grain—and practically everything else that people wanted—until the economy ultimately collapsed and the Soviet Union itself literally disappeared from the map in 1991. In China during the late 1950s, Chairman Mao Zedong also ruthlessly enforced public controls over what people could and must produce, with the tragic consequence a famine in which as many as thirty million people died.

The lessons learned, then, are these: wherever there is dictatorial control over an economy—even if the dictator has been democratically elected—and whenever economic liberties are denied, the aspirations and well-being of the citizens invariably decline to ultimate exhaustion.[37]

Notwithstanding such a steady devolution, however, there are noteworthy examples of sterling public-sector achievement. Among them, the U.S. military is a spectacular American public success story—as the nation spends a half-trillion dollars each year on defense—more than Russia, China, India, Japan, and all of Europe combined—to sustain the most powerful defense capability ever assembled relative to contemporaries of the age.

Indeed, thanks in large part to the foresight of Ronald Reagan in the 1980s, the qualitative edge enjoyed by the American military became such that, by 1990, the era of Desert Storm, no other country could compete with it in accuracy, mobility, or lethality.

Even today, despite disastrous Clinton-era military cutbacks, there is no martial counterbalance or competing funding source—as America's $13 trillion GDP equals that of Germany, France, the United Kingdom, Japan, and China, and it is more than that of all twenty-five countries of the European Union combined.[38]

Even so, however, at the bottom line, in its bureaucratic mode, the U.S. war-making capability remains a governmental program subject to petty, partisan public-sector oversight. Its future likewise stands in further peril because government itself generally doesn't work.

And as with all federal programs hamstrung by the inefficiencies of their bureaucracies, while the U.S. military is far more than just the post office in fatigues, it nonetheless administratively confronts many of the same parochial challenges confronted by typical bureaucracies, and is now simultaneously increasingly hampered by incessant meddling congressional oversight in its field operations as well.[39]

Accordingly, the case for systemic federal administrative reform could not be more compelling; as America remains a nation governed by monolithic late nineteenth-century federal public institutions and policies explicitly created to solve early twentieth-century socioeconomic problems. Indeed, "modern government," as most now know it, is a relic of the aftermath of the 1880s civil-service reform movement.

Yet this is an anachronism that cannot persevere—for to prevail in the modern global marketplace, a modern nation desperately needs a streamlined approach to governance addressed to twenty-first-century information age challenges.

Yet this nearly axiomatic public policy reality indelibly handwritten on the fiscal wall notwithstanding, America now finds herself frenetically attempting to provide twenty-first-century economic government while functioning at a nineteenth-century administrative pace—conjuring up vivid images of Cray computers operated by a run-amok bureaucracy framed within a backdrop of ink bottles, quill pens, gaslights, green shades, and ornate rolltop desks.

The examples of obsolescent bureaucratic dinosaurs roaming the inner environs of the Washington Beltway are legion. The Department of Commerce is advanced as the nation's frontline federal development agency. Yet it is regulation driven and woefully ill structured to promote balanced twenty-first-century economic growth—frequently requiring to promulgate a single policy as many as twenty-seven layers of bureaucratic management approval, or often even more, between the deputy assistant secretary and cabinet secretary levels.

Its obsolescent research and regulatory functions likewise were formulated in an age when mass assembly production operations were coming to the fore more than a century ago. Certainly, they are inadequately equipped to provide the levels of forward-looking collaborative technological research and policy vision needed to succeed in the dynamic new "information age."

Indeed, if the logo on the portal in the lobby of the CIA building at Langley—"You shall know the truth, and the truth shall keep you free"— accurately signals that agency's vital mission, then an analogous one prominently posted on the portals of the Herbert Hoover Commerce Building might appropriately warn business people: "Abandon all hope all ye who enter here!"

The Department of Agriculture has similarly grown big—its aggregate workforce size soon to rival the number of farmers in America—without concurrently growing strong in its ability to support modern farming. At the same time, the Treasury Department often appears more determined to, and more appropriate for, penalizing U.S. business interests than promoting them—and the Justice Department, of late, has likewise gotten into the business of forging new "industrial policy" by challenging the operational efficiencies of some of the nation's most successful corporations.

At an historic juncture in the nation's economic history when developing state-of-the-art workforce skills is paramount in global competition, moreover, federally funded job training programs remain monolithic, largely unstructured, inefficient mosaics of well-intended but ineffective "bureaucratic cures." Clearly, if America is to prevail within the modern global market, massive executive institutional reorganization is required.

Because the nation's public-policy management institutions are outdated and unresponsive to modern marketplace demand, moreover, the administrative rules that they develop and over which they preside are correspondingly arcane. Ownership and management of the nation's dynamic cellular telephone industry—one of its fastest-growing business sectors at more than 40 percent per year—for instance, continue to be governed by eight-decades-old FCC regulations designed to control operations of "1930s commercial radios."

The net result of all of this bottom-line "bureaucratic mission creep," of course, is that the index alone to the Code of Federal Regulations consists of now more than a thousand pages, spanning some fifty separate volumes, and is mushrooming each year. Americans are concurrently finding it increasingly difficult to pay their taxes not only because they are overtaxed, but also because the process itself is becoming increasingly difficult—as the U.S. Internal Revenue Code contains more than 7.5 million words, runs 16,845 pages, and is utterly unintelligible to anyone other than a trained professional.[40]

By contrast, the U.S. Constitution and its Bill of Rights are less than ten pages long combined—and upon reading those hallowed pages, it becomes readily evident that the Founding Fathers had no intention of permitting the state to claw its way ever deeper into citizens' daily lives.

Small wonder that a late 2006 CNN poll found that an overwhelming majority of Americans believe that the size and cost of their government are unwieldy and obtrusive; that 54 percent believe that government is "trying to do too many things that should be left to individuals and businesses"; and that only 37 percent believe that government should be seeking to do more.[41]

In increasing numbers, then, the American people are coming to know better. They have realized that government rarely solves the problems that it purports to solve; in fact, it usually merely reconfigures them. More profoundly, they have come to understand that life dependency upon government is not only impoverishing, it is utterly impoverished.

It is no accident, therefore, that the nation's voting trends for the past quarter century have been for much more limited government, despite the fact that the Congress itself has been slow in appreciating the magnitude of that message issuing from the street.[42]

Much of this systemic governmental inefficiency directly stems, of course, from the traditionally reflexive knee-jerk nature of the policy formulation process itself. For public problems invariably emerge in the form of "crises"—and the remedies proposed address immediate symptoms rather than their underlying causes. Superficial manifestations are treated, therefore, without their systemic determinants ever being effectively explored.

Yet when the actual causes are ultimately, and quite predictably, not abated by the short-term patchwork solutions, are the palliatives ever repealed? To the contrary, they are too often merely amended into infinite complexity until even the original purpose of the precipitating initiative is lost.

Thus it is that bureaucratic inefficiency and institutional obsolescence accrete within the federal system—to such a metastasizing degree that today, it is near axiomatic in definition that a dinosaur is a "governmentally owned lizard" and a pelican a bureaucratic compromise between a peacock and a swan.

Such ineffective, self-perpetuating public-sector approaches to the serious challenges of advanced technology development required to sustain global trade competitiveness obviously cannot continue if the nation is to remain an economic superpower.

Together with institutional reform, therefore, must come public policy management reform, and, to this end, prioritization of the commitment of finite public-sector resources—financial, physical, and human—becomes quintessential, while employing evaluative criteria that unequivocally distinguish the "indispensably vital" from the "merely useful."

In this process, policy makers must productively begin by more vividly conceptualizing and formulating the nation's requisite development policy goals—seeking to determine what their aspired concepts and tangible measures of progress really are—concurrently cognizant that such definition can be ambiguous and more illusive than it superficially seems.

As it is here that top-to-bottom critical reexamination of prevailing public-policy evaluative practice is invoked—reflecting a realization of the need for explicitly "benchmarked" criteria to measure progress, with the milestones established explicitly retrofitted to their specific operating milieus.

The need for exacting bureaucratic qualitative and quantitative analysis is intuitively obvious. In a country where cannibals prevail, where cannibalism is deemed moral, for instance, is it a sign of progress if the cannibal learns to eat with a knife and fork and eats only fishermen on Friday?[43]

In equal measure, in a nation that would aspire to greater administrative and fiscal responsibility, is it a mark of progress to perpetuate long-standing failed statist policies that are the essence of "big government" and, when they predictably fail, to repackage them as budget-breaking cornerstones of economic change.

Such is not good governance. It is instead its antithesis—the moral equivalent of running up huge bills on one's children's credit card while on a drunken binge. But doesn't logic suggest that if one's basic ideological premises are flawed, the policies that issue from them will be flawed as well?

For when the "bureaucratic cure" becomes the problem—as today it undeniably has—still more failed public-sector decision-making paradigms are invariably invoked and implemented until they ultimately reach the point where, piled one upon the other, their accumulation comes to resemble the federal government itself, which is precisely what it is—a nonresponsive aggregate of remedies mistargeted to superficial symptoms rather than to underlying causes.

As such, there are no "magic cures"—for such futile attempts, in themselves, create new problems faster than they solve old ones—as the problem creation process itself comes to subordinate, and eventually suffocate, any lingering hope for problem solution that may be genuine.

But this too should come as no surprise. For while the self-presumed wisdom required to manage the newly created problems grows geometrically, the knowledge needed to administer the requisite solutions grows merely arithmetically. The result, therefore, is one that starts as a contrived, top-down micromanaged bureaucratic fiscal panacea and evolves into an out-of-control, Jurassic bureaucratic monolith.

Yet isn't there a certain logic to suggest that the economy, and society itself, would be better off if America were to shed her penchant for liberal public-sector placebos and unfetter the "invisible hand" to let those natural free-market forces that have clearly stood the test of time work their economic wonders once again?

For as the lessons of economic history clearly teach, government most often does indeed "help best by helping least." In such instances, then, the causes both of prosperity and of freedom are better served by backing off and letting the private sector operate within the framework of Adam Smith's "invisible hand" of free-market process do what it does best. As a seemingly amazed economist Robert Samuelson recently concluded: "The less we understand the economy, the better it seemingly does!"[44]

Today, the economic numbers are clearly not on America's side. Total federal budgetary outlays grew by 46.3 percent between FY 2000 and FY 2007. The Congressional Budget Office projects them to grow at a minimum of another 41.3 percent through FY 2015. Demographics, as noted, likewise work to the national disadvantage as members of the baby boomer generation age.

The rising costs of health care, in particular, will contribute to the growth of programs for the elderly and low-income beneficiaries. As a consequence, total federal spending for Social Security, Medicare, and Medicaid, in itself, is projected to grow 25 percent faster than the economy at large over the next decade.[45]

Thereafter, moreover, if health care costs continue to exceed that of the economy, its requisite budgetary outlays will claim an even greater share of federal spending as the percentage of the population aged sixty-five or older continues to rise. Thus, in the long term, the increased resources required for such programs will exert pressures on the federal budget that will render current fiscal policies unsustainable.[46]

How We Got From "There" to "Here"

Preceding analysis has shown that America's government wasn't always dysfunctional, nor was it designed to be. Instead, it is clear, it was built upon the solid foundations of noble precepts derived from time-tested precedents devised by the Founding Fathers—foremost among them the capacity to deliver to citizens the blessings of "life, liberty, and the pursuit of happiness."

Indeed, in forging the nation's new political model, Benjamin Franklin explicitly acknowledged in his Constitutional Convention address in 1787: "We have gone back to ancient history for models of government, and examined the different forms of those Republics . . . and we have viewed modern states all round Europe."[47]

But two centuries—and modern political reality—intrude, and the resultant evolution has not been unequivocally positive. Thus today, because of bureaucratic incompetence in the pursuit of political excess, the nation is falling short of its historic promise.

Family values are declining, as the burden of taxes and regulation has too often forced both parents into the job market. As a consequence, children are not getting the home discipline that leads to educational excellence. Concomitantly, failing K–12 schools are turning out functional illiterates;

and the resulting disparities in education are dividing the nation into one of "haves" and "have nots."

Federal fiscal data document the extent of government's complicity in this devolution—that administrative complexity and its attendant bureaucratic costs, cancerous outgrowths of governance that precipitated the demise of Rome, are similarly threatening America today. Its manifestations are increasingly omnipresent and include the following grim realities.

- The government created to ensure the pursuit of happiness in liberty now runs up the costs of everything that consumers buy through excessive regulation.
- A government that can't carry out timely mail deliveries wants to control citizens' health care.
- A government that can't keep the peace in its own capital too often sends its troops on "peacekeeping" missions around the world.
- A government that can't teach children how to read nonetheless seeks to inculcate them with a faith in liberally favored social-engineering theories.
- The court system established to preside over a religious nation is now determined to drive every vestige of religion from its public, and often private, sectors.
- The government set up to protect private property now arbitrarily confiscates it in the name of *eminent domain* and other causes that it deems to serve the "public good"—in many cases, merely to consign it to a "higher economic use" to generate greater tax revenues for itself.
- As a consequence, the cost of government at all levels today takes more than 47 percent of the average citizens' paychecks—up from 7 percent in 1916 and 28 percent in1950.

Add in the more than 10 percent of national income in hidden regulatory costs, and it becomes readily evident that government consumes some 57 percent of all the earnings that the nation's workers had intended as commitments to sustain their daily lives—in effect, cutting potential private living standards by significantly more than half.[48]

This reality means that the average taxpayer works until the beginning of August each year for government before he or she starts working for himself or herself. And while some may be willing to pass a portion of that cost along to their children in the form of deficits, the interest on that debt must be paid annually, and now increases exponentially.

As a consequence, for many, the American Dream has become an ever-more-distant mirage—with John Kennedy's "boats lifted by the rising tide" now foundering in their moorings on a seemingly insurmountable bureaucratic reef. As today, government decides what products consumers buy;

whether they can have access to life-saving drugs; the lowest wages that employers can pay, often creating massive unemployment in the process; and the terms and conditions whereby small businesses can raise job-creating capital. The true tragedy in all of this political posturing is that at the bottom line, at the societal level, nothing the government does is voluntary. Everything it does is compulsory, either

- forcing someone to do something;
- forcing someone to pay for something; or
- forcibly preventing someone from doing something.[49]

Put another way, today government is society's monopolistic purveyor of coercion. It has no other raison d'être. Its ability to use force is the essence of modern law—a function that once began so nobly as servant to the people has now mutated into their oppressive master—for the whole business of authority is, by definition, to interfere in people's business. The mob is a mere fringe competitor by comparison.

Yet many contemporary socioeconomic problems evolve in areas wherein government has neither constitutional authority nor inherent competence—because that is not what it was designed to do. Nonetheless, it has snatched from otherwise responsible citizens responsibility for everything at whim, taxing away their God-given abilities to provide for their own well-beings—and then, moving in to fill the resulting void, offers the tender loving care of bureaucracies instead.

But since problems are the excuse for government, solving them is out of the question—for they have now become its constituency.[50] Why is this bad public policy? Here are but a few of the reasons:

- With government consuming nearly 60 percent of national income, in far too many families, both parents have to work, leaving children to learn about life on their own.
- Its welfare incentives undermine both family structures and community values.
- Its minimum-wage laws keep people from getting jobs and therefore from learning on-the-job skills.
- Its schools too often even work against parentally inspired values, teaching that somehow earned wealth is evil, that societal values are more important than family ones, and that one's own culture should not be foremost in a child's affections, thereby vitiating patriotic aspirations.
- In sum, it is destroying that socioeconomic mode of democratic capitalism that was the Founders' cherished vision—substituting the IRS for the traditional family and community, and offering its embedded statist values in remedy for the nation's every social problem.[51]

It was not always so. America's founding was, as has been shown, special in the world. It wasn't her natural resources or national character that made her great—through she has them in abundance. What made her unique was freedom—freedom *from* government—the first nation ever whose federal government was constrained by its constitution to a prescribed, but limited, number of fixed duties.

Anything not explicitly specified by it, as prescribed, then, was reserved to the states or to the people, if it was to be done at all. All else was forbidden, as the Ninth Amendment unequivocally stipulates: "The enumeration in the Constitution of certain rights shall not be construed to deny or disparage others retained by the people."

Yet today, the so-called multiculturalists argue that Constitution's safeguards are outdated and outmoded and should be subordinated to the pursuit of their particular parochial political interests. To these ends, historic constitutional safeguards have been bombarded with barrages of political correctness to effect self-serving social agendas. Indeed, in this quest, even direct extracts of those priceless constitutional safeguards embedded within the Bill of Rights have, at times, been voted down by recent Congresses.

In 1995, for instance, when Congressman Melvin Watt (D-NC), in a master stroke of legislative legerdemain, surreptitiously embedded the Fourth Amendment as an amendment to the ill-conceived and equally ill-fated Clinton crime bill then under debate to read: "provided that the right of the people to be secure in their persons, houses, papers, and effects, against unreasonable searches and seizures, shall not be violated; and no warrants shall issue, but upon probable cause, supported by oath or affirmation, and particularly describing the place to be searched, and the person or things to be seized"—it was defeated by the U.S. House of Representatives by a 303-121 vote.[52]

These were rights that could not be abridged. Yet somehow they have been summarily rejected by America's current elected and appointed leaders and self-assuming political elites. Where did the Founders' "grand experiment" go so wrong? When did government stop being servant and instead become master? Many argue that this civic devolution commenced with the Sixteenth Amendment empowering Congress to impose a federal income tax ratified in 1913. There is much to commend that argument, as the analysis that follows makes clear.[53]

WHAT MOTIVATES ECONOMIC MAN?

To fully fathom why the Founding Fathers' economic vision went so astoundingly awry, one must first understand the workings of business dynamics—profit motive—that fundamental factor that drives the aspirations of "economic man." As market history reveals that in the ascendancies of most free societies, a spiraling series of crucial economic interactions over time coalesce. To wit: that as man's *modus operandi* gradually ascends from merely acquiring the necessities of sheer survival to a more sedentary lifestyle, human ambitions concomitantly rise.

For *economic man* is "acquisitive man"—as his society matures, so do his objectives. In his quest for material gain, therefore, he is increasingly driven to convert current earnings into private savings in order to accumulate and commit "surplus capital" to investments that ensure his ability to procure future cherished goods and services. And these individual and collective savings, committed on the promise of a fair return, generate the investment funds that underwrite those productivity-enhancing technological breakthroughs that empower societies to progress.

It is free society's ability and willingness to divert those savings into noneconomic intellectual and aesthetic activities that produce the scientific, literary, and artistic achievements that are the hallmark of civilization. The accumulation of such wealth, in turn, enables its owners both to finance the development of "intellectual property" and to fund the activities of educational institutions.

It is the cumulative volume of a society's savings, made up of the contributions of its institutions and individual members, moreover, that ultimately determines its living standard—that liberates "economic man" from the need to focus exclusively upon basic necessities and, in the end, distinguishes between his merely eking out a living and attaining the highest levels of culture.

Though the desire to accumulate such "social overhead capital" is resilient, however, it would obviously be greatly diminished should some predatory external force—private mob extortion or public unjust governance, for example—arbitrarily intervene to expropriate the accumulated savings of individuals to fund its own objectives.

This is, in fact, precisely why communism died. It fell because it could not resolve the internal ideological contradictions between its steadfast commitment to radical equality and its belief that there was no need for incentives to individuals to optimize their full potentials—thereby rendering it largely incompatible with the motivational realities of human beings in a modern industrial age.

It follows, then, that those who would seek to restore or preserve a nation's historic economic strengths must commence by taking it back to its entrepreneurial roots—striving to reignite within it the competitive spirit of enterprising individuals while concurrently promoting both their desires to succeed and the rewards for those who actually do—cognizant that contrary to liberal contention, competition is not mean-spirited, acquisitive spirit is not selfishness, and profit is not greed. They are, in fact, the very factors that promote inventiveness.

Socialism, on the other hand, denies the workings of the free-market process and indeed is its antithesis, as it is contemptuous of individualism and personal achievement. Thus, socialism and freedom can never be effectively combined. Indeed, should an aspiring entrepreneurial nation ever cease to enjoy a "decade of greed," its underlying system of free democratic capitalism—historically capable of providing citizens with greater bounty than any other—will, at that moment, have commenced on its inexorable decline.

Yet modern nations are not the first to embark upon such a mistaken policy course, as the annals of economic history are strewn with the triage of imprudent tax and fiscal policies and replete with the political obituaries of those who tried to fool the market by masking private capital confiscation in the guise of serving the public good.

The reason for this stark reality is basic. "Profit motive" remains at the core of man's aspirations and accomplishments. Unfettered, it can be a powerful economic force. At the same time, it is perishable. It can be destroyed by inordinate taxation; and it can be ruined by rampant regulation—which is no more than indirect taxation in a more insidious form. Indeed, both threats have most frequently historically evolved in tandem to undermine the vitality of heretofore economically vibrant nation-states.

The reason for this reality is basic. As from a standpoint of disincentives, apart from overt penalties for noncompliance, even the tax itself is a penalty for engaging in the activity being taxed—effectively raising its price, thereby discouraging it from being performed. For in addition to the so-called sin taxes on alcohol and cigarettes, government punishes through taxation the requisite labor for, and investment in, socially constructive activities—that is, the proceeds from productive work and income earnings on capital. Economists call such disincentives a "deadweight loss" or a "welfare cost."[54]

Yet these are costs that no economically progressive society can long be expected to endure. Taxes matter because they are the foremost determinants of economic growth within any jurisdiction—and because, when they become repressive, they destroy private economic surplus by stifling initiative through vitiating profit motive. They matter because they are singularly most responsible for destroying the incipient economic vitalities of political jurisdictions.

Tax costs concurrently matter because they deny the basic growth dynamic that makes a market-driven private economy work. For government is not a generator of economic growth—prudent business people and diligent working men and women are. To vigorously expand, therefore, requires entrepreneurs able to create supported by investors willing to invest—and laborers willing to work harder in order to succeed.

Precisely for this reason, then, the Joint Economic Committee of Congress has estimated that, for every additional dollar of tax raised, overall

GDP growth is reduced by $1.20 to $1.60, while concluding that "high tax rates distort work and savings decisions and promote unproductive tax avoidance and evasive activities. These tax distortions thus create the aforesaid 'deadweight losses' that lower the nation's standard of living."[55]

The "disincentive effects" of such inordinate taxation are worthy of special contemplation, as they underlie a fundamental economic reality that is too often ignored. Imagine for a moment that the government of a trillion-dollar economy has decided to increase its annual spending by $10 billion—1 percent of national income. Linear mathematics might suggest that it could reach this spending goal by raising its tax rate by 1 percent—from 10 percent to 11 percent.[56]

But invariably, this increased levy will not yield sufficient revenue. Why? Because an increase in the tax rate will cause at least some discouraged taxpayers to work less diligently, or at least to dedicate fewer hours to their work. By diminishing the amount of income to be taxed, however, such a downsizing of work commitment shrinks the taxable income base—causing revenue yields to be reduced or even fall. In either event, then, it is clear that a 1 percent tax-rate hike will not produce a corresponding 1 percent increased revenue yield from aggregate national income.

Hence, to raise the targeted additional $10 billion, taxes will have to be raised by much more than 1 percent—perhaps by as much as 2 percent—thereby draining as much as $20 billion in financial capacity from the productive private economy while precipitating as much as a 3 percent drop in GDP growth. For in short, in order to benefit government by a measure of one, the private sector must generally be disadvantaged by at least a measure of two!

Indeed, this is among the foremost fraudulent premises of the "tax and spend" approach. Because it empowers a government to do things it should not be doing, it deprives it of the resources required for the things that it must do—the agenda that it is constitutionally mandated to carry out, such as providing for the jurisdiction's defense, ensuring equal access to public opportunity, securing neighborhoods, fighting drugs and crime, administering justice, and providing safe roads, transportation infrastructure, and other "public goods."

For eventually, the price must be paid—as "Santa Claus politics" is no more than "tooth fairy economics" that ignores one simple economic truth: the more you tax of something, the less you have of it—a reflection of the reality that in the free marketplace, there are indeed opportunity costs; there is no such thing as a "free lunch." To quote economist Walter Williams:

> How many times have we all heard of "free tuition," "free health care"—and free "you-name-it." If a particular good or service is really free, then we can have as much of it as we want without the sacrifice of other goods or services.

Take a "free" library. Is it really "free"? The answer is no. Had the library not been built, that $50 million could have purchased something else. That something else sacrificed is the cost of the library.

While users of the library might pay a zero price, "zero price" and "free" are not one and the same. So when the politicians talk about providing something for "free," ask them to identify the beneficent Santa or tooth fairy.[57]

Who, then, pays the price? The productive private sector, by the very definition of taxation, of course, does. As Winston Churchill once observed: "Some see private enterprise as a predator to be shot, others as a cow to be milked; But far too few see it for what it is, a steady horse pulling the entire wagon."[58]

Yet no economy can survive if it continues to be treated as the cow that everyone is milking but no one cares to feed. Today, it is too easy to forget that though some aspire to live at the expense of the state, it is actually the *state* that lives at the expense of everyone else—and that no nation can ever hope to create productive jobs by expanding businesses when facing the Hobbesian choice of "heads, the government wins, tails, the taxpayers lose"!

The fiscal bottom line, then, is this: the more public revenues spent, the less the volume of tax revenues collectable from, and investable by, private-sector sources. This is precisely the flawed economic premise of the tax systems that support "big brother" government—they are antithetical to market capitalism because they punish everything that decent citizens believe in: *productivity, competition,* and *success.*

That "economic surplus" is quintessential to the advance of civilizations is central to the workings of democratic capitalism. Its inverse corollary, however, is that whenever a government taxes away that surplus, it sows the seed corn of its own inevitable demise. For those individuals, empires, and eras most successful throughout history have invariably been those characterized by indomitable entrepreneurial spirit. The deaths of such empires and eras, in turn, have usually occurred when onerous public policies have suffocated that competitive spirit most often nurtured at the roots of its private enterprise foundation.

Succinctly stated, the costs of administrative complexity, when excessive, can vitiate an economy—making their moderation perforce a foremost policy priority. Thus, advocates of limited government must not be seen as "antigovernment" per se, as some would charge. Rather, they are merely hostile to concentrations of coercive power and to its arbitrary use. Equally attuned to the keen lessons of economic history and the perils of unconstrained bureaucracy, they stand for constitutionally limited government possessing the delegated authority and means to protect human rights, yet not being so powerful as to destroy or negate them.[59]

This, in essence, was what the English Magna Carta of 1215 A.D. was really all about—that taxation and regulation could not be imposed without the consent of the governed—as likewise was the vital message of America's Declaration of Independence and her Constitution, together with its Bill of Rights.

That the nation's Founders were avid students of economic history is evidenced in Thomas Jefferson's insightful observation in 1774 that "history has informed us that bodies of men as well as individuals are susceptible to the spirit of tyranny." It is this vigilance in the quest of liberty that has, to date, been this nation's priceless legacy and must now be preserved.[60]

7

The Tyranny of Taxation

I think we have much more machinery of government than is necessary, too many parasites living on the labor of the industrious.

—Thomas Jefferson

TAXATION AND THE FOUNDING FATHERS

Compounding the divisive social and civic issues heretofore considered, and the attendant bureaucratic complexity that they have engendered, the dollar costs of administering that complexity have been equally monumental. The tax challenges that they pose, however, are not new but instead are perils that have threatened polities from the onset of classic antiquity— as mankind since the dawn of history has sought a proper tax and public service balance.

Some have even said that such taxes are the price of civility and order. Such sentiments are attributed, in fact, to renowned former Supreme Court Justice Oliver Wendell Holmes, in famous words chiseled onto the portals of the IRS headquarters in Washington, D.C.: "Taxes are the price we pay for a civilized society."[1] Chief Justice John Marshall, in his time, was likewise moved to issue an equally dire tax warning, curiously not immortalized on the IRS building, holding that: "The power to tax is the power to destroy!"[2]

Sage insight, as at the bottom line, of course, the IRS is more than just the National Park Service with higher fees or the post office with less compassion. For such merits as there may be to public-sector benevolence, at the bottom line, it remains, as it has properly been called, the foremost authoritarian means to paternalistic public sector ends.

Taxation, of course, is the price of "big government"—not only taxation in the form of direct financial levies, but equally taxation in the form of regulation. This reality was realized early on by the ideological architects of the nation's creation. Indeed, the American Revolution itself was founded upon the cresting waves of objection to taxes deemed to be unjust—as the "Boston Tea Party," a protest against British commercial levies, was the critical catalyst that energized the momentous independence movement that soon would unfold.

Encapsulated in Benjamin Franklin's famed exhortation in 1789 that "in this world, nothing is certain except death and taxes," the nonconformist spirit of the age was captured in a groundswell of contemporary editorial commentary. In 1776, the exact year of the Declaration of Independence, for instance, Thomas Paine, in his pamphlet *Common Sense*, wrote: "Taxation, in its best state, is but a necessary evil; in its worst state, an intolerable one—drawn from the bitterness of want and misery."[3]

In that same year, the great free-market philosopher Adam Smith, author of *Wealth of Nations*, likewise concluded that inordinate taxation "can obstruct the industry of peoples and discourage them from applying to certain branches of business which might give employment to great multitudes."[4]

Smith, in a similarly enlightened statement demonstrating his firm understanding of the fundamental precepts underlying supply-side economics, further contended that "high taxes, sometimes by diminishing the consumption of the taxed commodities, sometimes by encouraging smuggling, often afford a smaller revenue to government than what might be drawn from more moderate taxation."[5]

Accordingly, while Smith openly acknowledged that certain levels of taxation are necessary to cover the essential costs of defense, justice, and public infrastructure, he concurrently recognized the inherent economic and fiscal dangers if those levies grew high. "Each tax should be so contrived," he wrote, "as to take out of the pockets of the people as little as possible."[6]

The early history of taxation in America thus grew tumultuously. Indeed, the thirteen colonies' independence movement first set root when their leaders met in 1776 to protest the levies imposed by the British "Stamp Act." Though the records show that this was, in reality, not an onerous levy, it was the very precept of seeking to impose foreign taxation upon an aspiring free people that triggered the revolt.[7] Indeed, even many of Britain's foremost opinion leaders, among them Pitt the Elder and Edmund Burke, sympathized with the colonies in their desire for tax remedy, with the latter asserting: "People must be governed in a manner agreeable to their tempers and dispositions."[8]

It is ironic, then, that America, a nation born in 1776 signaled by protest over moderate British taxation of tea, now confronts ever-rising taxes of her own making—as those factors that brought down the Greeks, Romans, Muslims, and French monarchy in succession pose growing threats to her own economic well-being.

Yet the nation had ample warning. Indeed, as early as its inception, James Madison, in *Federalist Paper No. 10*, wrote compellingly of the grave dangers arising within a democracy, of "over-taxation of the more productive few at the hands of the less productive many!"[9]

Little did Madison know just how prophetic his words would ultimately become. For until the onset of World War I, most of the federal government's revenues had come from tariffs. But from an initial 7 percent maximum marginal rate fixed when the federal income tax was instituted in 1913, the ceiling would soon rapidly rise to a top rate of 94 percent within the next three decades to support the welfare programs of the Great Depression and the World War II effort. Indeed, even on incomes in the lowest tax bracket of less than $2,000 per year, the maximum rate became a hefty 23 percent.[10]

While those exorbitant levies were subsequently, over time, substantially reduced, most notably through the Kennedy tax cut of 1964 which lowed the top marginal individual rate from 91 to 70 percent—and the Reagan tax cuts of the 1980s, which further dramatically reduced the maximum rate from 70 to 28 percent—they have now again risen to exceed 35 percent, a phenomenon also clearly anticipated by Madison when he warned: "Enlightened statesmen will not always be at the helm!"[11]

The concern of the Founding Fathers over prospective fiscal profligacy thus was consummate and profound. Indeed, the clear and present danger of tax dollar misuse—of needlessly extorting citizens to produce revenues allocated to parochial purposes—was clearly recognized by Thomas Jefferson when he wrote, "A wise and frugal government, which restricts men from injuring one another, must leave them free to regulate their own pursuits of industry, and shall not take from the mouths of men bread that they have earned."[12]

As Jefferson might well have concluded with the benefit of further prospective analysis, when governments tax too much, they also steal from their own citizens the fruits of their labor—and when more rigorous tax collection methods become necessary to enforce compliance, they rob from them their economic liberties as well.

For as Thomas Paine graphically wrote at the onset of the American Revolution in 1776: "When we survey the wretched condition of man under systems of government, dragged from his home by one power or driven out by another, and impoverished by taxes more than by enemies, it becomes evident that those systems are bad, and that a revolution in the principle and construction of government is necessary."[13]

This was a theme echoed as well in Jefferson's parallel assertion that:

Whenever any form of government becomes destructive to these ends, it is the right of the people to alter or abolish it, and to institute new government, laying its foundation on such principles, and organizing its power in such form, as to them shall seem most likely to affect their safety and their happiness.[14]

Yet history simultaneously makes clear that this was, by no means, a danger limited exclusively to the American experience. For the renowned political contemporary of Paine and Jefferson, the Baron de Montesquieu, at the time of the French Revolution in 1789, similarly warned his own country of "the dangers to all freedom-seeking peoples when their countries come to be ruined by the oppression of fiscal extortion by government—causing otherwise good men to fail to comply with its demands to be condemned as villains."[15]

The exacting remedies that issued from the early Founders' tax concerns thus came, foremost and explicitly, to be embedded in Article I of the U.S. Constitution as follows:

> Section 8. The Congress shall have power to lay and collect Taxes, Duties, Imposts, and Excises, to pay Debts . . . but all Duties, Imposts, and Excises shall be uniform throughout the United States. . . .
>   Section 9. No Capitulation or other Direct Tax shall be laid, unless in proportion to the Census of Enumeration herein before directed to be taken.

Would that their wise counsel had been heeded—for though they thought they had cast it in concrete in the very first article of the Constitution—and for a while, they had indeed—it would take a century and a half before their noble intent and handiwork would be undone by the Sixteenth Amendment sanctioning a federal income tax ratified in 1913.

CONTEMPORARY COSTS OF BUREAUCRATIC COMPLEXITY

Taxation

To understand the economic and political challenges that a jurisdiction faces in imposing inordinate taxation, it is first important to determine where it has historically been. America has traditionally employed a diverse range of federal revenue sources. From the beginning of the Republic until the onset of the Civil War, the country relied primarily upon customs duties to finance government at the national level. During the nineteenth century, however, publicly held land sales, over time, came to supplement tariffs as a prime revenue source. Excise taxes likewise eventually became an important source of federal receipts—and estate and gift taxes were collected sporadically through the end of World War I as well.[16]

While America did dabble in federal income taxation throughout the nineteenth century, specifically during the Civil War to support the military effort—in 1861 granting a $600 earnings exemption and thereafter imposing a 3 percent levy on net incomes between $3,000 and $10,000 and 5 percent on those above—later to be raised to 10 percent in 1864—its modern variant did not take shape until tax-levying enabling legislation issuing from the Sixteenth Amendment, occasioned by the looming of World War I, was formally ratified by forty-two states in June 1913.

Initially innocuous, it imposed a 1 percent tax on all individual incomes over $3,000 and on family incomes over $4,000—with a graduated 1 percent to 6 percent surcharge on brackets of incomes over $20,000, reaching a top marginal rate of 7 percent on taxable incomes of over $500,000. By 1916, with the country on a wartime footing, however, the maximum federal income tax rate had risen to 15 percent and by 1918 it had skyrocketed to 77 percent.[17]

In the subsequent four decades, moreover, these provisions were further greatly expanded—with the top marginal rate reaching 94 percent on all incomes over $200,000 in 1944 amid World War II—while slightly subsiding to 85 percent in the postwar era, only to be again raised to 91 percent during the Korean War, where it remained until the Kennedy tax cuts of the mid-1960s—at which point, they were codified and consolidated by the Federal Tax Act of 1954, as the modern income-tax era began earnest.[18]

Indeed, by 1930, income taxes had come to comprise some 60 percent of all federal receipts, with traditional customs duties and excise taxes accounting for 15 percent each of the federal receipts total. By 1944, that share, in fact, reached 80 percent of all of the federal collections vitally needed to pay for WWII. Since then, however, the income-tax share of federal receipts has fallen back to fluctuate between 55 percent and 65 percent, declining to as low as 52 percent in 2003, while more recently rebounding with the vibrant earnings produced by the robust 2003–2007 economic recovery.[19]

The passage of the Sixteenth Amendment thus was a watershed in U.S. political history—empowering the federal government radically by redefining the relationship of the citizen to the state; to wit, the higher its taxation, the greater their subjugation—thereby permitting politicians to preempt the people from building their own lives.[20]

Predicated upon the specious notion that all monies belong to the government, with that portion of it left to the people remaining at bureaucratic sufferance—hence, its notion that tax relief is actually a "tax expenditure"— in upholding its unlimited power to tax, the Supreme Court ruled in 1943 that "an income tax deduction is an act of *legislative grace*"—and in sustaining retroactive taxation in 1994, further held that "tax legislation is not a promise, as taxpayers hold no vested right in the Internal Revenue Code."[21]

Thus it is that the taxpayer is seen as always wrong in the eyes of the IRS, as abetted by the courts and their heavy-handed rulings—a circumstance that the Founders equated with tyranny—yet one with clear historic precedent, for to again quote Montesquieu, "As virtue is necessary in a republic, so fear is necessary in a despotic government."[22]

The reason that it is tyranny is basic. Government is force. It cannot create, only reallocate. Yet every increase in its ability to spend means an increase in its political power—and a new pretext for seizing private paychecks. Indeed, coercion is for government what profit is for private business.

But in a democratic system, politicians deserve no credit for seizing and bestowing, in the form of "government-issued happiness," that which they did not produce—as for every carrot that the public sector offers, it must commandeer a corresponding stick to extort the funds to pay for it. In other words, public benevolence today is made up of the proceeds of yesterday's tax plunder.[23]

Yet just as politicians cannot redeem people's souls by emptying their wallets, so government cannot make peoples lives more fair by making them less free—as governmental coercion is not an exercise in moral fine-tuning but instead a gross perversion of the Founders' unequivocal concepts of justice and equity before the law.[24]

While the devastating impacts of the subsequent rise of "big government" that it has engendered are omnipresent, however, nowhere are the adverse impacts of the transaction costs occasioned by bureaucratic complexity more evident than on the nation's private sector that builds the productive sinews of its economic might.

Indeed, the attenuating effects of federal taxation leaching the lifeblood from private economic vibrance have grown perilous today—and are particularly insidious given that the long course of financial history reveals that the economies of all great civilizations are impelled by profit motive. For in seeking to identify a civilization that has arisen that has denied profit motive and survived for countless centuries, one will find that there are none. The last ones, which survived for but seven decades, collapsed with the fall of the Iron Curtain.

Hence, today, even erstwhile communist China and the former Soviet satellites of Eastern Europe have adopted their own unique forms of "cowboy capitalism"—with Estonia, Georgia, Lithuania, Latvia, Romania, Serbia, Slovakia, the Ukraine, and even Russia herself all adopting the income "flat tax" in the wake of the 1989 fall of the Soviet Union—and with all likewise being richly rewarded with buoyant economic outcomes.

Equally positive results are now being realized in China, India, and throughout Southeast Asia as well. How? By cutting taxes, deregulating industry, and practicing that unique brand of entrepreneurial capitalism that a hundred years before contributed to making the twentieth century the "American Century."[25]

Yet the results are not surprising, for civilizations are powered by production—and production is fueled by profit motive, a reality with profound, sobering consequences for the nation's future economic course, as the current unfolding of U.S. industrial development makes clear.

Overall, manufacturing remains strong within America today. Employing fourteen million workers, and enjoying more powerful economic multiplier effects than any other sector, it owns the powerful pistons that drive the U.S. economy as well as the strength of its 2003–2007 dynamic recovery. More than one in six domestic jobs, in fact, directly depend on its productive processes.

The nation is the planet's premier manufacturer because it is its foremost leader in technology development and innovation, accounting for a more than one quarter of all global output. Indeed, were U.S. manufacturing an economy, it would be the eighth largest in the world. Manufactured goods likewise comprise more than 60 percent of total U.S. exports—as domestic producers ship abroad more than $60 billion in commodities each month.[26]

Yet manufacturing concurrently faces complex challenges. Not the least among them are inordinate bureaucratic transaction costs bred of misguided public policy. A recent National Association of Manufacturers (NAM) study has found, for instance, that compared to her nine largest trade rivals, American manufacturers face 31.7 percent higher operating costs in the areas of taxation, employee benefits, tort claims, and governmental regulation.[27]

Among the more egregious disparities, the U.S. corporate tax rate is more than 10 percent higher than the OECD (Organization for Economic Cooperation and Development) average, and annual costs of complying with federal regulation alone stand at more than $10,000 per employee—resulting in an aggregate $162 billion compliance burden for the nation's private producers. Indeed, the imprudent price of public policy does more direct damage to U.S. global trade competitiveness, and the dynamic job creation that derives from it, than does any other cause.[28]

The NAM findings are replicated in a July 24, 2007, Tax Foundation counterpart study, which similarly found that the United States continues to lag behind the OECD in corporate tax levels, stating:

> The United States has yet to catch the continuing wave of corporate income-tax reduction sweeping through many countries in the OECD. Five countries cut their corporate income tax rates in 2006, and eight more, including Germany, will have cut their rates by 2008. . . .
>
> As the OECD countries continue to lower their corporate income tax rates, moreover, they can expect to reap more foreign direct investment from the U.S. A recent study . . . found that when an EU member state cuts its corporate tax rate by 10 percent, from 30 to 27 percent, for example, it can expect to reap a 60-percent, short-run increase in investment by U.S. multinational corporations.[29]

As a consequence, among the thirty OECD member countries:

> Only Japan taxes corporate income at a tax rate higher than the United States. Japan has cut its rate recently, and its 39.5 percent rate now barely claims the world's title of highest corporate tax rate, just above the 39.3 percent in the United States. . . . Germany is one of several countries that had higher tax rates than the U.S. in 2000 but now levy a lower tax (38.9 percent). Ireland has [the] lowest rate at 12.5 percent.

The conclusion thus is inescapably simple. The United States needs new tax policy. It endures the second-highest corporate tax rate in the OECD and is one of only two countries that have not reduced their rates since 1994. Despite its high corporate tax rate, however, the United States collects less income tax revenue as a percentage of GDP than do other OECD countries with lower rates.[30]

The net results of America's globally out-of-touch tax policies are readily evident in other key economic indicators as well. At the onset of the twentieth century, federal taxes accounted for just 3 percent of GDP, and the tax code and related regulations filled just a few hundred pages.

Today, however, federal taxes take nearly 18 percent of GDP and are projected to rise to exceed 20 percent of GDP if the Bush II 2001 to 2003 tax cuts are permitted to expire in 2010 as scheduled—and aggregate federal tax rules and regulations now exceed 60,000 pages, with the U.S. Tax Code, in 2007, itself consisting of 16,845 pages, encapsulated in twenty volumes. The extraction of $2 trillion per year from American families and businesses, therefore, comes at equally enormous economic *and* administrative costs.[31]

Consequently, according to the Tax Foundation's annual cost calculation using the latest government data on income and directly imposed tax levies, "Tax Freedom Day"—the day that citizens can cease working for the government and start working for themselves "came on April 26, two days later in 2007 than it did in 2006 . . . and fully 12 days later than in 2003, when ("Bush II") tax cuts caused Tax Freedom Day to arrive comparatively early on April 14."[32]

The Tax Foundation report likewise compares the number of days Americans must work to pay taxes to the number of days they work to support themselves—revealing that Americans now work longer to pay for government (120 days) than they do for food, clothing, and housing combined (105 days). Since 1986, in fact, taxes have unfailingly cost more than the combination of all of these basic necessities.[33]

Indeed, Americans today work far longer to afford federal taxes alone (79 days) than they do to afford housing (62 days). In 2007, Americans worked another 41 days to afford their state and local taxes. That makes taxation a larger financial burden than housing and household operations (62 days), and health and medical care (52 days)—or food (30 days), transportation (30 days), recreation (22 days), and clothing and accessories (13 days) combined.[34]

The bottom line thus is that regulatory costs aside, the average American family head of household will work approximately twenty years out of a forty-year career just to pay direct monetary taxes to the more than 88,000 taxing jurisdictions that exist at all governmental levels today.[35]

Just the annual process of filling out federal tax forms takes an average individual an estimated twenty-seven hours—costing the productive economy more than 5.5 billion man-hours every year. Thus, not only does the U.S. government expropriate a third or more of tax-paying citizens' incomes, it, in effect, charges them even more to comply with its expropriation.[36]

Thus it is, as famed late nineteenth-century social philosopher William Granham Sumner succinctly put it, that: "The prosperity that we enjoy is the prosperity that God and nature has given us, less that which the legislator has taken from us."[37] "If it is indeed an outrage to lock up an innocent man for half his life in jail, therefore, is it not equally an outrage to compel an equally innocent man to forcibly donate half of his yearly earnings to his government?[38]

Taxation Disguised as Regulation

Taxation's adverse impacts on human motivation extend to regulation as well. Indeed, given the historic reality that property rights are central to America's concept of liberty, regulation is no less than taxation in a more insidious form. In fact, it is worse—as regulation of a citizen's business or property can reach a degree at which ownership is nullified and its value is destroyed.

If the government expropriates private property through eminent domain, for example, the "just compensation" clause of the Constitution requires that the aggrieved landowner be duly paid. Under "confiscation by regulation," on the other hand, there is no such compensation—yet if unchecked, the process can continue to metastasize to the point where the owner's only option is liquidation.[39]

For many, that point has been reached throughout America today. Indeed, a U.S. Small Business Administration study found that in 2006, regulatory compliance cost Americans $1.14 trillion. In a population of three hundred million, that total came to $3,713 per individual or $14,852 for an average family of four. That is $14,852 less they have to spend on consumer goods and lifestyle necessities that enrich their lives and enhance their health and safety.[40]

Astoundingly, that sum of hidden regulatory costs approached a value equal to half of that year's total U.S. federal spending of $2.6 trillion, and exceeded 9 percent of GDP—topping Canada's entire $1 trillion GDP. Combining regulation and spending, in fact, the national government's share of the American economy is a monstrous 29 percent. And that is just its direct public-sector cost.[41]

Factor in the reality that regulation adds as much as 33 percent to the cost of an airplane engine and 95 percent to the cost of a new vaccine, and it becomes readily apparent that its impacts upon America's socioeconomic well-being—its development of new technologies, its global market trade competitiveness, and the quality job creation that evolves from all of these dynamic processes—are both devastating and upwardly spiraling.[42]

Alas, the problem just keeps getting worse, not better—in 2007, the sixty-plus federal departments, agencies, and commissions were again busily at work creating 4,052 more rules. Of them, agencies report that 139 are "economically significant," meaning that they will cost the economy at least $100 million—and often, far more—while another 787 are expected to seriously affect small businesses. To put these regulatory costs into perspective, the entire federal budget didn't even hit a trillion dollars—approximately the total of what regulations now cost—until 1987.[43]

Yet Congress has no constitutional mandate to implement rampant private business regulation. The Constitution's opening section stipulates that "all legislative powers herein granted shall be vested in . . . the Congress." However, that power is conspicuously circumscribed, as noted, by Article 1, Section 8 of the Constitution, which stipulates that "The Congress shall have powers to regulate Commerce with Foreign Nations, and among the several States, and with Indian Tribes."

In other words, the federal government was empowered to regulate international and interstate commerce—but not private firms and individuals, and it was not vested with the latter powers until the establishment of the Interstate Commerce Commission in 1887. Consequently, whereas before the Civil War, the public sector maxim was that the best government is "that which governs least," that precept has, over time, permuted into a statist dogma extolling the best government as "that which regulates the most."[44]

Notwithstanding a federal government whose statutory reach is far greater than its constitutional grasp, moreover, for the past seven decades, Congress has ceded its authority to draft and approve final implementing rules to unelected regulatory agencies, restrained only by in-built constraints in the enacting legislation and the ineffectual Administrative Procedures Act. The present festering outgrowth of economic-growth-depressing federal regulation is the inexorable result.

All of this frenetic activity, one is concurrently reminded, takes place in the noble effort to "protect" the taxpayer using his own tax dollars. Yet like "protection" by the mob, the process that this so-called stewardship entails is itself arcane, sinister, and ultimately self-defeating. Libertarian Robert Ringer speaks precisely to this point:

> To argue that government gives people *services* in return for the money that it expropriates from them is, of course, irrelevant for exactly the same type of reason explained in connection with *eminent domain*. If someone takes your money at gunpoint in an alley, but gives you something in return that you either do not want or did not bargain for, it does not make him any less a robber.[45]

Irrespective of the original intent of this "robbery through regulation," however, the ultimate test of its substantive merits lies in its results. Viewed in this light, then, can anyone look at the scorecard of governmental oversight of private sector activity to date and say, "Well done! We need more of this"? Can the performance of government to date lead anyone to believe that it deserves a still-greater role in the competitive marketplace, that the nation needs still more public agencies to regulate free enterprise, or that government is even capable of managing itself?

Yet despite the woeful record of governmental intervention in the private marketplace, the social engineers of the liberal left continue to contend that their policies have failed only because they haven't gone far enough.

Instead, through a self-perpetuating policy promulgation process, like the addict to hard drugs, the excessive use of the "regulatory reflex" merely feeds an insatiable appetite on the part of an ever-expanding bureaucracy—as the cause of private-sector paralysis is resurrected as its cure, a reality invoking that legendary bureaucratic axiom: "The nearest thing to eternal life that one will ever encounter on earth is a governmental program." Or, to recall the insight of Ronald Reagan: "Government exists to protect us from each other. Where it has gone wrong is when it has sought to protect us from ourselves."[46]

As a consequence, the *Federal Register*—the compendium of all new federal regulation each year—which had totaled 14,479 pages in 1960 and 53,376 pages in 1988, the final year of the Reagan administration—has now exploded to a record-setting 75,000 plus pages annually.[47] By contrast, as President Reagan poignantly reminded while addressing NAM in 1982: "The Lord's Prayer contains 57 words. Lincoln's Gettysburg has 266 words. The Ten Commandments have just 297 words, and the Declaration of Independence has only 300 words. Yet a recent Agriculture Department's order setting the price of cabbage has 26,911 words."[48]

Thus, the cause of the complex mushrooming of the regulatory process is both elemental and regenerating, as government is supremely capable of creating, but wholly incapable of abandoning, the obsolete. Pursuing a motto that "nothing exceeds like excess," it knows how to "add" but not

"subtract"—how to "expand," but not "contract"—in producing its two principal outputs: bureaucratic structures and their attendant, invariably repressive, administrative rules. The reason is self-evident, as again expressed in the
cogent words of Ronald Reagan: "Governments don't solve problems; they
just continually rearrange them!"

The net effect, then, is that the taxpayers and consumers get stuck with
paying for everything that the government ever tries, as public-sector bureaucracy devolves into an amalgam of the sum total of all pubic-policy experimentation ever undertaken, good or bad—and, as shown in analysis, its
impacts upon entrepreneurial economic activity can be devastating.

As public bureaucracy, in this perverse manner, continues to metastasize
uncontrollably, one is reminded of the pungent, albeit insightful, observation of a former Michigan business analyst who—in arguing that the regi-
mented mentality of government is no substitute for the efficiency of a private form of management that must rely upon profits to survive—in
reflecting upon the time-proven maxim, "never trust a dog to guard your
food," notoriously allowed:

> I am always leery of any person or group compelled by a presumed greater wis-
> dom to provide gratuitous service to the public . . . especially since it is just
> such service that the bull has in mind when he contemplates the pretty heifer
> in the next pasture—and, unfortunately, the results are almost invariably the
> same![49]

Such "gratuitous public service" is likewise what well-meaning bureaucrats have in mind when they propose yet another market management
role for government. But wouldn't their arguments be more compelling if
government could manage its own affairs a little better? Is it sheer coinci-
dence that those sectors of the U.S. economy habitually in the greatest
trouble—railroads, farms, utilities, and the financial services sector—are
those that have traditionally been the foci of the most intensive "governmental help"?

For precisely this reason, then, Ronald Reagan—whose business take was
that "the liberal view of the economy is: if it moves tax it. If it keeps moving, regulate it. If it stops moving, subsidize it"[50]—concurrently warned that
"the most frightening words in the English language are: 'I'm from the federal government; I'm here to help!'"[51]

The challenges posed to democracy by excessive regulation thus are enormous and incompatible with the workings of democratic process. Democratic government is limited government for the simple reason that there
are economies of scale in its institutions, as in all others. Since it is imprac-
tical as well as unconstitutional to have multiple executive and legislative
branches, the alternative is recourse to quasi-independent rule-making bureaucracies, which lamentably is the case today.[52]

But more regrettably still, as government expands, its bureaucracies grow beyond the ability of elected representatives to control them, as the mechanics of governance themselves become increasingly complex. The end result is bureaucratic complexity in the form of serious institutional overload for all branches of government—and in the attendant devolution of public sector efficiency, the workings of democratic process become increasingly frustrated, if not altogether irrelevant, as they are not the means whereby the polity can most efficiently rule.[53]

The net result is tyranny through regulatory process—an outcome that serves well the interests of leftist liberals who continue to seek to win through bureaucratic and judicial co-option of that which they cannot achieve through popular will. To the extent that they have already succeeded, and in large measure they now have, therefore, true democratic government has not survived. Accordingly, since the survival of sound governance is quintessential to that of social progress, the quest for its effective preservation must continue further still.[54]

Tax Cuts Work

What is the solution? What path best serves the public social and fiduciary interests in seeking the most beneficial commitment of tax dollars to economic well-being? Evidence presented makes clear that "growth" is not a four-letter word—that though not produced by government, growth nonetheless can often be abetted by the workings of prudent public policy. There are, in fact, a multitude of examples—case studies of tax policies, those of Calvin Coolidge, John Kennedy, Ronald Reagan, and George W. Bush, in particular—that demonstrate that systematic economic development is a public good that can be fostered through market-based tax policies.

Such examples prove beyond a reasonable doubt, in fact, that a jurisdiction prospers most when its government focuses its quest for long-term economic expansion firmly upon a goal of tax moderation. As ultimately, tax levels are the principal determinant of economic growth within any jurisdiction—and prudently adjusting their impact incidence to support industrial and commercial development goals can make a significant difference at the economic bottom line.

The results are manifest in the industrial performance data. For the much of the past half century, despite the fact that it has labored under twin deadweight burdens of ill-advised tax and regulatory policies since the onset of Lyndon Johnson's "Great Society" in the mid-1960s, America's economy has nonetheless produced prosperity for most of its citizens.

But this outcome, it generally may be said, has been despite the efforts of the federal government, rather than because of them. In the process, government has extracted increasing shares of national resources from the private economy to satisfy the insatiable spending appetites of bureaucrats and special interests—and has then sought compensatory, but ultimately self-defeating, regulatory remedy through intervention into the free-enterprise system in vain quixotic efforts to fine-tune the resulting marketplace to better commercial and industrial returns.[55]

The inexorable result, however, has been a policy-induced economic slowdown forged of depressed private-sector activity. Census Bureau data reveal, for instance, that GDP averaged 3.5 percent annual inflation-adjusted growth in the century from 1870 to 1970.[56] By the twentieth century's end, however, after the tax costs of the Great Society had sapped private economic vigor, GDP had lost about one-third of its strength, slowing to a mere 2.3 percent annual pace.[57]

This is a critical industrial performance reversal, for were the U.S. economy to grow 3.5 percent rather than 2.3 percent for the remainder of the first half of the twenty-first century, through 2050, the resulting GDP would almost double—standing at $70 trillion rather than $36 trillion on its present course.

To do so, however, would require sound, tax-focused economic policy. Fortunately, there are ready remedies for preempting such underachievement. Foremost among them is to overhaul the federal tax code to make it fairer, simpler, and more capital friendly—as greater economic growth requires a tax system that stimulates it by encouraging higher rates of saving and investment.

Though the case for tax moderation is incontestable, however, it invariably faces stiff opposition from America's habitual tax-consuming crowd. Yet the positive returns on such a course are readily demonstrable, with the economic outcomes speaking for themselves. Foremost among them, from August 2003 to election day 2006, as a direct result of the 2001–2003 Bush II tax cuts, Bureau of Economic Analysis GDP data reveal that the American economy grew a spectacular 20.3 percent, larger, in fact, than the entire economy of China, which today stands at 19 percent of U.S. GDP.[58]

Indeed, as a direct result of the signature Bush tax cuts, in the four-year period from August 2003 through July 2007, the economy created a remarkable 8.3 million nonfarm jobs. In the process, average hourly earnings for production workers continued on a course of healthy growth as well.

Concurrently, and contrary to contentions that the reemerging federal deficit was a direct result of the Bush tax cuts, in the three years subsequent to their implementation, while the federal government revenues increased by 12 percent, spending concurrently grew by 8 percent. Had the latter been held to 6 percent, still twice the inflation rate, however, the federal budget would have been in balance in FY 2007.[59]

The results thus make clear that lowering business costs by reducing marginal tax rates on wage and capital incomes can unleash extremely powerful capital flows, both foreign and domestic. Examples of the efficacy of the approach are numerous. Commencing in 1964, President Kennedy's tax cuts lowered the marginal cost of expanding output by 4.5 percent—causing GDP to more than double its 2.5 percent 1950s growth average, indeed increasing to a high of 6.6 percent, as the economy added more than one million jobs by 1966.[60]

Similarly, two decades later, President Reagan's 1981 and 1986 tax cuts generated economic growth of 3.9 percent throughout the dynamic 1980s expansion. Not only was this exceptional growth rate noninflationary, it came during a period of highly deflationary Federal Reserve Board monetary policy resulting in *falling* inflation in the economy—as Reagan accomplished what no president has ever achieved before or since—presiding over significant concurrent declines in both inflation and unemployment. The Bush II tax cuts from 2001 to 2003, in turn, for the four years subsequent to their enactment, produced similar results in terms of precipitating economic growth without raising prices through stimulating increased industrial output.[61]

Tax cuts work! No one believes that the United States is richer than North Korea because she is better at managing aggregate demand. She is richer, in no small part, because she embraces supply-side tax and fiscal policies. Their merits are self-evident. Supply-side policies lower marginal tax rates to spur employment and growth, index tax brackets to inflation to offset "bracket creep," and tighten monetary policy to restore the stability of price levels and exchange rates.

That is precisely what Reaganomics accomplished. Top marginal rates were lowered from 70 percent to 28 percent, and tax brackets were indexed to inflation to create an inflation-immune tax structure. The spectacular prosperity enjoyed by the United States in the 1980s was the indisputable result.[62] Accordingly, following the Reagan tax cuts of 1981, the American economy in the next seven years grew a massive 34 percent—the equivalent then of a West Germany.[63]

Equally vibrant economic results resonated from the Coolidge tax cuts that produced the Roaring Twenties—cuts that included a reduction in the top marginal individual income-tax rate from 77 percent to 25 percent, and in so doing, reduced the share paid by the lowest income bracket of less than $10,000 from 21 percent to 5 percent, while increasing that paid by the highest income bracket of more than $100,000 from 29 percent to 51 percent—and from the Kennedy tax cuts that produced the "Prosperous Sixties"—which reduced the top marginal individual income tax rate from 91 percent to 70 percent with attendant buoyant growth—and whenever and wherever else dramatic tax cuts have been enacted as well.[64]

As a result of the "incentives effect" of the Reagan tax cuts of 1981 and 1986, moreover, despite reducing the top income marginal rate from 70 percent to 28 percent, and with inflation generally in check, federal tax yields nearly doubled over the 1980s decade—from $517 billion in 1980 to $990 billion in 1990!

Nearly half of the static losses from the Reagan tax reductions were, in fact, directly offset by increases in taxable income, and with the additional stimulatory effects of the tax cuts growing the economy, the U.S. Treasury collected an estimated $1.1 trillion more in total revenue in that decade than it would have had the original 1980s rates remained in effect.[65]

In the process, the wealthy not only paid more income taxes in real terms but also a greater share of income taxes as a percentage of their incomes than did any other income group. Indeed, by 1990, the top 1 percent of all Americans were paying 25 percent of all federal income taxes, up 40 percent from 1980, whereas the bottom 60 percent were paying just 11 percent of federal taxes, down 20 percent from that base year—with the revenue share paid by the top 10 percent of taxpayers rising from 48 percent to 57 percent, and with the top 50 percent of taxpayers paying 94 percent of all federal income taxes. Lower tax rates thus resulted in much larger, not smaller, tax payments by the liberally-labeled "rich."[66]

Why is this financial reality, in fact, the case? Why do tax rate cuts increase tax rate progressivity? A prime reason is that high-income-bracket taxpayers are then incentivized to shift their profits from tax shelters into productive investments that create jobs and incomes.

Alternately put, when tax rates fall, upper-income households shift assets out of instruments such as tax-free bonds that generate tax-exempt income, or from schemes designed to shelter income outright, into economic activity that produces taxable profits and wages that result in increased economic activity, and thereby, enhanced revenue flows to government.[67]

After President Reagan's 1981 tax cuts, in fact, total tax revenues climbed by 99.4 percent during the 1980s, and income tax revenues concurrently grew dramatically, increasing by 54 percent (28 percent after being adjusted for inflation) by1989. Indeed, more tax revenues were collected every year of the two Reagan terms than had ever been annually collected before.[68]

Yet this was, as noted, by no means, a unique outcome. It also happened during the tax cuts of the 1920s and the Kennedy tax cuts of the 1960s. Indeed, as part of the so-called Coolidge tax cuts, as embodied in the Revenue Acts of 1921, 1924, and 1926, federal income taxes were cut across the board—with top marginal rates reduced from 77 percent in 1922 to 25 percent by 1929.[69]

In the three years following the sweeping Kennedy tax cut of 1964, moreover, unemployment fell by 32.1 percent, a trend again paralleled in the three years that followed the Reagan tax cut (which took effect in 1982), as unemployment fell by 15.1 percent.

The reason for this dynamic growth is clear yet simple: the prime purpose of tax cuts is to generate industrial and commercial activity, and more economic activity generates more revenues, even at the lower rates, as tables 7.1 and 7.2, calculated from U.S. Department of Treasury historic budgetary data, reveal.[70]

Table 7.1. Revenue Impacts of Significant U.S. Federal Tax Cuts

Tax Cuts:	Marginal Cut:	Revenue Increase:	% Increase:
1920s Coolidge Tax Cuts	70% to 25%	$719 million in 1921 to $1,164 million in 1927	61%
1960s Kennedy Tax Cuts	91% to 70%	$94 billion in 1961 to $153 billion in 1968	total: 62% (inflation-adjusted 33%)
1980s Reagan Tax Cuts	70% to 28%	$517 billion in 1980 to $990 billion in 1990	total: 99.4% income: 54% (inflation-adjusted 28%)

Table 7.2. Tax Burden Shifts Resulting from U.S. Federal Tax Cuts

Tax Cuts:	Proportion Borne by the "Rich:"
1920s Coolidge Tax Cuts	Income over $50,000—from 44.2% in 1921 to 78.4% in 1928
1960s Kennedy Tax Cuts	Income over $50,000—from 11.6% in 1963 to 15.1% in 1928
1980s Reagan Tax Cuts	Top 10% of earners—from 48.0% in 1981 to 57.2% in 1988

Today, similar upward tax redistributions likewise are occurring as a result of the Bush II tax cuts, as determined by the Congressional Budget Office and arrayed in table 7.3. Indeed, recent analyses of revenue data show that whereas the highest earning 20 percent of all households would have paid 78.4 percent of all federal income taxes based on the year 2000 tax law, their share rose to 82.1 percent in 2004 after the three Bush II tax cuts—yet every other income group was bearing a smaller share of the total income tax burden.

Hence, it is no accident that today, the top 1 percent of U.S. income earners pay 33 percent, the top 20 percent pay 82 percent, the top 50 percent pay 94 percent, and the top 60 percent pay all of U.S. federal income taxes—with the bottom 40 percent paying none at all, as the Bush II tax cuts have fully erased the income-tax burden for more than 7.8 million families—with the consequence that after credits and deductions, a record 57.5 million Americans had no federal income tax liability whatsoever after the tax cuts cumulatively took effect in 2004.

Table 7.3.   Distributional Effects of the Bush II Tax Cuts

I. Effective Income Tax Rate Per Income Group After Bush II Tax Cuts:

Income Group:	2000 Tax Law:	Bush II Tax Cuts:	Differential:
Bottom 20%	−4.3%	−5.7%	−1.4%
Next 20%	1.9%	−0.1%	−2.0%
Middle 20%	5.2%	3.5%	−1.7%
Next 20%	8.5%	6.6%	−1.8%
Top 20%	17.1%	14.2%	-3.0%
Top 10%	19.4%	16.0%	−3.3%
Top 5%	21.4%	17.6%	−3.8%
Top 1%	24.5%	19.6%	−4.8%

II. Percent of Income Tax Burden Paid Per Income Group After Tax Cuts:

Income Group:	2000 Tax Law:	Bush II Tax Cuts:	Differential:
Bottom 20%	−1.6%	−2.7%	−1.1%
Next 20%	1.5%	−0.1%	−1.6.0%
Middle 20%	6.4%	5.4%	−1.0%
Next 20%	15.3%	15.2%	−0.1%
Top 20%	78.4%	82.1%	3.8%
Top 10%	63.5%	66.7%	3.2%
Top 5%	51.4%	53.7%	2.3%
Top 1%	31.6%	32.3%	0.6%

Source: U. S. Congressional Budget Office

The growth impacts of tax cuts are likewise manifest in GDP and employment data depicted in the four-year pre- and post-cut economic performances of the last three major tax cuts. They reveal that U.S. GDP increases averaged 2.91 percent in each of the three four-year run-up periods—and then were followed by 3.57 percent growth rates over the next four years, as the economic multiplier impacts of the tax reductions percolated through the economy—a combined 22.68 percent hike.

In like manner, private-sector employment growth averaged 1.44 percent in the pre-cut four-year run-ups, but spiked to 5.98 percent in the four-year post-cut periods of buoyancy—a 315.28 percent increase, as tables 7.4 and 7.5 reveal.

Table 7.4.   U.S. Real Gross Domestic Product (GDP) Growth

Presidency:	Pre-Tax Cut Period:	Post-Tax Cut Period:
Kennedy-Johnson	1960–1963: **+3.82%**	1964–1967: **+5.30%**
Carter-Reagan	1978–1981: **+2.77%**	1982–1985: **+3.47%**
Clinton-Bush II	2000–2003: **+2.15%**	2004–2007: **+2.95%**

Source: calculations performed on data contained in U.S. Department of Commerce, Bureau of Economic Analysis, Table 1.1.1. *Percentage Change From Preceding Period in Real Gross Domestic Product.*

Table 7.5.   U.S. Private Sector Labor Force Growth

Presidency:	Pre-Tax Cut Period:	Post-Tax Cut Period:
Kennedy-Johnson	1960–1963: **+0.87%**	1964–1967: **+2.94%**
Carter-Reagan	1978–1981: **+5.77%**	1982–1985: **+9.88%**
Clinton-Bush II	2000–2003: **−2.32%**	2004–2007: **+5.11%**

Source: calculations performed on data contained in the U.S. Department of Labor, Bureau of Labor Statistics, Historical Table B-1: *Employees on Non-Farm Payrolls by Industry Sector.*

Yet such results again come as no surprise. For as John Kennedy said: "An economy hampered by restrictive tax rates will never produce enough revenues to balance the budget, just as its trade will never produce enough jobs or profits. . . . It is a paradoxic truth that tax rates are too high and tax revenues are too low, and that the soundest way to raise revenues in the long run is to cut tax rates now."[71]

Subsequent revenue results would prove Kennedy absolutely right. For after the revenue effects of his reducing the top marginal tax rate from 91 percent to 70 percent began to officially register in the economic performance data in 1964, tax yields nearly doubled over the next four years.[72]

Moreover, it is becoming increasingly clear that economic redistribution among the earnings quintiles is likewise remarkably fluid—with great mobility both up and down—and that the income distribution within them can be dramatically impacted by tax policy, as economist Walter Williams observes:

There is considerable income mobility in our country. According to Internal Revenue Service tax data, 85.8 percent of tax filers in the bottom fifth in 1979 had moved on into a higher quintile, and often even the top quintile, by 1988.[73]

Indeed, of the bottom 20 percent of wage earners in 1975, 97 percent had moved out of the lowest income brackets by 1991—and of those, 39 percent had moved up to rank among the top 20 percent income earners.[74]

TAX CUTS AND ECONOMIC GROWTH

How Tax Cuts Work

As analysis has shown, from August 2003 to election day 2006, as a direct result of the Bush II tax cuts of 2001 to 2003, the American economy grew more than the equivalent of an entire China.[75] But this stellar economic performance was no isolated incident. For in the seven years immediately following the Coolidge and Reagan tax cuts, the U.S. economy likewise grew 42 percent and 34 percent respectively—and equally vibrant results have resonated whenever and wherever else dramatic tax cuts have been achieved. The critical question, from a policy formulation standpoint, thus becomes: Why is this documented reality invariably the case?[76]

Here, recent research lends a modicum of perspective. In a federally mandated study released in mid-2006, Gregory Mankiw, Harvard professor and former chairman of the U.S. Council of Economic Advisors, and Robert Carroll, U.S. Treasury Department deputy assistant secretary for tax analysis, effectively explained both why and how such tax cuts work—contending that tax relief generally does produce dynamic domestic economic growth, that not all taxes generate equally strong industrial and commercial activity, and that they work best when concurrently tied to spending cuts. Their principal findings are threefold.[77]

Lower Tax Rates Do Indeed Lead to Greater Economic Prosperity

According to the Mankiw-Carroll analysis, perpetuation of the 2001–2003 Bush II tax cuts will lead to a long-run increase in capital stock of 2.3 percent, and a long-run increase in GNP of 0.7 percent. In the 2007 economy, such a GNP expansion meant an extra $90 billion a year that the nation could spend on consumer goods to raise living standards, or on capital goods to sustain prosperity, more than two-thirds of which will occur within ten years.

Not All Tax Cuts Are Created Equal in Generating Growth

The Mankiw-Carroll analysis likewise found that certain tax-rate reductions have a profound impact upon economic growth, whereas others have minimal or even adverse effects—in the process, identifying particularly productive revenue returns from reductions in dividends and capital gains taxes.

How the Tax Relief Is Financed Is Equally Crucial for Its Economic Impact

In the last analysis, the Mankiw-Carroll study recognized, government eventually has to pay its bills. As a consequence, when taxes are cut, offsetting spending adjustments are required if a sound economy is to ensue—making a reduction in the size of government the logical complement to tax reform if stable economic growth is to be sustained.[78]

If spending is not cut, on the other hand, the results are strikingly different. Instead of increasing by 0.7 percent in the long run, GNP falls by 0.9 percent. The lesson learned: tax relief does stimulate economic growth, but only if the tax reductions are correspondingly matched by spending constraints. But there is one exception: lower taxes on dividends and capital gains promote growth even if they require higher income taxes to balance the federal budget.

Spending cuts, implemented in conjunction with tax cuts, thus are essential for long-term U.S. growth. If spending declines along with taxes, therefore, the economy optimally benefits from the restoration of federally confiscated financial resources back to optimal private economic use.[79]

There are valid economic reasons why this reality is, in fact, the case, and thus must be factored into the calculus of formulating prudent tax policy. For government affects growth in a variety of ways—among them, by the *character* of its spending, by the *focus* of its fiscal policies, and by the *sources* through which those policies are financed.

In theory, of course, governmental spending on investment can add to capital stock and thereby materially increase growth. On-the-ground reality, however, is often very different—as public-sector spending is typically taken up by governmental consumption and transfer payments, leaving little funding left over for investment. It is thus critical to explore how the impacts of tax cuts can best be optimized.[80]

Why Tax Cuts Work

The prime reason that tax cuts work goes to the heart of the American political process itself—as the liberal approach to taxation is "redistributive economics" reallocating capital, not creating it. For them, for taxation to be "fair," it must perforce be preferential, favoring the lower income strata.

To this end, they promote "progressive taxation," which they contend levels the economic playing field and narrows the income gap between the rich and poor. The revenues generated, in turn, must be committed to further leveling of the economic playing field through investments in public sector support infrastructure that again underwrites the "economically victimized and oppressed."

Conservatives counter by rejecting progressive "redistributive" taxation—opting instead for flatter, lower tax rates across the board. To this end, the Bush II tax cuts virtually eliminated taxation for the bottom 50 percent of taxpayers while creating incentives to work, save, and invest for all—cognizant that high tax rates penalize entrepreneurial risk-taking. For such recognition affirms the economic axiom that the higher the taxes on a good or service, the less of it will be produced; whereas the lower the taxes, the higher the level of dynamic economic activity, which will then produce better, lower-priced products for all.

The reasons for these financial phenomena are basic: when marginal tax rates are increased, incentives to produce are correspondingly diminished—in other words, the more investments are taxed, the less investment will take place, and the higher the taxes on savings, the lower the rate of savings taking place.

In sum, conservatives believe that the lower the taxes, the higher the level of that investment risk-taking that results in economic growth, job creation, and higher living standards; whereas liberals believe that government is a better arbiter than the free market of how hard-earned private-sector capital should be allocated. The profound public-policy question thus becomes: who is right?

The answer goes to the essence of macroeconomic performance. A prime reason for the inverse reciprocity between tax "productivity" and inequality, of course, is that while moderate tax rates will inspire greater personal and corporate investment in productive activity, rapidly progressive tax rates will seldom, if ever, actually redistribute income; they merely redistribute taxpayers from highly taxable to less taxable economic activities. Indeed, it is estimated that high-tax-driven recourse to tax shelters now costs the economy about 18 percent in growth each year—a massive $2 trillion loss in GDP.[81]

This phenomenon is also dramatically demonstrated in the fiscal reality documented in annual U.S. budgetary statistics revealing that immediately after the 1990 "Bush I–Democratic Congress" tax increase, in an exact replica of Roman fiscal policy in the fourth century, aggregate tax receipts in 1991 from America's uppermost tier of taxpayers actually declined by $6.5 billion, or 6.1 percent, even as their tax rates rose.

Conversely, when tax levels are decreased, the proceeds from their levies multiply. When the top capital gains tax rate was decreased from 39.9 to 28.0 percent in 1978, the federal revenue it produced rose from $9.1 billion to $11.9 billion. When President Reagan further cut the capital gains tax rate from 28 to 20 percent, revenue from its proceeds grew from $12.8 billion to $18.7 billion.

After the top capital-gains tax rate was restored to 28 percent by the Tax Reform Act of 1986, but was then again cut back to 20 percent in 1996, not only did the resulting tax yields again surge dramatically, but also the national economy grew by a dynamic 4.5 percent in 1997, 4.2 percent in 1998, 4.5 percent in 1999, and 3.7 percent in 2000.

In the first three years after President George W. Bush further reduced the capital gains tax rate from 20 percent to 15 percent, moreover, instead of declining by $5.4 billion as had been projected by the Congressional Joint Committee on Taxation, the tax yield more than doubled from a projected $57 billion to $133 billion.

Tax cuts thus do work. Indeed, as the course of fiscal history proves, cuts in *production output* tax levies invariably *enhance* public revenues, not attrite them. Want to attack the root causes of civilizational collapse, then? Cut taxes on those producers whose incomes underwrite the bureaucratic complexities created by cultural and civic alienation and the social welfare costs that they engender.

THE HUMAN CONSEQUENCES OF TAXATION WRIT LARGE

Yet such sage advice—predicated upon sound lessons of economic history—too often goes unheeded. As a consequence, for every full-time private worker in America today, there is a counterpart either holding down a governmental job or gaining a livelihood through a public sector handout—in effect, requiring every taxpaying American private sector employee to bear, on his shoulders, not only the burden of his own family, but concurrently that of a government employee or public supplicant—thereby dividing the nation, through the workings of public policy, into two economic classes: "those who earn paychecks" and "those who deem themselves more entitled to them."[82]

Regrettably, as noted, whatever the merits of public sector benevolence, such as they may be, the IRS may be euphemistically best described as the less-than-compassionate face of bureaucratic means to paternalistic ends. To give credit where credit is due, in consummate truth-in-packaging, the Treasury Department officially does define a "tax" as "a compulsory payment for which no specific benefit is due in return." Alternately put, in bureaucratic eyes, no matter how much a person pays in taxes, and despite promises of pandering politicians ever-solicitous of votes, taxpayers are not irrevocably entitled to a single benefit from their governmental investments.[83]

As a consequence, federal tax policy has now largely mutated into public sector oppression seeking revenue maximization. Indeed, in the past half century, the number of penalties that the IRS can impose has increased over tenfold—from 13 in 1950 to in excess of 150 now. In the process, bureaucratic management has focused upon the mechanics of tax collection—not on tax fairness—as for the IRS, rendering justice to the individual taxpayer is its lowest priority.[84]

In its relentless quest, then, it makes over ten thousand direct seizures of personal homes, cars, or other property each year—relying on a federal tax code that has increased in size over 850-fold, from fourteen pages to one approaching seventeen thousand, over the past century—at a direct administrative cost of $10.5 billion to the economy, not to mention the additional billions of productive opportunity cost in taxpayer compliance efforts.[85]

While the direct costs of taxation are severe, moreover, its indirect costs—in the forms of preempting personal savings, preventing firms from hiring, or otherwise suppressing economic growth—are more egregious still. The reason is basic: the more of a person's paycheck the government is allowed to take, the more it controls that citizen's destiny—as taxation, in excess, evolves into publicly sanctioned tyranny. In the words of Judge Learned Hand: "Taxes are enforced exactions, not voluntary contributions. To demand more in the name of morals is mere cant."[86]

This is a reality that America's first treasury secretary, Alexander Hamilton, doubtless had in mind when he said, "The genius of liberty reprobates everything arbitrary in taxation. . . . Whatever liberty that we may boast in theory, it cannot exist in fact while [arbitrary tax] assessments continue."[87]

In his assessment, Hamilton thus rightly recognized that liberty is an inherent right. The Bill of Rights did not "give" freedom to Americans; instead, it made a solemn pledge by government that it would not violate certain preexisting "unalienable" rights of individuals.

Regrettably, in 1913, the Sixteenth Amendment changed all of that by giving government the unlimited power to tax. It is disconcerting, but illuminating, therefore, to reflect how the transaction costs of bureaucratic complexity—in the forms of taxation and regulation—are jeopardizing America's economic future today.[88]

As within the government itself, there is no apparent serious desire to know about, nor systematic desire to alleviate, the onerous burdens of operating the federal tax system. For while the IRS, the General Accountability Office, and the Congress alike pay nominal lip service to the ideal of taxpayer assistance, they concurrently are endorsing, expanding, and extending repressive administrative support systems characterized by appalling irresponsibility and waste.

Small wonder, then, that America's massive bureaucratic complexity costs are coming to resemble those that precipitated the fall of Rome—as taxes, be they direct or in the form of regulation, destroy that powerful productive behavior that is the cornerstone of economically successful nation-states.[89]

Nevertheless, the federal tax system remains the very foundation of U.S. government—a force empowered by the threat of punishment for noncompliance—yet a phenomenon that runs contrary to both the workings of democratic process and the course of economic history. For a key development in the history of democratic governance has been a strict adherence to the rule of law—a universal precept that holds that the force of the state should be brought to bear in accordance with uniform rules that apply equally to everyone. The consummate advantage of such an approach is that it makes public actions both predictable and just.[90]

Today, however, to a significant extent, the federal tax system no longer adheres to the rule of law—as officials, at every level, make arbitrary decisions that cause similar cases to be treated differently and even unjustly—for when a bureaucratic system departs from legal rescript, abuses of power become inevitable—and in the resulting process, tax officials, given broad powers, far too often act fallibly human—thereby setting into motion arbitrary, bureaucratic machinations that threaten the system of democratic capitalism itself.[91]

Consequently, despite its spectacular, nearly unbroken string of success stories, traditional American democratic capitalism—economic determinism shaped by human motivation—called by some the "triumph of individuality," or indeed, "the ultimate triumph of motive over method"—today remains precariously under siege.

Its prime threat no longer comes from repressive socialism, perhaps, nor even from those who, for self-serving political purposes, would bureaucratically cap its productive capacity—*but instead from its own successes*. For elsewhere around the world today, the free-market system that America and Great Britain have done so much to create, promote, and export is now setting ever-deeper roots.

Real-time examples are legion. The fall of the Berlin Wall has, in itself, liberated a vast European marketplace of more than 300 million consumers, rivaling America in size. China is also employing its emerging economic freedoms to achieve a surging economic prosperity for its 1.3 billion population at levels unthinkable a mere two decades ago. With her 670 million citizens, India is rapidly following suit, doubling her economic growth rates and achieving dramatic 8-percent GDP annual growth rates.

Similarly, Margaret Thatcher's 1980 tax cuts for more than a decade made Britain the strongest European economy—and it remained so until Ireland implemented lower tax rates that enabled her to surpass Britain in economic growth. Russia and practically all of the erstwhile Soviet bloc countries, as noted, have moved to low flat-rate tax systems and are economically rebounding as well.

Paradoxically, then, while the United States is now economically recoiling from the threats of global competition as a consequence of her inordinate bureaucratic transaction costs—with some seeking remedy by calling for a return to trade protectionism and still higher taxation in the name of an ethereal "social justice"—the nation's global competitors have stumbled upon her erstwhile prized secret of trade competitiveness; to wit: *a regulatorily moderate, tax-friendly, free-functioning marketplace*.

THE ECONOMIC CONSEQUENCES OF COMPLEXITY AND ITS COSTS

Nearly two centuries ago, in 1831, Alexis de Tocqueville accurately foresaw the evolution of a feckless, indolent U.S. society dependent upon paternalistic government as the greatest threat to the nation's democratic experiment and warned that the republic must be vigilant in its guard against it.

His was a sagacious warning. For American civilization—the one that he knew firsthand—has historically not been a socialistic state steeped in industrial stasis, but instead a progenitor of dynamic, interactive private-sector economic growth processes—thereby fostering social motivations that foment creativity, opportunity, self-achievement, and fulfillment. To restore America, given the socioeconomic threats arrayed against her, the nation must now work its way back to its economic roots.

Critical times call for creative solutions and, at critical times, creates them. It clearly is no accident that in 1776, the challenge of America's quest for freedoms invoked the genius of the Founding Fathers. It is equally no accident that her Declaration of Independence and Adam Smith's *Wealth of Nations* both appeared that year.

It is likely no accident either that James Watt's perfected steam engine was patented in that same year. For as this inquiry has shown, personal freedom and economic prosperity through technological progress are inexorably linked. Great times invoke great ideas—and it is the Founders' great legacy that they established the intellectual and economic milieux propitious for great ideas, both intellectual and economic, to coalesce and flower.[92]

Their contributions are reflective of their intent. In seeking to guarantee "life, liberty, and the pursuit of happiness"—that "system of natural liberty" held out as an ideal by no less than Adam Smith—they established a democratic capitalistic administrative exemplar that has earned at once the awe and envy of the world.

Today, America remains blessed that two priceless principles, democratic freedom and economic freedom, came together two centuries ago to form the cornerstone of her governance. Embodied in the Bill of Rights appended to her Constitution, they remain an integral part of her national fabric. Her system of free-market capitalism is their vital offspring, and one that has provided unprecedented economic blessings. In the cogent words of Woodrow Wilson: "The American Revolution was a beginning, not a consummation.[93]

America's system of governance, as constituted by the Founding Fathers, was among the most daring experiments in democratic socioeconomic administration ever attempted by rational mankind. Indeed, it formed the crucible wherein the society was shaped that has become the world's foremost workplace for "economic man," presenting a case for unconstrained free markets that could not be more compelling —as free markets work because entrepreneurship works. The proof again is in the economic data.

Each year, the Fraser Institute in Canada and the Cato Institute and Heritage Foundation in Washington produce "economic freedom indices" calculated to demonstrate the strong relationship between a jurisdiction's economic freedoms and its economic growth—and more specifically, how its public policies promote or retard private prosperity. The components of each of the indices are largely the same—size of government, tax levels, extent of government control over markets, protection of private property rights, freedom of trade, freedom of capital markets, and so forth.[94]

Their findings are illuminating—making indelibly clear that not only taxation, but regulation and governmental control of production through state enterprises, all shrink the productive private-sector economic base. Except for spending to protect property rights, enforce the law, and protect citizens from aggression, both foreign and domestic, in fact, all government spending crowds out private spending and weakens the vitality of free market process.[95]

Hence, each annual publication of the "economic freedom indices" typically shows that the planet's freest countries enjoy per capita incomes as much as eight times larger than its least economically free countries, as table 7.6, depicting the Cato Institute's 2007 analysis of 141 separate countries, shows.[96]

Table 7.6.   Economic Freedom and Personal Income

Economic Freedom Index Per Capita Income (Quartiles)	(In U.S. $)
Top	$26,013
2nd	$10,733
3rd	$6,103
Bottom	$3,305

Source: Cato Institute. *Economic Freedom of the World, 2007 Annual Report*[97]

Succinctly put, the relationships between economic freedom and income tax level are absolute—leaving no doubt that there is no better solution to poverty and economic reconstruction than the unfettered working of free-market process.

This is a finding confirmed by the United Nations "Human Poverty Index," which reveals that the bottom quartile of the economic freedoms rankings endure a "poverty index" about two and one-half times larger than the top quartile of economically-freest country rankings. The reason is that free-market capitalism is the foremost path to economic upward mobility—and when its operational workings are frustrated, a jurisdiction is the poorer for the outcome.[98]

Regrettably, throughout America today, economic freedom *is* being frustrated by the workings of public policy—as the U.S. federal government has become a tax and regulatory behemoth ratcheting out of control. There is no president, no Congress, capable of its effective management. Indeed, two-thirds of its annual operating budget, as demonstrated in chapter 7, is already beyond the grasp of elected officials in the form of mandated nondiscretionary "entitlements."[99]

Consequently, bureaucratic complexity predictably continues to take its toll. For while government's ability to expand increases *exponentially*, its ability to administer increases only *arithmetically*. This, then, is a body grow-ing faster than its head—making it not an exaggeration to conclude that if this "bureaucratic elephantiasis" is not soon arrested, the American free-market system that has produced more prosperity than any other through-out history will not survive its domination.

With the confluence of these economic realities—exorbitant taxation combined with a national debt exceeding $9 trillion—$30,000 for every cit-izen, much held by foreign entities—America thus stands in economic peril. Today, her trade and fiscal deficits are financed by China, and her mortgage crisis is mitigated by financial bailouts from the Arab states.

Her economic future now held hostage to international interests, a pre-cipitous devaluation of the *yuan* or decoupling of the *riyal* from the dollar could prove financially disastrous. The decline of her housing market, upon which the finances of much of her citizenry are collateralized, is yet another harbinger of forthcoming danger—as today, as the relevance of her political leadership declines, that of foreign bankers rise. Reminiscent of the demise of Rome, the barbarians stand at the gate!

8

The Implosion of Ideology

The budget must be balanced, the treasury restored; the public debt must be reduced; the arrogance of public officials tempered and controlled; and aid to foreign lands must be curtailed lest Rome become bankrupt.

—Roman Senator Seneca in 63 B.C.

CULTURAL DISAFFECTION

"We are the Romans of the modern world," proclaimed Oliver Wendell Holmes in 1858, "the great assimilating people." There can be no question that Holmes was correct. Rome's melding ideals were indeed quintessential to her incipient power that emboldened her spectacular rise, yet, as Friedrich Hegel observed, the subsequent decline of Rome's civic ideals that such amalgamation ultimately produced was followed swiftly by the decline of Rome herself. As this analysis has repeatedly shown, similar declines in cultural and civic values are threatening America today.[1]

Such realities thus reinvoke the crucial question: Why do civilizations die? Yale historian Paul Kennedy blames the phenomenon on overextension of resources—"imperial overstretch"—a situation wherein a nation's commitments outrun its ability to fulfill them—whereas historian Joseph Tainter contends that the cause of the inevitable downward spiral in the life spans of civilizations is that as they mature, they become ever more complex—and that, as a consequence, their complexities over time endure diminishing returns until at the end, they collapse over their own accrued bureaucratic deadweights. Perhaps each hypothesis, in its own way, is right—or alternately, perhaps the correct answer is some hybrid of the two.

Notwithstanding the ultimate resolution of that paradox, however, analysis of this inquiry has explored and documented that, absent resource over-extension, invasion, or other *force majeure*, civilizations almost invariably disintegrate *from within*, usually collapsing in a three-stage process outlined in the introduction that incorporates the following:

1. *Increasing ethnic and social diversification*, causing gradual attrition of traditional culture produced by evolving internal ethnic and social diversity and alienation, as they transition from the core ethnicities that empowered their incipient dynamism into balkanized clans, thus precipitating;

2. *Growing cultural alienation and disaffection*, producing an undermining of adherence to the traditional civic and social values that had been initially established by those core ethnicities, now replaced by others espousing new and differing sets of cultural values, which in turn, initiates; and

3. *Mounting public cost to sustain the disaffected*, including attendant rapidly spiraling bureaucratic costs of adapting to the new cultural realities, among the latter, the social welfare costs of maintaining increasingly diverse societal sub-units—and requisite shifts in the underlying resources bases required to sustain them.

Such are the symptoms of decline readily evident throughout America today—socioeconomic challenges emerging with the elemental force of a cosmic cataclysm that must be expeditiously addressed if she is to confront the problems of her present and the perils of her future—realities that threaten her survival both as a civilization and as a coherent nation.

The evidence is forthright and compelling, as captured in the formula:

Deteriorating Cultural & Social Values	+	Increasing Civic Alienation	—>	Crescendoing Complexity & Cost	=	Core Causes of Civilizational Collapse

All such socioeconomic symptoms, as shown, today have been largely generated by the multiculturalist revolution and its ongoing quest for an ethereal "subcultural equality" bred not of opportunity but of outcome, reminiscent of the metastasizing societal cancers that have afflicted other great, but now defunct, civilizations and hastened their demise. America must thus take heed lest she face the fate of Rome.

America's French visitor Alexis de Tocqueville in 1831 concluded that America was a nation that loved equality more than she loved freedom. The closing line to his master work *Democracy in America*, in fact, forebodingly speculated that "the nations of our time cannot prevent the conditions of men from becoming equal but it depends upon themselves whether the principle of equality is to lead them to servitude or freedom, to knowledge or barbarism, to prosperity or wretchedness."[2]

Though de Tocqueville found that reality ominous, however, it was not until the twentieth century that the nation's pernicious quest for perceived equality through the overthrow of long-standing cherished tradition became a true threat to democratic freedom—ushered in by Franklin Roosevelt's "New Deal," sustained by Harry Truman's "Fair Deal," and culminating in Lyndon Johnson's "Great Society"—all anti-hierarchic movements aimed at socialistic collectivism, producing concomitant declines in the freedoms of business organizations, private associations, families, and individuals who have historically woven the nation's moral fabric—as the precepts of liberty and equality increasingly degrade into states of moral anarchy and tyrannical egalitarianism.[3]

Such ominous social trends would lead Rose and Milton Friedman a century and a half after de Tocqueville to admonish: "A society that puts equality—in the sense of equality of outcome—ahead of freedom will end up with neither equality nor freedom. The use of force to achieve equality will destroy freedom, and the force, introduced for good purposes, will end up in the hands of people who use it to promote their own interests."[4]

The Friedmans, though doubtless confidently on target then, perhaps had no idea how prescient their admonition would, over time, become—as America today finds herself confronting a mass countercultural insurgency evolving over the past half century that has shaken her to her historic roots. Indeed, its impact has been pervasive to the degree that it may no longer be impertinent to ask the question: Does the Constitution retain relevance today?

Those who lead the ongoing assault on the Bill of Rights do so wrapped in the mantle of "civil libertarianism." Infiltrating the nation's most cherished institutions, they have effected a profound social transformation throughout America—engaging in a perverse form of scholarly iconoclasm that determinedly seeks to deemphasize her language, rewrite her history, and refocus her values and beliefs—replacing her cultural and civic identities with those of quite different incoming subcultures.[5]

Though not the first time that her national well-being has been imperiled, this is the greatest peril America has encountered *from within*. Undeniably, throughout her first two centuries, as a nation of immigrants, she was bombarded with destructive ideologies and was endangered physically. But those threats were then was external: imperialism, communism, and fascism. Presently, beyond radical Islam—as the planet's last remaining military superpower, as well as the world's economic colossus—her greatest threats are instead internal: foremost among them, the perverse threat of multicultural correctness as a governing political doctrine compounded by invasive immigration at her southern border.[6]

The challenge now is thus profoundly different—as America faces a dogmatically driven attenuation of her traditional values and the sapping of her economic vitality by liberal academic, journalistic, and political elements who constitute the shock troops of an ongoing cultural revolution—a crisis that would be risible were it not so tragic, as two of America's historic mainstays in preserving her cultural legacy, academia and journalism, have forfeited their erstwhile powerful leadership roles as social melding forces.

More ominous still, these traditional twin bastions of American cultural strength have actually gravely undermined it—pursuing a divisive "deconstruction through diversity" crusade that has done a grave disservice to the country's civic culture. For instead of reinforcing its historic values, instead of being a progressive source of new ideas, its academia and media have degenerated into a cabal of leftist hate-mongering counterculturalists enforcing, in gestapo-like fashion, ethereal notions of what they put forth as "politically correct" social wisdom.[7]

Thus, moral indignation has become the controlling framework within the global views of such race-, class-, and gender-baiting cultural critics who have learned that a prime path to political power is to associate discrimination and oppression with even the most benign Eurocentric actions. So great is their paranoia that even Shakespeare is deemed to be compliant in this meanness of spirit that they deem to be the "great white moral sickness"— with academicians and their journalistic offspring decrying alleged cruelty of early Renaissance European explorers and attendant exploitation by their colonial regimes.[8]

Unable or unwilling to place history within the chronological socioeconomic context within which it evolved, in their paroxysms of indignation and indictment, they unabashedly proceed, oblivious to the cogent insight of famed historian Bernard Lewis that "in having practiced racism, sexism, and imperialism, the West was merely following common practices of mankind throughout the millennia of recorded history."[9]

As a consequence, the nation is today enduring a ragtag countercultural war being waged against its past. Western history is portrayed as a mass litany of crimes—genocide, massacres, slavery, colonialism, and imperialism—committed by those professing to be Christian. In the process, the nation's great scientific and technological accomplishments are being subordinated to a focus on its failures, as "Love Canal" has overtaken Neil Armstrong's 1969 moon walk in multiculturalist lore.

Thus it is that the city of San Diego banned the Boy Scouts from camping in a city park as a violation of church and state. Thus it is that the city of San Jose in 1994 was forced to remove its traditional *seasonal* crèche from its park display because it was deemed "insensitive" to non-Christian peoples.

But as columnist and social commentator Linda Chavez noted at the time: "The city officials showed no similar sensitivities two weeks earlier when a group of Christians protested the unveiling of a *permanent* exhibit in its public park of an eight-foot statue honoring the Aztec god Quetzalcoatl." The defining difference? The crèche was paid for with private funds. The ancient Indian statue, on the other hand, was financed with $500,000 in taxpayer dollars (!).[10]

In their histrionic campaign of political dissonance and venom, the nation is thus being indoctrinated by liberal elitists to believe that America is fatally flawed—that her history is one of nearly universal suffering, save for the white establishment. Columbus, Washington, Jefferson, and Lincoln, once national icons, are today under attack for allegedly victimizing humanity—replaced in stature, in their eyes, by the Vladimir Lenins, Ché Guevaras, and Malcolm Xs. No longer legends, only the faces of America's historic heroes sculpted on Mt. Rushmore remain as memories for some.[11]

Yet can anyone rationally argue that Harriet Tubman or Sojourner Truth, as important as they may have been, more profoundly affected the course of American history than did John Adams and Alexander Hamilton, or that "gangsta rap" is no less musical than Beethoven's Fifth Symphony? César Chávez and Susan B. Anthony—names fourth graders are now taught to instantaneously recognize—may have been great reformers, but there would have been nothing to reform save for the heroism and martial success of Generals John Pershing and George Patton whose genius and achievements during the first half of the twentieth century remain gaping *lacunae* within the historical literacy of the nation's youth.[12]

Accordingly, as the Constitutional Convention and Paul Revere are increasingly deleted from the nation's chronicles, America's heritage, history, and heroes are being trashed under the guise of a newly found neo-Marxist "political nirvana." Yet utterly overlooked in this would-be omnibus social revolution is the reality that it was this nation's Founders who introduced to the world the ideals of "God-given human rights" and "government of, for, and by the people."[13]

Concurrently, anyone who challenges the nation's ongoing massive onslaught of illegal immigration is called xenophobic, racist, nativistic, and overtly nationalistic—with patriotism now evolving as a pejorative term. Anyone who shows an affinity for God in a public place is deemed to be a miscreant. While multiculturalists rail endlessly that five of America's first seven presidents were slave owners, they do not concurrently point out that it was *this* nation that abolished slavery—not the indigenous African slave suppliers who grew rich selling their brothers into servitude.[14]

So zealous have been their efforts to project images of rampant minority victimization, however, that their machinations may well have inadvertently boomeranged—with it now becoming increasingly apparent that it is the would-be "beneficiaries" themselves who are the actual victims of this cynical and callous process, as *New Republic* columnist Michael Lind asserts: "The liberal strategy of de-emphasizing *genuine* progress made by blacks for fear of promoting political complacency has backfired, creating a distorted image of generic black degeneration, like something out of 1900s racist tracts in the minds of frightened whites."[15]

Accordingly, while the proponents of this *avant garde* liberal leftist "equality through diversity dogma" once looked to Marxism as their salvation, that ideology's recent global collapse as a viable system of political thought has left them in despondent disarray. Marxism had built its case on the specious notion that capitalism promoted unequal outcomes and thus was morally flawed—and that a successful socialist economy could be built without the competitiveness and unequal outcomes that a free market presupposes.[16]

But real-time experience over the past three decades has proven those ideas to be thoroughly mistaken—a historical evolution that poses profound problems for the purveyors of race, class, and gender politics in that their frameworks of thought and vocabulary have been utterly demolished—particularly in their alleged "exploitation" and "oppression" dimensions. For while previously "unequal outcomes" could be explained in terms of relative "exploitation" and "oppression," now, because of the abject failure of global communism, it is increasingly difficult to argue from that premise.[17]

No longer able to effectively make their case in the court of public opinion, therefore, the counterculturalists have sought their compensatory redress in the nation's courts of law. Often finding sympathetic hearings before the benches of judges who would be legislators, this is, of course, not a novel recourse. Deeply concerned about mounting court proclivities to abandon strict legal constructionism in favor of increasing judicial activism already evident in his time, Abraham Lincoln, in his first inaugural address, determined that

> the candid citizen must confess that if the policy of the Government upon vital questions affecting the whole people is to be irrevocably fixed by decisions of the Supreme Court . . . the people will have ceased to be their own rulers, having to that extent practically resigned their Government into the hands of that eminent tribunal.[18]

Recall as well the cogent counsel respecting courts of Churchill at Westminster College in 1946 that: "peoples of all countries have the right, and should enjoy the power by constitutional action . . . that freedom of speech and thought should reign; that courts of justice, independent of the executive, unbiased by any part, should administer laws which have received the broad assent of large majorities or which are consecrated by time or custom."[19]

Notwithstanding the preamble to the Constitution—"WE THE PEOPLE of the United States, in order to form a more perfect union, establish justice . . ."—what America today endures, at the hands of her courts and *cognescenti*, is not democracy at all. It is instead an imposition of the worst manifestations of a minority rule that seeks to rewrite the nation's noble history into something ignoble that it clearly wasn't. In the poignant warning of famed theologian Carl Henry, "We are today witnessing the twilight of a once great civilization."[20]

Small wonder, then, given the ongoing spate of culture-bashing, that the nation hasn't spawned even more garden-variety native America-haters of the ilk of Jane Fonda and John Walker Lindh. For with these ominous developments, the barbarians have broken down the gate—making more illuminating still the survey of how symptoms of the darkening twilight of imperial Rome play out through America today.

Is there recourse to remedy? Presently, both the nation's academic infrastructure and its media remain in denial respecting their cultural and political biases. And though many social commentators, are, in fact, aware that top-down pressures are continually pushing their professions in directions that they don't want to go, they have nonetheless been unable to forthrightly deal with the bedrock issues of ideological distortion and blatant bias that are its offspring to the degree needed to begin the requisite process of holistic reform, a phenomenon that merits further contemplation.[21]

CURBING CULTURAL ALIENATION'S COMPLEX COSTS

Such contemplation perforce begins with the economic price of governance in challenging times. As analysis has decisively demonstrated, aging empires, almost axiomatically, gradually grow so administratively complex that they ultimately collapse of their bureaucratic deadweights and their attendant tax and regulatory costs. Evidence is compelling, in fact, that America is today approaching that Plimsoll mark.

Perhaps indicative of the ongoing metastasizing of administrative complexity, a single recent legal measure, Sarbanes-Oxley—regulating professional business relationships in a post-Enron era—has single-handedly revived the entire profession of accounting in America—and that is but one example of ongoing "bureaucratic mission creep" and the productivity stasis that it engenders.

Were a foreign power to seize the United States and dictate that her citizens surrender 40 percent of their incomes to its agents, require them to submit to hundreds of authoritarian commands, prohibit many from using their real and personal property as they see fit, and deny others the opportunity to gain productive employment, is there doubt that such a course would be equated with tyranny? Yet the prime difference between that scenario and contemporary reality is that the despot's role is now seemingly sanctioned through the workings of democratic process.[22]

Yet such coercion is no less than public perfidy—and its sole remedy is to prevent still greater coercion, thereby making minimalist government the best form of governance. For if it is not necessary to coerce, then, for the well-being of society, it is necessary not to coerce—as political philosopher Herbert Spencer observed as early as 1884:

> It is not to the State that we owe multitudinous inventions from the spade to the telephone; it is not the State that made possible extended navigation through a developed astronomy; it was not the State that made the discoveries in physics, chemistry, and the rest which guide modern manufacturers; it was not the State which devised the machinery for producing fabrics of every kind, for transferring things from place to place, and for serving in a thousand ways our comforts.
>
> The worldwide transactions conducted in merchants' offices, the rush of productive traffic filling our streets, the total distribution system which brings everything within our easy reach and delivers the necessities of life to our doorsteps are not of governmental origin. All of those are the results of the spontaneous activities of private citizens, separate or grouped.[23]

Writing in a similar vein, twentieth-century philosopher C. S. Lewis observed:

> Of all tyrannies, a tyranny exercised for the good of its victims may be the most oppressive. It may be better to live under robber barons than under omnipotent moral busy-bodies. For a robber baron's cruelty may sometimes sleep; his cupidity may at some point be satiated; but those who torment us for our own good will torment us without end, for they do so with the approval of their own conscience.[24]

The cogency of such remarks is self-evident. For as nineteenth-century European political philosopher Benjamin Constant, in his seminal 1815 work, *Principles of Politics*, opined:

> Arbitrary public power destroys morality, for there can be no morality without security. . . . Arbitrariness is wholly incompatible with the existence of any government considered as a set of institutions. For political institutions are simple contracts; and it is in the nature of contracts to establish fixed limits. Arbitrariness, being precisely opposed to what constitutes a contract, thus undermines the foundations of all political institutions.[25]

Such quotes, taken in tandem, thus encapsulate John Stuart Mill's succinct, but precisely targeted, warning that to allow governmental beneficiaries to vote is tantamount to inviting them "to plunge their hands into their neighbors' pockets."[26]

Notwithstanding, such are realities now lost in the modern notion of the *body politic*—hence, that concept of a "social political contract" between the governors and governed extolled in chapter 2 does not exist today, as pulling the voting booth lever has now devolved into little more than a mechanistic process whereby citizens commit to a contract wherein the seller enjoys unlimited rights to deceive and defraud the buyer—validating the time-worn political maxim: "The more you promise, the less you have to deliver!"

Thus it is that onerous taxation and special interest regulation have ratcheted out of control throughout America today—dividing the country, in the 1930s words of H. L. Mencken, "between those [who] work for a living and those who vote for one."[27] To again make analogy to Rome, of the dying days of the Republic historian Plutarch observed: "The people were at that time corrupted by the gifts of those who sought office, and many made a constant trade of selling their votes."[28]

To which Montesquieu at the time of the 1789 French Revolution appropriately appended: "It is impossible to grant grand largesse to the people without extortion; and to counteract this, the state must be subverted. For the greater advantage that [the voters] seem to derive from the liberty [of voting], the nearer they approach that critical moment of losing it."[29]

IS ROME BURNING?

What, then, do these trends portend for the nation's economic future? As described in chapter 2, Richard Nixon, in his 1992 capstone masterpiece, *Seize the Moment*, observed that the "apogee of civilization"—the pinnacle of scientific and technological progress—has moved ever westward: from China to the Islamic East to Christian Europe in the Renaissance and on to America in the Industrial Revolution. He then presciently predicted that commencing in the twenty-first century, the "apogee of civilization" would again move back toward East Asia, empowering that region to inaugurate the "Century of the Pacific Rim."[30]

In discourse, Nixon spoke eloquently of those two great civilizations immediately preceding that one now called "Western civilization"—those of Rome and of the Muslim Arabs. Yet of the grandeur that was imperial Rome, of the majesty that was medieval Islam, no monument stands in greater tribute to their ultimate demises than the documentation of their downfalls at the hands of feckless rulers who proceeded as if responsible governance—equally in its civic and economic dimensions—played no role in sustaining domestic prosperity.[31]

Today, the challenges thus are many in addressing the imponderable: Was Nixon right? The critical strategic question becomes this: Can the seemingly inexorable course of American decline be reversed through more providently focused, prudently constructed public policy? Certainly, as the dynamic new economies of East Asia—the vast resource potentials of China, the industriousness of South Korea, the creativity of Singapore—increasingly become prime engines of global economic growth, signs of U.S. preeminence eclipse are concurrently more in evidence.

The trends are not transitory ones, as America's accelerating state of political drift cries out for a defining vision—a master policy for renewal that transcends partisan proclivities and policies. Before the crest of civilization crescendos on to the Orient, the nation must wake up to the reality that its continued prosperity is not a given. Instead, it is an aspiration, and an opportunity.

While time remains, therefore, it is not infinite—making incumbent upon America's leaders the need to take decisive action respecting the tax and regulatory bureaucratic overburden that now threaten her survival. For the challenge of effective governance today confronts not so much a socioeconomic crisis as a precursory public policy crisis. But if this policy crisis is not addressed with an agenda aimed at effective industrial and commercial regeneration, the full economic crisis will surely follow in its wake.

As analysis has made indelibly clear, free market capitalism is the modality that has forged America's spectacular commercial success. The concept underlying the term "capitalism," coined by no less than Karl Marx, was best captured by Scottish economic philosopher Adam Smith in his famed 1776 treatise *The Wealth of Nations* as: "Give me that which I want and you shall get this which you want." To wit: the act of buying and selling must always be mutually advantageous in benefiting both the buyer and the seller:

> Man has almost constant occasion for the help of his brethren, and it is in vain for him to accept it from their benevolence only. He will be more likely to prevail if he can interest their self-love in his favor, and show that it is for their own advantage to do so for him what he requires of them. . . .
>
> Give me that which I want, and you shall get this which you want is the meaning of every such offer, and it is in this manner that we obtain from one another the far greater part of the good offices of which we stand in need.
>
> For it is not from the benevolence of the butcher, the brewer, or the baker that we expect our dinner, but from their regard to their own interest. . . . No one but a beggar chooses to depend chiefly upon the benevolence of his fellow citizens.[32]

Capitalism, as defined by Smith, is thus founded equally upon unfettered markets, industrial ingenuity, and individual initiative. Indeed, entrepreneurial freedom is the indispensable prerequisite for capitalistic success. For entrepreneurs assume the risks, create the products, and invest the required resources in job-creating start-up businesses, and thereby employ the national workforce.[33]

Capitalism bred of entrepreneurial freedom works—the proof being in the economic data presenting overwhelming evidence that it is excessive taxation, overregulation, and other forms of public sector intervention that are private entrepreneurship's greatest enemy in its quest to abate poverty. The reason is that free market capitalism is the foremost path to economic upward mobility—and when its operational workings are frustrated, any jurisdiction is the poorer for the outcome.[34]

Notwithstanding capitalism's spectacular success in alleviating mass poverty, expanding economic opportunity, and raising living standards, however, many members of America's countercultural intellectual elite—an eclectic grouping that includes educators, journalists, editors, columnists, and clergy—have long been critical of it, conveying their messages framed in terms that Nobel laureate economist Friedrich Hayek calls "second-hand dealers in ideas."[35]

Having been educated in a higher education system dominated by socialistic ideology, he contends, such secondhand purveyors of shopworn ideas have historically been overwhelmingly critical of capitalistic concepts while highly sympathetic to socialistic, neo-Marxist ones. Their knee-jerk reactions to all the world's ills, therefore, is to unfailingly blame capitalism, while urging increased governmental intervention in the forms of taxation, regulation, and greater public sector spending in remedy.[36]

A prime reason that the countercultural intelligensia favor pseudo-communistic solutions is that they oppose the material inequality that they believe characterizes capitalism. Their ideal is instead absolute material equality—predicated on the premise that none should be economically better off than any others.

But there is yet a second, perhaps more overarching, reason why they are predominantly socialistic in their quest for remedies. Under a liberal regime of economic freedom and free market capitalism, there is no role for intellectuals to advise the state on how to best plan everyone else's affairs. They are so committed to achieving their utopian nirvana, therefore, that they are willing to defy the rules of law and markets to achieve their egalitarian ends.[37]

WHITHER, THEN, THE COURSE?

Yet the liberal extra-legal and contra-constitutional activities outlined in this treatise notwithstanding, the vacuity of their values should probably come as no genuine surprise, as it is wholly consistent with the miasma of multiculturalist misperception and misdirection that has been the focus of this inquiry.

Remedy, however, is quite another matter—and is a course that must be pursued with no small amount of trepidation. For while men of reason can differ, and men of reasoned intellect often differ, they remain men of reason. The lesson that they offer is this: when confronted with a serious challenge, one must proceed with consummate caution. But one must nonetheless proceed, cognizant that prudence mandates objectivity in evaluating the ideological handiwork of those in question—and then responding with countervailing strong resolve.

The lessons to be learned, then, are these. Socioeconomic forces do not operate in isolation, as one cannot enjoy the blessings of strong cultural values absent powerful economic ones in parallel, and conversely. Instead, they are inexorably intertwined. Indeed, when American heads of household stay up late at night these days, it is usually not in pondering the abstraction of whether school prayer should be made voluntary, but rather how to pay their bills and fund their children's educations.

Whatever the eventual provenance of, and catalyst for, America's socioeconomic regeneration, however, there can be no doubt that she needs it in large doses now. Her global legacy has been her historic willingness to fight for causes that she believes in. Today, that cause remains her foremost prospect for salvation—confronting the challenge of preserving those traditional values that define her as a culture—thereby seizing this moment to determine if the twenty-first century will again be the "American century."

For in the last analysis, a nation is the product of its values. America must be driven by American values if she is to remain American. If she does, if she comes to once again believe in herself as she once was, her preeminence will be preserved. For at the end of the day, neither multiculturalism, nor its political handmaiden, "political correctness"—"*Comintern* groupthink"—can defeat America. Only Americans can.

The manifestations of decline today are many. Education is infested with liberal bias and mediocrity. Civic traditions are today disregarded with impunity. Taxation is rising as regulation concomitantly grows to meet evolving bureaucratic complexity created to address the welfare burden occasioned by the resulting cultural dissonance and disconnect. The nation's longstanding self-correcting propensity for good thus is waning.

Indeed, the reasons for the decline of Rome rather than the nation's self-redeeming past may be a better guide to predicting her future, as her historic values are slowly being subsumed into a toxic counterculture best described by biblical Ephesians (5:11) as "the fruitless deeds of darkness." As the sun begins to set upon American global primacy at a time when it should be ascending to its zenith, then, it is fair to ask "why."[38]

And more importantly still, can she rebound? Arnold Toynbee has noted that in the process of decline, a civilization may rally from time to time, but its overall trajectory, the structural properties of its circumstance that determine its ultimate outcome. It is this debilitating process of devolution, then, that must be carefully contemplated.[39]

America remains the most advanced civilization in history—in the strength of her economy, the depth of her science and technology, the might of her military—and her ability to project the power that those sources of comparative advantage afford. Today, she has no equal. No rival superpower exists. No nation on earth has provided more security, stability, prosperity, and liberty to the peoples of the world than has the United States.

America was created as a land of promise, a venue for creative energy, a refuge from political tyranny, and a locus for economic freedom. In that quest, she has succeeded. She has advanced as history's most sophisticated civilization in technological capability and scientific knowledge. She has learned well from the legacy of her Founders, and the cause of her fortuitous outcome is compelling.

The sixty signers of the Declaration of Independence in 1776 committed themselves to the precept that all individuals are created equal and are to be ensured equal access to the pursuit of happiness. It bears repeating that they did not seek to foreordain equality of outcome, only equality of opportunity. They did not guarantee happiness—only, through the workings of due process of law, a level playing field in its pursuit.

Generally, they have succeeded. As a consequence, few Americans have experienced true poverty or starvation such as is today common throughout many countries of the world, indeed even some within her same hemisphere.[40]

For while far too many Americans subsist on welfare, few in America's major cities ever starve to death because they cannot find food. While many may lack affordable health insurance, few will die of diseases for want of medical attention. While too many remain illiterate, almost everyone has attended school, even if they did not graduate. Even for America's poor, color television is now commonplace—empowering them to witness live global events throughout the world.

The reason for America's success is intrinsic to her founding—as the Constitution begins with the proclamation: "We the people. . . ." The Declaration of Independence affirms the premise that all men are created equal. While St. Matthew opined, "the poor, ye shall always have with you," the Founding Fathers contemplated a contravening economic vision of alleviating poverty through productive pursuit of the "American dream." And the nation, in turn, has done well in overcoming immense odds by forging the "American dream" and making it well worth preserving.

Indeed, what the nation now judges as poverty would a century ago have been deemed a lavish lifestyle. As columnist Charles Krauthammer has cogently observed: "No country has been as dominant culturally, economically, technologically, and militarily in the history of the world since the Roman Empire."[41]

Thus, reflecting these realities, John Quincy Adams, in his July Fourth address in 1821, would proclaim: "America does not go abroad in search of monsters to destroy. She is the well-wisher to the freedom and independence of all. She is the champion only of her own. She will recommend the general cause by the countenance of her voice and the benign sympathy of her example."[42]

Beyond the great foresight of her founders, and the resilience and resourcefulness of her people, of course, America's unique strength has been the combination of her economic and military muscle, both of which she has employed decisively but judiciously. She is not an imperial power. Colin Powell perhaps described her best:

> Far from being the Great Satan, I would say that we are the Great Protector. We have sent men and women from the armed forces of the United States to other parts of the world throughout the past century to put down oppression.
>
> We defeated Fascism. We defeated Communism. We saved Europe in World War I and World War II. We were willing to do it. We were glad to do it. We went to Korea. We went to Vietnam. All in the interest of preserving the rights of people.
>
> And when those conflicts were over, what did we do? Did we stay and conquer? Did we say: "O.K., we defeated Germany; now Germany belongs to us? We have defeated Japan; so Japan belongs to us?"
>
> No. Instead, we built them up. We gave them democratic systems that they have embraced totally to their soul. Did we ask for any land? No. The only land that we ever asked for was enough land to bury our dead. For that is the kind of nation that we are.[43]

And thus it now is with Iraq and Afghanistan as well. Why would America want Iraq and the terrible burden of her unquenchable sectarian strife? Why would America want Afghanistan, a nation whose two most plentiful resources are opium and rubble? Instead, she is there because she is committed to the rights of people to self-determination.

Like Rome, she could have ruled the world had she elected to do so. Unlike Rome, she has contented herself within defensible borders framed by two great oceans—and for that reason, she is unique in history. After more than two centuries, America, therefore, need not apologize—her record of honor and good intent speaks for itself.[44]

As a nation, America does indeed enjoy a special destiny. Her greatness centers around the decency of her people framed by the socioeconomic vision of her Founders. It does not issue, in particular, from her brightest tenured academics, nor her Upper West Side Manhattan *cognoscenti*, nor the incisive analysis of her celebrity television anchor people, nor even from the remarkable foreign policy insights of her Hollywood entertainers.[45]

It stems instead from good citizens—working people who get up every day to build a better world, who fill the jobs and pay the taxes that ensure her effective governance and empower the nation to project force worldwide for the common good of all.[46]

Americans are a people who want limited government. They are willing to pay taxes, but they want to pay lower taxes. They want to protect the nation's borders. They will defend themselves when attacked. They still believe in "one nation under God indivisible"—and a "shining city on a hill."

They are, in sum, decent people working hard each day to preserve a nation that they love; and to pursue the American Dream, and are dedicated to Abraham Lincoln's determination "that this government of the people, by the people, and for the people shall not perish from this earth."[47]

In their quest, they will not be deterred by self-serving elitists who seek power under the socialistic mantra of the "politics of victimhood." They will not be driven down by those who would defame her culture. They will instead overcome the political and social challenges of the twenty-first century just as determined as they were when they overcame other menaces of parallel magnitude in the past. For they know well that should these elitists get their way, one day they will awake and the America that they know and have loved so long will be gone.[48]

The challenges are evident and ever-present, as America today is a land of perplexing paradox. She remains the greatest nation on earth: the land of opportunity; possessed of a vitality unlike that of any other. Her capacities are the envy of mankind. She is not yet a perfect union, but she is, by far, the world's most fair and just. How many have ever fled America for a better life in Mexico, Guyana, or Bangladesh?

Her preeminence, however, is at once the source of her strength and of her vulnerability. Indeed, those who would do her harm hate her less for what she does wrong than for what she has done right. She offers freedoms—freedom of the press and speech, freedom of religion, freedom to elect her leaders—rights not readily enjoyed in the lands from which most of her complainers and perpetrators of ill will now come.

A return to more faithful and prudent stewardship that restores her to her historic roots therefore is invoked. For if America retains the will, she possesses the way, as she remains the nation most blessed by God on earth.

Cognizant that contingent upon the strength of her resolve, she retains the resources—both natural and human—to prevail, therefore, the critical question must again be asked: Will ultimate demise be America's fate as well?

The answer to that question, which has been the principal focus of this inquiry, is addressed in the hopes embedded within the capstone "recipe for remedy" that follows—a regimen that proceeds mindful of the classic epitaph of Victor Hugo that

> The future has many foreboding names:
> For the weak: unattainability;
> For the fearful: ignominity;
> But for the bold: opportunity![49]

To these ends, America's leaders must articulate a clear new vision for her national purpose to restore those priceless ideals that shaped her founding. She must rebuild a strong and binding contract between her government and her citizens and reassert a powerful commitment to public policies that ensure the strength and survival of that contract.

Above all, she, and they, must recommit themselves to those values historically embedded within her culture and embodied in her Declaration of Independence and Constitution—reflecting that she is, at the end of the day, the United States of America.[50]

Part IV

RECIPE FOR RENEWAL

But Rome, tis thine alone, with awful sway,
To rule mankind and make the world obey,
Disposing peace and war in thy majestic way;
To tame the proud, the fettered slave to free,
These are imperial arts and worthy thee.

—Virgil, *The Aeneid*, VI

9

Pursuing Prudent Public Policy

Our plans miscarry because they have no aim. When a man knows not for
which harbor he is headed, no wind is the right wind.

—Seneca

PART I: THE POLICY FORMULATION CHALLENGE

The Noisome Nuances of Public Policy

The socioeconomic findings regarding America's future loom foreboding.
But however distressing the symptoms of cultural decay defined, the problems portrayed are not without prospective remedy—as various civilizations have, at times, reversed their courses of decline.

The quest for such remedies, however, must be circumspectly pursued—
as public policy can be a controversial, and at times capricious, benefactor.
Indeed, of late, in its fervent, albeit often naive, efforts to "protect the people" from all wrongs, government has, at times, caused more problems than
it has cured, and at a costly price.

As here it is that reality intrudes—for decision makers must be wary not
only of overtly bad policies *per se*, but of the unintended consequences of
seemingly more benevolent and benign ones. To cite but one classic example of the potentials for ambivalence in outcome issuing from the pursuit
of conflicting public sector goals, the 1973 Supreme Court's *Roe v. Wade* decision on abortion—castigated by some as sanctioning "child murder"—is
heralded by others as a case of "bad policy turned good."[1]

The equivocations, based on the data, are understandable. In the early 1990s, Bill Clinton's professed preoccupation with crime caused him to propose putting more one hundred thousand police on the nation's streets. Indeed, he lamented that fighting crime would consume the entire discretionary portion of his federal budget.

Yet that outcome didn't happen. Why? Because in the eyes of some, as a result of ready access to *Roe*-sanctioned abortions, those mothers most likely to produce criminals aborted them instead. In the words of Chicago economist Steven Levitt:

> Perhaps the most dramatic effect of legalized abortion, however, and one that would take years to reveal itself, was its impact on crime. In the early 1980s, just after the first cohort of children born after *Roe v. Wade* was hitting its late teen years, the crime rate began to fall.
>
> What this cohort was missing, of course, were the children who stood the greatest chance of becoming criminals. And the crime rate continued to fall as a whole generation came of age minus the children whose mothers had not wanted to bring them into the world. Legal abortion led to less unwantedness; unwantedness leads to high crime; legal abortion, therefore, led to less crime.[2]

Succinctly put, this argument holds a major reason that the national crime rate has come down in recent years is that mothers with the greatest propensities to produce children most likely to commit crimes elected instead to strike them dead in their infancies—a contention at the very least, demonstrating that Dr. Levitt, in discourse, has proven that if there are two public policy dots, it doesn't take a genius to connect them with a straight line.

By contrast, conservative commentator Pat Buchanan contends that *Roe*—in tandem with birth control, cohabitation without marriage, the rise of feminism, women seeking out-of-home careers, and dual-wage-earner families—is producing a deceleration in the births of native-born Americans toward zero population growth and below, thereby contributing to destruction of the requisite delicate balance between productive supporters and the support needed to sustain a requisite balance in human resources.[3]

The fulcrum of his argument is that as a society progresses, all social classes within it become more affluent and, in the process, begin to downsize their families by not spawning further children—adhering to a belief that traditional sex roles deny women full equality because they do not empower them to perform as men.[4]

When contraception fails to prevent unwanted children, therefore, abortion becomes a family values "Maginot Line," the second corridor of defense. The net result is a nation comprised of "double income, no kids" (DINK) couples. Logic follows, then, that the richer a society, the fewer its offspring, and the sooner it begins to die.[5]

Noting that a 2.1 child per family birthrate is required to sustain a population at zero population growth—and that the U.S. native-born fertility rate is slightly below 2.0 children per family, and with a massive influx of baby boomers soon to retire, he raises cogent questions: What happens when the ratio of productive workers to social services recipients becomes 1:1 or less? Who will pay for the health, welfare, and pensions of the elderly? Who will care for those confined to retirement centers and nursing homes? This dilemma, in Buchanan's view, is America's great social conundrum—its domestic demographic corollary to external "imperial overstretch."[6]

Sometimes, rather than being public policies misperceived or having unintended consequence, however, they simply are bad policies. Among them, government's mishandling of the Great Depression, as detailed in chapter 7, precipitated what some viewed as one of the most dangerous financial circumstances that the nation has ever faced. Yet in sheer order of economic magnitude, the crisis itself was not that severe. Other market crashes—among them that of October 1987—have been more pronounced.

Moreover, within six months of the 1929 crash, the Standard & Poors Index had rallied by more than 50 percent—one of the greatest rallies in market history. On these developments, Milton Friedman writes:

> The Great Depression, like most other periods of severe unemployment, was produced by serious governmental mismanagement rather than by any inherent instability of the private economy. A government-established agency—the Federal Reserve—had been assigned responsibility for monetary policy. In 1930 and 1932, it exercised this responsibility so ineptly as to convert what otherwise might have been a moderate contraction into a major catastrophe.[7]

Friedman's analysis is firmly based upon historic precedent, as the nation had indeed experienced sharp economic contractions before. There is a prevailing myth that the Great Depression started with an instantaneous crash, but such was not the case. For what the stock market then experienced, in reality, was no more than a significant retrenchment from its September 1929 peak until "Black Tuesday," October 29, 1929—losing about one-third of its value, which had nearly doubled in the previous year and a half.

Indeed, before 1929, the U.S. economy had suffered far sharper economic contractions than it has ever experienced since. From 1920 to mid-1921, it endured an acute, but short, depression. Wholesale prices dropped by 44 percent, the sharpest decline in U.S. history, and more than five hundred banks failed. By comparison, had not other factors intervened, there was no reason for the Great Depression to have resulted from the stock market crash of 1929.[8]

Indeed, all evidence suggests that the 1929 crash itself was more of a mere harbinger of impending financial danger than a coming economic catastrophe's cause—a warning of economic vulnerability and the need for effective remedy—a call for new free market–based medicine in the quest for a more holistic cure. It precipitated instead ill-conceived, misapplied public policy that actually caused the Great Depression.

Herbert Hoover initially sought to restore business confidence through the fiscal responsibility of a balanced federal budget on the hope that the economy would then right itself. By diverting monies from private sector to massive public spending, Franklin Delano Roosevelt's New Deal, in turn, merely prolonged the depression and made it worse, applying the wrong cure to the wrong disease—making it a policy epoch of transformational importance, ultimately generating tragic consequences throughout the nation's economy—as such policies reduced market demand further still, thereby contributing to the forthcoming economic collapse.[9]

The 1930 Smoot Hawley tariff regime likewise sought to "level the market playing field" by empowering domestically produced goods to better compete with imports—but again, by precipitating reciprocal tariffs elsewhere, thereby discouraging international trade, this misguided policy merely weakened the economy further still.

As in the last analysis, the New Deal, as an intended cure, was little more than symbolic public policy pablum motivated more by evocative political expediency than by economy insight, and the remedy that it provided proved woefully inadequate. Indeed, after Roosevelt's week-long "bank holiday" declared in March 1933, more than five thousand banks did not reopen their doors.[10]

After eight years, in fact, by 1940, the economic circumstance was worse than it had been a decade before—with over 20 percent of all nonfarm workers remaining jobless, and real wages 10 percent lower than they had been in 1931—and with the official unemployment rate, which had registered at 15.9 percent in 1931, standing at 17.2 percent in 1939. In short, after a decade of applying compensatory public spending palliatives, the nation's economy was worse off for the effort.[11]

Indeed, in the end, what really cured the Great Depression was World War II and the groundswell of private spending that it engendered. For it was the massive orders for durable goods to support the war effort that put America back to work and restored the nation's economic vigor—not the New Deal nor any of the other public sector economic placebos put into place over the preceding decade.

Contrast that approach with the experience of the present decade. For, despite the March 2001 burst of the techno-bubble, 9/11, and the attendant war on terror, at the close of 2007, the nation stood in better economic shape than at any time in her history—notwithstanding that economic danger signs—bred of tax and regulatory excess, together with irrational exuberant public spending made possible by the credit afforded by the superficial equity produced by an inflated housing market—remain clearly on the horizon. Still, inflation, save for energy prices, remains under control, the unemployment rate stands at a near-historic 5 percent "frictional level," and the budget deficit as a percentage of GDP is among the best of the past half century.

What are the public policy lessons to be learned from the economic and demographic consequences of these disparate public policies? Among them, the law of logic dictates that somewhere between Levitt and Buchanan—between Roosevelt and Reagan—there is a proper public policy balance that succeeds. Prudent policy formulation in quest of meaningful cure must thus perforce seek that crucial balance. The bottom line invoking prudent stewardship, then is that it is not tautological to conclude that if effective remedy is to be sought through productive policy, one has to get it right!

Partisanship and Public Policy

What, then, is the proper role of the nation's political parties in this policy formulation process? This dilemma, in fairness, it must be said, frames not sheer partisan concerns, but ones that span the political arena and are pandemic to its processes.

Throughout history, one could generally count on the Democrats to be fiscally and socially irresponsible. But today, the Republicans too have bought into the philosophy of boundless unearned public-sector largesse. Hence, while it used to be pithily observed that "God put Republicans on earth to cut spending and taxes," in the post-Reagan era, that homily is, at best, half right. Republicans have, in effect, become "big government conservatives."

For while they may run as libertarians—calling for tax cuts and governmental cutbacks—they now govern as liberal Democrats—lacking sufficient intellectual ambidexterity to keep one hand on the Bible and the other on the budget—thereby losing their erstwhile grip on the steering wheel of responsible federal governance that heralded their mid-1990s ascent to power, becoming instead "Democratic lite." "Great Society Republicans" is a phrase that comes to mind.

Hence, while Republicans lay claim to being closer to American core values in the issues of limited government, lower taxes, entrepreneurship, and national security, there is little in their governance in the new millennium to indicate that they believe their own longstanding, oft-professed, but seldom practiced, socioeconomic doctrine.

Former senator Malcolm Wallop (R-WY) pithily puts it this way: "If the Democrats were to suggest burning down every building on Capitol Hill tonight, the Republican moderates would counter: 'No, that's too radical. Let's do it one building at a time and spread it out over three years!'"[12]

Thus, Republican governance has devolved to the degree that it is distinguished from that of the Democrats only in degree and passion. As journalistic commentator Jonathan Rauch has aptly assessed the dichotomy:

"Conservatives would rather have fiscal deficits than higher taxes; whereas liberals would rather have deficits than smaller government."[13]

The Democrats, on the other hand, have generally remained true to their intellectual heritage by thriving on the politics of victimization and dependency—building their majorities by buying their constituencies with public-sector panaceas employing other people's money—usually that of America's economically hard-pressed middle class who would prefer to use their earnings to support their own families, not those of someone else.

In utter denial of the nation's pervasive subculture of crime and poverty, their remedies remain predicated on the flawed thesis that low-class criminals are derelicts depraved solely because they are deprived—hence, government must step in to "help."[14]

Thus, though Democrats have sought to expand their tent by buying off constituencies with other people's money, their agenda remains remarkably "idea free"—abandoning, under Senator Harry Reid (D-NV) and Speaker Nancy Pelosi (D-CA), their traditional flame-throwing, but no longer marketable, liberal lines, while shuffling between witless partisanship and nervous policy silence on the campaign trail—as there is today no "radical middle" for them to stake out. Their sole abiding political case for power is instead founded on the premise that they are not Republicans.[15]

In short, while Democrats continue to pursue class warfare as a mantra, Republicans proceed oblivious to the reality that there is a war at all. The net effect is that while Democrats are a lost cause in the quest to preserve the socioeconomic greatness of America, Republicans are, at best, reluctant warriors in the effort—producing a permuted admixture of the French Revolution's leitmotif and that of Karl Marx—as *liberté* and *fraternité* have been supplanted by *egalité* and *stupidité*!

At the philosophical bottom line, however, there is a defining difference. That difference lies in the separate approaches that conservative and liberal governance each bring to their perceived missions. For today, the economic analogue to liberal *social* elitism is liberal *fiscal* elitism—disliking the democratic nation-state for the same reason that they dislike the free market—both are systems that run on their own volitions without the need for top-down, micromanaged governmental intervention.[16]

Indeed, those who threaten the nation's traditional social fabric through historiographic revisionism and counterculturalism are likewise largely the same political subset who concurrently jeopardize it economically—seeking to substitute the tender mercies of federal bureaucracy for the bedrock nuclear family that has been the historic source of America's moral strength. This course, they believe, is altruistic.

Yet the economic lessons from the futility of this flawed policy course are not new. Indeed, common to all civilizations, they are embedded in an ongoing epic—almost cosmic—"conservative vs. liberal" confrontation. It is a clash of diametrically opposing ideological wills—a substantive debate on how pro-active governance should deploy.

In this case, the dichotomy is at once critical and clear—framing policy differences as profound and distinct as "darkness" is from "light"—a distinction that, to effectively define the political choices, must first be fathomed in its full policy dimensions by prudent decision makers and then vigorously pursued through legislative action.

As in their pursuit of the policy process, liberals unabashedly practice the "politics of victimization"—thereby creating "vast constituencies of dependency"—while portraying the economy as a "zero-sum" game wherein the affluent acquire wealth at the expense of the less powerful. In the defining words of Senator Hillary Clinton (D-NY) to a San Francisco audience on June 28, 2004: "We are going to take things away from you on behalf of the common good."[17] (Karl Marx, stand proud!)

The governing goal of any equitable political system, in their view, therefore, must be "economic justice"—promoting a "living wage" to ensure a "level playing field." For liberals, then, life begins at the point when a person is old enough to fill out food stamp applications. No ambiguous "first trimester" social welfare nonsense for these benevolent bureaucrats! In this quest, progressive taxation is needed to ensure that the rich "pay their fair share"—even if the outcome results in less public revenues— making raising worker's wages to job-destroying artificial levels an overarching goal.

Conservatives, on the other hand, believe in economic opportunity and freedom. They counter that workers are voluntary "wage-for service" *means*, not ends—that high wages and living standards are fortuitous by-products of dynamic economic growth issuing from the successful competition that occurs when businesses offer the best products at the lowest possible prices to consumers.

Businesses, in their view, thus exist to meet the needs and tastes of customers to generate profits—which are then reinvested in new technologies and production facilities—and thereby, higher quality jobs. In this dynamic market process, then, low-income consumers benefit by gaining access to the best products at the most competitive prices—thereby optimizing their purchasing power—while workers concurrently gain from those higher living standards bred of higher wages.

While liberals measure compassion for the poor by the numbers of individuals they force to the public trough through the "politics of dependency," then, conservatives gauge it not by the volume of governmental programs created, but by the number of individuals whom they lift out of poverty, thereby rendering governmental assistance unnecessary—all the while cognizant that productive jobs lead to wealth creation, self-reliance, and ultimate self-sufficiency.

Operating within the vast chasm of this ideological divide, therefore, while liberals believe that surplus capital is no more than unrequited governmental revenues that, through some unfortunate flaw or oversight in the public taxing system, still remains within the private sector at their sufferance—in their words, tax "expenditures"—conservatives know that it is the seed corn from which all future economic growth will issue.

Conservatives, in rejecting the flawed notion of redistributive economics, thereby identify onerous fiscal overburden as the prime cause of the economic stagnation that causes financial stress for America's wage earners and their households. They believe that liberals have—through class warfare and the politics of dependency and fear—for far too long, farmed out the nation's poor and minorities to the plantations of welfare politics. They view liberalism as a launch pad for sustained attacks on the nation's core values, precipitating its accelerating moral decline.

They see statist values as not only symbolic of, but a catalyst for, the deepening decay. They envision an America that is slowly toppling from its lofty role as a free-market beacon into the abyss of a subsuming welfare state. They believe in a return to limited government by and for the people, and they believe that the liberal notion that all rights and powers directly descend from Washington is not only patently absurd but singularly unconstitutional.

In this cosmic clash of coalescing visions, then, while liberal government is "big government," conservative government is "rationalized governance." While liberals offer "statist governance," conservatives counter with "private economic opportunity." While liberals argue a public-sector solution for every social problem, conservatives see in every one an underlying *public-sector* cause.

Accordingly, while liberals propose to dramatically expand the role of government in their quest for a cure, conservatives would significantly downsize it through tax cuts and budget-balancing amendments. While liberals seek to grow the government, conservatives seek to *expand the private sector* to keep the macroeconomy strong. When liberals oppose deficit spending, their solution is to "tax more." When conservatives oppose deficit spending, their solution is to "spend less." Thus, while for liberals, raising taxes is invariably a first recourse, for conservatives, it is relegated as a "last resort."[18]

The political clash thus is "Promethean" in scope and ideological in its underpinnings. While liberals extol the expansion of public rights, conservatives cite the importance of private responsibilities. Under the pretext of compassion, liberals sell repackaged socialism in their quests for empowerment through dependency, as theirs becomes a "quasi-religious disorder" that demands that all of life be controllable.

They thus demonstrate their compassion by randomly throwing money—other people's money—at perceived social problems. They denominate the degree of their compassion by the numbers of people that they have taken to the public sector trough. Hence, while conservatives call for "judicial restraint" in seeking ultimate recourse government to solve problems for which it is ill suited, liberals cry out for publicly imposed "social justice" to remedy all societal ills.

In the process, under the guise of "fairness," liberals confiscate the hard-won earnings of achievers and redistribute them to nonachieving pet constituencies—to those who have been rendered non-achievers by their deadly cocktails of taxation, regulation, and other disincentives to produce. Their battle cry—"the rich get richer while the poor get poorer"—thus culminates in their all-too-often successful efforts to ensure that no one ever gets much richer than anyone else.

Finally, when all else has failed, to prevent "starvation in Paradise," in true *"deus ex machina"* fashion, they proceed to entice their "beneficiary victims" with public-sector entitlements, which further reduces them to perpetual "ward of the state" status. As a consequence, it is no accident that today, over 47 percent of the nation's income is not spent by the workers who have earned it but by America's political class who have taxed it away from them.[19]

Pragmatic conservatives counter, in turn, not only that such a welfare state is unequivocally addictive but that it imposes dual drags upon economic efficiencies—first in misallocating resources by allowing individuals the option of not having to provide for themselves; and second, by permitting politicians to overburden the private economy through pandering to the whims of the indolent at the expense of the conscientiously productive to build electoral majorities.

Yet by thus weakening the private sector, the nation, as well as its individuals, are concurrently weakened—as the public welfare system institutionalizes dependency and perpetuates it from one generation to the next. The end result is an expanding ethical shortfall within the political system, which produces a corresponding moral shortfall in societal values, which ultimately results in devastating monetary shortfalls in the federal budget, precisely the sequential formula that, this analysis has shown, brings about the fall of civilizations.[20]

Compensatory social safety nets, moreover, most often merely serve to complicate the bureaucratic addiction problem by setting "welfare traps"— offering public-sector handouts at benefit levels that price alternate employment out of the open market—thereby often making dependency an economically more rational decision than seeking low-paying jobs.[21]

In sum, America's profound "dependency crisis"—her gradual devolution from an entrepreneurial ethic to an "entitlements ethic"—is a product of a profound loss of both her social and economic bearings. For while an able-bodied person who truly wants to make a productive contribution to society still can, liberal political leadership has effectively countered with a hybrid system of disincentives for productive effort blended with high rewards for indolent inactivity—a deadly combination that produces a poverty of human values by giving economic value to material poverty.

Thus it is that, under liberalism, the progenitive sources of socio-economic problems are inverted and recast as their cures—as the prime purpose of liberal politics is not to solve problems but to find problems to justify the empowerment of government. For liberalism itself is empowered only through the relative deprivation of others—much of which it has already been responsible for creating through the impacts of the taxes required to sustain it.[22]

The consummate irony, however, is that it is firmly founded upon an unadulterated, convoluted economic logic in terms of who ultimately winds up paying for their sublime largesse. As whenever any strategy focuses on "making the poor less poor" by "making the rich less rich," the tab invariably winds up being paid by a defenseless, struggling middle class.

At times, liberals actually do succeed in subduing political debate by treading upon the *terre sanctae* of Orwellian "big government political doublespeak," rechristening their big government programs with conservative-sounding names—patently misleading terms such as "deficit reduction," "reinventing government," "welfare reform," and the like.

Old-fashioned tax hikes thus become "revenue enhancements." Classic pork barrel patronage is promoted as an "economic stimulus package," budget deficits as "underfunded tax revenue investments," disposable personal income as "unavoidable tax expenditures," socialized medicine as "managed competition," employer mandates as "shared responsibility," welfare as "non-work-required human investments" . . . ad infinitum.

Indeed, at times, quite remarkably, they do succeed at the ballot box as well. Yet when the French political philosopher Rousseau advanced his general theory of democracy founded upon governance in accordance with the general will of the people in the eighteenth century, that concept was predicated upon the pretext of the promise that the electorate would somehow ultimately get some semblance of what it thought it voted.

Its premise held that were a politician to be elected by promising to cut taxes, for instance, then some effort probably should be devoted seeking to cut taxes after the election. Logic again follows that were a candidate elected upon the pretense of being a champion of the long-suffering middle class, then some post-election focus might be lent to formulating policy that, at the least, does no grave harm to middle-class economic interests.

Yet today, such is often not the case. For unlike the free market, wherein consumers vote their income dollars to purchase precisely what they want, in the contemporary political marketplace, the voter generally gets something quite different from what he or she voted for—often modified in the name of "changing economic circumstance."

But while political compromise is undeniably inevitable in, and intrinsic to, the democratic process, malleable and duplicitous responses to good-faith public commitments are not abiding strengths of character. For implementing the opposite of what was promised and what the electorate voted for is not a characteristic of democratic practice—it is what dictators do.

Former perennial Socialist Party presidential candidate Norman Thomas often presciently warned that "America's people will never knowingly adopt socialism, but under the name of liberalism, they will adopt every fragment of the socialist program until one day America will be a socialist nation without every knowing what had happened."[23]

It is sobering to reflect, therefore, that Thomas and Gus Hall, the long-standing American Communist Party presidential candidate, both dropped their bids for the nation's highest office in 1970, lamenting that the two major political parties had egregiously co-opted the substance of their platforms.[24]

In short, within a free society, income can be neither taken nor redistributed, it must be earned. The affluent are wealthy because they have worked for it. Take it away from them and, through ingenuity, they likely will reaggregate it once again. This is no less than a free market function, as the Constitution guarantees equal opportunity, not equal outcome—in this process, government is mandated to preserve parity at the starting gate, not to ensure the outcome at the closing line.

The role of government thus must be to ensure the operation of a robust and transparent business environment wherein producers can healthily produce and vigorously compete. Moderating tax and regulatory policies to ensure that they do not distort market price is quintessential to this end.

Who, then, is right in seeking to shape the public-policy macrocosm? There is no question that society is the more ambient when the better angels of conservatism win—as in pursuing the liberal logic to its inexorable, unfortunate end leads to no more than a menu of failed policy options consisting of minimum wages, public-sector job creation, and mandated equality of outcomes.

But to prevail, conservatives must far more aggressively advance their agendas, as success is not contingent upon faith alone. Politics, the pursuit of the possible, must thus not be confounded with religion in the pursuit of the ideal. Politics is about getting into office; religion is about getting into heaven.[25]

Hence, pursuing "business as usual"—seeking to win present battles with the staid techniques of the past—no longer works. In football, this approach is called a "prevent defense"—retreat from pursuing the attack to a consolidation strategy that is invariably the recourse of losers.

Preparing a dynamic remedial agenda for the threats to America's socio-economic future identified by this inquiry requires not only careful contemplation, then, but disaggregation by solution. It also requires systematic policy planning and dynamic implementational follow-through. The policy options that follow are dedicated to that end—addressing first the challenges of cultural and civic alienation; and then the socioeconomic welfare burdens that they engender.

PART II: REDUCING CULTURAL ALIENATION

Immigration

As analysis has shown, today, America's leftist elitists support countercultural causes that now threaten the nation's productive future. They support subcultural identity over national identity and patriotism, which they pejoratively label "nativist. They opposed teaching classic history in the nation's schools.

They oppose border control, oppose English as the nation's official language, and seek ways to allow everyone presently illegal in-country to remain. In fervently attempting to inflict this gravely flawed agenda upon a nation that rejects it in desperation, they resort to describing their critics as racist and xenophobic.

These are not utterly new challenges—as proper immigration policy has been an American policy concern from the founding of the Republic:

*George Washington, in a letter to John Adams, asserted that immigrants should be absorbed into American life so that "by an intermixture with our people, they or their descendants get assimilated to our customs, measures, laws: in a word, soon become one people."

*In a similar 1790 speech to Congress on the naturalization of immigrants, James Madison stated that America should welcome the immigrant who could assimilate but exclude the immigrant who could not "readily incorporate into our society."

*Alexander Hamilton, in turn, wrote in an 1802 missive: "The safety of a republic depends upon the energy of a common national sentiment; on a uniformity of principles and habits; on the exemption of the citizens from foreign bias and prejudice; and on that love of country which will almost invariably be found to be closely connected with birth, education, and family."[26]

Immigration policy has also been one of the American government's great public failures. In 1876, the Supreme Court ruled that the individual states could not set immigration policy, and the Congress responded with the Immigration Law of 1882, which barred "criminals, lunatics, idiots, and those likely to become a public charge" from entering the country. From this initial "high point," however, the federal record on immigration has proceeded downhill ever since.[27]

The findings of this inquiry have made clear that such failure cannot be tolerated if the Republic is to survive as an integral entity. To reach an effective remedy for America's burgeoning immigration problem, however, it must first be succinctly defined. Briefly, its parameters include the following:

- The line of immigrants waiting to enter America is endless, yet the funds available to support them are finite.
- Continuous immigration does not encourage dispersion and assimilation.
- Many immigrants are unskilled and often also illiterate.
- Admission of excessive numbers of unskilled and illiterate immigrants can lead to poverty and crimes associated with poverty, as well as to disease.
- Excessive immigration in inner cities can lead to the creation of ghettos and slums.
- The number of unskilled people seeking admission often exceeds the total needed, thereby creating unemployment anew.
- Immigrants tend to have large families, placing excessive demands on social services.
- Although single workers may initially be admitted, "chain immigration" policies allow them to bring in spouses, children, parents, in-laws, and so on, further straining social services.
- Sojourning immigrants often view the country as an economic stopover and have no real desire to assimilate.
- Large numbers of immigrants from a particular area often settle together in enclaves, which can lead to societal balkanization.
- *Economic costs* of excessive immigration usually exceed its *economic advantages* because of both liberal social welfare policies and the requisite municipal infrastructures needed to sustain them.
- Continuous immigration can lead to welfare demands that exceed the social services' abilities to meet those demands.
- Lack of security monitoring of immigration can lead to the admission of would-be terrorists and criminals.[28]

Because of the complexity and diversity of the challenge, pursuit of a responsive remedial agenda calls for a combination "carrot and stick" policy approach outlined as follows:

Who Should Come: . . .

Warmly welcome legal immigrants.   Make Foreign Service consular, Homeland Security, and Transportation Safety Administration activities for those seeking to comply with due process user-friendly—cognizant that those who feel welcome seldom set out to destroy their new homes.

Impose means and prospective contributions tests for legal entry. Rein-state requirements analogous to 1882 and 1891 U.S. statutory provisions that explicitly excluded from U.S. entry "paupers or persons likely to be-come a public charge." Instead of welfare and free education for illegal aliens, governments, at all levels, should develop legal sanctions and infra-structures to provide emergency services only—with a federal five-year mandatory waiting period for non-medical-emergency welfare assistance benefits.[29]

Succinctly put, immigrants should be chosen on their economic merits, not their family connections or welfare needs. Means-tested immigration was the clear intent of the Founding Fathers—with colonial assemblies en-acting restrictions against the admission of those "likely to become a pub-lic charge," and with the Massachusetts Pilgrims in 1639 imposing sharp fines for shipmasters discharging paupers and criminals into America. If such a formula results in only Mexicans, only Irish, or only Singaporeans admitted in a single year, so be it. America will have qualitatively improved the admixture of her society rather than merely adulterating it.[30]

Implement immigration meritocracy. Give priority to skilled immigra-tion over family reunification by replacing the family reunification focus of the Hart-Celler Immigration and Naturalization Act of 1965 with so-called designer immigration—a policy oriented toward job skills and potential economic contributions rather than social and political considerations. This approach again is consistent with the thinking of the Founders—as George Washington, in a letter to John Adams, wrote: "My opinion with respect to immigrants is that, except of useful mechanics and some particular de-scriptions professions, there is no use in encouragement."[31]

Making the case for skills-based admissions, economist George Borjas con-vincingly contends that based on "immigration surplus"—the cost-benefit per capita income balance sheet of admitting immigrants—"the per capita incomes of native Americans would rise substantially if the country switched from its current immigration policy, which admits a mix of skilled and unskilled workers, to one that admitted only skilled workers."[32]

Borjas further maintains that in the latter instance, the capital surplus benefit would more than double or triple—dramatically rising from in range from $7–21 billion to $42–126 billion—concluding: "Therefore, the economic benefits—for the nation as a whole—from pursuing a policy that attempted to maximize the immigration surplus could be sizable."[33]

The L-1 visa program, whereby senior-level managers may be brought in for up to seven years, and the H-1B program, whereby professional workers are brought in for up to six years to work primarily in the electronic and software industries, should be thus made the prime focus of future immi-gration policy; and as such, should be significantly expanded from the pres-ent 65,000 beneficiaries, with an additional 20,000 allowed for "high value" immigrants with degrees from American universities—to 500,000 workers yearly in the case of H-1B visas.[34]

The provisions of E-2 and EB-5 visas to facilitate the access of investors who invest $1 million or more in America in businesses that result in five or more jobs—or a minimal $500,000 investment that produces at least ten jobs—should likewise be expanded to encourage job-creating inward investments in the United States—making those who commit to such investments immediately eligible for immigration. Applicants possessing doctorates in science, engineering, or medicine should be made *immediately eligible for immigration.*

And Who Should Not: . . .

Implement a "zero amnesty" national immigration policy.   No one should be exempted from the nation's immigration due process laws nor excused from obeying them. "Zero amnesty" embodies the constitutional requirement of equity before the law, recognizing that banning illegal immigration ensures a more equitable immigration policy for everyone.[35]

Export illegal aliens without equivocation.   Replace "catch and release" with "catch, arrest, and deport," executing streamlined deportation procedures for illegal aliens while levying lengthy prison sentences for repeat offenders. Eliminate the "voluntary departure option." Those who should have been deported should not be allowed to run free. Such policies benefit no one save those who would deliberately abuse the U.S. immigration system's undeserved trust.[36]

Eliminate social service transfer payments to illegal immigrants.   Restrict welfare benefits, excluding emergency medical services, exclusively to certified Americans. Denying tax-funded public services to invaders will contribute to self-imposed voluntary deportation.

Ban "chain migration," whereby immigrants are able to bring extended family members and often even friends to the United States.   Immigration should be limited to only immediate members of nuclear families and not to extended families, cognizant that the present process expands geometrically in that the relatives legally sponsored by family members also become empowered to sponsor their own extended family members, *ad infinitum.*[37]

In the process, moreover, children born on U.S. soil, including those of illegal aliens, instantaneously become citizens, thereby qualifying them for the full range of public benefits provided by American taxpayers—and when they are twenty-one years of age, they too can sponsor all of their extended family relatives.[38]

Eliminate the citizenship of so-called anchor babies, offspring of noncitizens temporarily in the United States.   Originally implemented solely to prevent the states from denying citizenship to post–Civil War newly freed slaves, the

Fourteenth Amendment instead extended blanket citizenship to "all persons born or naturalized in the United States *and subject to the jurisdiction thereof.*"[39]

This provision notwithstanding, several categories of residents—among them transitory aliens, children of diplomats, and self-governing Indians on reservations—were to be explicitly excluded from the extension of this privilege because they were not subject to American jurisdiction.

As explained in 1866 by Senator Jacob Howard (R-MI), the amendment's coauthor: "This will not, of course, include persons born in the United States who are foreigners, aliens, who belong to families of ambassadors or foreign ministers accredited to the Government of the United States, but will include every other class of persons."[40]

However, because of judicial interpretations exactly opposite of the sponsors' professed original intent, Congress, which is constitutionally vested with control over citizenship and naturalization issues pursuant to Article I, Section 8, should enact a law denying citizenship to offspring of illegal entries who, by virtue of that illegality, have not subjected themselves to U.S. jurisdiction.

Today, an annual average of 300,000 women enter America to deliberately birth their offspring on U.S. soil solely to gain citizenship. These "anchor babies" then become wards of the welfare state. Banning this legal loophole law would not only eliminate present circumvention of the Constitution, it would, in the long term, save U.S. taxpayers billions of dollars in social service costs that could more providently be spent on the children of America's native born.[41]

Deny driver's licenses and in-state tuition rates to those not in the United States in legal status. The recent blatant attempt by former New York Governor Elliot Spitzer, among others, to grant driver's licenses to illegal aliens is catastrophically wrong. Not only is such a license a supposed indication of an ability to drive, it likewise is the ID of choice both for voter registration and for gaining onboard access to commercial aircraft—a folly beyond stupidity in an age of airborne terrorism.

Notwithstanding, *any* proposal to mandate presentation of photo ID as a condition of gaining access to the poll booth tends to generate serious concern among the liberal elite lest it disenfranchise the voting-friendly fraudulent. Democratic votes should be won on the merits of platforms and ideas, not through seeking to egregiously steal elections by attempting to orchestrate how many illegals can be surreptitiously afforded access to the polls.

Deny federal aid to all cities that deliberately harbor illegal aliens in contravention of federal law. Austin, Chicago, Houston, New York, San Diego, San Francisco, and Seattle, among others, are all jurisdictions that have designated themselves as so-called sanctuary cities—forbidding their police forces from working with federal authorities in curbing immigration violations. They should be denied any and all federal aid so long as they countenance such civil disobedience.[42]

Enact a federal constitutional amendment making English the official language of the United States. Modeled after a measure initiated by California Senator S. I. Hayakawa in 1983, the amendment proposed should read:

> Section 1: The English language shall be the official language of the United States.
> Section 2. The Congress shall have the power to enforce this Article by legislation.[43]

Making English America's de jure *lingua franca* is imperative not only because it is in English-speaking environs wherein citizens and residents will compete for most productive, upwardly mobile jobs, but because U.S. taxpayers will have to assume their maintenance costs if they cannot support themselves.

English—the language of Shakespeare and the language that empowers immigrants to seek employment both within and outside of their ethnic enclaves—is now spoken by more than a billion people, and far more books, the source of academic learning, are published in it than in any other language. Thus, while few would argue that immigrants should never speak their native language, reasonable people do contend that, for practical reasons, that they should learn English as quickly as they can.[44]

Viewed through a slightly different prism, in a shrinking world, a compelling argument can be made that while bilingualism in an individual is admirable, in a society, it can be culturally devastating. All Americans should learn a second language, but that to empower them to compete in a global economy, not of necessity to converse with fellow citizens.

In the words of Theodore Roosevelt: "We must have but one flag. We must also have but one language. That must be the language of the Declaration of Independence, of Washington's Farewell Address, of Lincoln's Gettysburg speech and second inaugural."[45]

This is a consensus held by most Americans. A 2007 Zogby poll shows that 84 percent of all Americans support making English the official national language.[46] A parallel poll reveals that by 87 percent to 11 percent, the American people favor English as the official language of government; and by 83 percent to 17 percent, they believe that new immigrants should be required to learn English.[47]

Establish English language proficiency as a critical criterion in evaluating immigration applications. Require U.S. subgovernments to provide English instruction free of charge—and mandate immediate English language immersion courses, from the first day of arrival, for those whose native tongue is not English. English today is already America's de facto national language, and the most rewarding jobs today require a solid command of it. For this reason, polls show that an overwhelming percentage of Hispanic parents want their children solidly schooled in English in the American K-12 system.[48]

Erect a two-thousand-mile-long fence across America's southern border. Mindful of poet laureate Robert Frost's wise counsel—"good fences make good neighbors"—build an impenetrable fence manned by armed guards across the entire U.S. border with Mexico. The imposition of such a barrier is an imperative as a security issue as much as it is a compelling immigration issue.

Whereas the Berlin Wall of the 1960s was constructed to keep freedom-loving peoples *in*, the Tijuana and Brownsville walls of the 2000s are needed to keep bureaucracy-exploiting illegals *out*.[49] Since Mexico professes to an inability to control its own borders, the U.S. Border Patrol should help them—and to that end, must be given sufficient manpower and fire-power to turn back illegal immigrants and outgun the drug cartels.

The U.S. government financed the maintenance along the Afghani-Pakistani border of 12,000 border police and the construction of 177 checkpoints at a cost of $300,000 per checkpoint a half decade ago. If it can protect that porous border, it owes it to its citizens to protect its own southern border as well.[50]

Mandate passport identification for all U.S. cross-border travel and develop attendant biometric identification to prevent its fraudulent use. Adopt national identification cards. Fully secured entry into the country requires closely monitored borders backed by universally held biometric ID cards in the heartland. In the current age of terror, the nation can no longer afford the luxury of not requiring secure, uniform individual identification. The ability to identify people readily is a critical component of defense. Without trackable ID cards for everyone living or traveling in-country, even secured borders will be insufficient.[51]

Enforce anti-dual-citizenship provisions, banning the all-too-prevalent practice of simultaneously holding more than one citizenship or nationality. Today, dual citizenship is not merely a wave of the future, it is a tidal surge of the present. Though there are now some ninety-three countries that sanction it, the United States is not one of them. The dual-citizenship phenomenon holds special import for America, for her renunciation oath implies that she is indeed something special, the bastion of liberty and opportunity, the "shining city on a hill." That oath explicitly states:

> I hereby declare, on oath, that I absolutely and entirely renounce and abjure all allegiance and fidelity to any foreign prince, potentate, state, or sovereignty of whom or which I have heretofore been a subject or citizen; that I will support and defend the Constitution and laws of the United States of America against all enemies, foreign and domestic; that I will bear true faith and allegiance to the same.[52]

This is a critical initiative—as those who deny meaning to American citizenship deny meaning to that social contract and to membership within the cultural and political community of which they have become a part.[53]

The exclusive privilege of citizenship thus is vitiated by the flagrant disregard of it by illegal immigrants. For with dual citizenship, U.S. identity is no longer distinctive or exceptional. It is, instead, no more that an appendage to another citizenship. It is a blatant attempt to exploit the best of two worlds, as well as a direct repudiation of the *biblical* admonition: "No man can serve two masters."[54]

Make unlawful presence in the United States a felony, make aiding and abetting illegal aliens also a felony, and increase the penalties for the smuggling of illegal aliens.

Implement harsh penalties for would-be terrorists who attempt to enter as illegal aliens.

Make employment verification necessary and actively enforce laws making it a crime to hire illegal aliens. Businesses who break the law by hiring illegal aliens should be aggressively pursued and severely fined. Because it takes two parties to break the immigration law by working illegally—both an illegal worker and an illegal employer—the nation must get serious about punishing employers who hire illegal workers.[55]

Actively enforce bans on noncitizen voting in U.S. federal, state, and local elections. The blatant mid-1990s Clinton-Gore efforts, empowered by the 1993 "Motor-Voter Act," to open the nation's southern Mexican and Caribbean borders to allow for the immigration of waves of new, often illegal, Democratic voters were particularly egregious—paving the way for concurrently setting up voter registration booths in every driver registration and food-stamp distribution center across the country.[56]

Deny dual-citizenship political enfranchisement. U.S. citizens, as a condition of their citizenship, should be prohibited from:

- holding elected or politically appointed offices abroad;
- voting in public elections abroad;
- serving in foreign militaries; and
- holding U.S. public elective or appointed offices while maintaining dual citizenship.[57]

II. Education

The challenges to the America's educational system posed by the multicultural movement have been amply described in chapter 3. The conclusions to be drawn are readily evident—no serious academic program can be built upon a foundation of double standards and preferential treatment.[58]

Not only is such a course educationally unsound, it is patently unconstitutional. Democracy is not predicated on the premise of equal endowment but of equal rights. It does not guarantee success, but it does aspire to equal opportunity—and it is an opportunity extended to individuals, not groups. For truly "liberal" education resolves issues based on idealism, not on special interest—in terms of the weight of moral right and not of political force or civil disobedience in its absence.[59]

Finally, the imparting of knowledge must take place absent cultural, political, or other parochial bias. As the case studies described in chapters 2 and 3 make clear, an uncritical examination of non-Western cultures in order to favorably contrast them with those of the West is nothing more than a reverse cultural imperialism whereby self-proclaimed intellectuals project personal prejudices onto other cultures to achieve self-serving political ends.

Such intellectual distortion has no place in an academia committed to genuinely objective scholarly inquiry. Given these manifest realities and complex challenges, then, the following proposals become policy imperatives.[60]

The Ideological Emancipation of Education

Confront the counterculturalism challenge head-on. When the enemy's express goal is to kill you, churning out platitudes and empty rhetoric about multicultural diversity, mutual respect, and dialogue buys nothing except contempt and still greater risk. It must not be forgotten that ultimately, "political correctness" did not ward off 9/11, London, or Madrid.

Enact as federal law the: "All Men Are Created Equal Civil Rights Contract of 2008" modeled after the California Civil Rights Initiative of 1996. In other words, allow "merit" to be the sole determinant in public sector admissions, employment, and contracting decisions.

Support efforts by the Students for Academic Freedom to enact legislation at the state level to invoke a student bill of rights on public campuses that preserves freedom of thought and intellectual diversity and protects students from academic reprisals by professors who hold contradictory beliefs. Intended as a document to secure intellectual independence on campus, this approach opposes all ideological or religious tests for faculty hiring and promotion, calls for intellectually balanced courses in the humanities and social sciences, advocates free speech on campus, and seeks restoration of research free from intellectual philosophy restriction.

Insist that academicians practice the First Amendment rights that they profess to believe. Adherence to a full "Academic Bill of Rights" should be unconditionally tie-barred to a learning institution's future receipt of federal funds—thereby incentivizing them to ensure its general implementation and follow on strict enforcement.[61]

Require by law that all higher education administrators operating within publicly funded institutions mandatorily receive eight hours of "sensitivity training" taught by a certified constitutional lawyer—not in racism, sexism, or homophobia but in the application and enforcement of First Amendment rights respecting free speech.

Mandate by federal law that efforts to promote partisan political agendas in the guise of education within the classrooms of publicly funded campuses must unequivocally result in the immediate suspension of all federal funding for such institutions.

Support ongoing initiatives to grant students at nonsectarian colleges that receive public funds the right to go to court to seek redress from the imposed indoctrination of educational institutions possessing patently unconstitutional speech codes as integral parts of parochial political agendas.[62]

Support the Campaign for Fairness and Inclusion in Higher Education initiative of the Center for the Study of Popular Culture, which articulates four principal demands:

- Conducting an inquiry into political bias in hiring processes for faculty and administrators, and seeking ways to promote fairness toward— and inclusion of—diverse, under-represented mainstream perspectives;
- Conducting an inquiry into political bias in the allocation of student program funds—including speakers' fees—and seek ways to promote fairness toward—and inclusion of—diverse, under-represented mainstream perspectives;
- Imposing a zero tolerance policy toward the obstruction of campus speakers and meetings and the destruction of informational literature distributed by campus groups; and
- Adopting a code of conduct for faculty members that ensures that classrooms welcome diverse viewpoints and not be used for political indoctrination, which is a violation of students' academic freedoms.[63]

The Pragmatic Implementation of Education

Make English language competency a nationwide mandatory requirement for graduation in the nation's K–12 system. This goal was the clear intent of America's earliest settlers, as evidenced in the literacy laws of the state of Connecticut enacted in 1690. To wit:

> The [legislature] observing that . . . there are many persons unable to read the English tongue and thereby incapable to read the Holy Word of God or the good laws of this colony . . . it is ordered that all parents and masters shall cause their respective children and servants, as they are capable, to read distinctly the English tongue.[64]

Make civics a nationwide mandatory course for graduation in the country's K–12 educational system. No individuals can be good citizens unless they are fully cognizant of the laws, rules, and institutions of the political jurisdictions wherein they participate. Civics classes can, in large part, solve that shortcoming—with such education focused upon immigrant students in particular.

Restore objectivity to history and historiography. America's universities, colleges, and public schools share a profound responsibility to teach history for its own sake as integral to the requisite intellectual armament of civilized persons—and not to denigrate or degrade it by permitting its contents to be dictated by political pressure groups, be they ideological, ethnic, racial, religious, or economic. The preservation of legacy and history is far too precious for parochial bias to be allowed to intervene. For national values are imbued by a sense of history, not by whim, happenstance, or parochial ethnic or racial bias.[65]

Promote merit-based pay in local school districts to reward teachers who excel while shedding those who are incompetent. This precept is precisely how every successful private enterprise imbued by profit motive now must operate to survive. Today, because of tenure and union rules, bad teachers cannot effectively be removed from the education system for years—notwithstanding that those hurt the most by this unionized approach of applying due process are the national interest and the children themselves. This approach must be summarily reversed if America is to remain a superpower.[66]

Set explicit standards for teacher qualifications and pay, class size, and length of school year. In addition, set standards for optimal student-to-teacher ratios that ensure that America's children receive the quality of education that they both need and deserve. The school year also should be lengthened to ensure parity with the classroom exposures of schools of principal industrial competitors.

Implement nationwide proficiency testing for both students and teachers. Each teacher should be tested for proficiency in the subjects taught. Those who excel should receive bonuses; those who fail should be dismissed. Schools that excel should be financially rewarded; schools that don't should go unfunded until they implement the reforms that ensure that they do; and school administrators who can't achieve the requisite prescribed excellence within their schools should be released.

Establish a mandatory federal curriculum of hardcore subjects and standards of discipline within the classroom. National standards for mathematics, science, and English should be implemented and continually raised. If America is determined to preserve her global leadership, she should restore her educational standards to levels consistent with those now operating as the highest in the world.

Ensure equal access to higher education to any graduating high school senior meeting stringent national testing levels and demonstrating a need for fi-

nancial assistance. A civilian equivalent of the GI Bill, providing national college scholarships for the study of engineering and the sciences to bright but needy students, should be universally created and federally funded.[67]

Grant automatic admission and financial support to the top 10 percent of every high school class, based on grades, to state colleges and universities, regardless of financial circumstance. The federal government should provide scholarships and financial aid for college tuition, room, and board for all students in the top 10 percent of their classes, irrespective of background, who require financial aid. Building the nation's next generation of leaders should be its foremost policy priority, and in that quest, the wallet should not serve as a constraint to will.

Offer tax subsidies to encourage employer training of employees. A tax credit patterned after those sanctioned for R&D would yield significant tangible results in qualitatively upgrading the capabilities of the nation's labor force. Such credits would encourage stronger linkages between employers and trainers and thereby promote greater efficiencies in the use of training dollars.[68]

III. Faith and Family

Enact a constitutional amendment allowing Supreme Court rulings to be overridden by a 60 percent vote in each of the House and Senate. Today, the precipitous rise of judicial activism—judges seeking to preempt the constitutionally defined prerogatives of legislators—has reached intolerable levels. Decisive remedy is required to revert the role of the courts to that of strict judicial interpretation intended by the Founders and prescribed by the Constitution.

Former U.S. Solicitor General Robert Bork has proposed that Supreme Court decisions be overturned by a simple majority congressional vote. But if Congress could merely reinstate previously passed statutory provisions declared unconstitutional by the judiciary with an identical vote, such an approach would serve to obviate the systems of separation of powers and checks and balances clearly contemplated by the Founding Fathers. A "supermajority" vote requirement would ensure that the provisions in question reflect the will of a significant majority of the American people.[69]

Reinstate the celebration of the nation's traditional holidays and institutions. A rebirth of that patriotism so manifestly evident in the *Federalist Papers*, the preserved deliberations of the nation's architects, clearly is invoked. Patriotism in America lasted for a considerable time. Celebrations such as those that attended the rededication of the Statue of Liberty in 1976 regenerate pride and enthusiasm for the virtues and achievements of the American nation.

The celebrations of Columbus Day, George Washington's and Abraham Lincoln's birthdays, the July Fourth Independence Day, Memorial Day, and the national day of Thanksgiving proclaimed by Abraham Lincoln in 1863 today stand as "holidays"—the word itself a derivative of the old English "Holy Day"—intrinsic to the nation's heritage.

America's reverence for her flag is paralleled by her respect for faith in a way unmatched by any other nation and should thus be formally respected. In the words of some, the flag is to Americans what the cross was to the crusaders. To survive as an integral nation, America must thereby restore a reverence for patriotism.[70]

Imbue a national appreciation for the primacy of families and the promotion of education within them. Strong faith and large, nurturing families go hand in hand. That is why the highest birth rate in America is in Mormon Utah. That is why Asian Americans now dominate the University of California-Berkeley admissions stream—driven by values that emphasize strong families, work ethic, discipline, learning, thrift, and a knowledge of English. It is noteworthy that among the first acts of Lenin when he came to power in 1917 was to institute "no-fault divorce" to destroy the Russian family as a precondition for institutionalizing communism.[71]

Restructure the federal tax system to promote the primacy of nuclear families. Instead of a tax deduction for day care in two-wage-earner families, a tax credit of $10,000 per child in single-wage-earner families should immediately be implemented. Such an approach would diminish the present onerous tax burden for working families, while signaling that the nation doesn't need tax-funded babysitters.

Abolish death taxes on family businesses, farms, and estates valued at less than $10 million. Such an approach would contribute to ensuring the perpetuation of those legacy family businesses upon which the economic greatness of America was initially founded.

Solve the health-care "portability problem" by making all medical expenses fully deductible from taxable income. Thus, employees would own their own policies, choosing the ones that best serve their needs, while taking them wherever they wish or need in quest of medical service.[72]

10

Curbing Complexity's Compliance Costs

> When a government becomes powerful, it is destructive, extravagant, and violent. It is a usurer that takes bread from innocent mouths and deprives honorable men of their substance for votes with which to perpetuate itself.
>
> —Cicero

INVERTING THE "TAX AND SPEND" CYCLE

I. Tax Cuts

Chapter 7 has demonstrated that tax level is a foremost determinant of economic growth. If it is onerous, civilizations die; if it is moderate, such is no more than an indispensable prerequisite for their prosperity. It has been thus from the dawn of history. The Rosetta Stone was a multilingual tax code. The Magna Carta was a rescript regulating taxes. The French Revolution commenced as a tax debate. The American Revolution began as a petty tax revolt. Tax level has thus made and broken many great empires.

Today, America's "tax and spend" cycle has spiraled to such extent that the federal government colossus need not be reinvented, it must be disinvented. In a utopian world, a "Constitutional Restoration Act" would identify and eliminate all functions of the federal government expressly reserved for the states and the people by the Constitution—to wit: all illegal agencies, farm subsidies, foreign aid, and the like—together with the income tax required to pay for them in the manner suggested in chapter 6.[1] Draconian perhaps—but in the words of economist Harry Browne, when

269

it is Rosemary's baby that is being thrown out with the bathwater, the choice is not that difficult.[2]

For as shown in analysis, the government cannot be trimmed back piecemeal. It must be deconstructed systemically, not one step at a time. A decade ago, while Speaker Newt Gingrich (R-GA) was calling for a "more user-friendly government," Vice President Al Gore was speaking of "reinventing it." Nothing, as of yet, has worked. Yet to solve taxation problems, one must attack taxation's premise—and that, by disabusing bureaucrats, judges, and lawmakers of the specious notion that a "tax expenditure " is merely money that they have yet to collect from hapless citizens.

The Founding Fathers' profound concern for the potential "tyranny of taxation" was clearly reflected in their deliberations. Indeed the remedies that resulted came to be explicitly embedded in Article I of the U.S. Constitution:

> Section 8. The Congress shall have power to lay and collect Taxes, Duties, Imposts, and Excises, to pay Debts and provide for the common defense and general welfare of the United States, but all Duties, Imposts, and Excises shall be uniform through the United States. . . .
>
> Section 9. No Capitulation or other Direct Tax shall be laid unless in proportion to the Census of Enumeration herein before directed to be taken.

While tax excess today runs rampant throughout the American public taxing system, particularly egregious is the onerous tax burden carried by U.S. corporations vis-à-vis their foreign trade competitors. This is a travesty perpetuated by a liberal notion known as the "myth of the corporate income tax"—a specious contention that corporations actually pay taxes. Yet in the history of civilization, not successful one ever has—only paying customers do.

This latter financial reality regrettably comes as an apparent revelation to many as for years, "tax and spend" politicians have perpetuated the illusion that they are committed friends of the voting middle class by seeking to shift taxes onto "rich corporations."

But commercial and industrial firms, by definition, cannot pay taxes because they are mere legal constructs. In this capacity, they act as governmentally enfranchised "tax collection pass-through agents" for downstream consumers who must bear the ultimate tax burden as capitalized into the prices of goods and services that they buy. In other words, while businesses do, in fact, write "tax checks," they are no more than financial intermediaries—collecting money from their shareholders, employees, and customers and transferring it to public treasuries.[3]

Levying "corporate taxation," therefore, is, in reality, no more than a dissembling political shell game—that of determining who should bear the brunt of the incidence of tax burden in the first round of collection—the firm or its customer to whom it is invariably passed on perforce. Were it any other way, in fact, the firm would soon be out of business—and thus it is that, in the last analysis, tax impact ultimately *always* falls only upon households and the consumers who comprise them.

It is not surprising, then, that traditional liberal politicians are so enamored of the *electoral utility* of the "corporate income tax myth." For in the guise of taxing the rich while giving to the poor, it is an extremely useful revenue tool for surreptitiously confiscating the earnings of middle-class constituencies to finance the agendas of parochial special-interest groups who provide the most activist political bases for their reelections.

But while there may be a perverse political virtue in collecting a hidden tax that no one is really sure that he or she pays, from a public policy formulation standpoint, the corporate income tax, or a "big oil" corporate profits tax, again must be clearly recognized for what they are: *regressive sales taxes that take their most devastating toll upon lower- and middle-class citizens.*[4]

What's worse, in levying upon the productivities of vital industrial job-generators in escalating relationship to their demonstrable degrees of success, it kills the geese that lay the jurisdiction's most prized "golden eggs"— meaningful, productive jobs. For job exportation, in the form of foreign *outsourcing,* can be, and indeed to some extent, often already is, the inexorable result.

The bottom line, then, though there are undeniably certain *political advantages* in disguising this on-the-ground "cost of doing business" workplace reality within a tax-levying Trojan Horse, there are no *economic* ones. For to quote an insight from the eighteenth-century Scottish philosopher David Hume: "It should be the policy of all governments . . . never to lay such taxes as will inevitably fall upon capital; since, in so doing, they impair the funds for the maintenance of labor, thereby diminishing the future production of the country."[5]

In sum, it is undeniable to the point of being axiomatic that high capital tax levels are deleterious to economic growth. This was the conclusion of such profound classic political economists as David Hume and David Ricardo; that was likewise the conclusion of two of the most articulate and creative modern free-market economic thinkers: Milton Friedman and George Gilder.[6]

It was also concurrently the conclusion of the two most successful political leaders in the developmental economics realm in the 1980s: Ronald Reagan and Margaret Thatcher. Today, though they no longer rule, their ideas remain—continuing to suggest worthy initiatives that speak to their "bureaucratic overburden" policy concerns while simultaneously dispelling the tandem "obscene profits" and "corporate income tax" myths. Among them:

- Enacting no federally funded program without first consulting the Constitution to ascertain if it is a constitutionally permitted function;[7]
- Restoring constitutional government by returning power and functions to the states and to the people wrongfully federally usurped over time by congressional action;[8] and
- Reversing the traditional "tax and spend" cycle by reconciling between the two.

For in sum, as shown in chapter 7, a return to the fiscal discipline mandated by the Constitution would enable both elimination of the federal income tax and a national-debt-free balanced budget. The reason is basic. To quote economist Milton Friedman:

> If taxes are raised in order to keep down the deficit, the result is likely to be a higher norm for government spending. Deficits will again recur and the process will be repeated. Those of us who believe that government has reached a size where it threatens to become our master should therefore (1) oppose any tax increase; (2) press for expenditure cuts; [and] (3) accept large deficits as the lesser of two evils.[9]

While opposing deficits in the abstract, therefore, Friedman explains the calculus of the political taxation process accordingly:

> By concentrating on the wrong thing, the deficit, instead of the right thing, total government spending, fiscal conservatives have become the unwitting handmaidens of the big spenders. The typical historic process is that the spenders put through laws that increase government spending and say: "My God, that's terrible; we must do something about that deficit."
>
> So they cooperate with the big spenders in getting taxes imposed. But as soon as new taxes are imposed, the big spenders are off again, and thus there is another burst in governmental spending and yet another deficit.[10]

Accordingly, prospective remedies must be both comprehensive and complementary, and include:

Tax all income just one time. End the present gluttony of government whereby earnings are taxed first as income when they are earned, a second time as capital gains and dividends when the after-tax earnings are invested, and yet a third time as estate taxes when the income earner dies. This recidivist revenue-generating approach is manifestly unfair for those who wish to subsist not off the largesse of government but from the proceeds of their personal ingenuity and productivity. It can be remedied by eliminating capitals gains, dividend, and estate taxation.

Tax all income at a uniform rate. Taxing at an equal rate not only invokes a fairness issue but one of equality before the law. Taxation, by definition, is the process of taking money away from those who have earned it while using it for the benefit of those who have not. A uniform tax rate transparently treats all Americans in the same manner—consistent with free-market philosophy while operating within a social system wherein equality before the law is not only central to a free and just society but is constitutionally guaranteed.

Shift to taxing consumption rather than income from production. This approach would thereby result in lowering marginal tax rates by flattening the levy structure, eliminating various deductions, and simplifying the overall tax system. The rationale of the approach: progressive taxation is, in reality, regressive, destroying the investment capital needed for job creation—thereby diminishing the reward for realizing the American Dream.

Harvard economist Robert Barro estimates that a shift to a flat-rate consumption tax, for instance, would raise the long-term U.S. growth rate by about 0.3 percent per year, resulting in an increase in annual real GDP growth of about $300 billion after ten years.[11] The tangible benefits to such a tax are thus readily and intuitively obvious, and include the following:

- An immediate powerful stimulant to economic activity;
- Enhanced incentives for work, savings, and investment;
- A curtailment of consumption, which would produce a dramatic jump in savings;
- A shift from consumption toward investment through capital gains tax elimination;
- Incentivizing capital use through immediate tax-expensing of job-creating investment;
- A reduction in producer prices accompanied by a rise in industrial outputs, and
- A dimunition of the ability to fund special-interest social engineering.[12]

The rationale for this more enlightened tax approach thus is basic. Today, it has become ever more clear that the most equitable and efficient forms of taxation are those structured as *consumption-based* levies on cash flow, and not as *production-based* levies on output. The distinction here is critical. For the use of consumption-based taxation promotes greater trade competitiveness based upon the propensities of people working harder to earn and save for the things that they need and want—in effect, enhancing export potentials while concurrently discouraging frivolous consumption. Production-based taxation, on the other hand, penalizes those incentives that promote productive work.[13]

Consumption-based taxation also is a *fairer* approach in that it is a better measure than income alone of an individual's ability to pay. For it forces consumers to make intelligent choices based upon accurate appraisals of the relative values and costs of their marketplace goods and services. In so doing, it drives an economy's resource utilization to "optimal use"— thereby reducing overall production-factor costs.

Conversely, production-based taxation—surreptitiously imposed to mask inordinate costs of public "bureaucratic services" provided to taxpayers— merely reallocates consumer spending while raising the costs of goods and services in the international marketplace, thereby reducing export prospects while destroying both domestic jobs and the productive assets of domestic job producers. The resulting commercial inequity is economically inane. Every other major industrial country employs consumption-based taxation extensively—it makes eminent economic sense that America now take recourse to it as well.[14]

For the facts of life remain largely economic—and taxes, both in the form of direct financial levies and indirect public sector regulatory overburden, remain the most significant determinants of growth in any jurisdiction— making its economic well-being, for consumers and producers alike, founded upon a necessary streamlining of its bureaucratically challenged administrative structures, instead of merely indiscriminately off-loading its costs onto consumers in ways that vitiate the innate strengths of its private productive base and thereby diminish its capacity.

Instead of taxing *initiative* and *success*, therefore, a prudent government must tax the outcomes of *productive* activity—its *output*, levying upon *sales*—rather than taxing its inputs—the *factors of production* themselves. To do less is to kill the working geese that lay the jurisdiction's revenue golden eggs.

The bottom line on income taxation is that the competitive market cannot be fooled—either domestically or internationally—with unrealistically high levy levels, however well disguised. For natural market forces will inevitably sort out the resulting price disparities and restore a competitive balance—as the "invisible hand" operates with more consummate guile than does the "deceiving mind," and consumers and wage earners ultimately and invariably pay the price of improvident taxation in economic opportunities foregone.

Within these policy parameters, then, several primary policy options commend themselves. They include the following:

Option #1:

Integrate federal corporate and personal income taxation. A number of current egregious tax inequities within the present business tax levy system would be effectively remedied by a "corporate-individual income tax" integration approach. Foremost among these inequities, as now constituted, is the corporate income tax, which, in its truest sense, is more of a tax on capital than on "capital intake." In other words, it taxes a firm on vital income that it must use, over and above depreciation, to replace worn out or obsolete machinery, equipment, tools, and buildings.[15]

Second, the corporate-individual income tax integration proposed would eliminate the present "double taxation" of corporate earnings produced by the tandem dual workings of the corporate income tax and the capital gains tax—in America now levied at rates that are second highest among OECD countries—that torque the effective allocation of available business capital and thereby prevent it from being put to its optimal economic use.

For today, as noted, undistributed corporate earnings are taxed twice to the extent that they become incorporated into the downstream value-added to corporate stock that is ordinarily levied upon at capital gains rates when stock is sold or exchanged in a taxable transaction. In other words, the firm pays corporate income taxes on its total profits, then individual owners of its shares are taxed again when those same corporate profits become taxable income in the form of capital gains and dividends.[16]

Hence, if an entrepreneur who pays corporate taxes at a 34 percent marginal rate elects to take his profits as capital gains, he is hit with yet another 15 percent tax levy. To put this inequity best into perspective, if the businessman has saved $40,000 and uses it to buy a Cadillac, he has the benefit of a highly utilitarian, durable vehicle whose use is not further taxed per miles driven. But if he uses that same money to buy stock, thereby providing the economy with job-creating equity capital, and then elects to sell that stock to buy other stock, he is left holding a nominal $40,000 paper instrument and has to pay an *additional* $6,000 tax on his own money's use.[17]

The taxes of Sub-Chapter S corporations, proprietorships, and partnerships, on the other hand, are taxed only once at the owner's level at the progressive rates specified for individuals. In like manner, under the approach proposed, full integration of both dividends and retained earnings would result in taxation of all corporate earnings at the shareholder level based upon the *pro rata* share of corporate earnings attributable to stock holdings. The corporate levy paid would then be treated in its entirety as a tax withheld and creditable by the shareholder.[18] Accordingly, under the tax shift proposed, the net positive effects would be twofold:

1. capital gains would be taxed only upon a *realization*, not an accrual, basis;
2. while retained corporate earnings would be taxed on an accrual basis and at full rates, but corporate income would be taxed only once.

The rationale for such an approach is intuitively obvious. If the corporate income tax is properly viewed within terms of its greatest utility—as an investment allocation mechanism, not as a revenue-generating mechanism per se—it can then more facilely be restructured to serve the nation's long-term goal of expanding its global market export share.

Such an approach is critical in fostering strategic investment. For as John Kennedy concluded in 1963: "The tax on capital gains directly affects investment decisions, the mobility and flow of risk capital . . . the ease or difficulty experienced by new ventures in obtaining capital, and thereby the strength and potential for growth in the economy."[19]

Federal Reserve Chairman Alan Greenspan concurred with this assessment in 1997: "Its major impact, as far as I can judge, is to impede entrepreneurial activity and capital formation. . . . I have argued that the appropriate capital gains tax rate is zero." The American people, by a 48 percent to 41 percent margin, it is worthy of note, currently fully agree with President Kennedy and Chairman Greenspan that the capital gains tax should be abolished.[20]

Option #2:

Reform the income tax by shifting to a percentage-based flat tax on all income—with no exemptions or deductions save for the exclusion from taxation of those heads of household whose annual earnings fall below $30,000, with additional $3,000 deductions for each dependent. The *individual* income tax corollary to eliminating, or at least radically modifying, the corporate income tax could thus come in the form of "flat rate" personal taxation, combined with the elimination of most exemptions and deductions save at the lowest income levels.

Such an approach would concurrently effectively respond to long-standing calls by tax experts for an across-the-board uniform marginal personal income levy—asserting that it would ensure greater tax equity than does the present system of progressively taxing private individuals, while in the process, eliminating all individual filing requirements and inherent transaction costs altogether.[21]

Pursuant to this model, then, the individual tax would be levied through paycheck deduction by the employer and forwarded to the federal government with no name attached—thereby eliminating altogether individual tax compliance expenditures. Corporate taxpayers and self-employed individuals would also pay an identical percentage flat tax on profits based on submitted profit and loss statements. In exchange, estate, gift, capital gains, and Social Security taxes would be abolished, thereby ensuring the solvency of the Social Security system.[22]

An ancillary, though not inconsequential, advantage to a flat tax-rate approach is that it would allow citizens, as public-sector consumers, to more accurately assess the prices that they pay for governance. For just as they now vote their consumer dollars for the best buys in the supermarket, so also could they cast their political votes for the most cost-effective policy options—thereby ensuring that the cause of bureaucratic efficiency is optimally served.

Within these options, there likewise are several promising policy sub-options. They include:

Sub-Option #1: Reducing the present corporate income tax rate to bring it more in line with those of America's principal global trade competitors. Today, as demonstrated in chapter 7, the United States levies the second highest corporate tax rate amongst the OECD (Organization for Economic Cooperation and Development) countries, below only economically moribund Japan. Hence, just as her competitors are cutting their corporate tax levies to compete optimally in the global market, America now must do so also if she is to remain a major economic player.

Sub-Option #2: Replacing investment amortization with "expensing." This tax reform is critical for preserving the vitality and primacy of American manufacturing. Under present tax rules, business investments in capital equipment may be depreciated for specified periods of up to a maximum number of years. This approach means that a machine purchased for a million dollars to be used in assembly-line production is eligible for a "tax write-off" at the rate of $100,000 per year for perhaps a decade.

"Expensing," on the other hand, permits deduction of the full million dollars in the year of purchase rather than apportioning it over a prolonged depreciation period. Revenue neutral, therefore—because the actual amount of write-off remains the same, with only the immediate deduction replacing a prolonged time-phased one—this approach can serve as a monumental incentive for job-creating investments in major manufacturing industries—auto, steel, other durable goods, and the like—that now endure high capital production expansion costs.

Sub-Option #3: Implementing a "negative income tax" to replace the multitude of social-welfare programs now financed by government. Pursuant to this policy approach, every individual would be guaranteed a certain means-tested minimum income that would vary as a function of family size. Characterized by simplicity and efficiency, it would unilaterally replace social security, public welfare, food stamps, housing support, and, in precept, all other governmental programs directly affecting personal living standards today.[23]

Sub-Option #4: Enacting universal savings accounts to make all savings free from taxation. With America enduring one of the lowest savings rates in the world—thereby denying future individual security, while depriving the capital markets of much-needed job-creating investable capital—incentivizing citizens to save for their futures rather than being consigned to the public dole serves the national interest in a multiplicity of ways—including ensuring long-term economic security for individuals while aggregating capital committable to future job-creating investments.

II. Spending Curbs

Enact no federally funded program without first consulting the Constitution to ascertain if it is a constitutionally sanctioned function. This landmark approach can be realized by enacting Congressman John Shadegg's (R-AZ) proposed "Enumerated Powers Act," which would provide that: "Each Act of Congress shall contain a concise and definite statement of the constitutional authority relied upon for the enactment of each portion of that Act."[24] This measure, if enacted, would thus require Congress to specify the statutory basis of authority in the U.S. Constitution as a basis for passage of the laws that it enacts.

Reduce bureaucratic inefficiencies through spending limits. Bureaucracy, in its essence, as shown, is little more than public plunder plucked from people's pocketbooks. With the term "tax expenditure" now central to public-sector jargon, an appropriate *riposte* might be "tax bureaucrats, not people"—making spending cuts in the quest for fiscal responsibility an overarching policy imperative.

Recognizing the twin fiscal realities that the people's money belongs to the people, not to officials, and that government spending doesn't create income, it merely redistributes existing funds, therefore, public sector costs can be significantly reduced by simply forcing government to live within its means, and then letting the bureaucrats themselves blend the proper admixture of management controls and incentives needed to administratively survive and function efficiently.[25]

Foremost among such options could include a constitutionally mandated federal balanced budget—with exceptions allowed only in times of war and other similarly carefully circumscribed dire public emergencies. The case for such a measure targeting "governmental right-sizing" needs no lengthy discourse here. For America's present fiscal problems are caused not because she taxes too little but because she spends too much—because governmental spending continues to grow faster than the national income required to sustain it.

Hence, in good times or in bad, in periods of recovery and recession, government expenditures go only in one direction—up! Yet this spending spiral invariably invokes even higher taxes, and higher taxes mean less take-home pay for citizens. The process, moreover, is self-generating. Because government spends more, taxpayers come to have less of their own revenues for *their* personal priorities. Thus, in a tragic cycle, still more people become still more dependent upon government, triggering the need for even more public-sector spending.

This recurring pattern of spiraling unconstrained public spending, and the attendant need for forcing government to budget itself, are ably captured by Nobel Prize–winning economist Milton Friedman:

> There is a fundamental bias in our present democratic structure. The bias is that special interests have a stronger weight in determining legislation than does the public interest in general. On the other hand, the costs of that legislation are spread over all of the people. . . .
> Let's have the vested interests fighting not against the taxpayers in general but against one another. . . . Let's not have each one of them trying to have their appropriations increased at the expense of the poor taxpayers who have nothing to say about the matter.[26]

That, in actuality, is what budget balancing is really all about. By compelling federal government to live within its means, citizens are merely asking it to do what every single American family must now do to survive—requiring elected officials who would call themselves responsible public servants to direct their focus to the fiscal bottom line: the national balance sheet.

Implement federal spending limits through a constitutional provision mandating that, except for partial indexing for inflation, the federal government can spend no more in a given fiscal year than it took in the year before. Such limits would have a stipulation that in case of emergency, that limitation could be waived in two-year increments by the vote of a 60 percent majority of those voting in each house of Congress.[27]

Restrict federal spending to a constant 20 percent share of GDP except for force majeure. Spending limitation, as indicated, is a natural complement to budget balancing, providing safeguards that preserve the goal of federal fiscal responsibility. This too is a critical imperative. For in addressing the question: which is preferable—a $2 trillion budget with a $500 million deficit or a $2.5 trillion balanced budget with 2 percent higher taxes?—the answer is "neither" if economic prosperity achieved through fiscal sanity is to prevail.[28]

The concept's critics invariably will contend that both a spending limitation and a balanced-budget requirement frustrate the process of "representative government"—and raise the cogent question: Isn't this what we elect our legislators to do? But the reality lies in the corresponding question: Are they doing it today? That answer is clearly no.

Conversely, when it is argued that mandatory limits to spending are required, such a démarche is not a denial of the workings of democratic process. It is instead merely a clarion call for a judicious separation of the power to tax from the power to spend—an approach deeply embedded in Western fiscal philosophy with the signing of the Magna Carta in 1215 A.D. Pursuant to it, the king could spend but could not tax; while the Parliament could tax but could not spend.

This separation of official functions by imposing external spending constraints thereafter became the cornerstone for future successful economic governance and remains a valid prototype to the present day as it pertains to the legislative capacity to collect and allocate tax dollars. For within its delimited process, legislators still retain their basic rights to conceptualize and legislate. But they are now compelled to do them more carefully, mindful of resource constraints. To this extent, then, mandated fiscal restraint is no less than a reaffirmation of the time-tested precept of responsible representative government: "There is your budget. Now manage it in the most effective way!"[29]

In the United States, federal spending predicated upon government's "capital take" from the economy for most of the past half century has hovered around this 20 percent of gross domestic product (GDP) level. In recent decades, however, it has, at times, crept well above the 20 percent "Plimsoll mark." Yet history's economic lessons make clear that such upward drifts in revenue spent must not be perpetuated for long if prosperity is to issue from the private sector. Hence, unyielding spending ceilings must be established to explicitly fix the relationship of public consumption to private production before the rapacious appetite of government ingests still more intolerable levels of productive job-creating private enterprise.

The case for such a revolutionary policy course thus is, at once, both compelling and simple. Relative shares of GDP are firmly fixed so that both the public and private sector are guaranteed proportional allocations of national productive output. By thus linking public spending to private production, the close connection between economic growth and government's capacity to distribute benefits from that growth is thereby underscored.

Directly tying public spending to GDP growth likewise makes psychological as well as economic sense—producing a powerful public sector incentive to promote private profits that does not now exist for bureaucrats. For with fixed budgetary constraints directly linked to economic growth, by actually contributing to private industrial and commercial productivity, bureaucrats can get ever-rising revenue flows—and hence get to spend more money, which is their native instinct!

In this "natural selection" process, moreover, those wasteful expenditures and needless regulations that now impose financial obligations upon private enterprises would no longer be regarded as "free," or even desirable, but would perforce be weighed against the opportunity costs of aggrandized bureaucracy foregone. Accordingly, albeit however inadvertently perhaps, public servants would come to be actively working to achieve cost savings that concurrently serve the private economic interest.[30]

For when every addition on the public-sector spending side mandates an equivalent subtraction, the process dramatically changes both the calculus and the equilibrium of the bureaucratic fiscal equation. Rather than ratcheting up spending through the unrestrained power to tax—rather than re-joicing in each other's spoils—for the first time, federal agencies would be put into direct competition with each other for fixed-value budgetary assets.

Indeed, in an era of finite fiscal resources, such an intramural quest for improved internal efficiency might even eventually come to be deemed a highly salutary in-house bureaucratic innovation. The true winner in such a scenario, however, would be America's taxpaying citizen. For not only would government be given an overt incentive to reduce both its spiraling spending and inflation, but its direct take from his or her wallet would be reduced in relative terms as well.

Create a federal "rainy day" trust fund. A budget-balancing constitutional amendment fixing federal outlays as a share of GDP could concurrently stipulate that revenues received in excess of the 20 percent threshold ceiling be consigned to a Federal Economic Stabilization Trust.

Such a fund could initially be structured to served as a "fiscal restoration fund"—with its proceeds dedicated to reducing the federal debt—and once the debt was eliminated, the fund could be retooled as a "rainy day" fund that forces government to save in economic upturns for subsequent less buoyant economic times. If such an approach sounds not radical but rather rational, that is because it is really no more than what heads of household who aspire to be financially prudent voluntarily do in their private lives.

Preceding analysis has made clear that economic growth through enhanced fiscal responsibility is a national challenge invoking federal solutions. There is thus no better place to start than within the U.S. government itself. To this end, creation of a federal rainy day fund would allow for countercyclical budgeting in times of economic downturn without raising taxes—using financial surpluses built up in good times to offset deficits incurred in bad times.

At the same time, this approach decisively rejects the conventional wisdom oft-held by those in government that the solution to recession is to remove capital from the productive private sector in the form of tax increases to underwrite the costs of pasting public financial band-aids over critical economic wounds. To the contrary, it moderates the rate of taxation while preserving essential services—thereby restoring revenue-producing income growth to private industry.

Provide "sunset clauses" for all new programs promulgated. It is a public-sector axiom that "the nearest thing to immortality in this world is a governmental bureau"! Yet were the promulgation of new bureaucratic programs to be accompanied by the devolution of old ones—if that crucial "creative destruction," breaking down the old to make way for the new, that now takes place in the free market also worked within the halls of government, its present problems of inefficiency and obsolescence would not be self-compounding.

Today, however, such is not the case—as bureaucratic dinosaurs remain very much alive and well, openly roaming bureaucratic alleyways within Washington's Beltway foraging on economically sustaining private profits. Incorporating "sunset provisions" into every newly created program requiring substantial recurring commitments of federal funds—thereby mandatorily subjecting its performance to periodic review for propriety and efficiency in the renewal process—would effectively attack this Jurassic anomaly.

For under this approach, public programs that do not produce demonstrably cost-effective positive review would be scrutinized on an ongoing basis to ascertain their continuing merit. Recognizing the efficacy of this approach, fiscal analyst Chris Edwards recommends that "Congress needs to get serious about the need to 'sunset' all federal programs on a rotating basis of every eight years. Programs would then be automatically terminated unless specifically reauthorized."[31]

Require privatization impact statements for all significant new federal programs. Together with oversight reforms for existing bureaucratic programs, prudent public-policy oversight could concurrently mandate that major recurring executive-branch program or policy initiatives underactive legislative consideration for implementation or renewal be accompanied by privatization impact statements.

Such statements should require that their proponent agencies justify why they can perform what they propose in more cost-effective ways than can the private sector—while employing the same types of stringent cost-benefit analyses that all private firms must undertake on a continuing basis to survive.

III. Reduce Rampant Regulation

If America is to preserve her global trade competitiveness, it is clear that in tandem with tax and spending reform, concerted policy efforts must be focused upon the regulatory dimensions to her exorbitant bureaucratic transaction costs. For as analysis has shown, if government is to be made more economic and efficient, it must first be forced both to rationalize the rules that govern its operation and to become more attuned to the impacts of its involvement in the private marketplace. Accordingly, if the American economy is to continue to prosper, greater regulatory reason must prevail.

These are critical imperatives. For as analysis reveals, without diligent oversight, the economic and bureaucratic transaction costs of public regulation can spiral out of control to the extent that they come to jeopardize the global competitiveness of U.S. workers and the industries that employ them. Indeed, profound regulatory reforms are policy goals so fundamental that they are nearly axiomatic—yet today, they are almost universally ignored by the disciples of the "big government fix." How, then, can they best be reinstated? From a public policy standpoint, several institutional reforms aimed at more rational regulatory processes readily suggest themselves.

Conduct a comprehensive constitutional review of all existing federal regulations. This review should span the entire corpus of the Federal Register—legislatively eliminating those regulations that exceed the confines of the law.

Reform how government promulgates administrative rules. A total revamping of how the government imposes regulation would contribute mightily to boosting long-term economic growth. Today, Congress has sub-delegated extraordinary rule-making authority to federal agencies that have frequently abused their authority—failing to conduct even routine cost-benefit analyses of the rules that they implement.

Not only must more focused analysis of the impacts of public policy be mandated, but the entire regulatory process must be overhauled to restore to the Congress the full legislative oversight role contemplated by the Constitution.[32] To this end, to preserve private prosperity, Congress must restore to itself its legally vested authority to approve all final federal rules.[33]

Institutionalize regulatory budgeting in the public-policy formulation process. To lend further focus to the costs of public regulation, mandatory promulgation of an annual federal regulatory budget should be made a policy priority. Pursuant to it, to empower effective Congressional oversight, the executive branch would each year be required to develop in significant detail accurate estimates of the regulatory costs imposed by the full operational spectrum of the agencies and programs over which it presides.

Each year, the Congress, in turn, would be statutorily required to formally approve the federal regulatory budget, making such adjustments as it prudently deems necessary. By making explicit the price of the federal regulatory burden, then, this process would enable direct cross-checks between the administrative costs officially sanctioned by government and those actually run up on an ad hoc basis by executive agencies in pursuit of their statutory mandates.

It would concurrently mandate legislative—as well as proponent agency—approval of customer compliance costs; and in so doing, it would make possible a "regulatory report card" by specific agency and program that would constitute a critical first step toward fiscal remedy by forcing bureaucratic and elected political officials alike to directly confront the market-costs of the regulations that they impose.

Provide for detailed cost-benefit analysis for each new rule proposed. Today, though there are ongoing initiatives to assess the economic impacts of regulation, such efforts, however laudatory, are perfunctory at best and clearly do not go far enough. To quote economist Richard Rahn: "Too few governmental regulations are today subjected to rigorous cost-benefit tests. Many governmental agencies do not take the requirement seriously, act in good faith, or even present accurate data. For regulators have a strong incentive to underestimate the true costs of their regulations."[34]

The reality that each year's new tranche of federal regulations costs the economy another $50 billion or more clearly mandates a new oversight approach—one requiring that all regulations subject to Congressional oversight be accompanied by objective cost-benefit analyses standardized across federal agencies in formats that provide both direct and "contextual" information, in so doing, monetizing the values of the *effects*, as well as accurately assessing the *costs*, of each promulgation proposed, thereby forecasting the net benefits to society over time.

Such statements—which would require a clear demonstration that the incremental benefits of a proposed initiative exceeds its incremental costs—should also incorporate not only economic assessments but technological risk and small business impact assessments and be developed by each proponent agency concurrent with its preparation of each proposed major regulation submitted for review.

Such analyses could thus become the basis for Congressional determination of whether any given federal rule or regulation has produced sufficient benefit as to justify its continuance over time. By making the agency cost-benefit review more discerning, the nation's "regulatory report card" can thus ensure that the unwarranted growth of the "regulatory state" is taken seriously by empowering better federal policy decision making through enhanced transparency derived from superior information.

Make the federal regulatory approvals process "elective" rather than "rejective." Reverting administrative rules approval directly to Congressional jurisdiction and explicit approval would likewise make a material contribution to restoring proper oversight in rules promulgation. Pursuant to such a "hands-on" approach, each Congressional committee would be made explicitly responsible for those rules promulgated by those federal agencies subject to its jurisdiction—and would be required to explicitly endorse each rule by record roll-call vote ninety days prior to its proposed effective date.

In effect, then, this approach would compel the Congress to approve those follow-on policy mechanisms implemented to enforce the laws that they pass, in addition to the laws themselves. By mandating that all new regulations be mandatorily endorsed, rather than merely tacitly accepted, by Congressional committees, this promulgation reform would thus effectively "regulate the regulators" by requiring greater managerial oversight on the part of America's elected officials.

In short, holding Congress accountable for the consequences of *regulation* in the same manner that it now is for creating and funding programs that it implements can head off spending excess—as requiring express approval of all new regulations would ensure that lawmakers bear direct responsibility to voters for each operating component of imposed new regulatory cost.

Establish market-driven ends, not bureaucracy-driven means. Selective use of market-based incentives, rather than punitive disincentives, likewise can ensure more uniform compliance with specific, predetermined regulatory standards. Indeed, it is becoming increasingly evident that the best way to regulate economic activity is to impose *financial* charges for noncompliance rather than to impose rigid conformity rules for operations across a broad range of industrial sectors.

Undeniably, there are compliance risks inherent in this approach. But risks are inherent to every public-policy approach. This is the essence of free-market capitalism. But the risks are not correspondingly reduced by simplistically off-loading them onto the taxpayers rather than onto the violators themselves—as the present regulatory process does.

Creating such regulatory opportunity costs rather than detailed operating procedures, of course, is not a new technique. Indeed, in an extreme, albeit undeniably effective, early application, the famed eighteenth-century B.C. Babylonian lawgiver Hammurabi promulgated a simple, albeit attention-getting, building code for contractors—"Should a building that you erected collapse, killing people, you will be executed—and should the owner's son be killed, your son will be executed!"—a superb example of how a rule should read: set goals, offer compliance incentives, but don't micromanage the compliance process!

Provide "sunset clauses" for all regulations promulgated. Just as for recurring federal *programs* described above, in addition to promulgations reform, termination reform—"sunset clauses" prescribing fixed-date expirations for each new federal *rule* enacted—can also ensure focused periodic, circumspect reconsideration of the impacts of long-term regulatory policies. For only through such systematic review can proper stewardship provide that rules continue to serve the public good for which they were originally intended.

Recourse to the sunset law approach thus introduces two highly salutary effects into the public-policy-making system. First, it requires elected officials to periodically validate whether past regulations presently remain valid. Second, it creates a deliberate natural policy inertia—by requiring bureaucracies to rectify past public policy follies, it reduces their time available to create new ones.

Implement tort reform. In addition to restructuring the way that the federal government makes rules to implement legislation, the nation must concurrently strive to fix its broken civil justice system. Rather than providing efficient and effective means of resolving disputes and enforcing contracts, the process has today created a litigious legal industry that feeds upon itself to the detriment of everyone but the lawyers who directly benefit financially from it.

In its course, its flagrant abuses have come to constitute a tremendous overburden on America's economy. When businesses have to pay needlessly staggering legal bills, they pass the costs onto consumers, whose marketplace demands, the economy's sustaining lifeblood, are then correspondingly markedly diminished, or are put beyond the reach of those who desperately need them, as is the case of the impacts of meritless malpractice suits upon equitable health care delivery in America today.

The United Kingdom's policy of requiring initiators of failed frivolous lawsuits to bear the full legal costs—not only those incurred by the initiator but also those incurred by the defendant and by the court—would constitute a critical first step to this end.

Endnotes

INTRODUCTION

1. O. Guinness 1993, p. 51.
2. John Adams quoted in H. Lottman 1982, p. 207; O. Guinness 1993, p. 52.
3. On this, see S. Huntington 2004b, passim; L. Ingraham 2003, p. 257.
4. J. Black 1994, pp. 229–30.
5. On this, see D. Moynihan 1993, pp. 17–20, and p. 19 in particular.
6. R. Bork 2003, pp. 3–4.
7. M. Berman 2006, p. 13.
8. T. Holland 2004, pp. 270–71; M. Berman 2006, p. 34.
9. Christopher Scarre quoted in M. Berman 2006, p. 305.
10. O. Guinness 1993, passim.
11. H. Luce 1941, pp. 61–65; O. Guinness 1993, pp. 9–10.
12. D. Ravich 1990, p. 342.
13. A. Schmidt 1997, pp. 3–4.
14. D. D'Souza 1995, p. 3.
15. A. Schmidt 1997, pp. 4–5.
16. A. Schmidt 1997, pp. 6–8, 65, 81; N. Glazer 1987, p. 11. Indeed, what the nation's architects referred to by the term "diversity," as political scientist Nathan Glazer has correctly pointed out, was "the differences amongst the laws of the several states, not to the diversity of religion, race, and religion."
17. R. Kimball 1998, p. 219.
18. Ibid.
19. Ibid.
20. E. Renan 1935, p. 284.
21. George Clemenceau quoted by M. Berman 2006, p. 157. T. LeBlanc 1997, p. 1; P. Buchanan 2002, pp. 84, 86, 94. This observation is also occasionally attributed to Oscar Wilde.
22. Voltaire quoted in F. Wooldridge 2004, p. 150.
23. Benjamin Franklin quoted in E. von Kuehnelt-Leddihn 1990, p. 67; A. Schmidt 1997, p. 179.

24. T. Jefferson 1859, vol. 2, p. 232.

25. Thomas Paine quoted in W. McDougall 1997, pp. 20, 23.

26. Albert Einstein quoted in F. Wooldridge 2004, p. 289; A. Schmidt 1997, pp. 191–94.

27. Admiral Halsey quoted in J. Bradley 2006, p. 343; Edmund Burke quoted in G. Heck 2007, p. 187.

CHAPTER 1: HISTORIC CAUSES

1. G. Cowgill 1991, pp. 246–49.

2. R. Netting 1977, p. 299; J. Taintner 1988, pp. 12, 152, 167, 175. However, the decline of arable land and agricultural productivity surely also played a role in the Mayans' ultimate demise.

3. M. Steyn 2005, p. 1; P. Buchanan 2002, pp. 227–28.

4. S. Huntington 1993, p. 24; J. Diamond 2005, p. 438.

5. L. Auster 1997, p. 20.

6. T. Holland 2004, pp. 270–71.

7. Ibid.; M. Berman 2006, pp. 304–5; J. Tainter 1988, pp. 134–36.

8. C. Scarre 1995, p. 221; M. Berman 2006, p. 305.

9. G. Vidal 1965, p. 431.

10. A. Gotlieb February 15, 2004, p. 12. Though as both Thomas Cahill (1995, pp. 181ff.) and Morris Berman (2002, p. 69) note, in the twilight phase of Rome, there was a "monastic class"—a tiny handful of savants—who, though they recognized that they could not reverse the rapidly spiraling downward trends, nonetheless strove to preserve those treasures of their civilization and ways of thinking and living that they believed might come to be appreciated in a future, healthier era.

11. Lactantius quoted in C. Freeman 2002, p. 322.

12. J. Black 1994, p. 12.

13. J. Kuntsler 2005, passim, pp. 17–19 in particular, also quoted in S. Leeb 2006, p. 20. Kuntsler concurrently describes, in somber terms, how a posited impending energy crisis could create shortages and financial costs that could cause American society to collapse as well.

14. Jared Diamond as quoted in S. Leeb 2006, p. 33.

15. J. Diamond 2005, pp. 20ff, 114, 118, 432.

16. P. Brimelow 1995, p. 245.

17. C. Northcote Parkinson 1959, passim, cited in J. Black 1994, pp. xvii–xviii, 2.

18. J. Tainter 1988, pp. 67–69, 93ff.

19. Ibid.; M. Berman 2000, pp. 17–18.

20. Joseph Tainter, as synopsized by M. Berman 2000, p. 18.

21. Ibid.

22. J. Tainter 1988, pp. 114–15, 124 (citing Frederic Scherer).

23. J. Tainter 1988, pp. 115–17.

24. J. Tainter 1988, pp. 93, 118ff.

25. J. Tainter 1988, p. 116.

26. J. Tainter 1988, p. 119.

27. J. Tainter 1988, pp. 195–96.

28. J. Tainter 1988, pp. 127ff., 187ff.

29. J. Jacobs 2005, pp. 23–24.

30. T. S. Elliot quoted in O. Guinness 2001, p. 90; G. Bowersocks 1991, p. 165.

31. J. Tolson, "Lessons from the Fall," *U.S. News and World Report*, May 1, 2007, p. 28.

32. Virgil quoted in J. Jacobs 2004, pp. 55, 174.

33. J. Jacobs 2004.

34. J. Jacobs 2004.

35. C. Murphy 2007, pp. 24–25.

36. See *Inscriptiones Latinae Selectae*, H. Dessau ed., no. 212; G. Bowersocks 1991, p. 75; W. Durant 1944, p. 666, J. Black 1994, p. 39.

37. H. Pflaum 1950, p. 106; C. Starr 1982, pp. 75–78; M. Grant 1968, pp. 53–54; C. R. Whittaker 2004, pp. 210–11.

38. P. Turchin 2007, p. 292. Eventually, over 100,000 Roman citizens came to receive free monetary distributions and another 250,000 received free food handouts.

39. P. Heather 2006, pp. 68–69; *History Guide* 2007, pp. 5–6.

40. Ibid.

41. Ibid.

42. *History Guide* 2007.

43. Juvenal quoted in P. Heather, loc. cit.

44. Augustine quoted in R. MacMullen 1988, p. 45.

45. T. Holland 2004, pp. 181–82.

46. B. Shabbath, fol. 33b, cited in P. Garnsey and C. Whittaker 1978, p. 268.

47. Livy 1967, preface to Book 1; quoted in J. Black 1994, p. 189.

48. Ibid.

49. Ammianus Marclllinus, *Roman History*, quoted in C. Murphy 2007, p. 59; W. Goffart 1980, p. 33; C. R. Whittaker 1994, p. 195.

50. C. Murphy 2007, p. 80; C. R. Whittaker 2004, p. 210.

51. C. R. Whittaker 2004, p. 203; Whittaker 1999, p. 168.

52. Whittaker 1994, pp. 185ff.

53. C. Murphy 2007, p. 133; C. R. Whittaker 2004, pp. 210–13. Indeed, Ammianus Marcellinus estimates that as much as one-third of Rome's civil service consisted of erstwhile foreign immigrants.

54. C. Murphy 2007, p. 31.

55. Cassio Dio, *Roman History*, quoted in C. Murphy 2007, p. 152.

56. P. Heather 2006, pp. 216–26; R. MacMullen 1988, pp. 186 ff., quoted in C. Murphy 2007, pp. 80, 168–69; W. Goffart 1980, p. 7; C. R. Whittaker 1994, p. 253; P. Heather 2006, p. 191.

57. P. Heather 2006, 191.

58. V. Hanson 2003, p. 1.

59. Ammianus Marcellinus cited in P. Heather 2006, p. 119. See also P. Heather 2006, 368ff., 375, 384.

60. P. Heather 2006, loc. cit.

61. Tacitus quoted in P. Heather 2006, loc. cit.; C. Freeman, loc. cit.; C. Murphy 2007, pp. 166–67; P. Turchin 2007, p. 60. The Romans called their frontiers *limites* (singular, *limes*), from which the English word "limit" derives.

62. C. Murphy 2007, p. 171.

63. W. Goffart 1980, p. 35.

64. L. Auster 1997, p. 46.

65. T. Cahill 1995, p. 29.

66. R. MacMullen 1988, p. 129; C. R. Whittaker 1994, pp. 263–64.

67. C. Murphy 2007, p. 209.

68. Ibid.

69. Will Durant 1944, p. 366, quoted by P. Buchanan 2006, p. 2; W. Goffart 1980, pp. 36, 50, 61, 69, 100.

70. W. Durant quoted in P. Buchanan 2006, p 2.

71. T. Sowell 1996, p. 387.

72. Dio Cassio 52:28 and Tacitus. *Histories*, 4:74, both cited in C. Starr 1982, p. 86. Yet as Roman historian Tacitus, describing the Roman conquest of Britain, succinctly despaired:"Ubi solitudinem faciunt pacem appellant." ("They create a desert and call it stability.")

73. P. Heather 2006, p. 63. Other estimates place Rome's early fourth-century military strength at as many as 645,000 soldiers.

74. M. Grant 1968, p. 44.

75. R. MacMullen 1988, pp. 39, 41. MacMullen believes that a more accurate number for the size of the Roman military at this time was about 400,000 troops.

76. S. Leeb 2006, p. 32.

77. J. Tainter 1988, 127ff., 187ff.

78. J. Thompson and E. Johnson 1937, pp. 15–18; A. Bernardi 1970, pp. 53ff.; P. Kennedy 1987, passim; H. Pirenne 1958, p. 27.

79. H. Pirenne 1958, p. 27.

80. J. Tainter 1988, pp. 188–91; A. Jones 1964, chapter 25, passim; P. Heather 2006, pp. 111–12.

81. Ibid.

82. Guglielmo Ferraro as described in J. Tainter 1988, p. 58.

83. S. Mazzarino 1966, p. 54.

84. S. Leeb 2006, p. 33.

85. M. Grant 1968, pp. 44–47; S. Clough 1951, pp. 153ff.

86. H. Mattingly 1960, p. 215; J. Tainter 1988, pp. 136–37.

87. M. Grant 1968, pp. 44–47; S. Clough 1951, pp. 153ff.

88. S. Clough 1951, pp. 153ff.; M. Grant 1968, p. 50; C. Starr 1982, p. 80.

89. J. Jacobs 2005, pp. 22–24, 181–82.

90. Ibid.

91. M. Grant 1968, p. 48; S. Clough 1951, p. 157; J. Tainter 1988, pp. 143, 150–51; J. Jacobs 2005, pp. 181–82.

92. Lactantius 1984, Book 7, p. 7; P. Heather 2006, p. 65.

93. Ibid.

94. A Bernardi 1970, pp. 38ff.; H. Adelson 1962, pp. 12–16; R. LaTouche 1967, pp. 16–17.

95. Ibid.

96. Lactantius 1984, pp. 2, 7. 23; A. Bernardi 1970, vol. 1, p. 33; J. Bury 1923, vol. 1, p. 33.

97. Lactantius quoted in J. Strayer and D. Munro 1942, p. 5.

98. Cited in R. MacMullen 1988, p. 162.

99. A. Bernardi 1970, pp. 65–69, 76ff.

100. J. Tainter 1988, p. 196.

101. C. Murphy 2007, pp. 183–84, 187.

102. On this, see G. Miles 1990, pp. 629–59, passim; C. Murphy 2007, pp. 190–91. Of these developments, historian Lynn White observes: "There is, in fact, no proof that any important skills of the Graeco-Roman world were lost during the Dark Ages, even in the unenlightened West."

103. A. Bernardi 1970, p. 81.

104. G. Luzzatto 1961, pp. 11–13; A. Bernardi 1970, pp. 23–29; R. LaTouche 1967, pp.16–17; S. Clough 1951, p. 159.

105. C. Freeman 2002, p. 322; K. Phillips 1990, p. 226.

106. S. Clough 1951, pp. 120–21; see also R. LaTouche 1967, p. 11; N. Baynes 1927, pp. 29ff.; D. Munro and G. Sellery 1914, p. 131; S. Katz 1955, pp. 95–96.

107. E. A. Gibbon 1969, as cited in S. Dill 1900, p. 129.

108. M. P. Charlesworth, as quoted in H. Heaton 1948, p. 53.

109. J. Black 1994, p. 40.

110. O. Guinness 1993, p. 214; J. Black 1994, p. 40.

111. J. Black 1994, pp. 39, 136.

112. Ibid.

CHAPTER 2: CONTEMPORARY CAUSES OF COLLAPSE

1. S. Lipset 1992, p. 58; S. Huntington 1993.

2. R Nixon 1992, pp. 230ff.

3. R. Nixon 1992, pp.147–48.

4. A. Schlesinger 1998, pp. 142, 144; S. Renshon 2005, pp. xvii, xviii.

5. S. Huntington 1961, p. 23.

6. Ibid.

7. G. K. Chesterton quoted in O. Guinness 2001, p. 263; A. Schlesinger 1998, p. 17.

8. R. Palmer 1964, vol. 1, p. 223.

9. S. Renshon 2005, p. 59; F. Wooldridge 2004, pp. 195–97.

10. D. Kupelian 2005, p. 86.

11. Ibid.

12. R. Bernstein 1994, p. 212.

13. D. Kupelian 2005, pp. 98–99; A. Kors and H. Silverglate 1998, pp. 193–94; S. Renshon 2005, p. 1.

14. Paul Craig Roberts quoted in D. Kupelian 2005, pp. 98–99; A. Kors and H. Silverglate 1998, pp. 193–94.

15. S. Renshon 2005, pp. 252–53.

16. S. Renshon 2005, pp. 2, 59.

17. S. Renshon 2005, p. 221; J. Black 2004, p. 58.

18. S. Renshon 2005, p. 82.

19. J. Black 2004, pp. 19, 33, 220–21.

20. Ibid.; H. Kramer and R. Kimball 1999, p. 14.

21. On them, and the so-called Frankfurt School of which they were members, see R. Wiggershaus 1995, passim; T. Blankley 2005, p. 100; J. Black 1994, pp. 184–86, 220–21; M. Berman 2000, pp. 107–8.

22. Sources cited, loc. cit.

23. H. Marcuse 1971, p. 17; H. Kramer and R. Kimball 1999, p. 14.

24. H. Marcuse 1966, p. xvii; R. Kimball 1998, p. 84.

25. H. Marcuse 1966, p. xvii; H. Kramer and R. Kimball 2000, pp. 7–8; H. Kramer and R. Kimball 1999, pp. 14–15.

26. R. Kimball 1998, pp. 15–16, 18; P. Buchanan 2002, pp. 85–86; J. Black 2004, p. 212; J. Leo 2001, p. 255; L. Ingraham 2003, p. 36.

27. Sources cited, loc. cit.

28. R. Bork 2003, pp. 17–19.

29. See M. Learner 1998, passim, quoted in J. Black 2004, pp. 343–44; H. Kramer and R. Kimball 1999, p. 17.

30. M. Lerner 1996, p. 97; quoted in J. Bovard 1999, p. 235.

31. J. Bovard 1999, pp. 236–37.

32. R. Dworkin 1977, p. 239; quoted in I. Kristol 1978, p. 179.

33. Andrew Hacker quoted in W. Elliot 1974, p. 29.

34. Samuel Butler quoted in F. Wooldridge 2004, p. 129; J. Black 1994, p. 185; P. Buchanan 2002, pp. 80, 85–86, 93, 216, 267.

35. J. Ellis 1997, p. 7.
36. J. Ellis 1997, p. 207.
37. R. Kimball 1998, pp. 191–92.
38. Ibid.
39. H. Gates 1989, p. 44; R. Kimball 1998, p. 92; J. Black 2004, pp. 175ff.; D. D'Souza 1991, pp. 17–18.
40. Henry Gates quoted in D. D'Souza 1991, p. 172.
41. J. Parini 1988, p. B-1; quoted in W. Williams, August 2002, p. 1; D. D'Souza 1991, p. 18.
42. Annette Kolodny quoted in A. Sanoff 1989, p. 54; D. D'Souza 1991, p. 18.
43. R. Bork 2003, p. 13.
44. R. Kimball 1998, pp. 216–17.
45. R. Bork 2003, pp. 51–53.
46. R. Nisbet 1975, p. 67.
47. D. Potter 1973, pp. 387–88.
48. A. Bloom 1987, p. 314.
49. See A. Schlesinger 1998, pp. 20ff., 112, 139; cited in T. Blankley 2005, p. 100; Vladimir Lenin quoted in M. Malkin 2002, p. 63.
50. J. Black 1994, p. 242.
51. Ibid.
52. S. Renshon 2005, p. 101.
53. S. Huntington 2004b, p. 141.
54. S. Huntington 2004b, p. 221.
55. Ibid.
56. S. Huntington 2004b, pp. 137–38.
57. A. Schlesinger 1998, p. 126.
58. J. Black 1994, pp. 134–35, 140–41.
59. Ibid.
60. L. Bartholemew 1994, p. 5; S. Huntington 2004b, p. 173.
61. U. S. Newswire, June 15, 1998, p. 1; S. Huntington 2004b, p. 142; P. Buchanan 2002, pp. 19, 141, 209; T. Tancredo 2006, pp. 42, 185; S. Renshon 2005, p. 39; H. Browne 1995, p. 50.
62. A. Schmidt 1997, p. 181.
63. Ibid.
64. S. Huntington 2004b, pp. 142–45.
65. T. Tancredo 2006, p. 34; S. Huntington 2004b, pp. 142–45, 272; A. Schmidt 1997, pp. 109–10, 143, 148, 172.
66. R. Kimball 1998, p. xii.
67. Alexis de Tocqueville quoted in A. Schlesinger 1998, p. 165.
68. A. Bloom 1987, p. 382.
69. Susan Haack quoted in M. Berman 2006, p. 126.
70. A. Schmidt 1997, pp. 20–21.
71. Ibid.
72. B. Goldberg 2005, p. 36.
73. B. Goldberg 2005, loc. cit.
74. A. Schmidt 1997, p. 26.
75. A. Schmidt 1997, pp. 26–28.
76. A. Schmidt 1997, p. 80.
77. K. Marx 1970, p. 21.
78. Diane Ravitch quoted in K. Winkler 1995, p. A11.
79. D. Murphey 1991, p. 349.

80. Examples are, in part, selected from A. Schmidt 1997, pp. 90–91.

81. J. F. Revel 1993, pp. 92–93.

82. V. Hanson 2004, p. 1; M. Malkin 2005, p. 8.

83. R. Kimball 1998, pp. 57–58.

84. Edmund Burke 1967, p. 42; E. Burke 1969, vol. 8, p. 138; E Burke 1961, p. 203; T. Sowell 2007b, pp. 56, 60, 64.

85. Ibid.

86. F. Wooldridge 2004, pp. 78, 138–39.

87. P. Buchanan 2002, pp. 89–90, 256–57; P. Buchanan 2006, pp. 172–73.

88. A. Schmidt 1997, pp. 85–86.

89. P. Collier and D. Horowitz 1996, pp. 245ff., 371.

90. Ibid.

91. A. Schmidt 1997, p. 86.

92. A. Bloom 1990, p. 367.

93. R. Bork 2005, pp. ix, x.

94. Justice Charles Evan Hughes quoted in D. Danelski and J. Tulchin 1973, p. 143; O. Guinness 1993, p. 365.

95. Cf. *Cooper v. Allen*, 358 U.S. 1 (1958) ("the federal judiciary is supreme in the exposition of the Constitution") and the Court's interpretation of the Constitution "is the supreme law of the land"); *Brown v. Allen*, 344 U.S. 443, 540 (1953) (Justice Robert Jackson concurring opinion); quoted in L. Graglia 2005, pp. 20, 28.

96. Thomas Jefferson quoted in N. Gingrich 2006, p. 78.

97. R. Bork 2005, p. xi.

98. Ibid.

99. Cf. *Texas v. Johnson*, 491 U.S. 397 (1989) (see also *United States v. Eichman*, 496 U.S. Code 310 (1990) (flag desecration); *Shad v. Mt Ephraim*, 452 U.S. 61 (1981) (nude dancing); *Abington School District v. Schempp*, 364 U.S. 203, 225 (1963) (school prayer); *Grutter v. Bollinger*, 539 U.S.305 (2003) (racial discrimination in college admissions).

100. Cf. *Cantwell v. Connecticut*, 310 U.S. 296 (1940); R. Bork 2005, p. xii, xv, xxii–xxiii, xxvi, xxxi; L. Graglia 2005, pp. 17, 41–42, 51.

101. *Plessy v. Ferguson*, 163 U.S. 537 (1896) (permitted); *Brown v. Board of Education*, 347 U.S. 483 (1954) (prohibited); *Swann v. Charlotte-Mecklenberg Board of Education*, 402 U.S. 1 (1971) (required); L. Graglia 2005, pp. 20–22.

102. L. Graglia 2005, pp. 31–32.

103. G. Himmelfarb 1974, pp. 46–47.

104. L. Graglia 2005, p. 24.

105. L. Graglia 1996, pp. 293, 298.

106. S. Levinson 1989, pp. 64–65.

107. Antonin Scalia dissenting opinion in *Board of County Commissioners, Wabaunsee County, Kansas v. Umbehr*, 518, U.S. 668, 688–689 (1996), cited in R. Bork 2005, p. xi.

108. Alexis de Tocqueville quoted in L. Graglia 2005, p. 1; T. Eastland 2005, pp. 110–11, 135.

109. G. McDowell 2005, p. 60.

110. J. Black 2004, p. 272.

111. A. Schlesinger 1998, pp. 22, 49.

112. S. Huntington 2004b, pp. 144, 147.

113. S. Huntington 2004b, pp. 148–49.

114. S. Huntington 2004b, p. 150.

115. S. Huntington 2004b, p. 151.

116. S. Lipset 1992, pp. 66–67; S. Huntington 2004b, p. 153.

117. Ibid.

118. All incidents related in A. Schmidt 1997, pp. 34–46, passim; V. Hanson 2003, p. 104.
119. Sir Charles Napier quoted in M. Steyn 2006, p. 193.
120. All incidents related in A. Schmidt 1997, pp. 34–46, passim; V. Hanson 2003, p. 104.
121. Ibid.
122. Ibid.
123. A. Schlesinger 1998, p. 133.
124. A. Schlesinger 1998, p. 135; G. Jackson 2007, p. 325.
125. S. Renshon 2005, pp. 83–84; J. Black 2004, pp. 178–79.
126. Sources cited, loc. cit.; A Coulter 2002, p. 201; R. Davis 1999, pp. 1–2.
127. Sources cited, loc. cit.
128. R. Bork 2003, p. 260.
129. A. Schmidt 1997, p. 189.
130. Ibid.
131. R. Kimball 1998, pp. 226–27; G. Jackson 2006, pp. 321ff.
132. R. Kimball 1998, p. 236.
133. Lord Thomas Macaulay cited by J. Black 1994, p. 246.
134. Walter Lippman quoted in O. Guinness 2001, p. 32.
135. J. Ortega y Gassett 1957, p. 76; R. Bork 2003, p. 313.
136. W. Churchill 1946, passim.
137. Winston Churchill 1946, quoted in J. Black 2004, pp. 292–93.
138. J. Black 2004, pp. 292–93.
139. Ibid.
140. R. Kirk 1992, passim, replicated in J. Black 2004, p. 318.
141. D. Kupelian 2005, p. 103.
142. A. Schlesinger 1998, pp. 135, 165; D. Kupelian 2005, p. 103.
143. D. Kennedy 1997, p. 355; S. Huntington 2004b, p. 259.

CHAPTER 3: EXCESSES OF EDUCATION

1. J. S. Mill 1915, pp. 948ff. in general, and p. 953 quoted.
2. Will and Ariel Durant in *The Lessons of History*, cited at www.uga.edu/ihe/perspectives/perpect/0102.
3. H. G. Wells in *The Outline of History*, cited at www.classicreader.com/author.php/aut.
4. Franklin Roosevelt, the "Four Freedoms," cited at www.americanrhetoric.com/speeches/fdrthefourfreedoms.html; home.att.net/-jrhsc/fdr.html.
5. Henry David Thoreau quoted in L. Peter 1977; cited at www.quotationspage.com/quotes/Henry_David_Thoreau.
6. D. Kupelian 2005, p. 156.
7. H. G. Good 1956, pp. 3, 10, 13.
8. H. G. Good 1956, p. 31.
9. H. G. Good 1956, p. 87.
10. George Washington quoted in John Fitzpatrick 1932, vol. 15, p. 55; D. Barton 2002, p. 85.
11. Ibid.
12. Washington, Jay, and Madison all quoted in H. G. Good 1956, pp. 91–93.
13. George Washington, John Adams, and Thomas Jefferson quoted in E. Burns 2006, p. 7; C. Johnson 2006, p. 59; W. McDougall 2004, p. 285; O. Guinness 2001, p. 149.
14. C. Reese 2007, p. 15.
15. Ibid.
16. John Adams quoted in E. Sandoz 1984, p. 67.

17. M. Malbin 1978, pp. 14–15; G. Demar 1995, pp. 154–55; E. Gaustad 1993, p. 177; D. Barton 2002, p. 41; A. Schmidt 1997, p. 175. On Continental Congress deliberations leading to enacting of the Northwest Ordinance, see E. Gaustad 1993, pp. 151–56.

18. D. Barton 2002, pp. 41–42.

19. Guinness 1993, p. 228.

20. S. Steinberg 1981, p. 54; S. Huntington 2004, p. 134; S. Renshon 2005, p. 57; W. Berns 2001, passim.

21. Ronald Reagan quoted in J. Black 2004, p. 13.

22. A. Kors and H. Silverglate 1998, pp. 2–3.

23. Ibid.

24. A. Kors and H. Silverglate 1998, pp. 4ff.

25. Judge Learned Hand quoted in A. Kors and H. Silverglate 1998, p. 66.

26. A. Kors and H. Silverglate 1998, p. 67.

27. A. Kors and H. Silverglate 1998, pp. 68ff.

28. A. Kors and H. Silverglate 1998, p. 68.

29. On this, see H. Marcuse 1969, pp. 81–123 passim.

30. A. Kors and H. Silverglate 1998, p. 68.

31. H. Marcuse 1969, pp. 81–123 passim; also quoted in A. Kors and H. Silverglate 1998, p. 69.

32. H. Marcuse quoted in A. Kors and H. Silverglate 1998, p. 70.

33. Ibid.

34. Ibid.

35. Ibid.

36. H. Marcuse quoted in A. Kors and H. Silverglate 1998, p. 71.

37. H. Marcuse as synopsized in A. Kors and H. Silverglate 1998, p. 71.

38. Ibid.

39. T. Sowell 1994, p. 62; A. Kors and H. Silverglate 1998, p. 71.

40. A. Kors and H. Silverglate 1998, pp. 27, 71ff.

41. J. Ellis 1997, p. 6.

42. Ibid.

43. J. Ellis 1997, pp. 7–8.

44. J. Ellis 1997, p. 10.

45. J. Ellis 1997, p. 11.

46. J. Ellis 1997, pp. 31–32.

47. J. Ellis 1997, p. 32.

48. Ibid.

49. Polling results displayed at www.zogby.com/news/ReadNews.dbm?ID=1334, dated July 10, 2007; Alan Kors quoted in D. D'Souza 1991, p. 257.

50. A. Kors and H. Silverglate 1998, p. 96.

51. A. Kors and H. Silverglate 1998, pp. 192, 205–6.

52. Julia Harume quoted in A. Sears and C. Osten 2005, p. 56.

53. A. Kors and H. Silverglate 1998, pp. 192, 205–6.

54. Ibid.

55. A. Kors and H. Silverglate 1998, p. 193; R. Bork 2003, p. 304; J. Ellis 1997, p. 75.

56. R. Bernstein 1994, p. 58.

57. R. Bork 2003, p. 306.

58. Dennis Prager quoted in B. Goldberg 2005, p. 38.

59. B. Wilson 2003, pp. 1ff.

60. John Adams quoted in A. Schmidt 1997, p. 43.

61. C. Crawford 2006, p. 43.

62. Justice Robert Jackson quoted in A. Kors and H. Silverglate 1998, p. 209.

63. A. Kors and H. Silverglate 1998, pp. 277–78; J. Black 2004, pp. 134ff., 145.

64. Sources cited, loc. cit.

65. A. Kors and H. Silverglate 1998, pp. 99ff.; J. Black 2004, p. 134.

66. Quotations are from N. Hentoff 1992, p. 7; B. Cerveny 1994, p. 4; A. Schmidt 1997, pp. 92–93.

67. Camille Paglia quoted in A. Schmidt 1997, p. 94.

68. R. Bernstein 1994, p. 22.

69. A. Kors 1989, p.1; R.Kimball 1998, pp. 64ff.; D. D'Souza 1991, pp. 9–10; R. Bernstein 1994, p. 60.

70. R. Bernstein 1994, p. 65.

71. A. Kors and H. Silverglate 1998, pp. 231–32; R. Bernstein 1994, pp. 191–92; B. Goldberg 2005, pp. 52–53.

72. Ibid.

73. A. Kors and H. Silverglate 1998, p. 276.

74. Ibid.

75. Judicial settlement presented to University of Pennsylvania student replicated in A. Kors and H. Silverglate 1998, p. 212.

76. N. Hentoff 1989, p. A23; D. D'Souza 1991, p. 148.

77. A. Schmidt 1997, p. 100.

78. *New York Times*, April 25, 1989, p. 1.

79. R. Kimball 1998, p. 87.

80. R. Kimball 1998, pp. 87–88.

81. A. Kors and H. Silverglate 1998, pp. 277–78.

82. A. Kors and H. Silverglate 1998, pp. 278, 290–91, 310.

83. Ibid.

84. A. Kors and H. Silverglate 1998, pp. 313–14, 328–32, 335.

85. Sources cited, loc. cit.

86. A. Kors and H. Silverglate 1998, pp. 248–49.

87. A. Kors and H. Silverglate 1998, p. 149; R. Bullock 1993, p. 1; A. Schmidt 1997, p. 94; W. Berns 2006, p. 173. R. Bernstein 1994, p. 86.

88. Related in the *Education Reporter* and cited in J. Black 2004, p. 58.

89. A. Kors and H. Silverglate 1998, pp. 259–61.

90. D. D'Souza 1991, pp. 140ff., 151–53, 195.

91. D. D'Souza 1991, p. 153.

92. Ibid.

93. Donald Kagan quoted in D. D'Souza 1991, p. 239; A. Kors and H. Silverglate 1998, p. 146.

94. Cardinal John Henry Newman, *The Idea of a University* (1852), quoted in R. Kimball 1998, p. ix.

95. A. Schlesinger 1998, pp. 59ff.; S. Huntington 2004b, pp. 176–77.

96. D. D'Souza 1991, p. 208.

97. Ibid.

98. S. Frederick Starr quoted in D. D'Souza 1991, pp. 214, 239.

99. Ibid.

100. A. Schmidt 1997, p. 165.

101. Ibid.

102. A. Schmidt 1997, p. 164; J. Black 2004, pp. 124, 132, 152, 156–57, 255–56, 296–97; R. Bork 2003, pp. 89, 247–48; J. Kaylin 1995, p. 39; J. Leo 2001, p. 78–80; L. Ingraham 2003, p. 240.

103. All quoted in J. Black 2004, pp. 218–19; J. Martin and A. Neal 2003, passim; M. Malkin 2005, pp. 104–5; L. Ingraham 2003, pp. 235ff.

104. Sources cited, loc. cit.

105. All cited in J. Black 2004, pp. 224–25.

106. Ibid.

107. Ibid.

108. Howard Zinn quoted in J. Jacoby 2007, p. 10; B. Shapiro 2007, p. 13.

109. J. Black 2004, pp. 4, 55, 118ff., 190ff.

110. Ibid.

111. Ibid.

112. J. Black 1994, pp. 8, 33, 137.

113. R. Kimball 1998, pp. 14–15, 44; A. Schmidt 1997, pp. 79–80, 164.

114. A. Schmidt 1997, pp. 29, 81; R. Kimball 1998, pp. 14–15, 44.

115. R. Bernstein 1994, p. 295.

116. *The California Patriot* quoted in J. Black 2004, pp. 172–73.

117. J. Black 1994, p. 138; J. Black 2004, pp. 142–45; J. Fallows 1997, p. 107.

118. See F. Snowden 1970, passim; F. Snowden 1983, p. 73; A. Schmidt 1997, p. 167.

119. A. Schmidt 1997, p. 81.

120. A. Schmidt 1997, p. 95.

121. A. Schmidt 1997, pp. 66–69.

122. Ibid.

123. Ibid.

124. *Washington Times* 2007a, p. A15.

125. All cited in J. Black 1994, pp 8, 153; J. Leo 2001, pp. 74–75; L. Ingraham 2003, p. 16. In the late 1990s, feminists at the University of Massachusetts-Amherst proposed a new watchdog program called "Vision 2000" wherein each academic program would be compelled to hold an annual seminar on gender issues, and gender studies would be "introduced into all pertinent programs of institutional research." All professors and students would undergo mandatory gender sensitivity training. Faculty would be held accountable if men were "over-represented" in the curriculum, or if their pedagogies were not "women friendly"—with "women-friendly pedagogies" mandated for all classes. Teachers who did not comply were to be denied promotions and raises.

126. W. Berns 2006, p. 176; J. Leo 2001, p. 47.

127. C. Chumley, September 2000, p. 1; J. Black 1994, pp. 139–40, 192ff., 310–11; A. Schmidt 1997, pp. 74–76; D. D'Souza 1991, p. 161.

128. D. S'Souza, loc. cit. On one occasion, it is reported that a student at the University of Texas asked what was wrong with being a black conservative, to which his professor responded that any individual who is black and conservative simply isn't "black enough," and that such a person is not working for the best interests of the black community (!) (Indeed, Stanford advertises for homosexual residence advisors; and at Cornell, they have to undergo "homosexual activity" training.)

129. Ibid.

130. Robert Berdahl quoted by T. Schevitz 2002, p. 1.

131. H. Hewitt 2003, p. 1.

132. A. Kors and H. Silverglate 1998, p. 354; also quoted in J. Black 2004, p. 299.

133. J. Black 2004, pp. 147–48.

134. J. Black 2004, p. 148.

135. See R. Bork 2003, pp. 250ff.

136. J. Black 2004, pp. 43ff., 70, 75, 94.

137. See A. Kors and H. Silverglate 1998, pp. 3–6; J. Black 2004, pp. 5, 107.

138. J. Black 2004, pp. 34–35; D. D'Souza 1991, p. 14; National Endowment for the Humanities 1989, pp. 33–56.

139. Sources cited, loc. cit.

140. J. Black 2004, pp. 165–69.

141. P. Schlafly 2007, p. 18.

142. Ibid.

143. Thomas Jefferson quoted in W. Berns 2001, p. 65.
144. W. Berns 2001, p. 79.
145. Alexis de Tocqueville quoted in W. Berns 2001, p. 64.
146. Ibid.
147. W. Berns 2001, pp. 79–80.
148. Ibid.
149. M. Gross 1997, p. 116.
150. J. Black 2004, pp. 105, 273.
151. J. Black 2004, p. 7.
152. R. Baldwin 1998, pp. 1–2.
153. J. Black 2004, pp.111, 115–18, 305.
154. John McWhorter quoted in W. McGowan 2001, p. 158.
155. Ibid.
156. R. Bork 2003, p. 247.
157. R. Baldwin 1998, p. 8.
158. Ibid.
159. R. Kimball 1998, pp. 10–11, 21.
160. Ibid.
161. Ibid.
162. Polling results cited in J. Black 2004, pp. 74–75; B. Goldberg 2005, p. 52.
163. J. Black 2004, pp. 227–28, 248; G. Jackson 2006, p. 167.
164. Ibid.
165. D. Flynn 2005, passim; A. Mangino 2007, pp. 1–2.
166. *Feminism and Geography: The Limits of Geographical Knowledge,* as quoted in W. Henry 1994, p. 117; R. Kimball 1998, pp. xiii–xiv.
167. Alvin Thornton quoted in D. D'Souza 1991, pp. 109–10, 126.
168. M. Bernal 1989, vol. 1, pp. 73, 242; D. D'Souza 1991, p. 116.
169. M. Angelou 1985, p. 1; also quoted in D. D'Souza 1991, p. 157.
170. S. Sontag 1969, p. 203.
171. S. Renshon 2005, p. 145; J. Black 2004, p. 222.
172. A. Schlesinger 1998, pp. 67–74, 124–26; J. Black 1994, p. 14.
173. Sources cited, loc. cit.; D. Stannard 1992, passim.
174. R. Bernstein 1994, pp. 51–56.
175. Ibid.
176. J. Black 1994, pp. 179–80.
177. Charles Pierce quoted in G. Demar 1997, v. 3, p. 248; J. Black 2004, p. 50.
178. J. Leo 2001, pp. 43–44, 141–42, 227.
179. R. Bernstein 1994, p. 275.
180. Ibid.
181. A. Schlesinger 1998, p. 132.
182. John Adams quoted in O. Guinness 2001, p. 88; C. Campbell 1994, p. C-6.
183. E. Gaustad 1993, p. 103; G. Demar 1995, pp. 84, 163–65.
184. J. Adams 1850, p. 34; Thomas Jefferson quoted in G. Demar 1995, pp. 192–93; D. Barton 2002, p. 163.
185. Norman Cousins quoted in F. Wooldridge 2004, p. 77.
186. A. Schlesinger 1998, pp. 77, 80–81, 98–99, 101, 104 (quoted); A. Schlesinger 1990, p. 1.
187. D. D'Souza 1991, pp. 188, 229.
188. Ibid.
189. Roy Wilkins and Bayard Rustin both quoted by T. Sowell 1989, p. 118; D. D'Souza 1991, p. 205.
190. S. Renshon 2005, p. 152

191. E. J. Dionne 1999, p. 1.
192. G. Heck 2007a, p. xix; D. Kupelian 2005, p. 119.
193. John Searle, *The New York Times Review of Books* (1991), quoted in R. Baldwin 1998, p. ix.
194. Margaret Thatcher quoted in O. Guinness 2001, p. 242.
195. D. Martin 1999, p. 13.
196. See D. Thompson 1970, passim; S. Renshon 2005, p. 150.
197. S. Renshon 2005, p. 150.
198. R. Bernstein 1994, p. 11.
199. R. Kimball 1998, pp. 93ff.; J. Black 1994, p. 35.
200. V. Hanson 2003, p. 1.
201. A. de Tocqueville 1969, pp. 464–65.
202. A. Kors and H. Silverglate 1998, p. 354.
203. A. Kors and H. Silverglate 1998, pp. 371–73; J. Black 2004, p. xii.
204. Louis Veuillot qouted in J. Burnham 1964, p. 237. Sources cited *supra*, loc. cit.
    Quand je suis le plus faible, je vous demande la liberté,
    parce que tel est vôtre principle;
    mais quand je suis le plus fort, je vous l'ôte,
    parce tel est le mien.
205. J. Black 2004, p. 319.
206. See R. Conquest 1999, passim, cited in J. Black 2004, p. 267.
207. Benno Smith quoted in A. Neal 2003, p. 1; J. Black 2004, p. 269.
208. George Santayana quoted in R. Bernstein 1994, p. 342; J. Black 2004, p. 269.

CHAPTER 4: MANIPULATION OF THE MEDIA

1. Thomas Jefferson quoted in *Encyclopedia Britannica Online* at www.britannica.com/ebi/article-927666.
2. H. G. Good 1956, p. 25.
3. Ibid.
4. Justice Holmes in *Chaplinsky v. New Hampshire*, 1942, quoted in G. Stone 2004, pp. 8, 33–34. To the contrary is the admonition of Congressman James A. Bravard at the time of the passage of the "Sedition Act of 1798" that the notion that truth prevails over falsehood is "a fine moral sentiment, but our limited knowledge of events does not verify it."
5. H. G. Good 1956, pp. 26–27.
6. G. Stone 2004, pp. 5–6.
7. H. G. Good 1956, p. 27.
8. Cf. E. Burns 2006, pp. 19ff., 35ff., 203–9; J. Fallows 1997, p. 48.
9. J. Fallows 1997, p. 48.
10. Ibid.
11. J. Fallows 2007, pp. 48–49.
12. G. Stone 2004, p. 9.
13. G. Stone 2004, pp. 12–13, 120, 146ff., 530ff., 540, 552ff.
14. G. Stone 2004, p. 548.
15. Thomas Jefferson quoted in J. Miller 1951, p. 231; G. Stone 2004, pp. 63, 71, 73.
16. G. Stone 2004, p. 73.
17. Ibid.
18. D. Kupelian 2005, p. 186.
19. B. Goldberg 2003, pp. 81–83.
20. B. Goldberg 2003, pp. 9, 14, 99.

21. B. Goldberg 2003, pp. 103, 110–11.

22. D. Moynihan quoted in G. Heck 2007a, p. 109.

23. D. Kupelian 2005, p. 169.

24. Ibid.

25. P. Buchanan 2002, pp. 145–46; D. Kupelian 2005, p. 182.

26. D. Kupelian 2005, p. 169.

27. B. Goldberg 2002, p. 131. John Kennedy's Commerce Secretary Luther Hodges once allowed that "if ignorance paid dividends, most Americans could make a fortune on what they don't know about the U.S. economic system." But this hypothesis holds true only to the extent that citizens actually believe what their media tell them on a daily basis—and that the media continues to persevere in promoting its perverse anticapitalistic bias, which it undoubtedly will—for after all: "it's their story, and their stickin' to it."

28. B. Goldberg 1996, p. 1.

29. J. Fallows 1997, p. 35.

30. P. Mulhern 2001, p. 1; B. Goldberg 2005, pp. 163ff.; M. Malkin 2005, pp. 123–25.

31. J. Fallows 1997, p. 33.

32. J. Fallows 1997, pp. 31–32.

33. J. Fallows 1997, pp. 60–61.

34. J. Fallows 1997, p. 81.

35. Ibid.

36. Lisa Myers quoted in T. Patterson 1994, p. 102.

37. Lisa Myers quoted in T. Patterson 1994, p. 131.

38. H. Fineman and A. McDaniel 1992, p. 28.

39. Nina Totenberg quoted in B. Goldberg 2002, p. 187.

40. Julianne Malveaux quoted in B. Goldberg 2002, p. 187.

41. All examples cited are from B. Goldberg 2003, pp. 124–26, 146–47; W. McGowan 2001, p. 235.

42. Jonathan Alter quoted in B. Goldberg 2003, pp. 224–26.

43. N. Henry 2007, p. 13; Eric Engberg quoted in B. Goldberg 2002, pp. 23, 69ff., 221ff.

44. Will Durant quoted in E. Burns 2006, p. 24.

45. Lisa Myers quoted in J. Fallows 1997, p. 131.

46. B. Goldberg 2002, pp. 6ff., 9, 13, 63. For the verbatim text of the op-ed, see B. Goldberg 2002, pp. 221–24.

47. Ibid.

48. A. Schmidt 1997, p. 154

49. D. Kupelian 2005, p. 182.

50. B. Goldberg 2003, pp. 129–31; L. Dobbs 2006, pp. 85–86; A. Coulter 2002, p. 71.

51. B. Goldberg 2002, p. 131.

52. *Washington Times,* October 9, 2007b, p. A6.

53. B. Goldberg 2002, p. 130; G. Jackson 2006, p. 169.

54. David Frumm quoted in W. McGowan 2001, p. 229; B. Bozell 2007, p. 11.

55. Sources cited, loc. cit.

56. B. Goldberg 2003, pp. 106–7.

57. B. Goldberg 2003, p. 106.

58. Ibid.

59. B. Goldberg 2003, pp. 36, 270.

60. Ibid.

61. B. Goldberg 2002, p. 222; B. Goldberg 2005, p. 205.

62. Editorials as identified by B. Goldberg 2005, pp. 298–99.

63. B. Kohn 2003, pp. 21, 141ff.

64. B. Kovach and T. Rosenstiel, *The Elements of Journalism* (New York: 2003), quoted in B. Kohn 2003, p. 31.

65. B. Kohn 2003, p. 35.
66. B. Goldberg 2002, p. 66; A. Coulter 2002, p. 155.
67. B. Goldberg 2002, p. 64.
68. James Sleeper quoted in W. McGowan 2001, p. 246.
69. W. McGowan 2001, p. 248.
70. J. Fallows 2007, p. 49.
71. Ibid.
72. B. Goldberg 2003, p. 257.
73. B. Goldberg 2003, p. 259; B. Goldberg 2002, pp. 30ff.
74. B. Goldberg 2002, p. 30.
75. Evan Thomas quoted in B. Goldberg 2002, pp. 187–88.
76. Eleanor Clift quoted in B. Goldberg 2002, p. 191.
77. Dan Rather quoted in B. Goldberg 2002, p. 189.
78. B. Goldberg 2002, pp. 31, 114.
79. B. Goldberg 2002, p. 203.
80. A. Cohen 2003, p. 1.
81. Dan Rather quoted in B. Goldberg 2002, p. 203.
82. Carl Rowan quoted in B. Goldberg 2002, p. 204.
83. Richard Lacayo quoted in B. Goldberg 2002, p. 203.
84. Nina Easton quoted in B. Goldberg 2002, pp. 203–4.
85. David Broder quoted in B. Goldberg 2002, pp. 203–4.
86. P. Fosl 1995, p. 1
87. Pauline Kael quoted in B. Goldberg 2002, p. 30.
88. T. Patterson 1994, pp. 37, 79; L. Ingraham 2003, p. 39.
89. Vaclav Havel cited in J. Fallows 2007, p. 12.
90. Alexis de Tocqueville quoted in W. McGowan 2001, p. 248.
91. W. McGowan 2001, pp. 248–49.
92. W. Lippmann 1965, pp. 19, 54–55, 222, 229.
93. Terry Moran quoted in H. Hewitt 2006, p. 49.
94. B. Goldberg 2003, p. 203.
95. Lord Salisbury quoted in M. Barone 2007, p. 25.
96. A. J. Leibling quoted in B. Goldberg 2003, p. 37.
97. H. Browne 1995, pp. 140–142.
98. On this, see J. Bradley 2006, pp. 280–95; H. Browne 1995, p. 140; N. Henry 2007, p. 99.
99. The Meuse-Argonne offensive was the largest American battle of World War I. In six weeks, the Allied Expeditionary Force lost 26,277 killed and 95,786 wounded.
100. Sir Robert Thompson quoted in N. Gingrich 2008, p. 116.
101. For the source of these calculations, see N. Ferguson 2006, pp. 46–52.
102. Ibid.
103. M. Schermer 2002, p. 1.
104. B. Goldberg 2003, pp. 229–31; M. Malkin 2005, p. 90.
105. B. Goldberg 2003, pp. 232–34.
106. Don Imus quoted in B. Goldberg 2003, p. 230.
107. S. Huntington 2004b, pp. 125ff.
108. O. North. "Mullah Meetings—'Negotiating' with Radicals," *Conservative Chronicle*, August 1, 2007, p. 28.
109. "George S. Patton's Speech to the Third U.S. Army" at www.historyfilmcom/patton/bio.htm
110. Thomas Paine quoted in J. Bradley 2006, p. 75.
111. J. Bradley 2006, pp. 281–95; A. Zolberg 2006, pp. 435–36.
112. P. Buchanan 2002, p.107.

113. Charles Gibson quoted in B. Goldberg 2003, p. 199.
114. L. Ingraham 2003, p. 316.
115. D. Limbaugh 2007, p. 1.
116. P. Buchanan. "How Empires End: the Ruin of Acre," *Conservative Chronicle*, August 1, 2007, p. 5.
117. T. Sowell. "After the Terrorists' War On Us: Part II," *Conservative Chronicle*, July 25, 2007, p. 18.
118. Thomas Jefferson quoted in J. Yablon 2007, p. 1.
119. Thomas Jefferson quoted in C. Crawford 2006, p. 3.
120. See B. Goldberg 2003, pp. 284–87.
121. T. Patterson 1994, p. 250.
122. Pew polling reported in N. Henry 2007, p. 32.
123. Theodore Roosevelt quoted in T. Goldstein 2007, p. 235.
124. Harry Truman quoted in T. Goldstein 2007, p. 131.
125. Lord Macauley quoted in T. Goldstein 2007, p. 241.
126. N. Henry 2007, p. 214.

CHAPTER 5: CRISIS OF CITIZENSHIP

1. O. Handlin 1973, p. 2.
2. G. Jackson 2007, pp. 351ff.
3. S. Renshon 2005, pp. 180, 183. It is noteworthy that those Americans of non-Mexican origin who seek to become naturalized in Mexico are required to formally renounce their U.S. citizenship.
4. P. Brimelow 1995, pp. 5, 242.
5. S. Renshon 2005, p. 158.
6. George Washington quoted in M. Malkin 2002, p. 123.
7. Thomas Jefferson cited in A. Zolberg 2006, p. 24; J. F. Kennedy 1964, p. 28; R. Daniels 2004, p. 6.
8. Thomas Jefferson quoted in A. Zolberg 2006, p. 58.
9. Alexander Hamilton quoted in D. Tichenor 2002, pp. 37, 51, 53.
10. James Madison quoted in A. Zolberg 2006, p. 58.
11. John Jay quoted in R. Bork 2003, p. 207; W. Berns 2006, p. 76.
12. A. Zolberg 2006, p. 432; R. Daniels 2004, p. 6.
13. Sources cited, loc. cit.
14. S. Huntington 2004a, p. 38.
15. A. Schlesinger 1998, p. 34; S. Huntington 2004a, pp. 40–41, 59.
16. P. Schaff 1961, p. 72; S. Huntington 2004a, pp. 59–63.
17. Alexis de Toqueville, Edmund Burke, and Franklin Roosevelt quoted in S. Huntington 2004a, pp. 38, 59–62; J. F. Kennedy 1964, p. 18.
18. D. Moynihan 1986, p. 58; S. Huntington 2004b, p. 189.
19. S. Huntington 2004a, p. 45; T. Tancredo 2006, p. 175.
20. F. J. Grund 1968, pp. 355–56; W. Williams 2002, p. 30.
21. President Clinton quoted in S. Huntington 2004, p. 70.
22. On this, see R. Brookhiser 1991, pp. 34ff.
23. S. Huntington 2004, pp. 94, 191; A. Zolberg 2006, p. 129; P. Buchanan 2006, p. 127; J. F. Kennedy 1964, p. 26; O. Graham 2004, p. 6.
24. A. Schmidt 1997, p. 184.
25. T. Roosevelt 1941b, p. 16; A. Schmidt 1997, p. 184.
26. J. F. Kennedy 1964, p. 10.

27. S. Renshon 2005, pp. 1–2, 39, 186.

28. S. Renshon 2005, pp. 25–26.

29. S. Renshon 2005, pp. 73–75.

30. J. Edwards 2006, p. 1; P. Buchanan 2002, pp. 2–3; P. Buchanan 2006, pp. 9, 47, 55–56, 133; S. Huntington 2004b, pp. 177–78, 227, 248; A. Zolberg 2006, p. 439; S. Renshon 2005, pp. xvii ff., 103, 171; P. Brimelow 1995, pp. 4, 15; G. Hanson 2005, pp. 11, 19; O. Graham 2004, p. 68; G. Borjas 1999, pp. 154–75.

31. A. Zolberg 2006, p. 439; S. Renshon 2005, pp. xvii ff., 103, 171; P. Brimelow 1995, pp. 4, 15; G. Hanson 2005, pp. 11, 19; O. Graham 2004, pp. 68, 133; A. Schmidt 1997, pp. 190–91.

32. Sources cited, loc. cit.

33. Loc. cit.

34. G. W. Bush 2001, p. 2; P. Brimelow 1995, p. 46.

35. J. Leo 2001, p. 126.

36. L. Dobbs 2006, p. 131; F. Wooldridge 2004, p. 174.

37. V. Hanson 2007, pp. 5–6.

38. V. Hanson 2007, pp. 7, 87.

39. Ibid.

40. On the so-called Atzlan Project, see J. Dougherty 2004, p. 44; P. Buchanan 2006, pp. 107–13, 131–33; D. Sheehy 2006, pp. 8–9, 57, 59–62, 71, 76, 93, 165–68, 172, 176, 206, 209, 255; V. Hanson 2007, p. 32.

41. *Voz Fronteriza*, March 1995, cited in A. Kors and H. Silverglate 1998, p. 237; A. Schmidt 1997, p. 118.

42. *Voz Fronteriza*, May, 1995, cited in A. Kors and H. Silverglate 1998, loc. cit.

43. J. Dougherty 2004, pp. 5, 103, 124–31.

44. Ibid.

45. Lou Dobbs 2006, p. 131; P. Buchanan 2006, p. 221; S. Huntington 2004b, pp. 317–18; P. Brimelow 1995, p. 81.

46. R. Justich and B. Ng 2005, p. 1; L. Dobbs 2006, pp. 132–33; S. Huntington 2004b, pp. 205, 211; D. Sheehy 2006, pp. 11–12.

47. Sources cited, loc. cit.

48. Sources cited, loc. cit.

49. T. DeWeese 2003, p. 1; J. Dougherty 2004, p. 35; J. Faux 2006, p. 139.

50. Vincente Fox quoted in T. Tancredo 2006, p. 143, 156–57; D. Kennedy 1996, p .67; S. Huntington 2004a, pp. 228, 280; P. Brimelow 1995, p. 252; J. Dougherty 2004, p. 38.

51. G. Borjas 1999, p. xvi; Ernesto Zedillo quoted in P. Brimelow 1995, p. 282; J. Dougherty 2004, p. 37; D. Sheehy 2006, pp. 23ff., 67; O. Graham 2004, p. 131–32. Today, Zedillo is director of Yale University's Center for the Study of Globalization. Heralding a *reconquista*, in 1998, Mario Obledo, chairman of the California Coalition of Hispanic Organizations, would assert: "We are going to take back all of the political institutions of California in five years. We are going to be the majority population of this state." (Mario Obledo quoted in D. Sheehy 2006, p. 67.)

52. Felipe Calderon quoted in P. Buchanan. "Mexico to America: Buenas Noches," *Conservative Chronicle*, September 18, 2007, p. 30.

53. J. McKinley 2005, p. 1; S. Renshon 2005, p. 173.

54. S. Francis 2001, p. 1; D. Sheehy 2006, p. 25.

55. Sources cited, loc. cit.

56. S. Renshon 2000, p. 3; S. Renshon 2001, p. 15; P. Buchanan 2002, p. 132; P. Buchanan 2006, pp. 127–28, 131; S. Huntington 2004b, pp. 204ff., 209–10, 281–82; L. Ingraham 2003, p. 193.

57. P. Belluck 2000, p. 1; S. Renshon 2005, pp. 173–76, 200–1; P. Brimelow 1995, p. 194; F. Romero 1993, p. 1; V. Hanson 2003, pp. 32–33; J. Faux 2006, pp. 210–11.

58. Sources cited, loc. cit.

59. J. Vargas 1996, p. 3; A. Corchado 1995, p. 1; M. Powell 2005, p. 1; S. Renshon 2005, pp. 27, 173–76; P. Buchanan 2006, pp. 127–28, 131.

60. Sources cited, loc. cit.

61. L. Dobbs 2006, pp. 149–50.

62. V. Hanson 2003, p. 27.

63. Ibid.

64. Ibid.

65. V. Hanson 2003, p. 28.

66. V. Hanson 2003, pp. 29–30.

67. R. Beck and S. Camarota 2002, p. 1; S. Sailer 2006a, p. 12.

68. T. Tancredo 2006, pp. 108–9, 155–56, 159; L. Dobbs 2006, pp. 134, 188; V. Hanson 2007, p. 8; G. Jackson 2007, pp. 357–58.

69. G. Hanson 2005, passim, and pp. 3 and 20 in particular; L. Dobbs 2006, pp. 138–39; J. Black 1994, p. 185; P. Buchanan 2002, pp. 80, 85–86, 93, 216, 267; F. Wooldridge 2004, p. 143; G. Borjas 1999, pp. 103–4, 212; G. Borjas 2003, passim; D. Sheehy 2006, p. 28; P. Brimelow 1998, p. 1.

70. G. Borjas 1999, pp. 103–4, 212.

71. Sources cited, loc. cit.; Milton Friedman quoted in P. Brimelow 1998, p. 1.

72. S. Renshon 2005, pp. 243–45; G. Jackson 2006, pp. 355, 358.

73. Heritage Foundation study cited; C. Thomas, "No More Trust on Immigration," *Conservative Chronicle*, June 13, 2007, p. 16; P. Schlafly. "Immigrant Bill Will Raid Pockets of Taxpayers," *Conservative Chronicle*, June 13, 2007b, p. 14; D. Limbaugh. "Bogged Down in the Immigrant Debate," *Conservative Chronicle*, May 30, 2007, p. 2.

74. P. Buchanan 2006, pp. 43–44; T. Tancredo 2006, pp. 163–65; S. Huntington 2004a, p. 236; P. Brimelow 1995, p. 187; F. Wooldridge 2004, p. 84; D. Sheehy 2006, p. 15; M. Cosman 2005, p. 1; D. Sheehy 2006, p. 15; V. Hanson 2007, pp. xvii, 148. Indeed, some 70 percent of the enrollment in the Los Angeles School District reportedly is Latino.

75. Sources cited, loc. cit.

76. T. Tancredo 2006, p. 203; S. Renshon 2005, p. 224; D. Sheehy 2006, pp. 24ff.

77. S. Huntington 2004b, p. 316.

78. V. Hanson 2003, p. 77.

79. M. Malkin 2006, p. 1; T. Tancredo 2006, p. 14; P. Buchanan 2002, pp. 124–26; P. Buchanan 2006, pp. 60, 80–81, 110–11, 125; V. Hanson 2007, pp. xiv–xv. Thousands more that day simultaneously marched in solidarity in the streets of Mexico City.

80. S. Huntington 2004a, p. 10; *Los Angeles Times*, February 16, 1998, p. B1.

81. S. Renshon 2005, pp. 102–3, 106.

82. James Madison quoted in B. Fein 2005, p. 1.

83. George Washington quoted in J. Fonte 2005, p. 5; A. Schlesinger 1998, p. 30.

84. All quoted in M. Spaulding 1994, pp. 39–40 and P. Brimelow 1995, p. 191.

85. Alexander Hamilton cited in P. Brimelow 1995, p. 191.

86. G. Geyer 2006, p. A-18; P. Buchanan 2006, pp. 153–54.

87. S. Waterman 2005, p. 1; T. Tancredo 2006, pp. 111–12.

88. T. Tancredo 2005, p. 1.

89. Steven Camarota quoted in J. Dougherty 2004, p. 32. See also pp. 53–54.

90. T. DeWeese 2003, p. 1; D. Tichenor 2002, pp. 246ff. On Castro's *Mariel Port* boat lift which commenced on April 20, 1980, and brought 125,000 Cubans to Florida, including several thousand known criminals and psychotics, see also J. Dougherty 2004, pp. 67–68; P. Buchanan 2002, p. 137; G. Borjas 1999, pp. 70–73; R. Daniels 2004, pp. 205–7.

91. On the physical threat to home and homestead owners posed by immigrants, see J. Dougherty 2004, passim; F. Wooldridge 2004, passim; D. Sheehy 2006, pp. 20ff., passim; D. Tichenor 2002, p. 3.

92. L. Dobbs 2006, pp. 188, 209; P. Brimelow 1995, pp. 240–41; J. Dougherty 2004, p. 32.

93. Sources cited, loc. cit. George Washington quoted in transcript of National Public Radio 2000, p. 2; or as Thomas Jefferson later more eloquently rephrased it: "Peace, commerce, and enduring friendship with all nations; entangling alliances with none."

94. P. Noonan 2005, p. 1; T. Tancredo 2006, pp. 21–23; P. Buchanan 2006, p. 113.

95. P. Buchanan 2006, p. 31.

96. Congressman Elton Gallegly quoted in D. Sheehy 2006, p. 11; P. Buchanan 2006, p. 35.

97. Pat Buchanan 2002, pp. 3–5, P. Brimelow 1995, p. 57; cited in G. Michael 2006, p. 281.

98. On this, see S. Huntington 2004a, p. 1; S. Huntington 2004b, pp. 243, 298, 340; S. Huntington 2003, pp. 204–6, 205; G. Michael 2006, pp. 281, 304.

99. S. Huntington 2003, p. 305.

100. Ibid.

101. G. Borjas 1999, p. xvi; Samuel Huntington cited in R. Samuelson 2006, p. A-21.

102. S. Camarota 2005, p. 2; E. Rubenstein 2005, p. 1; P. Buchanan 2006, p. 38.

103. Theodore Roosevelt originally cited in P. Davis 1920, pp. 648–51; also quoted in L. Dobbs 2006, p. 209; A. Schlesinger 1998, p. 118; P. Buchanan 2002, p. 133.

104. T. Roosevelt 1941a, p. 10; O. Guinness 2001, p. 233.

105. D. Schweikert 1999, p. 1; T. Tancredo 2006, p. 37.

106. Calvin Coolidge quoted in P. Brimelow 1995, p. 211; Franklin Roosevelt cited in A. Schlesinger 1998, p. 43; P. Buchanan 2006, p. 146; G. Borjas 1999, p. 38.

107. J. Jay 1787, p. 1; also cited in S. Huntington 2004a, p. 44.

108. A. Schlesinger 1998, p. 142; P. Buchanan 2002, p. 145.

109. D. Sheehy 2006, pp. 13–15.

110. Alexander Hamilton quoted in O. Graham 2004, p. 5.

111. A. Schlesinger 1998, pp. 112–13.

112. A Schlesinger 1998, pp. 113–15.

113. S. Francis, *Mass Integration and the Disintegration of American Culture,*" quoted in F. Wooldridge 2004, p. 25.

114. A. Schmidt 1997, pp. 111, 116–17.

115. James Scheuer quoted in A. Thernstrom 1990, p. 45.

116. Ibid.

117. Ibid. Theodore Roosevelt quoted in T. Roosevelt 1898, p. 26.

118. A. Schmidt 1997, pp. 125–26.

119. A. Schmidt 1997, pp. 126–27, 190–91.

120. R. Carlson 1975, pp. 6–7; S. Huntington 2004b, pp. 131–32.

121. E. Hartmann 1948, p. 92; G. Korman 1967, pp. 147, 158–59; S. Huntington 2004b, pp. 132ff.; L. Ingraham 2003, p. 206.

122. Arthur Schlesinger 1998, pp. 20–21; P. Buchanan 2006, p. 249.

123. S. Huntington 2004b, pp. 183–84.

124. P. Brimelow 1995, p. 144; D. Sheehy 2006, p. 17; G. Borjas 1999, p. 45; D. Tichenor 2002, pp. 3, 89ff, 99ff., 106–10, 115; R. Daniels 2004, pp. 3, 19, 20, 134ff.; M. Ngai 2004, pp. 5, 227ff., 258ff.

125. Sources cited, loc cit.

126. Senator Ted Kennedy quoted in D. Sheehy 2006, p. 15.

127. P. Brimelow 1995, p. 144.

128. On this, see D. Sheehy 2006, pp. 17ff.

129. D. Sheehy 2006, pp. 18–19; D. Tichenor 2002, pp. 243ff., 267ff.; R. Daniels 2004, pp. 219ff., 233ff.; L. Ingraham 2003, p. 202.

130. Sources cited, loc. cit.

131. A. Zolberg 2006, pp. 337, 436; P. Brimelow 1998, p. xvii; P. Buchanan 2006, pp. 237–40; F. Wooldridge 2004, p. 1.

132. P. Brimelow 1995, p. 158.

133. P. Brimelow 1995, pp. 55, 61.

134. D. Sheehy 2006, pp. 18–19; O. Graham 2004, pp. 103, 158.

135. T. Tancredo 2006, pp. 101–2; P. Buchanan 2006, pp. 245–46, 250; S. Huntington 2004b, pp. 178–79; J. Dougherty 2004, p. 31; F. Wooldridge 2004, p. 174; D. Sheehy 2006, pp. 18–19.

136. U.S. Census Bureau, Current Population Survey, cited in T. Tancreo 2006, p. 175.

137. S. Renshon 2005, p. 160.

138. Ronald Reagan quoted by P. Brimelow 2004, p. 1; Arnold Toynbee quoted by P. Buchanan 2006, pp. 245–46.

139. D. Sheehy 2006, p. 35. On the "quick as hell" theory of full employment, as articulated by its progenitor, see R. Ringer 1977, passim.

140. J. F. Kennedy 1964, pp. 40–41, 58; A. Zolberg 2006, pp. 183ff.; T. Tancredo 2006, p. 33.

141. T. Tancredo 2006, pp. 33–34.

142. P. Buchanan 2006, p. 46.

143. T. Blankley 2005, p. 190.

144. T. Tancredo 2006, p. 183; P. Brimelow 1995, pp. 266–67; G. Jackson 2007, pp. 358–59.

CHAPTER 6: THE BURDENS OF BUREAUCRACY

1. U.S. Department of Treasury 2007, pp. 5, 10, 11, 15, 17–19.

2. M. Friedman 1993, pp. 6, 11.

3. George Washington cited in J. Bovard 1999, p. 10; H. Browne 1995, p. 38.

4. John Adams quoted in J. Bovard 1999, p. 10.

5. James Madison quoted in G. Heck 2007b, p. 46.

6. Thomas Jefferson quoted in G. Heck 2007b, p. 46.

7. Ibid.

8. C. Adams 1993, p. 192.

9. J. Makin and N. Ornstein 1994, pp. 6, 265, 284, 303; R. Samuelson 1994, p. 41.

10. On this, see L. Silk 1996, p. 38.

11. See T. Brokaw 2000, passim.

12. Ibid.

13. P. Drucker 1969, p. 198.

14. See P. Ford 1894, vol. 8, p. 481; A. Wildavsky and C. Webber 1986, p. 370; P. Peterson 1993, pp. 43, 223–24; H. Figgie 1992, p. 143; L. Hunter July 25, 2001, p. 5.

15. Sources cited, loc. cit.

16. Proverbs 13:22. See also Ecclesiastes 18:33: "Be not made a beggar by banqueting on borrowing;" and II Corinthians 12:14: "Children should not save up for their parents but the parents for their children."

17. T. DiLorenzo 2004, pp. 6, 63.

18. Thomas Jefferson quoted in T. DiLorenzo 2004, pp. 63–64.

19. On this, see W. McDougall 2004, pp. 202ff.; T. DiLorenzo 2004, pp. 65–69.

20. T. DiLorenzo 2004, pp. 70–71.

21. T. DiLorenzo 2004, p. 71.

22. T. DiLorenzo 2004, pp. 71–73.

23. Adam Smith 1937, p. 745.

24. S. Huntington 2004b, p. 122.

25. H. Browne 1995, pp. 39–40.

26. H. Browne 1995, pp. 40–42.

27. Ibid.

28. H. Browne 1995, pp. 43–46.

29. H. Browne 1995, p. 43.

30. J. Powell 2003, pp. ix–xv, 263–66.

31. J. Powell 2003, pp. 245–46; N. Boortz and J. Lindner 2005, p. 46.

32. Walter Lippman quoted in G. Best 1991, p. 213.

33. H. Browne 1995, pp. 44–45.

34. H. Browne 1995, p. 47.

35. Ronald Reagan quoted in L. Kudlow, "The Big Easy's Billion Dollar Boondoogle," *Conservative Chronicle*, September 12, 2007, p. 2.

36. J. Powell 2003, pp. 265–66.

37. J. Powell 2003, p. 266.

38. R. Haass 2005, pp. 7–8.

39. H. Browne 1995, pp. 144–46.

40. D. Harsanyi 2007, p. 10; R. Hall and A. Rabushka 2007, pp. 6ff.

41. D. Harsanyi 2007, pp. 9–10.

42. Cato Institute 2005, p. 20.

43. A question attributed to Stanislaw J. Lee in L. Peter 1977, p. 410; likewise see Samuel Butler's quote on cannibalism, L. Peter 1977, p. 183, and that of Emily Lotney, L. Peter 1977, p. 429.

44. P. O'Rourke 2007, p. xi.

45. Calculations made on data presented in U.S. Department of the Treasury 2004, Table 1; U.S. Congressional Budget Office 2005, pp. xv ff.

46. Sources cited, loc. cit.

47. H. Gilpin 1840, vol. 2, p. 984.

48. G. Heck 2006, p. 50; H. Browne 1995, pp. 2–4, 51–52. This 47 percent represents a combination of federal, state, local, and Social Security taxes, both personal and corporate, capitalized into price. The Social Security tax alone has risen from a combined 2 percent employee rate in 1935 to 12.4 percent today.

49. H. Browne 1995, pp. 4, 10, 28, 32.

50. H. Browne 1995, pp. 72–73.

51. On these, see H. Browne 1995, p. 189.

52. H. Browne 1995, p. 50.

53. H. Browne 1995, p. 36.

54. J. Payne 1993, pp. 87–88, 98–99.

55. Joint Economic Committee of Congress, April 2001, "Executive Summary," pp. 12–13; likewise cited in L. Hunter July 25, 2001, p. 22; W. Gentry and R. G. Hubbard, April 30, 2004, p. 21; W. Gentry and R. G. Hubbard, June 2004, p. 39; W. Gentry and R. G. Hubbard, November 2003, p. 26.

56. J. Payne 1993, pp. 87–91.

57. W. Williams, August 11, 2004, p. 1.

58. Winston Churchill quoted in "John Petrie's Collection of Political Quotes," cited at www.arches.uga.edu/~jpetrie/Political_Quotes.html.

59. Cato Institute 2005, pp. 9–10.

60. Thomas Jefferson quoted in Cato Institute 2005, pp. 10–12.

CHAPTER 7: THE TYRANNY OF TAXATION

1. Oliver Wendell Homes quoted in S. Moore 2000, p. 1.

2. Chief Justice John Marshall quoted in P. Drucker 1989, p.70.

3. Thomas Paine 1969, p. 206, cited in C. Adams 1993, p. 275.

4. A. Smith 1909/1937, p. 835, quoted in C. Adams 1993, p. 286; B. Friedman 1989, p. 237.

5. Sources cited, loc. cit.

6. A. Smith 1979, v. 2, b. 6, p. 826, quoted in J. Muller 1993, pp. 152–52.

7. G. Heck 2007a, p. 88.

8. *Burke: Selected Works* 1881, pp. 95ff., quoted in C. Adams 1993, p. 302.

9. J. Madison quoted in C. Adams 1993, p. 365—making it doubly ironic that no monarchy in Western history *ever* taxed its subjects as heavily as *every* modern democracy does today. (On this, see J. Sobran, January 2, 2002, p. 7.)

10. J. Makin and N. Ornstein 1994, pp. 104–5.

11. J. Madison quoted in C. Adams 1993, pp. 365ff., 465.

12. Thomas Jefferson quoted by President Ronald Reagan proclaiming America's "Economic Bill of Rights," July 3, 1987, p. 4, at www.reagan.utexas.edu/archives/speeches/1987/070387a.htm; also quoted in G. Heck 2007a, p. 89.

13. Thomas Paine. *Common Sense* (1776), quoted in C. Adams 1993, pp. 276 (cited), 448.

14. Thomas Jefferson cited in N. Gingrich 2008, p. 69.

15. Montesquieu, *Spirit of Laws,* vol. 1, ch. 8, quoted in C. Adams 1993, pp. 474, 476.

16. U.S. Department of the Treasury, *Budget of the United States,* 2004, p. 6.

17. R. Hall and A. Rabushka 2007, pp. 30–31.

18. See W. Pennick 1983, passim; U.S. Department of the Treasury, *Budget of the United States,* 2004, p. 6. Historically, the highest marginal rates for income taxation have been 94 percent for personal, 82 percent for corporate. On this, see S. Steinmo 1993, pp. 75ff., 101–2; K. Friedman 2003, p. 14; R. Hall and A. Rabushka 2007, pp. 32–33.

19. U.S. Department of the Treasury, *Budget of the United States,* 2004, p. 6.

20. J. Bovard 1999, p. 22.

21. *Interstate Transit Lines v. Commissioner,* 319 U.S. 590, 593 (1943); *U.S. v. Carlton,* 512 U.S. 19, 33 (1994); both cases cited in J. Bovard 1999, p. 199; N. Boortz and J. Lindner 2005, p. 86.

22. Montesquieu 1949, p. 26.

23. J. Bovard 1999, pp. 28, 185, 188, 220–21, 225–26.

24. Ibid.

25. R. Hall and A. Rabushka 2007, pp. viii ff.; G. Jackson 2006, pp. 298ff.

26. NAM 2006b, passim; NAM 2006a, pp. vi, 2ff.

27. NAM 2006b, pp. 52–53, 59.

28. Ibid.

29. Tax Foundation, July 27, 2004, p. 1.

30. Tax Foundation, July 27, 2004, p. 1.

31. Cato Institute 2005, pp. 118–19; R. Hall and A. Rabushka 2007, pp. 31ff.

32. Tax Foundation, April 30, 2006, p. 1.

33. Tax Foundation, April 30, 2006, p. 2.

34. Ibid.

35. N. Boortz and J. Lindner 2005, p. 119.

36. Heritage Foundation 1995, pp. 66–67; N. Boortz and J. Lindner 2005, pp. 40–42.

37. W. Sumner 1888, p. 62; quoted in J. Bovard 1991, p. 272.

38. J. Bovard 1999, p. 247.

39. R. Reagan 1987, p. 3.

40. C. Crews, June 22, 2007, p. 1; Heritage Foundation 1995, pp. 1–4. See also "Regulatory Burden Reaches Record Level," Cato Institute, June 25, 2007, at www.cato-at-liberty.org/2007/06/25/regulatory-burden-reaches-record-level.

41. Sources cited, loc. cit.

42. Heritage Foundation 1995, p. 3.

43. Ibid.

44. J. Bovard 1999, p. 5; H. Browne 1995, p. 92.

45. R. Ringer 1977, pp. 196–97; W. Williams, May 7, 2003, p. 2.

46. Ronald Reagan quoted in Cato Institute 2005, p. 269.

47. C. Crews 2007, pp. 1, 8.

48. F. Ryan 1995, p. 87.

49. Walter Boris, Michigan Consumers Power Executive, speech in Jackson, Michigan, July 1973.

50. Reagan speech to Republican local officials on March 22, 1998, in Washington, D.C., at www.reagan.utexas.edu.com.

51. Reagan remarks to the White House Conference on Small Business, August 16, 1986, at www.presidentreagan.info/speechs/quotes.

52. R. Bork 2003, p. 324.

53. Ibid.

54. R. Bork 2003, p. 330.

55. J. Kemp. 1998, pp. 1–2.

56. J. Tobin 1998, pp. 27–28; R. Shapiro 1998, p. 119; U.S. Bureau of the Census 1975, Table F, 10–16.

57. Sources cited, loc. cit.

58. See U.S. Bureau of Economic Analysis, "National Income Accounts Data," "Gross Domestic Product," at www.bea.gov/national/txt/dpga.text.

59. U.S. Bureau of Economic Statistics, August 3, 2007, pp. 1–8.

60. G. Jackson 2006, pp. 292ff.

61. Idem, p. 10; O. Guinness 1993, p. 116; F. Rohatyn, "Ways to Achieve Higher Growth," in J. Jasinowski 1998, pp. 1–2.

62. R. Mundell 1998, pp. 202–3.

63. See G. Heck, January 24, 2007, passim.

64. R. Hall and A. Rabushka 2007, pp. 32–33, 64–66.

65. M. Forbes 1994, p. 25.

66. G. Gilder, 2004, p. 3; T. Savage, April 15, 2004, p. 2.

67. R. Hall and A. Rabushka 2007, pp. 65ff.

68. D. Mitchell, August 13, 2003, p. 2. But while revenues were rising by 28 percent in the Reagan years, federal expenditures were growing by 36 percent—producing exorbitant budget deficits—a phenomenon for which his tax cuts are often erroneously blamed.

69. G. Jackson 2006, p. 292.

70. Paradigms are extrapolations derived from D. Mitchell, August 13, 2003, p. 2; T. Sowell, July 23, 2003, p. 15; S. Steinmo 1993, pp. 95–96.

71. President Kennedy quoted in the *New York Times* 1984, p. 1; G. Jackson 2006, p. 293; G. Heck 2007b, p. xvi.

72. Sources cited, loc. cit.

73. W. Williams, September 8, 2004, pp. 1–2.

74. On this, see B. Bartlett 2002, passim.

75. See U.S. Bureau of Economic Analysis, "National Income Accounts Data," "Gross Domestic Product," at www.bea.gov/national/txt/dpga.text.

76. See G. Heck, January 24, 2007, passim.

77. R. Carroll and G. Mankiw July 26, 2006, p. 1.

78. J. Tobin 1998, p. 43; R. Barro 1998, p. 194.

79. R. Mundell 1998, pp. 200–1.

80. Ibid.

81. N. Boortz and J. Lindner 2005, p. 49.

82. J. Bovard 1999, p. 127.

83. Cited in "Tax Notes," *Wall Street Journal*, September 14, 1979, p. 1; quoted in J. Bovard 2000, p. 259; J. Bovard 1999, p. 22.

84. J. Bovard 2000, pp. 259, 266, 268, 275; J. Payne 1993, pp. 119ff.

85. Sources cited, loc. cit.

86. Judge Learned Hand quoted in J. Payne 1993, p. 103.

87. Alexander Hamilton quoted in H. Syrett 1962, vol. 3, p. 104; J. Bovard 2000, pp. 288–91.

88. J. Bovard 2005, p. 234.

89. J. Payne 1993, p. 3.

90. J. Payne 1993, pp. 5, 35, 138.

91. J. Payne 1993, pp. 138–39.

92. L. Thurow 1996, pp 10, 279.

93. Woodrow Wilson quoted in L. Peter 1977, p. 49; W. Simon 1978, pp. 19ff.

94. Cf. Fraser Institute 2006, passim; Cato Institute 2007, passim; T. DiLorenzo 2004, p. 24.

95. T. DiLorenzo 2004, pp. 24–25.

96. T. DiLorenzo 2004, p. 24.

97. Cato Institute 2007, Executive Summary, p. 4.

98. See United Nations 2000, passim; T. DiLorenzo 2004, pp. 25–26. All of this presupposes, of course, the operation of an informed electorate.

99. T. DiLorenzo 2004, pp. 3–4, 25–26.

CHAPTER 8: THE IMPLOSION OF IDEOLOGY

1. Oliver Wendell Holmes quoted in S. Ahlstrom 1975, vol. 2, p. 328; Friedrich Hegel quoted in O. Guinness 1993, p. 156.

2. A. de Tocqueville 1945, vol. 2, p. 352.

3. R. Bork 2003, pp. 67, 82–83.

4. R. and M. Friedman 1980, p. 148.

5. J. Banks 1994, p. 3.

6. T. Blankley 2005, pp. 125, 129.

7. W. McGowan 2001, p. 247; J. Ellis 1997, p. 215.

8. J. Ellis 1997, pp. 89–90.

9. Bernard Lewis quoted in D. Davis 1993, p. 35; J. Ellis 1997, p. 87.

10. L. Chavez 1994, p. A11; A Schmidt 1997, pp. 147–48.

11. J. Jacobs 2005, p. 170; R. Bernstein 1994, pp. 49–50; H. Kramer and R. Kimball 1999, p. 72.

12. V. Hanson 2003, pp. 122–23.

13. G. Demar 1997, vol. 3, p. 174.

14. P. Buchanan 2006, pp. 83–84, 158, 199.

15. Michael Lind quoted in W. McGowan 2001, p. 244.

16. J. Ellis 1997, p. 116.

17. Ibid.

18. Abraham Lincoln quoted in R. Bork 2003, p. 318.

19. Winston Churchill 1946, quoted in J. Black 2004, pp. 292–93.

20. Carl Henry quoted in J. Black 1994, p. 222; G. Demar 1997, vol. 3, p. 178; P. Buchanan 2006, pp. 83–84, 158, 199.

21. J. Fallows 1997, pp. 4–5.

22. J. Bovard 1999, pp. 97–98.

23. H. Spencer 1969, quoted in J. Bovard 1999, pp. 238, 257–58.

24. C. S. Lewis quoted in D. Harsanyi 2007, frontispiece.
25. B. Constant 1988, pp. 290–91.
26. John Stuart Mill quoted in J. Sobran 2002, p. 1.
27. J. Bovard 1999, pp. 122, 125.
28. Plutarch 1935, p. 943.
29. Montesquieu 1949, p. 110.
30. Ibid.
31. R Nixon 1992, pp. 147–48.
32. A. Smith 1937, p. 422; T. DiLorenzo 2004, pp. 1–2.
33. T. DiLorenzo 2004, p. 22.
34. T. DiLorenzo 2004, pp. 3–4, 25–26; L. Von Mises 1985, p. 102.
35. Friedrich Hayek quoted in T. DiLorenzo 2004, p. 30.
36. T. DiLorenzo 2004, pp. 30, 223.
37. T. DiLorenzo 2004, pp. 30–34.
38. M. Berman 2006, pp. 302–4.
39. Arnold Toynbee cited in M. Berman 2006, p. 303.
40. J. K. Blackwell 2006, p. 221.
41. Charles Krauthammer quoted in L. Ingraham 2003, p. 318.
42. John Quincy Adams quoted in W. McDougall 1997, p. 36.
43. Colin Powell quoted in L. Ingraham 2003, pp. 319–20.
44. L. Ingraham 2003, p. 320.
45. L. Ingraham 2003, pp. 338–39.
46. Ibid.
47. Abraham Lincoln quoted in L. Ingraham 2003, p. 339, 2–4.
48. L. Ingraham 2003, p. 4.
49. Victor Hugo quoted in P. Moine 2002, p. 1.
50. W. McDougal, 2004, p. 15; M. Berman 2006, pp. 299–300; L. Dobbs 2006, p. 212; P. Buchanan 2002, p. 267.

CHAPTER 9: PURSUING PRUDENT PUBLIC POLICY

1. See *Roe v. Wade*, 410 US 113, 93 S.C. 705, 35 L.Ed 2nd 147 (1973).
2. S. Levitt and S. Dubner 2005, p. 139; J. Rifkin 2004, pp. 81–82; M. Berman 2006, pp. 288–89. Notwithstanding that the average rate of homicides per 100,000 people in the United States from 1997 to 1999 was 6.26, contrasted with 1.7 throughout the European Union, about one-fourth that number; and that the homicide rate for American children was five times higher than that of the other twenty-five wealthiest nations combined.
3. P. Buchanan 2002, pp. 15, 25–27, 34ff. Today, America's native-born fertility rate stands at slightly under 2.0 percent—below the 2.1 percent needed to sustain zero population growth. The nation's massive population surge, then, is coming instead from immigration, much of it illegal.
4. Ibid.
5. Ibid.
6. P. Buchanan 2002, pp. 14, 97–98; M. Berman 2000, p. 32.
7. M. Friedman and A. Schwartz 1963, p. 299; M. Skousen 2005, p. 38; S. Leeb 2008, p. 65.
8. L. Ebenstein 2007, p. 119. By contrast, on October 19, 1987, the U.S. stock market lost nearly 23 percent of its value in a single day, and not even a recession, much less a depression, followed.
9. S. Leeb 2006, pp. 65–66.
10. L. Ebenstein 2007, p. 121.

11. S. Leeb 2006, p. 66; L. Ebenstein 2007, p. 121; H. Browne 1995, p. 43.
12. Malcolm Wallop quoted in R. Bork 2003, p. 333.
13. J. Rauch 1989, p. 39.
14. J. Klein 2006, pp. 92–93.
15. J. Klein 2006, p. 232.
16. P. Brimelow 1995, p. 230.
17. H. Clinton 2004, p. 1.
18. Here, no value judgments are intended. These are convictions genuinely espoused on each side of the intellectual divide.
19. J. Muller 1993, p. 3.
20. R. Kuttner 1984, pp. 179, 232; R. Nixon 1992, p. 295.
21. A. Wildavsky and C. Webber 1986, p. 370; R. Kuttner 1984, p. 37.
22. On this, see P. Drucker 1949, p. 19.
23. J. Black 2004, p. 247.
24. Ibid.
25. D. Horowitz 2000, pp. 47ff.
26. George Washington, James Madison, and Alexander Hamilton quoted in M. Malkin, "The Forgotten 'A' Word: Assimilation," *Conservative Chronicle*, July 11, 2007, p. 20.
27. O. Graham 2004, p. 9.
28. As defined by F. Wooldridge 2004, pp. 176–77.
29. A. Zolberg 2006, pp. 224, 419–20; D. Tichenor 2002, p. 3.
30. J. Simon 1989, passim; A. Zolberg 2006, p. 390; P. Brimelow 1995, p. 148; O. Graham 2004, p. 4.
31. George Washington quoted in O. Graham 2004, p. 4.
32. On this, see G. Borjas 1999, pp. 99–101.
33. Ibid.
34. A. Zolberg 2006, p. 381; P. Brimelow 1995, p. 88; G. Hanson 2005, pp. 9, 56.
35. T. Tancredo 2006, pp. 130, 171.
36. M. Malkin 2002, pp. 220, 231ff.
37. F. Wooldridge 2004, pp. 1–2.
38. P. Brimelow 1995, p. 263; P. Buchanan 2002, pp. 234–35; D. Sheehy 2006, pp. 22–23.
39. P. Brimelow 1995, p. 4; R. Daniels 2004, p. 11.
40. J. Dougherty 2005, p. 1; P. Buchanan 2006, pp. 258–59; T. Tancredo 2006, p. 167; F. Wooldridge 2004, pp. 1–2.
41. Sources cited, loc. cit.
42. P. Buchanan 2006, pp. 22–26, 268; T. Tancredo 2006. pp. 187, 198; S. Renshon 2005, pp. 240–41; F. Wooldridge 2004, pp. 101ff.; M. Malkin 2002, pp. 47ff.
43. A. Schmidt 1997, p. 121.
44. A. Schlesinger 1998, pp. 114–15; S. Renshon 2005, p. 87; G. Borjas 1999, p. 33.
45. Theodore Roosevelt quoted in S. Huntington 2004b, p. 324.
46. P. Schlafly. "Many Want English as the National Language," *Conservative Chronicle*, June 27, 2007c, p. 17.
47. N. Gingrich 2008, p. 129.
48. S. Huntington 2004a, pp. 169ff., 170; S. Renshon 2005, pp. 226ff.
49. T. Tancredo 2006, p. 171; P. Buchanan 2006, pp 254ff.; M. Malkin 2002, pp. 233ff.
50. T. Tancredo 2006, p. 149; J. Dougherty 2004, p. 195; G. Putnam 2002, p. 1.
51. T. Blankley 2005, p. 174.
52. U.S. "Oath of Citizenship" replicated by M. Malkin 2002, p. xv.
53. S. Renshon 2005, pp. 3ff.
54. S. Huntington 2004a, pp. 212–15; P. Buchanan 2006, pp. 260–64.
55. G. Borjas 1999, p. 206.

56. J. Bovard 1999, p. 124.
57. See S. Renshon 2005, pp. 196ff.
58. D. D'Souza 1991, p. 249.
59. D. D'Souza 1991, p. 250.
60. Ibid.
61. On this, see John Zogby at www.zogby.com/news/ReadNews.dbm?ID=1334, dated July 10, 2007; J. Black 2004, pp. 106, 160–62.
62. A. Kors and H. Silverglate 1998, pp. 351–52.
63. D. Horowitz 2002, passim; also replicated in J. Black 2004, pp. 302–3.
64. E. Kendall 1809, vol. 1, pp. 270–71; D. Barton 2002, p. 81.
65. A. Schlesinger 1998, p. 146.
66. L. Dobbs 2006, p. 168.
67. F. Rohatyn 1998, p. 23.
68. A. Carnevale 1998, p. 140.
69. See R. Bork 2003, pp. 117ff.; J. Leo 2001, p. 164.
70. S. Huntington 2004b, pp. 125ff.
71. D. Kupelian 2005, p. 119.
72. H. Browne 1995, p. 109.

CHAPTER 10: CURBING COMPLEXITY'S COMPLIANCE COSTS

1. As budgetarily delineated in chapter 7. On this, see H. Browne 1995, pp. 195–98.
2. H. Browne 1995, p. 185.
3. On this, see L. Thurow 1980, pp. 97–99, 171–72; L. Thurow 1985, pp. 223–30.
4. Sources cited, loc. cit.
5. David Hume cited in R. Kuttner 1984, p. 188.
6. See R. Norton 1992, p. 46.
7. Cato Institute 2005, pp. 19, 26ff., 41ff.
8. Ibid.
9. M. Friedman 1967, p. 68.
10. See M. Friedman 1978, passim.
11. See R. Barro 1998, pp. 191–93; R. Hall and A. Rabushka 2007, passim; G. Jackson 2006, pp. 311ff.
12. D. Jorgenson 1998, pp. 223–24; Cato Institute 2005, pp. 128–29.
13. On the case for consumption-based taxation, see G. F. Break in D. Skadden 1978, pp. 6ff.; L. Thurow 1985, p. 239.
14. On this, see J. Makin and N. Ornstein 1994, p. 195; D. Calleo 1991, p. 90; P. Peterson 1993, pp. 292ff.; L. Thurow 1992, p. 270; R. Kuttner 1984, pp. 223. Alternately, in the quest for greater tax equity as well as a corporate revenue replacement, the deductibility of state and local taxes could be eliminated from all federal income taxation. This approach would, in fact, strike at the very heart of the "tax fairness" issue. For why should the citizens of the "no income tax" states—jurisdictions that have properly perceived the direct linkage between tax level and economic growth and have knowingly opted for the latter—be penalized by being forced to subsidize high-tax, low-growth states to provide the latter with public services that they are unwilling to pay for themselves? Eliminating state and federal local tax deductibility would thus be a commendable "tax equity" reform as well as a suitable instrument for replacing the revenue foregone in eliminating or replacing the federal corporate income tax.
15. B. Stanley in D. Skadden 1978, p. 105.

16. B. Stanley in D. Skadden 1978, p. 116; J. Leonard 2003, p. 10. While a modicum of relief from this inequity, in the form of a "partial" dividend tax deduction, was in fact incorporated into the U.S. Job Growth and Tax Relief Reconciliation Act of 2003, it is scheduled to "sunset" at the close of fiscal year 2008.

17. R. Kuttner 1984, p. 195.

18. R. Barkley 1992, p. 66.

19. S. Moore 2003, p. 1.

20. John Kennedy and Alan Greenspan quoted in N. Gingrich 2008, p. 139.

21. Former Representative Dick Armey of Texas, for instance, long promoted a revenue-equivalent 17 percent flat rate tax substitute for the present progressive individual income tax that would grant a married couple a baseline tax exemption of $26,200, with each dependent entitled to another $5,300 exemption. Thus, a family of four wouldn't be liable for taxation until its income exceeded $36,800. Congressman Armey estimated that such an approach would eliminate a present $200 billion drag on the economy—$100 billion in reduced paperwork and compliance costs and another $100 billion now wasted in needless investments made for tax avoidance rather than economic purposes. (On this approach, see M. Forbes July, 1994, p. 23.)

22. H. Browne 1995, pp. 182–83. An alternate approach could be the levy of a 5 percent national sales tax.

23. S. Leeb 2006, p. 174.

24. Cato Institute 2005, pp. 19, 26ff., 41ff.; W. Williams 2007, p. 9.

25. On the case for constitutional *tax* limitation, see J. Perry 2004, passim; G. Jackson 2006, pp. 87ff.

26. On this, see, M. Friedman 1978, p. 19.

27. H. Browne 1995, p. 184.

28. See M. Friedman 1978, p. 16. Such constitutionally mandated spending limits are preferable to taxation limits in that they concurrently restrict the ability to engage in public borrowing to accommodate deficit spending.

29. See A. Wildavsky and C. Webber 1993, pp. 11ff.

30. Ibid.

31. C. Edwards, February 2, 2004, p. 2

32. J. Kemp 1998, pp. 10–11.

33. W. Niskanen 1998, p. 220.

34. R. Rahn, July 11, 2004, p. 1.

Bibliography

Abrams, J. "Murtha's Statement on War Being Unwinnable Draws Sharp GOP Response," Associated Press, May 6, 2004.

Adams, C., ed. *The Works of John Adams, Second President of the United States.* Boston: 1850–1856.

Adams, C. *For Good and Evil: the Impact of Taxes upon the Course of Civilization.* London: 1993.

Adams, J. Q. *An Oration Delivered Before the Inhabitants of the Town of Newburyport at Their Request on the Sixty-Fifth Anniversary of the Declaration of Independence.* Newburyport: 1837.

———. *Letters of John Quincy Adams to His Son on the Bible and Its Teachings.* Auburn: 1850.

———. *Memoirs of John Quincy Adams.* Philadelphia: 1874.

Adams, S. *Writings.* ed. S. Peabody. New York: 1880.

Adelson, H. *Medieval Commerce.* New York: 1962.

Adler, M. "The Mayflower Compact," in *Annals of America.* Chicago: 1968, vol. 1.

Ames, F. *The Works of Fisher Ames.* Boston: 1809.

Ahlstrom, S. *A Religious History of the American People.* Garden City, NY: 1975.

Andrews, M. *The Founding of Maryland.* Baltimore: 1933.

Andrus, S. *The Code of 1650, Being a Compilation of the Earliest Laws and Orders of the General Court of Connecticut.* Hartford: 1822.

Angelou, M. "Journey to the Heartland," Address to the National Assembly of Local Arts Agencies, Cedar Rapids, Iowa, June 12, 1985.

Auster, L. *The Path to National Suicide.* Monterey, VA: 1990.

———. *Hidden Clichés: Exposing the Fraudulent Arguments that Have Opened America's Borders to the World.* Monterey, VA: 1997.

Banks, J. *Multiethnic Education: Theory and Practice.* Boston: 1994.

Bancroft, G. *History of the Colonization of the United States.* Boston: 1837 et seq., vols.1–6.

Bark, W. *The Origins of the Medieval World.* Stanford: 1958.

Barkley, R. *The Seven Fat Years.* New York: 1992.

Barone, M. "We, Not Our Enemies, Are the Evil Oppressors," *Conservative Chronicle*, April 25, 2007.

Bartlett, B. "Remember Reagan-Kemp-Roth Tax Cut," *Human Events*, July 22, 2002.

Barro, R. "Government Can Boost Growth," in J. Jasinowski, ed. *The Rising Tide.* New York: 1998.

Bartolemew, L. "Introduction," in A. Nava et al., eds. *Educating America in a Multicultural Society.* New York: 1994.

Barton. D. *The Truth about Thomas Jefferson and the First Amendment.* Aledo, TX: 1992.

———. *The Foundations of American Government.* Aledo, TX: 2000.

———. *Original Intent: The Courts, the Constitution, and Religion.* Aledo, TX: 2002.

Bassler, R. ed. *The Collected Works of Abraham Lincoln.* New Brunswick: 1953.

Bawer, B. *While Europe Slept.* New York: 2006.

Baynes, N. "M. Pirenne and the Unity of the Mediterranean World," 1927, in A. F. Havighurst, ed. *The Pirenne Thesis: Analysis, Criticism, and Revision.* London: 1969.

Beardsley, E. *Life and Times of William Samuel Johnson.* Boston: 1886.

Beck, R., and Camarota, S. "Elite vs. Public Opinion: An Examination of Divergent Views on Immigration," *Backgrounder,* Center for Immigration Studies, December 2002, at www.cis.org.

Belluck, P. "Mexican Presidential Candidates Campaign in the United States, *New York Times,* July 1, 2000.

Bennett, J. *The Anglosphere Challenge.* Lanham, MD: 2004.

Bennett, W. *Index of Leading Cultural Indicators.* New York: 1994/1999.

———. *America; the Last Best Hope.* Nashville: 2006.

Bergh, A. ed. *The Writings of Thomas Jefferson.* Washington: 1904.

Berger, P., and Neuhaus, R. *To Empower People: from State to Civil Society.* Washington: 1996.

Berman, M. *The Twilight of American Culture.* New York: 2000.

———. *Dark Ages America.* New York: 2006.

Bernal, M. *Black Athena: The Afroasiatic Roots of Classical Civilization.* New Brunswick, NJ: 1989.

Bernardi, A. "The Economic Problems of the Roman Empire at the Time of its Decline," in C. M. Cipolla, ed. *The Economic Decline of Empires.* London: 1970.

Berns, W. *Making Patriots.* Chicago: 2001.

———. *Democracy and the Constitution.* Washington: 2006.

Bernstein, C. "It's Press vs. Bush: A Bruising Fight," *Los Angeles Times,* October 15, 1992.

Bernstein, R. *Dictatorship of Virtue: Multiculturalism and the Battle for America's Future.* New York: 1994.

Best, G. *Pride, Prejudice, and Politics: Roosevelt vs. Recovery, 1933–1938.* Westport, CT: 1991.

Bieler, A. *La Pensée Éonomique et Sociale de Calvin.* Geneva: 1959.

Black, J. *When Nations Die.* Wheaton, IL: 1994.

———. *Freefall of the American University.* Nashville: 2004.

Blackwell, J. K. *Rebuilding America.* Nashville: 2006.

Blankley, T. *The West's Last Chance.* Washington: 2005.

Bloom, A. *The Closing of the American Mind.* New York: 1987.

———. "The Democratization of the University," in *Giants and Dwarfs: Essays 1960–1990.* New York: 1990.

Boaz, D. *Toward Liberty: The Idea That is Changing the World.* Washington: 2002.

Boortz, N., and Lindner, J. *The Fair Tax Book.* New York: 2005.

Borjas, G. *Heaven's Door.* Princeton: 1999.

———. "The Labor Market Curve Is Downward Sloping: Reexamining the Impact of Immigration on the Labor Market," *Quarterly Journal of Economics,* November 2003, vol. 118, no. 4.

Bork, R. *Slouching toward Gomorrah.* New York: 2003.

———. "Introduction," in R. Bork, ed. *A Country I Do Not Recognize.* Stanford: 2005.

Boskin, M. "The Role of Technology," in J. Jasinowski, ed. *The Rising Tide.* New York: 1998.

Bovard, J. *The Fair Trade Fraud.* New York: 1991.

———. *Freedom in Chains.* New York: 1999.

———. *Lost Rights: the Destruction of American Liberty.* New York: 2000.

———. *Attention Deficit Democracy.* New York: 2005.

Bowersocks, G. "The Dissolution of the Roman Empire," in N. Yoffee and G. Cowgill, eds. *The Collapse of Ancient States and Civilizations.* Tucson: 1991.

Bozell, B., and Baker, B. *And That's the Way It Isn't*. Washington: 1990.

———. "NBC's Massive Al Gore Donation," *Conservative Chronicle*, July 11, 2007.

Bradley, J. *Flags of Our Fathers*. New York: 2006.

Brewer, D. *The United States: A Christian Nation*. Philadelphia: 1905.

Brimelow, P. *Alien Nation*. New York: 1995.

———. "Milton Friedman, Soothsayer," *Hoover Digest*, 1998, vol. 2, at www.hoover.stanford .edu/publications/digest/982/friedman3.html.

———. "In Memoriam: Ronald W. Reagan," *VDARE*, June 5, 2004, at www.vdare.com/pb/ rwr/_memoriam.htm.

Brokaw, T. *The Greatest Generation*. New York: 2000.

Bronson, B. "The Role of Barbarians in the Fall of States," in N. Yoffee and G. Cowgill, eds. *The Collapse of Ancient States and Civilizations*. Tucson: 1991.

Brookhiser, R. *The Way of the Wasp*. New York: 1991.

Browne, H. *Why Government Doesn't Work*. New York: 1995.

Buchanan, P. *The Death of the West*. New York: 2002.

———. *State of Emergency: The Third World Invasion and Conquest of America*. New York: 2006.

———. "America Is Now an Auto Graveyard," *Conservative Chronicle*, February 28, 2007.

———. "Free Trade and Funny Math," *Conservative Chronicle*, March 7, 2007.

———. "How Empires End: The Ruin of Acre," *Conservative Chronicle*, August 1, 2007.

Bullock, R. "Race Riders Strike Another Paper," *Campus Report*, December 1993.

Burke, E. "Speech on Moving Resolutions for Conciliation with the Colonies," in R. Hoffman and P. Levack, eds. *Burke's Politics*. New York: 1949.

———. *Speeches and Letters on American Affairs*. New York: 1961.

———. *Reflections on the Revolution in France*. New York: 1967.

———. *The Correspondence of Edmund Burke*. Chicago: 1969.

Burnham, J. *The Suicide of the West*. New York: 1964.

Burns, E. *Infamous Scribblers*. New York: 2006.

Bury, J. *A History of the Later Roman Empire*. London: 1889/1923.

Bush, G. W. "Inaugural Address," Washington, January 20, 2001.

Butler, J. *Awash in a Sea of Faith: Christianizing the American People*. Cambridge: 1990.

Cahill, T. *How the Irish Saved Civilization*. London: 1995.

Calderon, Felipe, quoted in P. Buchanan. "Mexico to America: Buenas Noches," *Conservative Chronicle*, September 18, 2007.

Calleo, D. *The Bankrupting of America*. New York: 1991.

Camarota, S. "Immigrants at Mid-Decade: A Snapshot of America's Foreign-Born Population in 2005," *Backgrounder*, Center for Immigration Studies, December 2005.

Campbell, C. "Our Semi-Pagan Forebears," *Atlanta Constitution*, June 19, 1994.

Caplow, T. et al. *The First Measured Century*. Washington: 2001.

Carlson, R. *The Quest for Conformity: Americanization through Education*. New York: 1975.

Carnevale, A. "Investing in Education and Training for Higher Growth," in J. Jasinowski, ed. *The Rising Tide*. New York: 1998.

Carroll, R., and Mankiw, G. "Dynamic Analysis," *Wall Street Journal*, July 26, 2006.

Cato Institute. *Cato Handbook on Policy*. Washington: 2005.

———. *Economic Freedom of the World, 2007 Annual Report*. Washington: 2007.

Cerveny, B. "Counter-Coup: Rolling Back the Attack on Free Speech," *The Defender*, March 1994.

Channing, W. "Religion: The Only Basis of Society," in W. McGuffey. *McGuffey's Fifth Eclectic Reader*. New York: 1879.

Chavez, L. "Aztec Idols, Yes; Mary and Jesus, No," *USA Today*, December 7, 1994.

Cheney, L. "The End of History," *Wall Street Journal*, October 20, 1994.

Chumley, C. "Education Foundation Highlights Ridiculous Classes," at www.CBSNews.com, September 3, 2000.

Churchill, W. "The Iron Curtain Speech: 1946," National Center for Public Policy Research, at www.nationalcenter.org/ChurchillIronCurtain.html.

Clinton, H. "We Are Going to Take Things Away from You on Behalf of the Common Good," *Free Republic*, June 29, 2004, at www.freerepublic.com/focus/f-news/1162094/posts.

Clough, S. B. *The Rise and Fall of Civilization*. Westport, CT: 1951.

Cohen, A. "Oklahoma City Bombing vs. Sept. 11," CBS News, *Court Watch*, April 2003, at www .cbsnews.com/stories/2003/04//20/news/opinion/courtwatch/main550231.

Collier, P., and Horowitz, D. *Destructive Generation: Second Thoughts about the '60s*. New York: 1996.

Columbia University. *Columbia Rules*. New York: 1785.

Commager, H., ed. *Documents of American History*. New York: 1958.

Conquest, R. "Liberals and Totalitarianism," in H. Kramer and R. Kimball. *The Betrayal of Liberalism: How the Disciples of Freedom and Equality Helped Foster the Illiberal Politics of Coercion and Control*. Chicago: 1999.

Coolidge, C. *Foundations of the Republic—Speeches and Addresses*. New York: 1926.

Constant, B. *Political Writings*. Cambridge: 1988.

Cooper, D. *The Death of the Family*. New York: 1971.

Cooper, R. *The Breaking of Nations*. New York: 2003.

Copperman, P. *The Literary Hoax*. New York: 1978.

Corchado, A. "Mexicans Study Dual Citizenship: Implications of an Idea Intriguing to Many," *Dallas Morning News*, July 15, 1995.

Cosman, M. "Illegal Aliens and American Medicine," *Journal of American Physicians and Surgeons*, Spring 2005, vol. 10, no. 1.

Coulter, A. *Slander*. New York: 2002.

———. *Godless: The Church of Liberalism*. New York: 2006.

Cowgill, G. "Onward and Upward with Collapse," in N. Yoffee and G. Cowgill, eds. *The Collapse of Ancient States and Civilizations*. Tucson: 1991.

Crawford, C. *Attack the Messenger*. Lanham, MD: 2006.

Crews, C. "Washington's Ten Thousand Commandments," *Investors Business Daily*, June 22, 2007.

Cunningham, N. *In Pursuit of Reason: The Life of Thomas Jefferson*. Baton Rouge: 1987.

Cushing, H., ed. *The Writing of Samuel Adams*. New York: 1907.

Danbury Baptist Association. "Letter of October 7, 1801 to Thomas Jefferson," Thomas Jefferson Papers, Manuscript Division, Library of Congress.

Danelski, D., and Tulchin, J., eds. *The Autobiographical Notes of Charles Evans Hughes*. Cambridge: 1973.

Daniels, R. *Guarding the Golden Door*. New York: 2004.

Davis, D. "Slaves In Islam," *New York Review of Books*, October 1993.

Davis, P., ed. *Immigration and Americanization*. Boston: 1920.

Davis, R. "Al–Gor(e)ing Blacks Again," National Center for Public Policy Research, October 1999, at www.nationalcenter.org/P21NVDavisVote1099.html.

Demar, G. *America's Christian History: The Untold Story*. Atlanta: 1995.

———. *God and Government*. Atlanta: 1997.

———. *Whoever Controls the Schools Rules the World*. Powder Springs, GA: 2007.

Dennett, D. *Darwin's Dangerous Idea: Evolution and the Meaning of Life*. New York: 1995.

Derekhshani, T. "At God's Funeral, Biographer Describes 'Killers' of the Deity," *Arizona Republic*, August 29, 1999.

DeWeese, T. "The Outrages of the Mexican Invasion," American Policy Center, Monograph 22, February 2003.

Dewey, J. "My Pedagogic Creed," *School Journal*, January 16, 1997, vol. 54, no. 3.

Dexter, F., ed. *The Literary Style of Ezra Stiles*. New York: 1901.

———. *Documentary History of Yale University*. New Haven, CT: 1916.

Diamond, J. *Collapse: How Societies Choose to Fail or Succeed*. New York: 2005.

DiBacco. T. "Simple Creed Sums Up Basics," *Washington Times*, October 1, 2001.

Dill, S. "Rome and Byzantium,"*Quarterly Review*, no. 383. London: 1900.

Dionne, E. J. "The Civics Deficit," *Washington Post*, November 30, 1999.

DiLorenzo, T. *How Capitalism Saved America*. New York: 2004.

Dobbs, L. *War on the Middle Class*. Washington: 2006.

Donohue, W. *Twilight of Liberty: The Legacy of the ACLU*. New Brunswick, NJ: 1994.

Dorchester, D. *Christianity in America*. New York: 1988.

Dougherty, J. *Illegals*. Nashville: 2004.

———. "Anchors Away," *Voices*, May 10, 2005.

D'Souza, D. *Illiberal Education: The Politics of Race and Sex on Campus*. New York: 1991.

———. *The End of Racism: Principles for a Multiracial Society*. New York: 1995.

Drucker, P. *The New Society*. New York, 1949.

———. *The Age of Discontinuity*. London: 1969.

———. *The New Realities*. New York: 1989.

Durant. W. *Caesar and Christ*. New York: 1944.

Dworkin, R. *Taking Rights Seriously*. Cambridge: 1977.

Eastland, T. "A Court Tilting against Religious Liberty," in R. Bork, ed. *A Country I Do Not Recognize*. Stanford: 2005.

Ebenstein, L. *Milton Friedman*. New York: 2007.

Edwards, C. "Farm Subsidies at Record Levels," Cato Institute, Washington, February 2, 2004.

———. "The Era of Big Government," Cato Institute, Washington, February 2, 2004.

———. "Downsizing the Federal Government," Cato Institute, Washington, June 2, 2004.

Edwards, J. "Two Sides of the Same Coin: The Connection between Legal and Illegal Immigration," Center for Immigration Studies, 2006, at www/cis.org/articles/2006/back106.html.

Eisenstadt, S. *The Political Systems of Empires*. Glencoe, IL: 1963.

Elliot, W. *The Rise of Guardian Democracy*. New York: 1974.

Ellis, J. *Literature Lost: Social Agendas and the Corruption of the Humanities*. New Haven, CT: 1997.

Etzioni, A. *The Spirit of Community: Rights, Responsibilities, and the Communitarian Agenda*. New York: 1993.

Fallows, J. *Breaking the News: How the Media Undermine Democracy*. New York: 1997.

Fanfani, A. *Catholicism, Protestantism, and Capitalism*. Norfolk, VA: 2003.

Faux, J. *The Global Class War*. Hoboken, NJ: 2006.

Federer, W. *The Ten Commandments and Their Influence on American Law*. St. Louis, MO: 2003.

———. *Why America Should Be Under God*. St. Louis, MO: 2004.

Fein, B. "Divided Loyalties," *Washington Times*, December 13, 2005.

Ferguson, N. "Empires with Expiration Dates," *Foreign Policy*, September–October 2006.

Figgie, H. *Bankruptcy 1995*. Boston 1992.

Fineman, H., and McDaniel, A. "Bush: What Bounce?" *Newsweek*, August 31, 1992.

Fitzpatrick, J., ed. *The Writings of Washington*. Washington: 1932.

Flynn, D. *Deep Blue 2004 Campuses*. Clarendon: 2005.

Fonte, J. "Why There Is a Cultural War," *Policy Review*, December 2000–January 2001.

———. "Dual Allegiance: A Challenge to Immigration Reform and Patriotic Allegiance," *Backgrounder*, Center for Immigration Studies, November 2005.

Forbes. "Thoughts on the Business of Life," July 18, 1994.

Forbes, M. "Who Can Give Them Courage," *Forbes*, March 14, 1994.

Ford, P. *The Writings of Thomas Jefferson*. New York: 1894.

Fosl, P. "Conservatives Should Own Up to Their Share of Blame," *Roanoke Times & World News*, May 6, 1995.

Fournier, K. *In Defense of Liberty*. Virginia Beach: 1993.

Francis, S. "Mexican Government Sends Illegal Immigrants to Death—Knowingly," Creators Syndicate, May 28, 2001.

Franklin, B. *Aims and Morals of Benjamin Franklin*, W. Pfaff, ed. New Orleans: 1927.

Fraser Institute, *Economic Freedom of the World, Annual Report*. Vancouver, Canada: 2006.

Freeman, C. *The Closing of the Western Mind*. London: 2002.

Fridson, M. *Unwarranted Intrusions: The Case against Government Intervention in the Marketplace.* Hoboken, NJ: 2006.

Friedman, B. *Day of Reckoning.* New York: 1989.

Friedman, M. "Fiscal Responsibility," *Newsweek,* August 7, 1967.

———. "The Limitations of Tax Limitation," *Policy Review,* Summer 1978.

———. *Why Government Is the Problem.* Stanford: 1993.

Friedman, M., and Friedman, R. *Free to Choose.* New York: 1980.

———. *Two Lucky People: Memoirs.* Chicago: 1998.

Friedman, M., and Schwartz, A. *A Monetary History of the United States.* New York: 1963.

Fukuyama, F. *The End of History and the Last Man.* New York: 2006.

———. *America at the Crossroads.* New Haven, CT: 2007.

Garcia, P. "Dual Language Characteristics and Language: Male Mexican Workers in the United States," *Social Science Research,* 1984.

Gates, H. "Whose Canon Is It Anyway?" *New York Times,* February 26, 1989.

Gaustad, E. *Neither King nor Prelate: Religion and the New Nation, 1776–1826.* Grand Rapids, MI: 1993.

Gentry, W., and Hubbard, R. G. "Taxes and Wage Growth," National Bureau of Economic Research, Washington: November 2003.

———. "Success Taxes, Entrepreneurial Entry, and Innovation," National Bureau of Economic Research, Washington: April 13, 2004.

———. "Tax Policy and Entry into Entrepreneurship," National Bureau of Economic Research, Washington: June 2004.

Geyer, G. "Orchestration from Mexico," *Washington Times,* April 6, 2006.

Gibson, J. *The War on Christmas.* New York: 2005.

Gibbon, E. A. *The Decline and Fall of the Roman Empire.* London: 1969.

Gilder, G. *Wealth and Poverty.* New York: 1981.

———. "Ronald Reagan and the Spirit of Free Enterprise," *Imprimis,* Hillsdale College, Summer 2004.

Gilpin, H., ed. *The Papers of James Madison.* Boston: 1840.

Gingrich, N. *Rediscovering God in America: Reflections on the Role of Faith in Our Nation's History and Future.* Nashville: 2006.

———. *Real Change: From the World that Fails to the World that Works.* Washington: 2008.

Glazer, N. "The Constitution and American Diversity," *Public Interest,* Winter 1987.

Goffart, W. *Barbarians and Romans, A.D. 418–584: The Techniques of Accommodation.* Princeton, NJ: 1980.

Goldberg, B. "Networks Need a Reality Check," *Wall Street Journal,* February 13, 1996.

———. *Bias: A CBS Insider Exposes How the Media Distort the News.* Washington: 2002.

———. *Arrogance: Rescuing America from the Media Elite.* New York: 2003.

———. *100 People Who Are Screwing Up America.* New York: 2005.

Goldman, A. *The Search for God at Harvard.* New York: 1991.

Goldstein, T. *Killing the Messenger.* New York: 2007.

Goldwater, B. "Nomination Acceptance Speech," American Rhetoric: Top 100 Speeches, at www.americanrhetoric.com/speeches/barrygoldwater1964rnc.htm.

Good, H. G. *A History of American Education.* New York: 1956.

Gotlieb, A. "Review of Freeman," *New York Times Book Review,* February 15, 2004.

Graglia, L. "It's Not Constitutionalism, It's Judicial Activism," *Harvard Journal of Law and Public Policy,* Winter 1996.

———. "Constitutional Law without the Constitution: The Supreme Court's Remaking of America," in R. Bork, ed. *A Country I Do Not Recognize.* Stanford: 2005.

Graham, O. *Unguarded Gates.* Lanham, MD: 2004.

Grant, M. *The Climax of Rome.* Boston: 1968.

Grant, M., and Davison, C. *The Founders of the Republic on Immigration, Naturalization, and Aliens.* New York: 1928.

Gross, M. *The End of Society: Social and Cultural Madness in America.* New York: 1997.

Gross, P., and Levitt, N. *Higher Superstition: The Academic Left and Its Quarrels with Science.* Baltimore: 1994.

Grund, F. J. *The Americans in Their Moral, Social, and Political Relations.* New York: 1968.

Guinness, O. *The Death of Dust.* Downers Grove, IL: 1979.

———. *The American Hour.* New York: 1993.

———. *The Great Experiment: Faith and Freedom in America.* Colorado Springs: 2001.

Haass, R. *The Opportunity.* New York: 2005.

Halberstam, D. *The Next Century.* New York: 1991.

Hall, R., and Rabushka, A. *The Flat Tax.* Stanford: 2007.

Hall, T., and Ferguson, J. *The Great Depression.* Ann Arbor, MI: 2001.

Haltiwanger, J. "Aggregate Productivity and Job Growth," in J. Jasinowski, ed. *The Rising Tide.* New York: 1998.

Handlin, O. *The Uprooted.* Boston: 1973.

Hanson, G. *Why Does Immigration Divide America?* Washington: 2005.

Hanson, V. "Bomb Texas," *Commentary,* January 16, 2003.

———. *Mexifornia.* New York: (2003) 2007.

———. "Brace Yourself," *National Review Online,* September 2, 2004, at www.nationalreview .com/script/printpage. p?ref=hanson/hanson200409022149.asp.

Harrington, A. "The New Anti-Civilization," *Chronicles,* June 2001.

Harsanyi, D. *Nanny State.* New York: 2007.

Hartmann, E. *The Quest to Americanize the Immigrant.* New York: 1948.

Hatch, N. *The Democratization of American Christianity.* New Haven, CT: 1989.

Hazard, E., ed. *Historical Collections: Consisting of State Papers and Other Authentic Documents: Intended as Materials for an History of the United States of America.* Philadelphia: 1792.

Heather, P. *The Fall of the Roman Empire.* London: 2006.

Heaton, H. *Economic History of Europe.* London: 1948.

Heck, G. *The Islamic Code of Conduct for War and Peace.* Riyadh, Saudi Arabia: 2006.

———. *Building Prosperity: Why Ronald Reagan and the Founding Fathers Were Right on the Economy.* Lanham, MD: 2007a.

———. "Energy Bill Ripple Effect," *Washington Times,* January 24, 2007b.

———. "Reduce Deficit Reagan's Way: With Tax Cuts," *Investors Business Daily,* February 28, 2007c.

Henry, N. *American Carnival: Journalism under Siege in an Age of New Media.* Berkeley: 2007.

Henry. W. *In Defense of Elitism.* New York: 1994.

Hentoff, N. "Watching What You Say on Campus," *Washington Post,* September 14, 1989.

———. "Students Quickly Losing Their Freedom of Speech," *Campus Report,* May 1992.

Heritage Foundation. *Strangled by Red Tape.* Washington: 1995.

Heritage Foundation study, cited in C. Thomas. "No More Trust on Immigration," *Conservative Chronicle,* June 13, 2007.

Herman, A. *Joseph McCarthy: Reexamining the Life and Legacy of America's Most Hated Senator.* New York: 2000.

Hewitt, H. "Larry Summers Is Bucking the Faculty in Trying to Remake Undergraduate Education at Harvard," *National Review Online,* June 12, 2003.

———. *Painting the Map Red.* Washington: 2006.

Himmelfarb, G. *On Liberty and Liberalism; the Case of John Stuart Mill.* New York: 1974.

History Guide. "Lectures on Ancient and Medieval Europe: A Brief Social History of the Roman Empire," 2007, at www.historyguide.org/ancient/lecture13b.html.

Hitti, P. *Capital Cities of Islam.* Minneapolis: 1973.

Holland, T. *Rubicon: The Last Years of the Roman Republic.* New York: 2004.

Hook, S. "Stanford Documents," Sidney Hook, ed., in *Partisan Review*, Fall 1988, *seriatim*.

Horowitz, D. *The Art of Political War*. Dallas: 2000.

———. "The Problem with America's Colleges and the Solution," *FrontPage Magazine.Com*, September 3, 2002.

Hudson, W. "Growth Is Not a Four Letter Word," in J. Jasinowski, ed. *The Rising Tide*. New York: 1998.

Human Events. "$16,344 per Student, but Only 12 Percent Read Proficiently," March 20, 2006.

Hunter, L. Who's Afraid of the National Debt?" Institure for Policy Innovation, Washington, July 25, 2001.

Huntington, S. *American Politics: The Promise of Disharmony*. Cambridge, MA: 1961.

———. "The Clash of Civilizations," *Foreign Affairs*, Summer 1993, vol. 72, no. 3.

———. "The Erosion of American National Affairs," *Foreign Affairs*, September–October 1997, vol. 76, no. 5.

———. *The Clash of Civilizations and Remaking of the World Order*. New York: 2003.

———. "The Hispanic Challenge," *Foreign Policy*, March–April 2004a.

———. *Who Are We? The Challenges to America's National Identity*. New York: 2004b.

———. "Dead Souls: the Denationalization of the American Elite," *National Interest*, Spring, no. 75, 2004c.

Hurst, L. "The First Immigrant," *Toronto Star*, October 12, 1991.

International Monetary Fund (IMF), IMF Center, "EconEd Online," at www.imf.org/external/np/exr/center/econed/index.html.

Ingraham, L. *Shut Up and Sing*. Washington: 2003.

International Herald Tribune. "America Is Not a 'Christian Nation,'" October 9, 2007.

Iserbyt, C. *The Deliberate Dumbing Down of America*. Ravenna, OH: 1999.

Iyengar, S. *Is Anyone Responsible? How Television Frames Political Issues*. Chicago: 1994.

Jackson, G. *Conservative Comebacks to Liberal Lies*. Ramsey, NJ: 2006/2007.

Jacobs, J. *The Death and Life of Great American Cities*. New York: 1993.

Jacobs, J. *Dark Age Ahead*. New York: 2005.

Jacoby, J. "Toward Understanding Why We Fly the Flag," *Conservative Chronicle*, Washington: July 18, 2007.

Jasinowski, J., ed. *The Rising Tide*. New York: 1998.

Jay, J. *The Federalist, No. 2*. October 31, 1787.

Jefferson, T. *Notes on the State of Virginia*. Philadelphia: 1794.

———. *Works*, H. A. Washington, ed., New York: 1859.

———. *The Writings of Thomas Jefferson*. A. Bergh, ed. Washington: 1904.

Johnson, C. *Blowback*. New York: 2000.

———. *The Sorrows of Empire*. New York: 2004.

———. *Nemesis: The Last Days of the American Republic*. New York: 2006.

Johnson, H., ed. *Correspondence and Public Papers of John Jay*. New York: 1893.

Jones. A. *The Roman Empire: A Social, Economic, and Administrative Survey*. Oxford: 1964.

———. *The Roman Economy: Studies in Ancient Economic and Administrative History*. Oxford: 1974.

Jorgenson, D. "The Growth-Boosting Power of a Consumption Tax," in J. Jasinowski, ed. *The Rising Tide*. New York: 1998.

Justich, R., and Ng, B. "The Underground Labor Force Is Rising to the Surface," Bear Sterns Asset Management, January 3, 2005.

Kanter, R. "Small Business and Economic Growth," in J. Jasinowski, ed. *The Rising Tide*. New York: 1998.

Katz, S. *The Jews in the Visigothic and Frankish Kingdoms of Spain and Gaul*. Cambridge: 1937/1955.

Kaylin, J. "Bass, Yale, and Western Civ," *Yale Alumni Magazine*, Summer 1995.

Kemp, J. "The Mandate for Higher Growth," in J. Jasinowski, ed. *The Rising Tide*. New York: 1998.

Kendall, E. *Kendall's Travels*. New York: 1809.

Kennedy, D. "Can We Still Afford to Be a Nation of Immigrants?" *Atlantic Monthly*, vol. 278, November 1996.

——. "Culture Wars: The Sources and Uses of Enmity in American History," in *Enemy Images in American History*. Providence, RI: 1997.

Kennedy, J. F. *A Nation of Immigrants*. New York: 1964.

Kennedy, P. *The Rise and Fall of the Great Powers*. New York: 1987.

Kimball, R. *Tenured Radicals*. Chicago: 1998.

Klein, J. *Politics Lost*. New York: 2006.

Kirk, R. "Renewing a Shaken Culture," *Heritage Foundation*, Lecture 434, December 11, 1992.

Kohn, B. *Journalistic Fraud: How the New York Times Distorts the News and Can No Longer Be Trusted*. Nashville: 2003.

Kolb, C. *White House Daze*. New York: 1993.

Korman, G. *Industrialization, Immigrants, and Americanization*. Madison, WI: 1967.

Kors, A. "It's Speech, Not Sex, the Dean Bans Now," *Wall Street Journal*, October 12, 1989.

Kors, A., and Silverglate, H. *The Shadow University: The Betrayal of Liberty on America's Campuses*. New York: 1998.

Kovach, B., and Rosenstiel, T. *The Elements of Journalism*. New York: 2003.

Kramer, H., and Kimball, R. *The Betrayal of Liberalism*. Chicago: 1999.

——. "The Betrayal of Liberalism," in *The New Criterion*, 2000, at www.newcriterion.com:81/ constant/books/betrayal/betrayintro.

Kristol, I. *Two Cheers for Capitalism*. New York: 1978.

Kudlow, L. "Witnessing the Bush-Bernanke Boom," *Conservative Chronicle*, February 28, 2007.

von Kuehnelt-Leddihn, E. *Leftism Revisited: From Sade and Marx to Hitler and Pol Pot*. New York: 1990.

Kunstler, J. *The Long Emergency*. New York: 2005.

Kupelian, D. *The Marketing of Evil*. Nashville: 2005.

Kuttner, R. *The Economic Illusion*. Philadelphia: 1984.

——. *The End of Laissez Faire*. New York: 1991.

Lactantius. *De Mortibus Persecutorum*. J. L. Creed, ed. New York: 1984.

Lambro, D., "Read Their Lips: More Taxes for All," *Conservative Chronicle*, February 28, 2007a.

——. "Success Stories Fly under the Radar," *Conservative Chronicle*, February 28, 2007b.

Lamm, R. "The Destruction of America: Immigration or Invasion," synopsis of speech, Washington, DC, April 2006, replicated in Smerconish, M. "The Man with the Plan to Destroy America," *Philadelphia Daily News*, May 4, 2006, at www.freerepublic.com/focus/news/ 1629745/posts, May 10, 2006; and www.spearboard.comn/showthread.php?t=28300.

Lasch, C. *The Revolt of the Elites and the Betrayal of Democracy*. New York: 1995.

LaTouche, R. *The Birth of Western Economy*. London: 1967.

The Laws of Harvard College. Boston: 1790.

Leach, W. *Land of Desire: Merchants, Power, and the Rise of a New American Culture*. New York: 1993.

Leaming, A., and Spicer, J., eds. *The Grants, Concessions, and Original Constitutions of the Province of New Jersey*. Philadelphia: 1758.

LeBlanc, T. "Western World Not Doomed after All," *University Wire*, November 3, 1997.

Leeb, S. *The Coming Economic Collapse*. New York: 2006.

Lefler, H., ed. *North Carolina History*. Chapel Hill, NC: 1956.

Leo, J. *Two Steps Ahead of the Thought Police*. New York: 1994.

——. *Incorrect Thoughts: Notes on Our Wayward Culture*. New Brunswick, NJ: 2001.

Leonard, J. *How Structural Costs Imposed on U.S. Manufacturers Harm Workers and Threaten Competitiveness*, National Association of Manufacturers, Washington: 2003.

Lerner. M. *The Politics of Meaning*. New York: 1996.

——. "Marcuse at 100," *Tikkun*, September–October 1998.

Lesthaeghe, R. "A Century of Cultural and Demographic Change in Western Europe: An Exploration of Underlying Dimensions," *Population and Development Review*, Fall 1983.

Levinson, S. *Constitutional Faith*. Princeton, NJ: 1989.

Levitt, S., and Dubner, S. *Freakanomics: A Rogue Economist Explains the Hidden Side of Everything*. New York: 2005.

Levy, J. *The Economic Life of the Ancient World*. Chicago: 1967.

Lewis, B. "The Arabs in Eclipse," in C. M. Cipolla, ed. *The Economic Decline of Empires*. London: 1970.

Lichtenberg, F. "Technology Investment Is Driving Economic Growth," in J. Jasinowski, ed. *The Rising Tide*. New York: 1998.

Lieven, A. *America Right or Wrong*. Oxford: 2004.

Limbaugh, D. "On a Mission for Marriage," *Creators Syndicate*, September 7, 2000.

————. "Bogged Down in the Immigrant Debate," *Conservative Chronicle*, May 30, 2007.

Limbaugh, R. *See, I Told You So*. New York: 1993.

Link, A., ed. *The Papers of Woodrow Wilson*. Princeton, NJ: 1966.

Lippman, W. *Public Opinion*. New York: 1965.

Lipset, S. "Equal Chances versus Equal Results," *Annals of the American Academy of Political and Social Science*, vol. 523, September 1992.

Livy. *The History of Rome from Its Foundation*. A. DeSelincourt, trans. Baltimore: 1967.

Lot, F. *La Fin du Monde Antique et le Début du Moyen Âge*. Paris: 1927.

Lottman, H. *The Left Bank*. Boston: 1982.

Luce, H. "The American Century," *Life*, February 17, 1941.

Luskin, D. "Bush Fails to Get Deserved Credit for Tax Cut Benefits," *Detroit News*, August 27, 2004.

Luther, M. "Against the Heavenly Prophets in the Matter of Images and Sacraments," in *Luther's Works*, B. Ehrling, trans., and C. Bergendorf, ed. Philadelphia: 1958.

Luttwak, E. *The Grand Strategy of the Roman Empire: From the First Century A.D. to the Third*. Baltimore: 1976.

Luzzatto, G. *Breve Storia Economica dell'Italia Medievale*. Picolla: 1958.

————. *An Economic History of Italy from the Fall of the Roman Empire to the Beginning of the Sixteenth Century*. P. Jones, trans. London: 1961.

MacMullen, R. *Corruption and the Decline of Rome*. New Haven, CT: 1988.

Malbin, M. *Religion and Politics: The Intention of the Authors of the First Amendment*. Washington: 1978.

Malkin, M. *Invasion*. Washington: 2002.

————. *Unhinged: Exposing Liberals Gone Wild*. Washington: 2005.

————. "Racism Gets Whitewash from the Press," *Conservative Chronicle*, April 5, 2006.

Makin, J., and Ornstein, N. *Debt and Taxes*. New York: 1994.

Malloy, W. *Treaties, Conventions, International Acts, Protocols, and Agreements between the United States of America and Other Powers, 1776–1909*. New York: 1968.

Mangino, A. "Profs Donate Heavily to Dems," *Yale Daily News*, September 12, 2007, at www.yalenews.com/articles/view/21235.

Mann, M. *Incoherent Empire*. London: 2003.

Marcuse, H. *Eros and Civilization: A Philosophical Inquiry into Freud*. Boston: 1966.

————. "Repressive Tolerance," in R. Wolff et al., eds. *A Critique of Pure Tolerance*. Boston: 1969.

————. *Counter-Revolution and Revolt*. New York: 1971.

Marsden, G. *Fundamentalism and American Culture*. Oxford: 2006.

Martin, D. "New Rules on Dual Nationality for a Democratizing Globe: Between Rejection and Embrace," *Georgetown Immigration Law Journal*, 1999, vol. 14.

Martinez, J. "More that Half of State's Juniors Fail Math, Writing, in New High School Test," *Detroit News*, August 15, 2007.

Marx, K. *A Contribution to the Critique of Political-Economy*. New York: 1970.

Mattingly, H. *Roman Coins*. Chicago: 1960.

Maurice, C., and Smithson, C. *The Doomsday Myth*. Stanford: 1984.

Mazzarino, S. *The End of the Ancient World*. London: 1966.

May, H. *The Enlightenment in America*. New York: 1976.

McDougall, W. *Promised Land, Crusader State*. New York: 1997.

———, ed. *Freedom Just Around the Corner*. New York: 2004

McDowell, G. "The Perverse Paradox of Privacy," in R. Bork, ed. *A Country I Do Not Recognize*. Stanford: 2005.

McFarland, N. "A July 4 Meditation on the Faith of the Founders: One Nation under God," *Orange County Register*, July 2, 1995.

McGowan, W. *Coloring the News: How Crusading for Diversity Has Corrupted American Journalism*. San Francisco: 2001.

———. *Coloring the News: How Political Correctness Has Corrupted American Journalism*. New York: 2003.

McKinley, J. "Mexican Manual for Illegals Upsets Some," *New York Times*, January 6, 2005.

Michael, G. *The Enemy of My Enemy*. Kansas: 2006.

Miles, G. "Roman and Modern Imperialism: a Reassessment," *Comparative Studies in Society and History*, vol. 32, no. 4, October 1990.

Mill, J. S. *Principles of Political Economy*, W. Ashley, ed. 1915.

———. *Considerations on Representative Government*. London: 1993.

von Mises, L. *Liberalism: In the Classical Tradition*. Irvington, NY: 1985.

———. *Human Action: a Treatise on Economics*. Auburn, AL: 1998.

Miller, J. *Crisis in Freedom: The Alien and Sedition Acts*. New York: 1951.

Mitchell, D. "The Historical Record of Lower Tax Rates," Heritage Foundation, Washington, August 13, 2003.

———. "Making American Companies More Competitive," Heritage Foundation, Washington, September 25, 2003.

Moine, P. "Victor Hugo House of Literature," *SGI Quarterly*, January 2002.

Montesquieu. *The Spirit of the Laws*. New York: 1949.

Moore, S. "Distortions that Don't Ease the Agony," Cato Institute, Washington, DC, 2000, at www.cato.org/pub_display/php?pub_id=4721.

———. "Remembering the Real Economic Legacy of JFK," *Human Events*, May 19, 2003.

Morris, B. F. *Christian Life and Character of the Civil Institutions of the United States, Developed in the Official and Historic Annals of the Republic*. Philadelphia: 1864.

Moynihan, D. "The Sonnet about the Statue of Liberty," *New York*, vol. 19, May 1986.

———. "Defining Deviancy Down," *The American Scholar*, Winter, 1993.

Mulhern, P. "Media Bias and Campaign Finance, *Nevada Journal*, August 3, 2001.

Muller, J. *Adam Smith in His Time and Ours*. New York: 1993.

Mundell, R. "A Pro-Growth Fiscal System," in J. Jasinowski, ed. *The Rising Tide*. New York: 1998.

Munro, D., and Sellery, G. *Medieval Civilization*. New York: 1914.

Murphey, D. "The Historic Dispossession of the American Indians: Did It Violate American Ideals?" *Journal of Social, Political, and Economic Studies*, vol. 16, Fall 1991.

Murphy, C. *Are We Rome?* Boston: 2007.

NAM (National Association of Manufacturers). *The Escalating Cost Crisis*. Washington: 2006a.

———. *The Facts about Modern Manufacturing*. Washington: 2006b.

National Center for History in the Schools. *National Standards for United States History: Exploring the American Experience, Grades 5–12*. Los Angeles: UCLA, 1994.

National Endowment for the Humanities. *A Survey of College Seniors: Knowledge of History and Literature*. Washington: 1989.

National Public Radio. "The Third Choice," at www.pbs.org/thinktank/thirdchoice/transcript .html, Washington: 2000.

National Tax Foundation. "America Celebrates Tax Freedom Day," Washington, April 30, 2007.

Neal, A. "Intellectual Diversity Endangered," Center for Individual Freedom, November 7, 2003.

Netting, R. "Maya Subsistence: Mythologies, Analogies, Possibilities," in *The Origins of Maya Civilization*. Albuquerque, NM: 1977.

New York Times. "Rationale for Kennedy's Tax Cut," September 18, 1984.

——. "Drives by Campuses to Curb Race Slurs Pose a Speech Issue," April 25, 1989.

——. "Excerpts from Supreme Court Opinions on Prayers," June 20, 2000.

Ngai, M. *Impossible Subjects: Illegal Aliens and the Making of America*. Princeton, NJ: 2004.

Nisbet, R. *The Twilight of Authority*. New York: 1975.

Niskanen, W. *Reaganomics: An Insider's Account of the Policies and the People*. New York: 1988.

——. "Growth Burden of Federal Regulation," in J. Jasinowski, ed. *The Rising Tide*. New York: 1998.

Nixon, R. *Seize the Moment*. New York: 1992.

Noble, J. "Discovering Columbus," *New York Times Magazine*, August 11, 1992.

Noll, M. *Eerdmans' Handbook to Christianity in America*. Grand Rapids, MI: 1983.

Noonan, P. "The American Way," *Opinion Journal*, December 8, 2005, WSJ.com, at www.opinion journal.com.

North, O. "Mullah Meetings—'Negotiating' with Radicals," *Conservative Chronicle*, August 1, 2007.

Norton, R. "Taking on Public Enemy No. 1," *Fortune*, October 19, 1992.

——. "Our Screwed Up Tax Code," *Fortune*, September 6, 1993.

Novak, R. *Completing the Revolution*. New York: 2000.

O'Rourke, P. *On the Wealth of Nations*. New York: 2007.

Ortega y Gassettt, J. *The Revolt of the Masses*. New York: 1957.

Palmer, D. *George Washington and Benedict Arnold*. Washington: 2006.

Palmer, R. *The Age of Democratic Revolution: A Political History of Europe and America, 1760–1800*. Princeton, NJ: 1964.

Parini, J. "Academic Conservatives Who Decry Politicization Show Staggering Naivete about Their Own Biases," *Chronicle of Higher Education*, December 7, 1988.

Parkinson, C. N. *The Evolution of Political Thought*. Boston: 1959.

Patterson, T. *Out of Order*. New York: 1994.

Payne, J. *Costly Returns: the Burdens of the U.S. Tax System*. San Francisco: 1993.

Pennick, W. "Evolution of the Federal Tax System: 1954-1983,"*Federal Tax Policy Memo*, National Tax Foundation, Washington, July 1983.

Perry, J. *The Case for Constititional Tax Limitation*. Americans for Tax Reform. Washington: 2004.

Peter, L. *Peter's Quotations: Ideas for Our Time*. New York: 1977.

Peterson, P. *Facing Up*. New York: 1993.

——. *Running on Empty*. New York: 2004.

Pflaum, H. *Essai sur les Procurateurs Équestres sous le-Haut-Empire Romain*. Paris: 1950.

Phillips, K. *The Politics of the Rich and Poor*. New York: 1990.

——. *Boiling Point*. New York: 1993.

——. *American Theocracy*. New York: 2006.

Pierce, B. *A History of Harvard University*. Cambridge: 1833.

Pirenne, H. *A History of Europe*. New York: 1958.

Plutarch. *The Lives of the Noble Grecians and Romans*. New York: 1935.

Potter, D. *History and American Society*. New York: 1973.

Powell, J. *FDR's Folly: How Roosevelt and His New Deal Prolonged the Great Depression*. New York: 2003.

Powell, M. "New Tack against Illegal Immigrants," *Washington Post*, June 10, 2005.

Putnam, G. "One Reporter's Opinion: Citizens' Militia on the Border," www.newsmax.com, December 13, 2002.

Rahn, R. "Regulatory Therapy," *Washington Times*, July 11, 2004.

Rauch, J. "Is the Deficit Really So Bad," *Atlantic Monthly*, February 1989.

Ravich., D. "Multiculturalism," *American Scholar*, Summer 1990.

——. *The Language Police*. New York: 2003.

Reagan, R. "Remarks Announcing America's Economic Bill of Rights," Washington, July 3, 1987, at www.reagan.utexas.edu/archives/speeches/1987/070387a.htm.

——. quoted in L. Kudlow, "The Big Easy's Billion Dollar Boondoogle," *Conservative Chronicle*, September 12, 2007.

Rededaugh, C. "Berkeley Holiday Honors Indigenous People," *University Wire*, October 10, 2000.

Reese, C. "Merv Griffin and Benjamin Franklin," *Conservative Chronicle*, August 29, 2007.

Rehnquist, W. "United States Not Founded on Absolute Church-State Separation," 1985, at www.belcherfoundation.org/wallace_v_jaffrey_dissent.htm.

Renan, E. "Qu'est Qu'une Nation?" in R. Bradley and R. Mitchel, eds. *French Literature of the Nineteenth Century*. New York: 1935.

Renshon, S. *Dual Citizens in America*. Washington: July 2000.

——. *Dual Citizenship and American National Identity*, Center for Immigration Studies, Paper 20, Washington, October 2001.

——. *The 50% American*. Washington: 2005.

Revel, J. F. *Democracy against Itself*. R. Kaplan, trans. New York: 1993.

Rice, C. *The Supreme Court and Public Prayer: The Need for Restraint*. New York: 1964.

Richardson, J. ed. *A Compilation of the Messages and Papers of the Presidents*. Washington: 1907.

Rifkin, J. *The European Dream*. New York: 2004.

Ringenberg, W. *The Christian College: a History of Protestant Higher Education in America*. Grand Rapids, MI: 2006.

Ringer, Robert. *Restoring the American Dream*. New York: 1977.

Rohatyn, F. "Ways to Achieve Higher Growth," in J. Jasinowski, ed. *The Rising Tide*. New York: 1998.

Romero, F. "Mexico's Influence Growing in the U.S.," *San Diego Union-Tribune*, August 22, 1993.

Roosevelt, T. "True Americanism," in *American Ideals and Other Essays: Social and Political*. New York: 1898.

——. "American People," in A. Hart and H. Ferleger, eds. *Theodore Roosevelt Encyclopedia*. New York: 1941a.

——. "American, Hyphenated," in A. Hart and H. Ferleger, eds. *Theodore Roosevelt Encyclopedia*. New York: 1941b.

Rorty, R. "The Unpatriotic Academy," *New York Times*, February 13, 1994.

——. *Achieving Our Country: Leftist Thought in Twentieth Century America*. Cambridge: 1998.

Rubenstein, E. "The Stupid American? Look Again," VDARE.com, December 22, 2005, at www.vdare.com/rubenstein/015222_nd.htm.

Rush, B. *Essays, Literary, Moral, and Philosophical*. Philadelphia: 1798.

Russo, M. "Free Speech at Tufts: Zoned Out," *New York Times*, September 27, 1989.

Ryan, F., ed. *The Wisdom and Humor of the Great Communicator*. San Francisco: 1995.

Sachs, J. "Global Competition Drives Economic Growth," in J. Jasinowski, ed. *The Rising Tide*. New York: 1998.

Sada, G. *Saddam's Secrets*. Brentwood, TN: 2006.

Sailer, S. "Americans First: What's Best for the Citizens We Already Have," *American Conservative*, February 13, 2006a.

——. "Cesar Chavez, Minute Man," *American Conservative*, February 27, 2006b.

Samuelson, R."The Budget: Back to the Future," *Newsweek*, February 14, 1994.

———. "We Don't Need Guest Workers," *Washington Post*, March 22, 2006.

Sandoz, E. "Power and Spirit in the Founding," *This World*, no. 9, Fall 1984.

Sanoff, A. "'60s Protestors, 80s Professors," *U.S. News and World Report*, January 16, 1989.

Savage, D. *Skipping Towards Gomorrah*. New York: 2003.

Savage, T. "Let's Clear Up a Couple of Misconceptions on Tax Cuts," *Chicago Sun Times*, April 15, 2004.

Scarre, C. *Chronicle of the Roman Emperors*. London: 1995.

Schachner, N. *Alexander Hamilton*. New York: 1946.

Schaff, P. *America: A Sketch of Its Political, Social, and Religious Character*. Cambridge: 1961.

Shermer, M. "Why ET Hasn't Called," *Scientific American*, August 2002.

Schevitz, T. "Cramped Speech at UC-Berkeley," *San Francisco Chronicle*, May 10, 2002.

Schlafly, P. "If NEA Delegates Get Their Way," *Washington Times*, weekly edition, August 7–13, 1995.

———. "Lesson Plan Could Forestall 'Citizenship Crisis,'" *Conservative Chronicle*, April 18, 2007a.

———. "Immigrant Bill Will Raid Pockets of Taxpayers," *Conservative Chronicle*, June 13, 2007b.

———. "Many Want English as the National Language," *Conservative Chronicle*, June 27, 2007.

Schlesinger, A. "When Ethnic Studies are Un-American," *Wall Street Journal*, April 23, 1990.

———. *The Disuniting of America: Reflections on a Multicultural Society*. New York: 1998.

Schmidt, A. *The Menace of Multiculturalism: Trojan Horse in America*. Westport, CT: 1997.

Schumpeter, J. *Capitalism, Socialism, and Democracy*. New York: 1962.

Schweikert, D. "Cultural Wars: General Ignorance of Language, Logic, and Philosophy," *E-NewsViews*, June 27, 1999.

Sears, A., and Osten, C. *The ACLU vs. America*. Nashville: 2005.

Settel, T. S., et al. *The Quotable Harry Truman*. New York: 1967.

Shapiro, B. "In Defense of Patriotism in the United States, *Conservative Chronicle*, July 11, 2007.

Shapiro, R. "The Economic Power of Ideas," in J. Jasinowski, ed. *The Rising Tide*. New York: 1998.

Sheehy, D. *Fighting Immigration Anarchy*. Bloomington, IN: 2006.

Shermer, M. "Why ET Hasn't Called," *Scientific American*, August 2002.

Silk, L. *Making Capitalism Work*. New York: 1996.

Simon, J. *The Economic Consequences of Immigration*. Cambridge: 1989.

Simon, W. *A Time for Truth*. New York: 1978.

Singer, C. *A Theological Interpretation of American History*. Phillipsburg, NJ: 1981.

Sivan, G. *The Bible and Civilization*. New York: 1973.

Skadden, D., ed. *A New Tax Structure for the United States*. Indianapolis, IN: 1978.

Skousen, M. *Vienna and Chicago: Friends or Foes*. Washington: 2005.

Smiley, G. *Rethinking the Great Depression*. Chicago: 2002.

Smith, A. *An Inquiry Into the Nature and Causes of the Wealth of Nations*. New York: 1937.

Smith, R. "The American Creed and American Identity: the Limits of Liberal Citizenship in the United States," *Western Political Quarterly*, vol. 41, 1987.

Snowden, F. *Blacks in Antiquity: Ethiopians in the Graeco-Roman Experience*. Cambridge: 1970.

———. *Before Color Prejudice*. Cambridge: 1983.

Sobran, J. "Reflections on Elections," November 5, 2002, at www.sobran.com.

Sommers, C. *Who Stole Feminism?* New York: 1993.

Sontag, S. "What's Happening in America," in *Styles of Radical Will*. New York: 1969.

Sowell, T. "The New Racism on Campus," *Fortune*, February 13, 1989.

———. "The Road to Hell Is Paved with Good Intentions," *Forbes*, January 17, 1994.

———. *Migrations and Cultures: A World View*. New York: 1996.

———. *A Conflict of Visions*. New York: 2002.

———. "Artificial Stupidity," Creators Syndicate, March 26, 2003.

———. "A Dose of Economic Reality," *Conservative Chronicle,* July 1, 2003.

———. "The New 'Yellow Peril,'" *Conservative Chronicle,* January 17, 2007a.

———. *A Conflict of Visions.* New York: 2007b.

———. "After the Terrorists' War On Us: Part II," *Conservative Chronicle,* July 25, 2007.

Sparks, J. *The Life of Gouverneur Morris.* Boston: 1832.

Spaulding, M. "From Pluribus to Unum," *Policy Review,* vol. 67, Winter 1994.

Stannard, D. *American Holocaust: Columbus and the Conquest of the New World.* New York: 1992.

Starr, C. *The Roman Empire, 27 B.C.–A.D. 476: a Study in Survival.* New York: 1982.

Steinberg, S. *The Ethnic Myth: Race, Ethnicity, and Class in America.* New York: 1981.

Steinmo, S. *Taxation and Democracy.* New York: 1993.

Steyn, M. "A Weird Stockholm Syndrome," *National Review Online,* July 18, 2005.

———. *America Alone.* Washington: 2006.

Stokes, A., and Pfeffer, L. *Church and State in the United States.* New York: 1964.

Stone, G. *Perilous Times: Free Speech in Wartime.* New York: 2004.

Strayer, J., and Munro, D. *The Middle Ages: 395–1500.* London: 1942/New York: 1959.

Sumner, W. *Protectionism.* New York: 1888.

Syrett, H., ed. *The Papers of Alexander Hamilton.* New York: 1962.

Szamuely, G. "The Real Shame of the West," *American Outlook,* Winter 1999.

Tacitus. *The Complete Works of Tactitus.* New York: 1942.

Tainter, J. *The Collapse of Complex Societies: New Studies in Archaeology.* Cambridge: 1988.

Tancredo, T. "Proposal Is 'Wrong-Headed,'" *USA Today,* March 23, 2005.

———. *In Mortal Danger: The Battle for America's Border and Security.* Nashville: 2006.

Tawney, R. *Religion and the Rise of Capitalism.* New York: 1926/London: 1960.

Tax Foundation. "America Celebrates Tax Freedom Day," S. Hodge and C. Dubay. Washington: 2006, 2007.

———. "U.S. Still Lagging Behind OECD Corporate Tax Levels," Fiscal Fact No. 96, C. Atkins and S. Hodge. Washington: July 27, 2004.

Thernstrom, A. "Bilingual Miseducation," *Commentary,* February 1990.

Thomas, C. "England May End Up Just History," *Lansing State Journal,* September 3, 2007.

Thompson, D. *The Democratic Citizen.* New York: 1970.

Thompson, J. W., and Johnson, E. N. *An Introduction to Medieval Europe.* New York: 1937.

Thurow, L. *The Zero Sum Society* New York: 1980.

———. *The Zero Sum Solution.* New York: 1985.

———. *Head-to-Head.* New York: 1992.

———. *The Future of Capitalism.* New York: 1996.

Tichenor, D. *Dividing Lines.* Princeton, NJ: 2002.

Tobin, J. "America Can Grow Faster," in J. Jasinowski, ed. *The Rising Tide.* New York: 1998.

Tocqueville, A. de. *Democracy in America.* Garden City, NY: 1851/New York: 1945/1969.

Tolson, J. "Lessons from the Fall," *U.S. News and World Report,* May 1, 2007.

Trowbridge, G., and Hornbeck, M. "CEOs to Governors: Schools Don't Make the Grade," *Detroit News,* July 22, 2007.

Trumbull, B. *A Complete History of Connecticut, Civil and Ecclesiastical, from the Emigration of its First Planters from England.* Hartford, CT: 1797.

Tuchman, B. *In March of Folly: From Troy to Vietnam.* New York: 1984.

Turchin, P. *Historical Dynamics: Why States Rise and Fall.* Princeton, NJ: 2003.

———. *War and Peace and War.* New York: 2007.

United Nations. *Human Development Report 2000.* New York: 2000.

———. *World Population Prospects: The 2000 Revision: Highlights.* New York: 2001.

U.S. Bureau of the Census. *Historical Statistics of the United States, Colonial Times to 1970.*

U.S. Bureau of Economic Analysis. "National Income Accounts Data," "Gross Domestic Product," at www.bea.gov/national/txt/dpga.text.

U.S. Bureau of Labor Statistics. "Current Employment Statistics, July, 2007," Washington, DC: August 3, 2007.

U.S. Congress. *Debates and Proceedings of the Congress of the United States*. Washington, DC: 1834, vol. 1, June 8 to September 25, 1789.

U.S. Congressional Budget Office. *U.S. Budget and Economic Outlook: 2006–2105*. Washington: 2005.

U.S. Department of Education. "A Nation at Risk," Report of the National Commission on Excellence in Education. Washington, DC: 1983.

———. "The Nation's Report Card," National Assessment of Educational Progress (NAEP), September 1990.

U.S. Department of Treasury. *Budget of the United States: Historical Tables*. Washington: 2004.

———. *2007 Financial Report of the U.S. Government*. Washington: 2007.

U.S. Government Printing Office. *Art in the U.S. Capitol*. Washington: 1978.

U.S. Newswire. "Transcript of Clinton Remarks at Portland State University Commencement," June 15, 1998.

Vargas, J. "Dual Nationality for Mexicans," *Chicano-Latino Law Review*, vol. 18, no. 1, 1996.

Vidal, G. *Julian*. New York: 1965.

Vobejda, B. "Which Legacy? Explorer's Image Changes with the Times," *Washington Post*, October 11, 1992.

Wall Street Journal. "Tax Notes Column," September 19, 1979.

Warsh, D. *Knowledge and the Wealth of Nations*. New York: 2006.

Washington, G. *Address of George Washington, President of the United States, Preparatory to His Declination*. Baltimore: 1796.

———. "Farewell Address," Philadelphia, PA, September 17, 1796, at www.virginia.edu./gwpapers/farewell/transcript/html.

Washington, George, James Madison, and Alexander Hamilton, quoted in M. Malkin, "The Forgotten 'A' Word: Assimilation," *Conservative Chronicle*, July 11, 2007.

Washington Post. "Racial Tension On Campus," March 23, 1987.

———. "Pratfall in Damascus: Nancy Pelosi's Foolish Shuttle Diplomacy," April 5, 2007.

Washington Times. "Ivory Tower Decay," October 9, 2007a.

———. "GOP Sees Press as Untrustworthy," October 9, 2007b.

Waterman, S. "Analysis: Porous Borders a Backdoor for Terrorists?" *Washington Times*, March 14, 2005.

Weber, M. *The Sociology of Religion*. Boston: 1922/1963.

———. *The Protestant Ethic and the Spirit of Capitalism*. New York: 1958.

Webster, N. *History of the United States*. New Haven, CT: 1832.

Weiss, B. *God in American History: A Documentation of America's Religious Heritage*. Grand Rapids, MI: 1966.

Wells, W. *The Life and Public Service of Samuel Adams*. Boston: 1865.

White, L. "Technology and Invention in the Middle Ages," *Speculum*, vol. 15, no. 2, April 1940.

Whitman, M. "Trade and Growth: Restoring the Virtuous Circle," in J. Jasinowski, ed. *The Rising Tide*. New York: 1998.

Whittaker, C. R. *Frontiers of the Roman Empire: A Social and Economic Study*. Baltimore: 1994.

———. *Rome and Its Frontiers: The Dynamics of Empire*. London: 2004.

Wiggershaus, R. *The Frankfurt School, Its History, Theories, and Political Significance*. Cambridge: 1995.

Wildavsky, A., and Weber, C. *A History of Taxation and Expenditure in the Western World*. New York: 1986.

Williams, W. "Improve Education: Fire the Experts," Creators Syndicate, August 26, 2002.

———. "Threats to the Rule of Law," *Conservative Chronicle*, June 12, 2002.

———. "The Morality of Markets," *Conservative Chronicle*, May 7, 2003.

———. "Economics 101," *Conservative Chronicle*, August 11, 2004.

———. "Income Inequality," *Conservative Chronicle*, September 8, 2004.

———. "Academic Slums: U.S. 33rd and 27th," *Conservative Chronicle*, December 8, 2007.

Wilson. B. "Free Speech, Civility, and the Campus Community," National Association of Scholars, September 9, 2003.

Windschuttle, K. *The Killing of History*. San Francisco: 1996.

Winkler, K. "Who Owns History," *Chronicle for Higher Education*, January 20, 1995.

Wood, G. *The Radicalism of the American Revolution*. New York: 1992.

Wood, P. *Diversity: The Invention of a Concept*. San Francisco: 2003.

Woodward, K. "Hymns, Hers, and Theirs," *Newsweek*, February 12, 1996.

Wooldridge, F. *Immigration's Unarmed Invasion*. Bloomington, IN: 2004.

Yablon, J. "Taxing Ideas," *American*, April 17, 2007, at www.american.com.

Zogby, J. "Zogby Poll: Most Think Political Bias among College Professors a Serious Problem," July 10, 2007, at www.zogby..com/news/ReadNews.dbm?ID=1334.

Zolberg, A. *A Nation by Design*. New York: 2006.

Zuckerman, M. "What Scandal Cannot Dim," *U. S. News and World Report*, July 12, 2002.

Index

Marshall, John, 199
Martin, David, 97
Marx, Karl, 43, 100, 236, 250, 251
Marxism, 34, 43–44, 47; education and, 66,
  68–69, 79, 85, 97, 100. *See also* neo-
  Marxism
Matthew, Saint, 239
Mayans, 4, 6, 53, 288n2
McCarran-Warren Act of 1952, 54
McCarthy, Joe, 104
McCarthyism, xvii, 42, 77, 99
McGinness, Joe, 109
McGovern, George, 112
McGowan, William, 116
McVeigh, Timothy, 118–19
McWhorter, John, 90
media, 101–32; Adams, J., and, 104, 106;
  belief/trust in, 122–23, 130, 300n27;
  Bush, G. W., and, 104, 107, 108, 111,
  112, 113; celebrities and, 119, 126;
  censorship and, 104–5; Clinton, B., and,
  108, 110, 112, 117; education and, 102;
  fair and balanced, 131; Founding Fathers
  and, 101–5; Franklin and, 103; free
  speech and, 102–3; Hamilton and, 103;
  Iraq and, 108, 121–31; Jefferson and,
  101–2, 103, 131; Kennedy, J., and, 108,
  128; loaded language of, 115;
  mainstream, 102, 105–7, 110, 116–32;
  military and, 102, 120–28, 130;
  multiculturalism and, 103, 105; 9/11
  and, 104, 118–19, 126, 127; Paine and,
  103, 126; patriotism and, 121, 123, 125,
  127; political correctness and, 105, 129;
  politics and, 102–19, 128–32; public
  policy and, 119; Reagan and, 106–7,
  111; religion and, 112, 115; role of, 65,
  101, 102–3; terrorism and, 118–19,
  125–26; Tocqueville on, 120; values and,
  xvi, 102, 105–6, 230; wars and, 104,
  120–30. *See also* journalism; journalists;
  press
media bias: economy and, 108, 300n27;
  incipient sources of, 111–16; modern
  manifestations of "mainstream,"
  116–32; values and, 105, 230
"melting pot," 16, 41, 57, 78, 95, 139,
  158–59, 164
Mencken, H. L., 235
Mending Wall (Frost), 153, 262
Mexico, on immigration, 143–48, 153,
  303n51, 304n79

Migrations and Cultures (Sowell), 19
military: Clinton, B., and, 127–28, 184;
  conscription/draft, 181, 182; costs of,
  19–24, 184–85; foreigners in, 4, 16–18;
  immigrants in, 139; media and, 102,
  120–28, 130; Reagan and, 127, 184;
  Rome and, 12–18, 19–24, 290n73,
  290n75; size of, 127–28; taxes for, 9, 14,
  17, 21–24, 201, 202–3. *See also* wars
Miller, Dennis, 121
Mill, John Stuart, 49–50, 61, 77, 98, 235
Milton, John, 42, 63, 81
Mongol invasion, of Central Asia, 4
Montaigne, Michel de, 63
Montesquieu, Baron de, 63, 174, 202, 203,
  235
moral relativism, 88, 91
moral values, 40
Moran, Terry, 120–21
Motor-Voter Act, 263
MoveOn.Org, 129
Moynihan, Daniel, xiii, 106, 137
multicultural, as term, 33
*Multicultural Experiences at Penn: What You
  Can Do*, 73
multiculturalism: defined, xv, 86; education
  and, 44, 70–74, 81–86, 263;
  ethnocentrism and, 55; goals of, 32–33,
  39–42, 47–48; impacts of, xv–xvii, 10,
  230–31; media and, 103, 105
multilingual/bilingual education, xv, 40, 83,
  147, 150, 158–59
Murphey, Dwight, 44
Murtha, John, 127
Myers, Lisa, 110

NAM. *See* National Association of
  Manufacturers
nanny state, 183
Napier, Sir Charles, 52–53
Napoleon, 123
nation-building: Iraq and, 129–31;
  patriotism and, 43, 152
National Association of Manufacturers
  (NAM), 205, 209
national ID cards, 262
national identity, 31–32, 39, 40, 98, 140,
  155, 256
National Industrial Recovery Act, 182
national security, 32–33, 123, 249;
  immigration and, 148, 153–54, 157,
  163, 257

About the Author

Gene W. Heck is a senior business development economist operating in Saudi Arabia and throughout the Middle East. Prior to joining the private sector, he was a member of the United States Diplomatic Corps, with postings to the U.S. embassies in Saudi Arabia and Jordan.

Dr. Heck has served as U.S. commercial attaché to Saudi Arabia, as senior U.S. treasury economic advisor to the Saudi Arabian Ministry of Finance and National Economy, as well as a governmental relations officer with Arabian American Oil Company (ARAMCO).

Dr. Heck holds a doctorate and three master's degrees from the University of Michigan, Ann Arbor; earned a master's degree (MPA) in public administration from Golden Gate University, San Francisco, California; and has completed the requisite coursework for a master's degree in Arab economic history from the University of Jordan. He also serves as an adjunct professor of government and history with the University of Maryland.

Dr. Heck has also won numerous national awards for economic strategies that he has developed and implemented. He likewise is the author of a dozen books, including *When Worlds Collide: Exploring the Ideologial and Political Foundations of the Clash of Civilization* (2007) and *Building Prosperity: Why Ronald Reagan and the Founding Fathers Were Right on the Economy* (2006), both published by Rowman & Littlefield.